Can you remember what you discussed at your last meeting? Perhaps you started a weekend shopping list. Keep track of all these miscellaneous details by using the Notes folder. See Chapter 12.

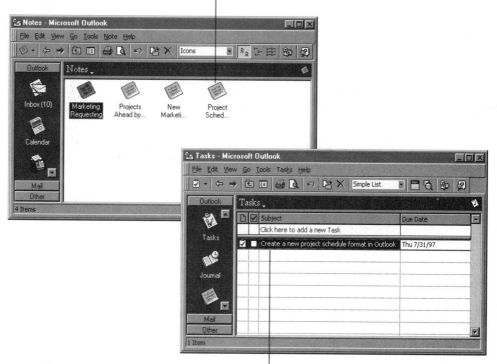

The Journal folder records what you've accomplished. It's like your memory bank, and it allows you to add or remove entries whenever you want to. You can also view your accomplishments in a variety of ways, such as on a timeline, or in a table, as shown here. For details, see Chapter 11.

Don't forget that monthly meeting or important birthday, and keep yourself on schedule by establishing due dates and reminders using the Tasks folder. For details, see Chapter 9.

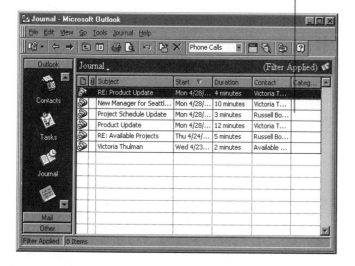

About the Author

Russell Borland started as a technical writer for Microsoft Corporation in 1980, and quickly rose to Manager of Technical Publications. In 1984, Bill Gates asked him to join a team to help design and develop a new product, code-named Cashmere. This project evolved into Opus, the code name for Microsoft Word for Windows version 1. Borland helped develop the product specification, the interface design, and the messages in version 1, and wrote the printed documentation.

In 1992, at the age of 46, Borland took up motorcycle riding. His first bike was a 1992 Harley-Davidson FXRS-Con Low-Rider Convertible.

Borland transferred to Microsoft Press in 1988 to write a book about Word for Windows version 1, called *Working with Word for Windows*. He has since revised this book several times under the title *Running Microsoft Word for Windows*. Borland, now a Master Writer, is also the author of *Microsoft WordBasic Primer*, *Microsoft Word for Windows 2.0 Macros*, *Getting Started with Microsoft Windows 3.1*, *Running Microsoft Mail for Windows 3*, and *Microsoft Exchange in Business*. He is coauthor of *Windows 3.1 Companion* and *Windows for Workgroups Companion*. All of these books are published by Microsoft Press.

Borland earned a bachelor of arts degree from Whitworth College, a master of arts from Portland State University, and a Ph.D. from the University of Washington.

In 1992, at the age of 46, Borland took up motorcycle riding. His first bike was a 1992 Harley-Davidson FXRS-Con Low-Rider Convertible. He named this bike "Gloria" and its engine "Lore, the Evo Twin." In 1993, Borland traded Gloria for a blue 1993 Harley-Davidson FLHS Electra Glide Sport, which he named "Blake." Whenever possible, Borland rides Blake back and forth the 90 miles from his home at the base of Sauk Mountain to Microsoft.

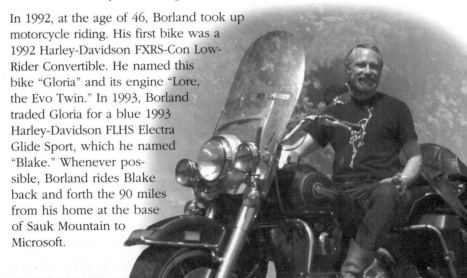

RUNNING
Microsoft® Outlook™ 97

Russell Borland

PUBLISHED BY
Microsoft Press
A Division of Microsoft Corporation
One Microsoft Way
Redmond, Washington 98052-6399

Library of Congress Cataloging-in-Publication Data
Borland, Russell, 1946-
    Running Microsoft Outlook 97 / Russell Borland.
        p.   cm.
    Includes index.
    ISBN 1-57231-608-X
    1. Microsoft Outlook.   2. Time management--Computer programs.
    3. Personal information management--Computer programs.   I. Title.
    HD69.T54B674   1997
    005.369--dc21   97-14337
                                                 CIP

Printed and bound in the United States of America.

4 5 6 7 8 9   WCWC   2 1 0 9 8

Distributed to the book trade in Canada by Macmillan of Canada, a division of Canada Publishing
Corporation.

A CIP catalogue record for this book is available from the British Library.

Microsoft Press books are available through booksellers and distributors worldwide. For further
information about international editions, contact your local Microsoft Corporation office. Or contact
Microsoft Press International directly at fax (425) 936-7329.

Acquisitions Editor: Kim Fryer
Project Editors: John Pierce, Victoria Thulman
Manuscript Editor: Mary Renaud
Technical Editors: John Pierce, Roslyn Lutsch

Chapters at a Glance

Table of Contents

/a/

the beloved

two

Acknowledgments

I extend my thanks to John Pierce, who acted as both project editor and technical editor for most of this book. Late in the process, Victoria Thulman took over as project editor, and Roslyn Lutsch took over as technical editor. I thank them for their attention to the details of the production process and the details of the technical material in this book. Their questions and corrections enabled this book to become the volume you are holding.

I thank Mary Renaud, who acted as manuscript editor. Mary has edited other books of mine, and why she should volunteer to edit another one is beyond my comprehension. I thank her for undertaking this unenviable task and for performing it with sterling dedication.

I wish to thank Kim Fryer, acquisitions editor, who helped me think aloud during the formative stages of this project.

I wish to thank Elisabeth Thébaud Pong, principal compositor, for her work folding all the changes that the author and editors wanted into the book pages. Composition work is a bit like needlepoint—painstaking, painful, tedious, slow, but beautiful when finished. I also want to thank William Teel for cleaning up and processing the screen art—more needlepoint. And I thank Travis Beaven for his artistic skills.

I wish to thank Cheryl Penner, principal proofreader, and the proofreading team for catching "gefluegelties" and for making sure we got the text right. Proofreaders are an author's better angels.

And I thank all the Press staff in marketing, sales, manufacturing, and distribution for their valiant attempts to get this book into the minds and hands of the people who might find it useful.

And complaints should come only to me.

Lazaruss Acres 1997

Introduction

Microsoft Outlook 97 combines a variety of communication, record-keeping, and documentation tools into a single program that enables you to efficiently manage the details of your work life and personal life. Outlook comes with standard tools and customization options that allow you to set up an environment that encourages your highest level of productivity. In this book, you'll learn how to manipulate folders, folder items, and forms to meet your unique needs and the needs of your organization. Best of all, Outlook is easy to use.

Parts I and II of the book walk you through the basic features of the Outlook environment and explore how to manage communications by using the e-mail, fax, and address book features as well as remote work options.

Parts III and IV look in-depth at how to schedule people, appointments, tasks, events, and so on, and show you how to create your contacts list and keep it up-to-date. You'll learn to take full advantage of the Journal folder and the Notes folder.

Part V provides all the details about folders and folder items—how to work with them and manage their contents efficiently. Part VI gets into more advanced work with forms, which you use constantly in Outlook to record, display, and relay information.

Folders and Folder Items

In Outlook, folders (which are similar to the folders you find in the My Computer and Microsoft Windows Explorer windows) contain all the various bits of information you create and work with on a day-to-day basis. Each Outlook folder contains its own particular type of folder item, as does any folder you add. You'll learn to create, store, view, and revise the following types of information in Outlook's built-in folders:

- Electronic mail (e-mail) messages

- Appointments and meetings

- Contacts (names, addresses, phone and fax numbers, and other personal information)

- Task lists (to-do lists)

- Journal entries (records of your activities in Outlook and in Microsoft Office applications as you perform them)

- Notes

- Disk folders on a disk connected to your computer (a shortcut for the My Computer window)

- Discussions (postings and replies in public folders)

You'll also learn to add new folders for items that don't quite fit into Outlook's standard folders, and how to set folder properties. To help you find and view items in folders, Outlook provides view options. You can modify these views and create your own.

Forms

All folder items are based on Outlook forms. Just about everything you'll do in Outlook, such as reading and composing messages, creating notes, and recording appointments, will use Outlook forms. Outlook supplies standard built-in forms, but you can also create your own forms or modify existing ones (including the standard built-in forms) by using Outlook's form design tools. Custom forms can enhance your ability to manage your work efficiently.

Outlook and Servers

Outlook is a "client" for an e-mail server. This means that you use Outlook to work with information and communications systems that are stored and passed through a server set up as a post office. It's likely that a majority of people who use Outlook will be connected to a server that runs with Microsoft Exchange Server. Because of the intimate connection Outlook has with Microsoft Exchange Server, in this book you'll see several illustrations of dialog boxes that show "Exchange" in their title bars. If you're on an e-mail system that doesn't use Microsoft Exchange Server, you'll see "Windows Messaging Service" in the title bars instead of "Exchange." Also note that in some cases, certain features of Outlook are available only on systems that use Microsoft Exchange Server.

What's On the CD?

This book comes with a CD that is loaded with the following software and book information:

■ A powerful, searchable HTML version of the book that enables you to quickly locate specific information, such as a procedure or a definition, with only a click of the mouse

■ Outlook add-ins

■ One free month of MSN

■ Information about related Microsoft Press books

■ Articles about Outlook from the Microsoft Knowledge Base.

Installing the CD

To install the CD, follow these steps:

1 Exit all open applications, and insert the CD into your CD-ROM drive.

2 Click the Start button, and select Run.

3 In the Open box, type your CD-ROM drive letter, and then type *Setup*—for example, *d:\Setup*.

4 Click OK. Follow the on-screen prompts to complete the installation.

Installing MSN

The enclosed CD-ROM also contains the client software for Microsoft Network, or MSN, which is Microsoft's Internet online service. When you install MSN, you get *one month free* unlimited access to MSN and the Internet. To try MSN, follow these steps:

1 On the taskbar at the bottom of your screen, click the Start button, and then click Run.

2 Type *d:\MSN\Msnstart.exe* (or, if your CD-ROM drive uses a drive letter other than "d," substitute the correct drive letter).

3 Click OK, and then follow the directions on the screen to install MSN.

4 When prompted for a registration number, enter *9126*.

PART I

Getting Started

CHAPTER 1

Starting Out

L et's begin with the basics: starting and exiting
Microsoft Outlook 97, logging on, and logging off.
This chapter also takes a look at your personal profile,
which sets up the options you'll use in each Outlook session. Outlook's profile wizard makes it easy to create, use,
change, and remove profiles.

Starting Microsoft Outlook

Microsoft
Outlook

Starting Outlook is really complicated—you have to double-click an icon. And, in case that proves to be inconvenient (or overly complex), several other methods are available, too. To start Outlook, take one of the following actions:

- Double-click the Outlook icon on the desktop.

- Click the Start button on the Microsoft Windows 95 Taskbar, point to Programs, and then click Microsoft Outlook.

- Click one of the six Outlook buttons on the Microsoft Office Shortcut Bar, which starts Outlook and opens a new item that corresponds to the button you click.

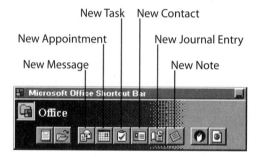

Logging On

If you are logged on to your organization's computer network, Outlook knows who you are and doesn't ask for your logon name and password. Outlook will start connecting you to your e-mail server, usually. (See the sidebar "The Lines Are Down! What Now?" on page 7, for a different situation.) Your e-mail server is the computer that stores the messages you send and receive.

 TIP

If you want to have Outlook request a logon every time you start the program, do the following: Start Outlook, and choose the Tools Services command. In the Services dialog box, select Microsoft Exchange Server and click the Properties button. In the Microsoft Exchange Server dialog box, click the Advanced tab and turn off the Use Network Security During Logon check box.

If you're not logged on to a network, you'll see a dialog box that you use to log on. Follow these steps:

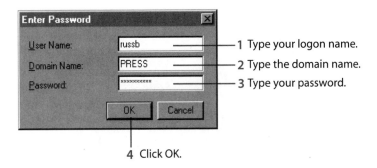

1 Type your logon name.

2 Type the domain name.

3 Type your password.

4 Click OK.

When you're logged on, Outlook will start connecting you to your e-mail server.

To determine which options you'll be using, Outlook refers to your user profile. (You'll find all the details on profiles later in this chapter; see "Developing Your Profile," on page 8.) The first time you start Outlook you will probably have only one profile set up—a profile that was established when you (or someone else) installed Outlook. If that's the case, Outlook simply begins using the profile when you log on, without asking you any questions. But if you happen to have more than one profile set up, and if you have turned on the option that prompts you to choose a profile, Outlook displays the Choose Profile dialog box, shown here:

1 Select the profile you want to use.

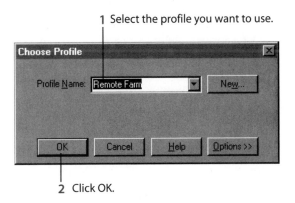

2 Click OK.

If the profile you're using is set up for use away from your network connection, Outlook then displays a dialog box like the following, which asks whether you want to connect to the network or work offline:

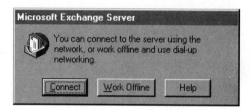

- If the network is available and you want to connect to your e-mail server to send and receive messages, click the Connect button.

- If you regularly connect to an online service (such as MSN, the Microsoft online network; CompuServe; America Online; or AT&T) and you want to connect to it to send and receive messages, click the Connect button.

- If you want to work offline (because the network is down, because you don't have a direct connection to it, or because you want to compose messages or perform other tasks before you connect), click the Work Offline button. When you work offline, you can compose messages for sending later, and you can review any messages that you have stored on your computer (rather than on your e-mail server). Later you can connect to the network or online service to send your messages and to receive any messages that are waiting for you.

When Outlook is running, you see the Outlook window. Chapter 2, "Looking Out into Outlook," explains what this window contains and how to use it.

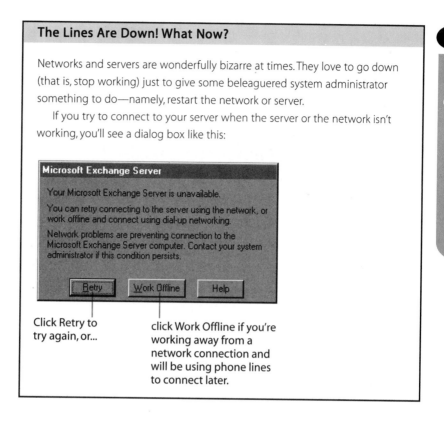

The Lines Are Down! What Now?

Networks and servers are wonderfully bizarre at times. They love to go down (that is, stop working) just to give some beleaguered system administrator something to do—namely, restart the network or server.

If you try to connect to your server when the server or the network isn't working, you'll see a dialog box like this:

Microsoft Exchange Server

Your Microsoft Exchange Server is unavailable.

You can retry connecting to the server using the network, or work offline and connect using dial-up networking.

Network problems are preventing connection to the Microsoft Exchange Server computer. Contact your system administrator if this condition persists.

[Retry]   [Work Offline]   [Help]

Click Retry to try again, or...

click Work Offline if you're working away from a network connection and will be using phone lines to connect later.

Getting Off and Out—Quitting Outlook

You've got a couple of ways to quit Outlook: you can exit, or you can exit and log off. You can quit Outlook by exiting (closing only Outlook) in all the usual Windows ways. Here's the list:

- Choose the File Exit command.

- Choose the Close command from the Control menu (or press Alt+F4).

- Double-click the Control menu icon.

- Click the Close button on the title bar.

- Right-click the title bar, and then choose Close from the shortcut menu.

When you quit Outlook by exiting and logging off, you close Outlook and log off any services you were connected to. The only way to exit and log off is to choose the File Exit And Log Off command.

Developing Your Profile

Outlook keeps track of who you are and what you like. Whenever you log on, Outlook sets itself up to accommodate you—the way you work and the way you want Outlook to work. Each Outlook session is governed by a personal profile—either the profile that was created when you (or some techno-guru) installed Outlook on your computer, a profile you created and told Outlook to use each time you run Outlook, or the profile that you select when you start the program.

If you always use Outlook in one place and in one way—say, on your desktop at work—a single profile is all you need. But if you use Outlook in different locations or to perform more complicated tasks, you might want several profiles. For example, you can set up one profile to use with Outlook when you're at your office, connected to a network. You can create other profiles for when you take your computer home with you or when you take it on your travels, business or otherwise. Or you might want a separate profile for those times when you send faxes from your computer over a telephone line that you also use for connecting to your mail server.

To set up, use, change, and remove profiles in Outlook, you run the Inbox Setup Wizard.

Creating a Profile

Suppose that Outlook is set up for your office, where you connect to your server through your organization's network. Now you go on the road with your laptop, and you want to connect to your server to read mail messages, to consult public folders, and to schedule appointments and tasks. Your original profile can be set up for both the home and away games, but you'll face a slower startup for Outlook because you'll see several dialog boxes on the way in.

For a more convenient and well-tailored startup, you can define a new profile for this situation. To do that, you start the Inbox Setup Wizard and create a new profile, which you'll use when you're away from your office. (And you'll edit the original profile for use when you're back in the office, right?)

 TIP

If you have set up Outlook to prompt you to select a profile each time you start Outlook, you can click the New button in the Choose Profile dialog box to start the profile wizard. See "Using a Different Profile," on page 18.

To create a new profile, follow these steps:

1 Open Windows Control Panel, and double-click the Mail And Fax icon in the Control Panel window.

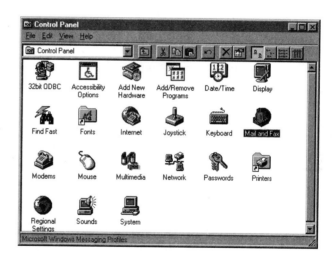

2 In the Properties dialog box, shown on the following page, you'll see a list of the information services set up for the existing profile. Click the Show Profiles button.

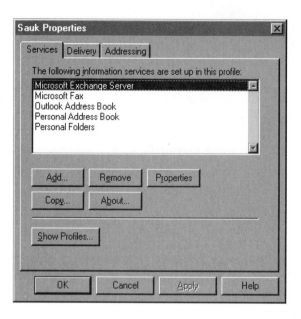

3   Click the Add button in the Mail And Fax dialog box to start creating a new profile.

4   The first panel of the Inbox Setup Wizard lets you select the services you want to include in the new profile. To include all possible services, leave all the check boxes turned on. To omit a service, click its check box to turn it off. (If you really know what you're doing, you can select the Manually Configure Information Services option and then select individual services and set them up the way you want. This book won't tell you all the things you need to know to take this path. You're better off letting the wizard supply the list and then selecting and omitting the services you want for each profile.)

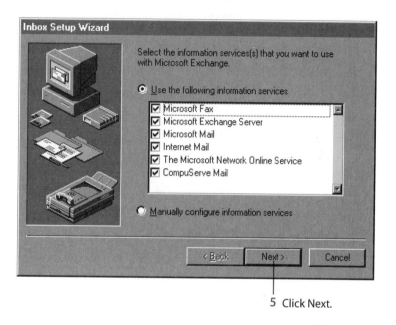

5 Click Next.

6 Type a name for the new profile.

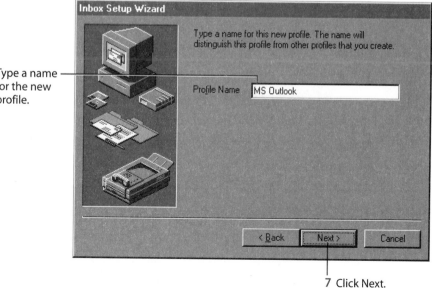

7 Click Next.

8 From this point on, the wizard displays only those panels that apply to the services you selected in step 4. Fill in the information on each panel, and click the Next button until you get to the last panel, shown here. If you don't know the information you need, check with your service administrator.

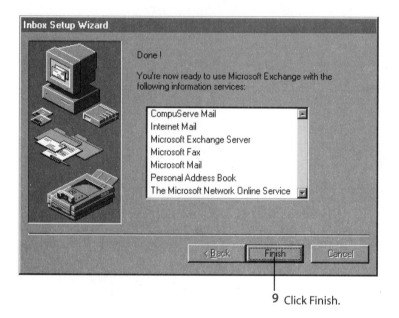

9 Click Finish.

10 In the Mail And Fax dialog box, click the Close button.

You can use the Inbox Setup Wizard to create profiles specific to each location from which you use Outlook: office, home, and on the road. Or you can set up profiles specific to the different services you use in Outlook, such as Internet Mail, MSN, or CompuServe.

Changing a Profile

You signed up for a new online service and want to add it to one or more of your profiles. You bailed out of an online service that wasn't giving you what you wanted. Your profile is now out of date, so you want to update the online service information. Here's how you do it:

1 Double-click the Mail And Fax icon in the Control Panel window to open the Properties dialog box.

2 Click the Show Profiles button to display the Mail And Fax dialog box.

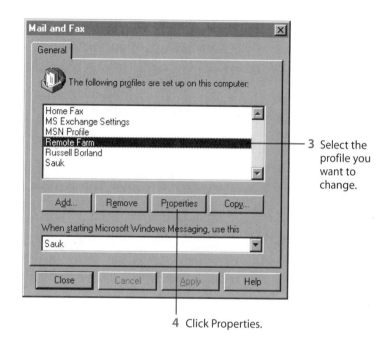

3 Select the profile you want to change.

4 Click Properties.

5 On the Services tab of the Properties dialog box (shown on the next page), you can add an information service to the profile by clicking the Add button and then selecting the service you want to add in the Add Service To Profile dialog box. To remove an information service from the profile, select the name of the service, click the Remove button, and then click Yes in the message box. To see or change the properties of a specific information service, select the name of the service and then click the Properties button.

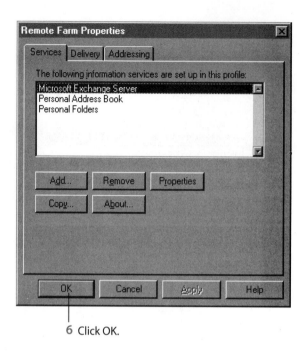

6 Click OK.

7 If you want to make changes to another profile, repeat steps 3 through 6. Click the Close button in the Mail And Fax dialog box when you've finished.

Notice that the Properties dialog box also contains two other tabs: Delivery and Addressing. You can use these tabs to make additional changes to your profile.

On the Delivery tab, you can change the location to which your mail is delivered, and you can specify an alternate location for mail delivery if the location you usually use is unavailable. If your profile includes two or more services that support mail with the same address type (for example, Outlook and Internet Mail), you can specify the order in which those services should process outgoing mail.

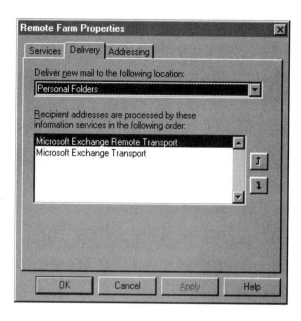

On the Addressing tab, you can specify which address list to display when you first open the address book, where to save new entries in your address book, and in which order to search address lists for recipient names.

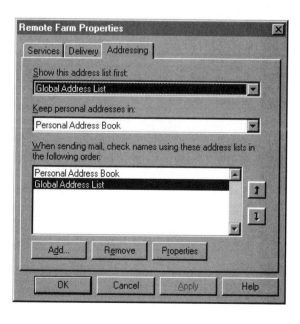

Adding Fax Service to a Profile

 SEE ALSO

For detailed information about sending and receiving faxes with Outlook, see "Facts About Fax," on page 123.

Sending faxes is a popular form of communication. The trouble with a stand-alone fax machine is that you need to print your message before you can send it. If your computer has a fax modem installed, you can create your message on the computer and then use Outlook to send the fax to its destination.

Before you can add fax service to Outlook, you need to install your fax modem and accompanying software. Installing a fax modem can be a tricky process. You can use the Windows Install New Modem Wizard to help you. Also consult your operating system manuals for instructions on how to install your fax modem software.

TIP

> If you use a single telephone line to connect to your mail server and to send faxes from your computer, set up a separate profile containing only Microsoft Fax service.

After you set up the software, take these steps to add fax service to an Outlook profile:

1   If you want to change the profile you're currently using while working in Outlook, choose the Tools Services command.

    To change a profile other than the one you're using, open the Control Panel window, double-click the Mail And Fax icon, and then click the Show Profiles button. Select the profile you want to change, and then click the Properties button. When the Properties dialog box appears, be sure that the Services tab is showing and that the name of the profile you want to change appears in the title bar.

    To add a profile, follow the steps outlined in "Creating a Profile," on page 8.

2   Click the Add button on the Services tab.

3   In the Add Service To Profile dialog box, select Microsoft Fax, and then click OK.

4   A message box asks whether you want to set up your fax modem for Outlook. Click Yes.

5   When the Microsoft Fax Properties dialog box appears, fill in as much of the information as you can. You *must* provide your fax number on the User tab.

6   If more than one modem is available to you, click the Modem tab, select the modem you'll be using, and then click the Set As Active Fax Modem button.

7   Click the Dialing tab, and then click the Dialing Properties button.

8   If you send faxes from only one location, you can set up the Default Location with the information that's needed. If you'll be sending faxes from several locations, click the New button, type a location name, and then click OK. Set up the necessary information for this new location. Click OK in the Dialing Properties dialog box.

9   If you will be dialing long-distance numbers within your area code, click the Toll Prefixes button. In the Local Phone Numbers list, select a prefix in your area code that requires you to dial 1 plus the area code before you dial the number, and then click the Add button. Repeat this step for each long-distance prefix that you will be dialing within your own area code.

⭐ **TIP**

If most of the prefixes in the list require you to dial 1 plus the area code first, click the Add All button, and then remove the few prefixes that are local to your number. If you aren't sure about which prefixes are toll and which are toll free, you can work around this when you set up a fax entry in your address book.

10   Click OK in the Toll Prefixes dialog box, and then click the Message tab.

11   In the Time To Send area, select the time you want your faxes to go out.

12 In the Message Format area, select a message format. Click the Paper button to select how you want your fax transmitted: the size of paper, the image quality, and the orientation of the fax image on the paper.

13 If you don't want a cover page, click the Send Cover Page check box to turn it off. If you do want a cover page, select the one you want to use.

If you want to change the cover page or see what it looks like, click the Open button. Or, if you want to create a new cover page of your own, click the New button. In both cases, the Fax Cover Page Editor starts up so that you can modify the existing cover page or create a new one.

If you have cover page files available, you can click the Browse button to open one of them for use.

14 When you've finished setting fax properties, click OK in the open dialog boxes. If Outlook is running, you'll see a message telling you that you can't use the service until you log off and restart Outlook. The next time you start Outlook, you can send faxes.

? SEE ALSO

For information about setting up fax addresses, see the sidebar "Fax Addresses," on page 135.

To send a fax, you must first set up a fax address. Then you simply send your message to that address. Outlook sends the message by fax rather than through your e-mail server mail transport.

Using a Different Profile

When you have more than one profile set up, you can select which profile to use when you start Outlook. You can tell Outlook to use a particular profile all the time, or you can tell Outlook that you want to choose a profile each time you start the program.

To use the same profile all the time, do this:

1 In Outlook, choose the Tools Options command, and then select the General tab if it isn't already displayed.

2 Select the Always Use This Profile option, and then select the profile from the drop-down list.

3 Click OK.

If you prefer, you can choose a profile at the start of each Outlook session. For this option, follow these steps:

1 In Outlook, choose the Tools Options command, and then select the General tab if it isn't already displayed.

2 Select the Prompt For A Profile To Be Used option.

3 Click OK.

Once the Prompt For A Profile To Be Used option is turned on, you'll need to select a profile in the Choose Profile dialog box each time you start Outlook. (See "Logging On," on page 4.)

Removing a Profile

So you moved to a new dwelling. It's in a different area code. You can edit one or more profiles, but maybe you no longer need a couple of the profiles that you've already set up. To simplify your Outlook life, you can remove the unwanted and unnecessary profiles.

To remove a profile from Outlook, follow these steps:

1 Double-click the Mail And Fax icon in the Control Panel window.

2 In the Properties dialog box, click the Show Profiles button.

3 Select the profile you want to remove.

4 Click the Remove button, and then click Yes when asked whether you want to remove this profile.

5 Click the Close button.

CHAPTER 2

Looking Out into Outlook

After Microsoft Outlook 97 starts up, you see the Outlook window with your Inbox folder open, as shown in Figure 2-1 on the next page. Using the various elements displayed in this window as a starting point, this chapter describes the group panels of the Outlook Bar, shows you how to customize the Outlook window (including the Outlook Bar and toolbars), and explains how to set up your Outlook Assistants and how to set options for Outlook services.

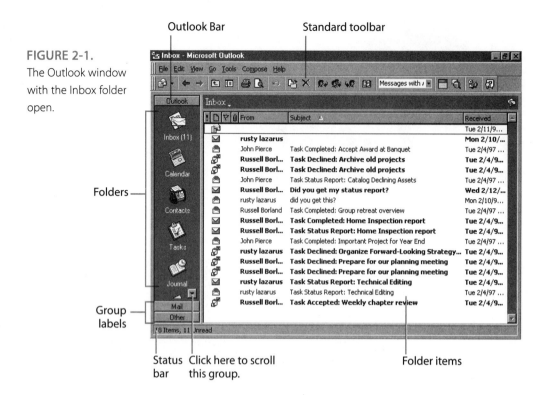

FIGURE 2-1.
The Outlook window
with the Inbox folder
open.

The Outlook Bar

The Outlook Bar, on the left side of the Outlook window, displays one of three groups of folders: the Outlook group, the Mail group, or a group called Other. When you click a group's label, the label moves to the top of the Outlook Bar, and the folders in that group appear on the bar. To open a particular folder, all you need to do is click it.

If the group contains a lot of folders (as the Outlook group does), you'll see small up and down arrows on the Outlook Bar, which you can click to scroll through the complete folder display. You can easily add folders to any of the three groups; for details, see "Adding a Folder to the Outlook Bar," on page 30.

Outlook Group

On the Outlook Bar, the Outlook group is displayed by default. On the panel for this group, you'll find at least these standard Outlook folders: Inbox, Calendar, Contacts, Tasks, Journal, Notes, and Deleted Items.

Inbox Folder

SEE ALSO

For details about working with messages, see Chapter 3.

The Inbox folder contains new messages you haven't read, plus any messages you've read and haven't deleted or moved to another folder. Figure 2-1 shows examples of Inbox folder items. You'll typically work in your Inbox folder to create new messages and to read, forward, or reply to messages you've received.

Calendar Folder

SEE ALSO

For more information about working with your calendar, see Part III, "Scheduling Your Time and Tasks."

The Calendar folder displays a calendar showing the appointments you have made and, depending on how you've arranged the window, a list of tasks you have recorded. Here's a view of a typical Calendar folder:

Date Navigator

Time slots   Appointment slots   Task list

Contacts Folder

SEE ALSO

For more information about setting up and working with your list of contacts, see Chapter 10.

You can use the Contacts folder to store names, street addresses, telephone numbers, e-mail addresses, and other information about people you deal with on a business or a personal basis. A typical Contacts folder looks like the illustration on the following page.

Getting Started

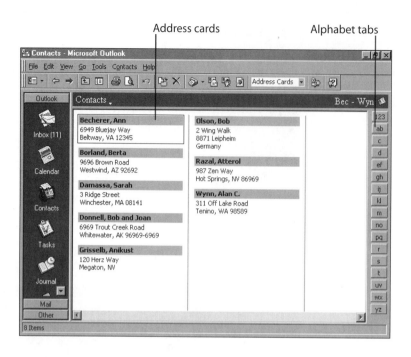

Address cards   Alphabet tabs

Tasks Folder

For more information about setting up and working with your list of tasks, see Chapter 9.

In the Tasks folder, you can compile a list of projects and the tasks that are involved in each project. You can describe and categorize each task, record its due date, and track its status. You can also sort the list in various ways—by category or by the name of the person assigned to the task, for instance. Your Tasks folder might look something like the illustration at the top of the facing page.

Journal Folder

SEE ALSO

For more information about your journal, see Chapter 11.

The Journal folder contains a record of various actions you've taken, such as sending and receiving messages, assigning tasks (and the responses), creating documents in the other Microsoft Office 97 applications—even making phone calls. You can track the actions on a timeline, and you can sort the list of journal entries in different ways. The illustration at the bottom of the facing page shows a typical Journal folder.

Click the minus sign to hide entries.

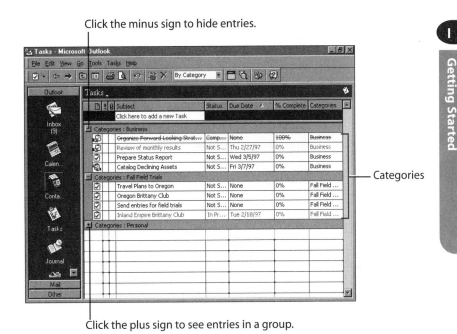

Categories

Click the plus sign to see entries in a group.

Click the plus sign to see entries.   Timeline

Entry Type groupings

Click the minus sign
to hide entries.

Notes Folder

? SEE ALSO

For more information about the Notes folder, see Chapter 12.

In the Notes folder, you can record notes about anything you like: meetings, personal reminders, comments, bits of useful information. This is a sample Notes folder:

Notes can appear in any of five colors.

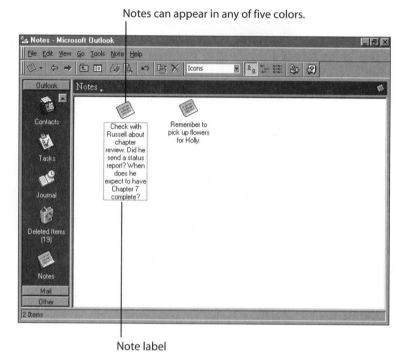

Note label

Deleted Items Folder

When you delete an item from any of your other folders, Outlook moves it to the Deleted Items folder. You can retrieve items from this folder as long as you haven't emptied it, but after you empty the folder, the folder items are gone forever. (You can empty the folder by right-clicking the Deleted Items icon and then choosing Empty "Deleted Items" Folder from the shortcut menu.) Until you empty the Deleted Items folder, it can contain any of the various kinds of folder items that you can set up or receive in Outlook—messages, appointments, task entries, contact entries, journal entries, notes, and documents. Each entry displays a distinctive icon to indicate what type of item it is. Here's an example of the Deleted Items folder:

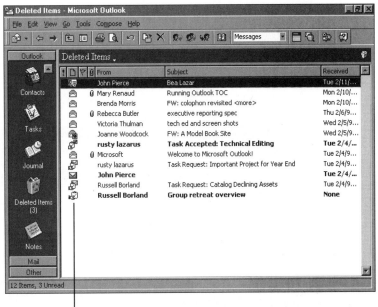

Icons indicate the type of item.

Mail Group

When you click the Mail label on the Outlook Bar, you see at least the four standard folders in the Mail group: Inbox, Sent Items, Outbox, and Deleted Items. The Inbox and Deleted Items folders are the same as those described in the preceding section.

Sent Items Folder

The Sent Items folder contains copies of messages you've sent. You can use this folder as a record of the messages you've generated in case you need to refer to them again or in case you need to resend a message.

Outbox Folder

The Outbox folder temporarily holds messages you've sent that have not yet been pulled from your computer to your e-mail server for delivery. When you're connected to your server, messages stay in your Outbox folder only a short time. If you're working offline, the Outbox folder holds your sent messages until you're connected again. When you're back online, Outlook sends your messages from the Outbox folder to your e-mail server.

Other Group

The third label on the Outlook Bar refers to a miscellaneous group called Other. When you click this label, you see four or five folders: My Computer (the same as the My Computer icon on the Windows desktop), My Documents, Personal Folders (if they are set up in Outlook), Favorites, and Public Folders. You can add other disk folders, as well as Outlook folders, to the Other group; for details, see "Adding a Folder to the Outlook Bar," on page 30.

My Computer Folder

? SEE ALSO

For more information about viewing disk contents in Outlook, see "Opening Documents or Starting Programs from Outlook," on page 382.

When you click the My Computer folder, the Outlook window displays icons for your computer's disk drives, the same icons you see when you double-click the My Computer icon on your desktop. You can then switch to any disk drive on your computer or to any network drive, just as you can in the My Computer window on your desktop. In this way, you can use Outlook as a substitute for My Computer and Windows Explorer to locate and open any folder, file, or document.

My Documents Folder

The My Documents folder on the Other group panel is a shortcut to the My Documents folder on your computer's hard disk. If, like me, you keep most of your documents in the My Documents folder or in a subfolder inside it, you can use the My Documents shortcut to find and open most any file or document that you want to work on.

When you open a file or document from the Outlook window, Windows starts the application that was used to create the document.

Personal Folders

? SEE ALSO

For information about setting up personal folders and using Outlook for remote mail, see Chapter 5 and Chapter 6.

On the Other group panel, you might also see an icon labeled Personal Folders. This folder contains duplicates of your four Mail folders (Inbox, Deleted Items, Sent Items, and Outbox) and can include other folders as well. Personal folders are located on your computer's hard disk rather than on a server. These duplicate folders work in a manner similar to the Mail folders when you're working offline. In fact, you must install personal folders if you plan to use Outlook for remote mail. They also work as backup folders in which you can keep duplicates of the messages in your Mail folders.

Favorites Folder

? SEE ALSO

For details about
adding shortcuts to
programs, folders,
documents, and web
pages, see "Adding
Items to the Favorites
Folder," on page 368.
For details about
adding shortcuts to
favorite public folders
to your Favorites folder,
see "Public Folder
Favoritism," on page
439.

Outlook's Favorites folder is a shortcut to the Favorites folder on your
hard disk. This folder is inside the folder in which Windows is installed (usually called Windows). Icons or labels for the items in your
Favorites folder also appear on the Favorites toolbar of your Office 97
shortcut bar (if you have set it up) and on the drop-down list of the
Favorites button on the Microsoft Internet Explorer toolbar. You can
set up and click the items in the Favorites folder to quickly jump to
any disk folder, World Wide Web site (URL), application, or disk file.

Public Folders

If your e-mail server uses Microsoft Exchange Server, it provides some
variety of public folders. These are folders that most people can use,
containing messages that can be read by everyone who can open the
folder. A public folder can also contain postings—notes that ask
questions, provide answers, or state opinions and facts—as well as
documents. Public folders are intended to present and record public
discussion of a specific topic.

? SEE ALSO

For more information
about public folders,
see Chapter 16.

Some public folders might have limited access—that is, they might be
available only to certain people. For example, only the members of a
project team might have access to a project folder.

Depending on the generosity of your Exchange administrator and on
the capacity of your Exchange server, you might have use of hundreds
of public folders (especially if your Exchange administrator sets up
public folders for Internet newsgroups) or possibly only a few.

Customizing the Outlook Window

Outlook allows you to customize the appearance and functionality of
the main Outlook window to fit the way you work and the tasks you
perform most often. You can choose whether to hide or display such
components as the Outlook Bar, the Folder List, the Outlook toolbars,
and the status bar. You can also add, remove, rename, resize, or
reposition various elements in the Outlook window.

Modifying the Outlook Bar

The Outlook Bar sits along the left edge of the Outlook window, as
you saw in Figure 2-1, on page 22. Earlier, this chapter described the

three groups that initially appear on this bar: Outlook, Mail, and Other. But you can do more with the Outlook Bar than switching groups and clicking on a folder icon to open a folder. The following sections explain the various ways you can change the Outlook Bar.

Turning the Outlook Bar Off and On

? SEE ALSO

For details about how to widen columns in the folder items list, see "Changing Column Width," on page 460.

When you are working with your e-mail messages or a list of tasks, at times you might want a better view of the columns of information displayed in the folder items list. If so, you'll want to use the entire width of the Outlook window for folder items so that you can widen the columns. To use the entire width of the Outlook window for the folder items list, you can turn off the Outlook Bar.

To turn off the Outlook Bar, do one of the following:

- Choose the View Outlook Bar command.

- Right-click the Outlook Bar, and then choose Hide Outlook Bar from the shortcut menu.

To turn the Outlook Bar back on, choose the View Outlook Bar command again.

Changing the Size of Icons on the Outlook Bar

Initially, the folder icons on the Outlook Bar appear in large size, but you can make them smaller. When you change the size of the icons on the Outlook Bar, you change them only for the current group. When the folder icons are smaller, you can see more of them without scrolling the group, and you can also narrow the Outlook Bar to allow more space for the folder items list or to display the Folder List.

To display the Outlook Bar icons in small size, right-click the Outlook Bar, and choose Small Icons from the shortcut menu. To return the icons to large size, right-click the Outlook Bar again, and choose Large Icons from the shortcut menu.

Adding a Folder to the Outlook Bar

You can add any existing Outlook or disk folder to any group on the Outlook Bar. To add a folder to a group on the Outlook Bar, take these steps:

1 Switch to the group on the Outlook Bar to which you want to add the folder.

2 Right-click the Outlook Bar and choose Add To Outlook Bar from the shortcut menu, or choose the File Add To Outlook Bar command.

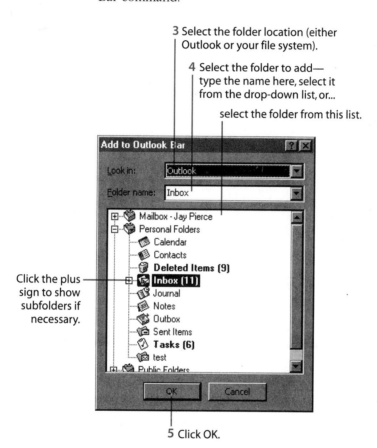

3 Select the folder location (either Outlook or your file system).

4 Select the folder to add— type the name here, select it from the drop-down list, or...

select the folder from this list.

Click the plus sign to show subfolders if necessary.

5 Click OK.

Removing a Folder Icon from the Outlook Bar

To remove a folder icon from the Outlook Bar, follow these steps:

1 Switch to the group on the Outlook Bar from which you want to remove the folder icon.

2 Right-click the folder icon you want to remove from the Outlook Bar.

3   Choose Remove From Outlook Bar from the shortcut menu.

4   Click Yes in the message box that asks whether you're sure you want to remove the folder icon.

> Removing a folder icon from the Outlook Bar doesn't remove the folder from Outlook. If you want to remove the folder, see "Removing a Folder," on page 436.

Renaming a Folder Icon on the Outlook Bar

The icons on the Outlook Bar are shortcuts to the actual folders. You can change the name of any icon that appears on the Outlook Bar.

> Changing the name of a folder icon on the Outlook Bar does not change the name of the folder itself. For information on renaming folders, see "Renaming a Folder," on page 435.

Here's how to rename a folder icon on the Outlook Bar:

1   Right-click the folder icon you want to rename.

2   Choose Rename Shortcut from the shortcut menu. The icon's name becomes active (highlighted).

3   Type or edit the name of the folder icon, and then press the Enter key.

Adding a Group to the Outlook Bar

You might find that you'd like to add another group (or several more groups) to the Outlook Bar. You can easily add a group by following these steps:

1   Right-click the Outlook Bar.

2   Choose Add New Group from the shortcut menu. Outlook adds a group label and activates it for naming.

3   Type a name for the new group, and then press the Enter key.

You can now add folder icons to your new group; see "Adding a Folder to the Outlook Bar," on page 30.

Renaming a Group on the Outlook Bar

If you want to change the name of a group on the Outlook Bar, take these steps:

1   Right-click the label of the group you want to rename.

2   Choose Rename Group from the shortcut menu. Outlook activates that group label for renaming.

3   Type a new name for the group, and then press the Enter key.

Removing a Group from the Outlook Bar

If one of the groups on the Outlook Bar is no longer useful to you, you can remove it from the bar. Simply right-click the label of the group you want to remove, choose Remove Group from the shortcut menu, and click Yes in the message box that asks whether you're sure you want to remove the group.

Displaying the Folder List

The first time you start Outlook, you see only a list of messages in your Inbox. If all you do with Outlook is read and send messages, this might suit you. But at some time or other, you'll more than likely want to open other folders and work with the items they contain. The easiest way to do this is to click the folder you want to open. If this folder is already on the Outlook Bar, you're golden. If the folder you want isn't on the Outlook Bar, you can add it there (which can make the bar cluttered and slower to use), or you can display the Folder List.

Displaying the Folder List can be extremely useful if your work takes you frequently from folder to folder. Still, there might be times when you want to see more of the columns in the folder items list without having to scroll horizontally. In this case, you can either hide the Folder List or change the width of the folder item list. (For information about the latter choice, see the next section, "Changing List Widths," on page 35.)

To show or hide the Folder List, use one of the following methods:

Folder List

- Click the Folder List button on the Standard toolbar to display the list; click this button again to hide the list.

- Choose the View Folder List command to display the list; choose this command again to hide the list.

- Click the down arrow on the right side of the folder's name in the folder title bar. This method displays a drop-down folder list temporarily: when you click the folder you want to open, the list disappears. If you decide not to open a folder, simply click the down arrow again to hide the list.

Click here to display the drop-down folder list.

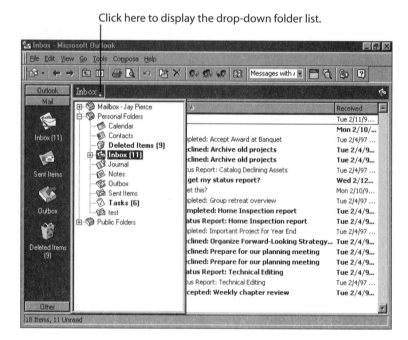

Changing List Widths

? SEE ALSO

The Calendar folder has additional sections that you can size. For details, see "Adjusting the Calendar Panes," on page 218.

When you have the Outlook window set up to show the Outlook Bar, the Folder List, and the folder items list, you might want to change the width of one or more of these elements in order to see the full width of large-size Outlook Bar icons, to see all the folders you've expanded in the Folder List—particularly when the subfolders run several levels deep—or to see more columns in the folder items list.

Here's how to change the width of the Outlook Bar or the lists:

1 Position the mouse pointer on the vertical dividing line between the Outlook Bar and the lists or on the line between the lists. The mouse pointer changes to a vertical line with two arrowheads pointing horizontally.

2 Drag the vertical dividing line to the left or to the right to adjust the width of the Outlook Bar or the lists.

Working with Toolbars

Like all good applications with a graphical user interface, Outlook provides toolbars in its windows. Clicking the toolbar buttons gives you a fast, easy way to take specific actions or perform common tasks. You can turn Outlook's toolbars on and off, you can reposition them, and you can change the size of the toolbar buttons.

Outlook contains three types of toolbars:

- A Standard toolbar contains buttons appropriate to the actions you usually take for the type of item you've selected or opened. You'll see a version of the Standard toolbar in every folder you open in Outlook. The buttons on the Standard toolbar change for each type of folder or folder item.

- A Formatting toolbar contains buttons for formatting text. Each type of Outlook item (except Notes) can display a Formatting toolbar, which you use to format the text of messages and comments.

- A Remote toolbar contains buttons for running a remote mail session. (See "Checking Out the Remote Toolbar," on page 199, for details.) You can see the Remote toolbar only in e-mail folders, which are designed primarily to hold messages.

Turning Toolbars Off and On

Obviously, toolbars take up a certain amount of window space. If you'd prefer to use this space to see more folders or folder items, you can turn a toolbar off in either of these two ways:

- Choose the View Toolbars command. On the submenu, click the box beside the toolbar name to clear the check mark. (A check mark in the box means that the toolbar is currently turned on.)

- Right-click any toolbar. On the shortcut menu, click the box beside the name of the toolbar you want to turn off to clear the check mark.

Only the names of toolbars that apply to the current folder or to the open folder item appear on the View Toolbars submenu or on the Toolbars shortcut menu.

To turn a toolbar back on, you can use either of the two methods just described, with the difference being that you click the appropriate box on the submenu or the shortcut menu to restore the check mark beside the name of the toolbar you want to turn on.

If all the toolbars are turned off, you can right-click the menu bar to display the Toolbars shortcut menu, where you can turn on the toolbars you need.

Changing the Position of a Toolbar

You can reposition a toolbar on the screen by moving it to the top edge, bottom edge, right edge, or left edge of the Outlook window or by floating the toolbar. (If the Outlook window is not maximized, you can even drag a toolbar outside the Outlook window.) To move a toolbar to a new position, drag the vertical "wrinkle" at the left end of the toolbar to a different edge of the Outlook window or into the middle of the window.

You might want to float a toolbar that is too wide to display all of its buttons on the screen. (This sometimes occurs on monitors that have a 640 × 480 resolution.) You'll know the toolbar has more buttons than you can see if it shows a right-pointing chevron at the right end of the toolbar.

 TIP

To quickly float a toolbar, double-click its "wrinkle." When a toolbar is too wide to display all of its buttons, you can double-click the right-pointing chevron at the right end of the toolbar to float the toolbar. To quickly return a floating toolbar to the edge where you last parked it, double-click its title bar.

When a toolbar is floating, you can change its size in much the same way as you change the size of a window. To change the size and shape of a floating toolbar, simply drag a side of the toolbar frame.

Changing the Size of Toolbar Buttons

Outlook is initially set up with small toolbar buttons. If you like larger toolbar buttons (the better to see them), take these steps to display larger buttons:

1 Choose the Tools Options command.

2 Click the General tab.

3 Click here to turn on Large Toolbar Icons.

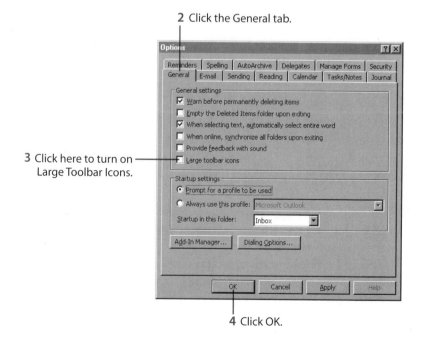

4 Click OK.

Large toolbar buttons are easier to see, but obviously, they also take up more space on your screen. With large toolbar buttons displayed, it's unlikely that the Standard toolbar can display all of its buttons within the width of the Outlook window, even on higher resolution screens. In this case, you might want to float the toolbar (or switch back to small toolbar buttons).

Displaying the Status Bar

The status bar at the bottom of the Outlook window shows helpful information. In many windows, the status bar displays the number of items in the open folder and how many of the items are unread. In some form windows (if the form's designer set up the form this way), the status bar also provides messages that indicate what you should type or choose in a form field.

If none of this information is important to you—if you never or only rarely look at the status bar—you might want to hide the status bar to gain some extra space in the window. To hide or display the status bar, choose the View Status Bar command.

Outlook Assistants

Outlook provides two assistants to help you work with messages that come to your Inbox: the Inbox Assistant and the Out of Office Assistant. The Inbox Assistant can be set up to automatically sort messages or to forward messages that you always treat the same way. For those times when you're out of the office, you can set up the Out of Office Assistant to tell people who send you messages that you are away, when you'll be back, and whom to contact or what to do during your absence. The Out of Office Assistant can also automatically sort, move, forward, and delete messages while you are away.

You can use the Inbox Assistant or the Out of Office Assistant only if you are using Outlook with Microsoft Exchange Server. In addition, you must have the Exchange Extensions add-in installed in Outlook to use the Inbox Assistant or the Out of Office Assistant. For information about installing add-ins, see "Add-In Manager Button," on page 49.

Inbox Assistant

For a variety of reasons over which you might have little control, your Inbox can become flooded with messages and items that you want to act on in very specific ways. You can, of course, take these actions yourself, attending to each message manually. But if you find a category of messages that you act on in a specific way every time, you can set up your Inbox Assistant to take care of these actions for you. The Inbox Assistant can automatically delete, forward, reply, move, and perform several other actions on items delivered to your Inbox.

To set up your Inbox Assistant, first choose the Tools Inbox Assistant command to display the following dialog box:

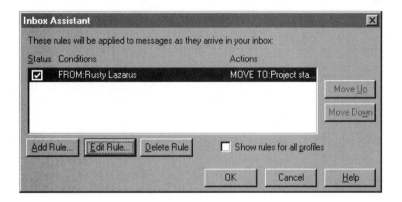

In the Inbox Assistant dialog box, click the Add Rule button to open the Edit Rule dialog box, shown in Figure 2-2 on the following page. In the Edit Rule dialog box, you identify the kinds of items for which you want the Inbox Assistant to take a specific action (or actions). The fewer settings you make in the upper area of the dialog box (When A Message Arrives...), the fewer items the Inbox Assistant is asked to deal with. The more settings you make in this area, the more items the Inbox Assistant must deal with. Table 2-1 (on the following page) lists the kinds of items the Inbox Assistant can act on.

FIGURE 2-2.

The Edit Rule dialog box.

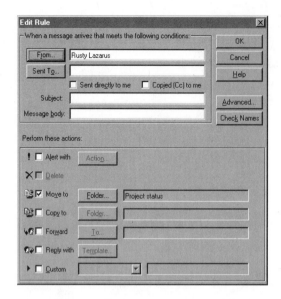

TABLE 2-1.   Edit Rule Dialog Box Options for Identifying Items.

Setting	What the Inbox Assistant Acts On
From	Items from a particular sender
Sent To	Items sent to a particular recipient
Sent Directly To Me	Items with your name in the To box
Copied (Cc) To Me	Items with your name in the Cc box
Subject	Items that include the specified text in the Subject box
Message Body	Items that contain the specified text somewhere in the message body

If you need to identify the items further, you can fine-tune your description by clicking the Advanced button in the Edit Rule dialog box. Clicking this button opens the Advanced dialog box, shown in Figure 2-3, which provides additional settings. Consult Table 2-2 for a list of these settings and the items they describe. When you have set up the Advanced dialog box, click OK to close it and return to the Edit Rule dialog box.

FIGURE 2-3.

The Advanced
dialog box.

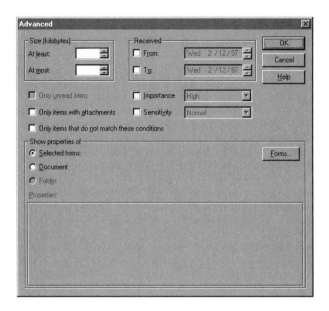

> ⭐ **TIP**
>
> You can choose settings in the Advanced dialog box without making any settings in the Edit Rule dialog box.

TABLE 2-2.   Advanced Dialog Box Options for Identifying Items.

Setting	What the Inbox Assistant Acts On
Size At Least	Items that are larger than the size you set
Size At Most	Items that are smaller than the size you set
Received From	Items received after the date you set (For items between two dates, also set a Received To date.)
Received To	Items received before the date you set (For items between two dates, also set a Received From date.)
Only Unread Items	Items you haven't read yet
Only Items With Attachments	Items that contain attachments (files or messages)
Importance	Items set to the specified level of importance—High, Normal, or Low

(continued)

TABLE 2-2. *continued*

Setting	What the Inbox Assistant Acts On
Sensitivity	Items with the specified level of sensitivity—Normal, Personal, Private, or Confidential
Only Items That Do Not Match These Conditions	Uses the reverse of all the settings in both the Edit Rule and the Advanced dialog boxes
Show Properties Of Selected Forms	Displays fields in the forms you select with the Forms button
Show Properties Of Document	Displays document properties
Show Properties Of Folder	Displays fields in the custom forms associated with the folder whose name appears after the Folder label

After you return to the Edit Rule dialog box, having selected the kinds of items you want the Inbox Assistant to act on, you need to specify the actions you want the Inbox Assistant to take for these items. In the lower portion of the Edit Rule dialog box, choose the actions that should be taken for this set of items. Table 2-3 explains these action options and how to set them up.

TABLE 2-3. **Edit Rule Dialog Box Options for Actions to Take.**

Action Option	How to Set Up the Option
Alert With	Select the Alert With check box, and then click the Action button to open the Alert Actions dialog box. To have the Inbox Assistant notify you with text, select the Notify With The Text check box, and type the text for the notification in the box. To be notified with sound, select the Play box. Then type the name of the sound file in the Sound box; or click the Sound button, select the sound file, and then click the Open button. Click the Test button to test the sound notification. When you have made your selections, click OK in the Alert Actions dialog box.

Action Option	How to Set Up the Option
Delete	Select the Delete check box.
Move To	Select the Move To check box, click the Folder button, select the folder to which you want the items moved, and then click OK.
Copy To	Select the Copy To check box, click the Folder button, select the folder to which you want the items copied, and then click OK.
Forward	Select the Forward check box, and then either type the names in the To box or click the To button to open the Choose Recipient dialog box. Select the names in the list on the left, and then click the To button in the Choose Recipient dialog box. When you have made your selection, click OK in the Choose Recipient dialog box.
Reply With	Select the Reply With check box, and then click the Template button. Follow the directions given in the following section, "Automatic Replies."
Custom	Select the Custom check box, and then select the action you want from the drop-down list. (You will probably find the list empty; custom actions are additional features that are not provided by Outlook.)

When the settings are complete, click OK in the Edit Rule dialog box to accept all the settings and return to the Inbox Assistant dialog box. If you want to specify different actions for other types of items, you can reopen the Edit Rule dialog box as described earlier, identify a new set of items, and select the appropriate actions. Repeat this procedure for each set of items that you want the Inbox Assistant to take care of—closing the Edit Rule dialog box and returning to the Inbox Assistant dialog box each time. For example, for messages from Joe Smith about working overtime, you can set up a rule to reply with a thank-you and forward the message to your payroll department. For messages that contain the words "project status" in the Subject line, you can set up a rule that moves the messages to a project folder. Finally, when you've finished setting up the rules you want, click OK in the Inbox Assistant dialog box.

Automatic Replies

To send an automatic reply using the Inbox Assistant, follow these steps:

1 In the Edit Rule dialog box, click the Reply With check box, and then click the Template button.

2 Click the To button to select names, or...

type names here (in addition to the sender).

3 Leave the Subject line blank so that "RE:" and the original subject can be inserted in the reply.

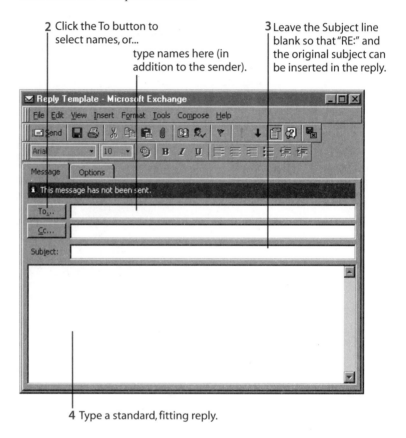

4 Type a standard, fitting reply.

5 Close the Reply Template window, and click Yes in the message box to save your changes.

Out of Office Assistant

When you're away from your office—on vacation, for example—and you want to notify people that you're not available for a while, you can set up the Out of Office Assistant to automatically send a reply when you receive a message. Also, the Out of Office Assistant can automatically perform specific actions on incoming items.

To set up the Out of Office Assistant, take these steps:

1 Choose the Tools Out Of Office Assistant command.

2 Select this option to turn on the Out of Office Assistant.

3 Type the message you want the Out of Office Assistant to send.

4 Click Add Rule to have the Out of Office Assistant act on incoming items during your absence.

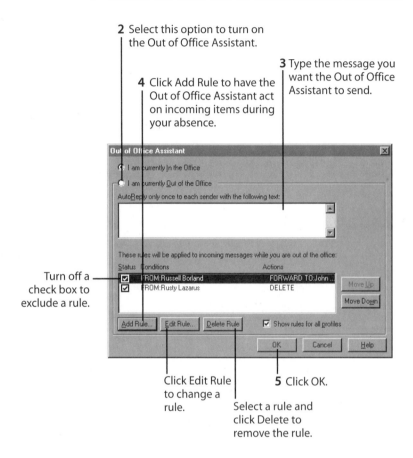

Turn off a check box to exclude a rule.

Click Edit Rule to change a rule.

Select a rule and click Delete to remove the rule.

5 Click OK.

Using the Add Rule button and the Edit Rule dialog box (shown in Figure 2-2, on page 40) allows you to set up the rules for the types of items you want the Out of Office Assistant to act on and the actions it should take for those items. You can create as many rules as you need. Consult Table 2-1, Table 2-2, Table 2-3, and the text in the earlier section, "Inbox Assistant," for details about these options.

TIP

You can set up the Out of Office Assistant in advance and then turn it on and off as you need. You can leave rules you create intact so that you have to set them up only once. You can, of course, change the rules at any time to better suit your needs.

When the Out of Office Assistant is turned on, the next time you start Outlook (if you connect to your e-mail server), you'll see a message telling you that the Out of Office Assistant is on and asking whether you want to turn it off. Click Yes to turn off the Out of Office Assistant; click No to leave it turned on.

The rules stay intact so that you can use them the next time you're out of the office without having to set them up again. Out of Office Assistant rules are inactive as long as the assistant is turned off.

Setting Outlook Options

The Tools Options command gives you a number of ways to customize Outlook to suit you and the way you work. The Options dialog box contains as many as 13 tabs. This indicates just how much you can muck around with Outlook—with the way it works and the way it looks. The following sections describe the options on each tab.

Here's the general procedure for adjusting options:

1 Choose the Tools Options command.

2 Click the appropriate tab.

3 Set the options you want to adjust.

4 Click OK.

 TIP

> When you want to set options on more than one tab, you can click the Apply button instead of OK to apply your changes right away and keep the dialog box open. The Apply button is especially useful for options that change the appearance of the Outlook window. That way, you have a preview of the new look—and you can change it back before you close the dialog box if you don't like it.

General Tab

On the General tab of the Options dialog box, you'll find options for how Outlook should act in general at startup and while running. You'll also find buttons for adding other programs that work with Outlook and for setting your dialing options for remote mail.

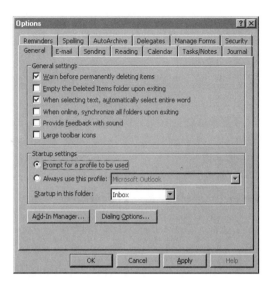

General Settings

SEE ALSO
For information about the Large Toolbar Icons setting on the General tab, see "Changing the Size of Toolbar Buttons," on page 37.

In this area you can choose settings for managing deleted folder items, making selections in message text, synchronizing your offline folders, choosing sound or silence when you take an action in Outlook, and displaying toolbar buttons.

Warn Before Permanently Deleting Items. If this option is turned on, Outlook prompts you to confirm that you want to permanently delete items from the Deleted Items folder when you empty the folder or when you manually delete an item from it. (This option is turned on by default.) When you see the message, click Yes to delete the items. Click No to keep the messages in your Deleted Items folder. (You'll see a slightly different message if your Deleted Items folder contains subfolders or remote message headers.)

Empty The Deleted Items Folder Upon Exiting. With this option turned on, Outlook empties your Deleted Items folder each time you quit Outlook. If you prefer to clear out your Deleted Items folder more selectively, be sure that this option is turned off.

When Selecting Text, Automatically Select Entire Word. When you're editing a message and need to select text that includes a space, as soon as you select a single character beyond the space, Outlook selects the entire word. This setting can be handy if you usually select entire words. But if you need to select parts of two neighboring words, you will find this option frustrating and disruptive. If necessary, you can turn it off.

? **SEE ALSO**

For details about synchronizing folders, see "Synchronizing Folders," on page 176.

When Online, Synchronize All Folders Upon Exiting.   One variation of using Outlook remotely involves setting up offline folders. (See the sidebar "Offline Folders Vs. Remote Mail," on page 165, for details.) When you use offline folders, you'll occasionally connect to your e-mail server, either over a network or over a telephone line. With this option turned on, Outlook synchronizes all your offline folders with your online (server) folders when you exit Outlook. (Synchronizing means that Outlook updates the contents of the offline folder and the online folder so that they contain the same items.) This way, your offline folders are consistent with your online folders when you start to work offline. Leave this check box turned off only if you prefer to manually synchronize your offline folders (with the Tools Synchronize command) while you're online. You can, of course, manually synchronize folders at any time you're online, even if this check box is turned on.

Provide Feedback With Sound.   Turn on this check box if you want Outlook to produce a sound for each action you take in the program—deleting a message, opening a file, and so on. If you don't have a sound card in your computer, the sound will be a simple beep. If you have a sound card, you can set the sound for each action by selecting the .WAV file you want Outlook to play when that action occurs. You set up these sounds through the Sound icon on the Windows 95 Control Panel.

Startup Settings

The options in this area of the General tab let you control which profile Outlook will use and which folder Outlook opens when it starts.

? **SEE ALSO**

For more details about profiles, see "Logging On," on page 4, and "Developing Your Profile," on page 8.

Prompt For A Profile To Be Used.   If you switch between two or more profiles because you connect to several online services, or if you travel with your computer and you sometimes connect to your e-mail server, you might want to select the Prompt For A Profile To Be Used option. When this option is turned on, Outlook displays the

Choose Profile dialog box when it starts up. This dialog box lists your profiles, allowing you to select the one you want to use for the current session.

Always Use This Profile.   If you use only one profile, turn on the Always Use This Profile option, and then select the profile name from the list below the label. This option is most useful when your computer is always in one place and you use the same profile all the time.

Startup In This Folder.   By default, Outlook starts up in your Inbox folder, on the assumption that you use Outlook most often for e-mail. If you use Outlook primarily for other purposes, you can designate one of the other Outlook folders—Calendar, Contacts, Tasks, Journal, or Notes—as the startup folder.

Add-In Manager Button

Add-ins provide additional functionality to Outlook. Outlook comes with several add-ins, including ones for features such as Digital Security and Delegate Access. Add-ins can also be third-party programs. Some add-ins are installed when you set up Outlook. To use certain Outlook add-ins (including Digital Security), you must be running Outlook with Microsoft Exchange Server. If you need to install another of Outlook's add-ins or want to use a third-party add-in, you can install it by using the Add-In Manager button on the General tab. To install or remove an add-in, take these steps:

1   Click the Add-In Manager button on the General tab.

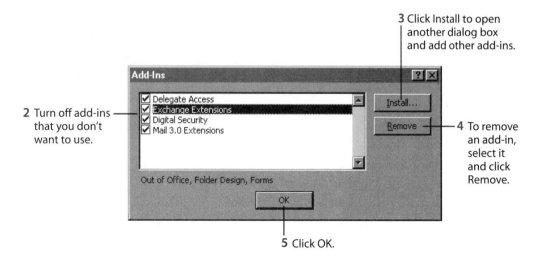

3 Click Install to open another dialog box and add other add-ins.

2 Turn off add-ins that you don't want to use.

4 To remove an add-in, select it and click Remove.

5 Click OK.

NOTE

For information about the add-ins that come with Outlook, see the Outlook online help.

Dialing Options Button

SEE ALSO

For details about setting dialing and modem properties, see "Setting Dialing Options," on page 125, and "Setting Modem Options," on page 128.

If you will be dialing from Outlook to connect to your e-mail server, to send faxes, or to call a contact, you probably need to set up your dialing options. You can also set up speed dialing. When you set up a speed-dial number, you can choose the Tools Dial command, and the number appears on the Speed Dial submenu. There, you simply click the speed-dial number to place the telephone call.

To set your dialing options, follow these steps:

1 Click the Dialing Options button on the General tab.

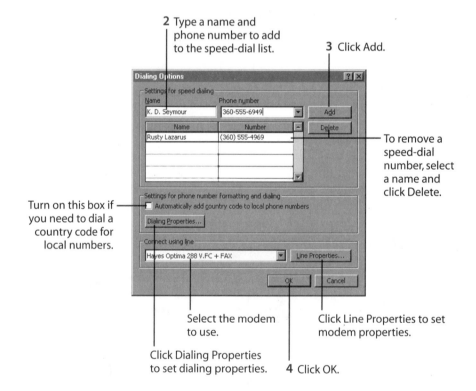

2 Type a name and phone number to add to the speed-dial list.

3 Click Add.

To remove a speed-dial number, select a name and click Delete.

Turn on this box if you need to dial a country code for local numbers.

Select the modem to use.

Click Line Properties to set modem properties.

Click Dialing Properties to set dialing properties.

4 Click OK.

E-Mail Tab

On the E-Mail tab of the Options dialog box, you select which e-mail services Outlook should automatically check for new messages and set options for how Outlook should notify you when a new message arrives and how Outlook should process new messages. You can also set up Microsoft Word 97 as your e-mail editor.

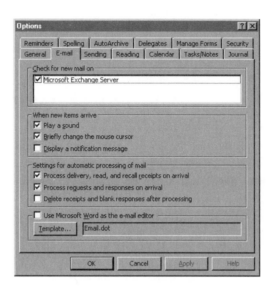

Check For New Mail On

When Outlook is originally set up, you have at least one "service" as part of your profile—for example, Microsoft Exchange Server. As time goes by (or maybe even right away), you might have access to online services such as CompuServe, America Online, AT&T, or MSN (the Microsoft online network). The Check For New Mail On box lists the services that are set up for the profile you're currently logged on with. You can control which services Outlook checks for new messages: turn off the check box beside the name of any service you do not want Outlook to check automatically; turn on the check box for each service you do want Outlook to check.

If you turn off automatic checking of some services, you can still direct Outlook to check these services by choosing the Tools Check For New Mail On command and then selecting the name of the service in the dialog box that appears.

When New Items Arrive

You can choose how you want Outlook to notify you when a new message arrives in your Inbox.

Play A Sound. With this option turned on, you hear a beep when new messages arrive. (This option is turned on by default.) If you have a sound card installed in your computer, you can set the new-message sound to any .WAV file (using the Sound icon on the Control Panel). Turn off this option to squelch the beep or sound.

Briefly Change The Mouse Cursor. With this option turned on, you see the mouse pointer change briefly to an envelope when new messages arrive. (This option is turned on by default.)

Display A Notification Message. Turn on this option to have the following dialog box appear when new messages arrive:

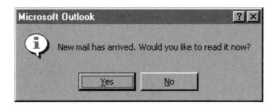

To read new messages right away, click Yes in this dialog box. Outlook then opens the first new message for you to read, without activating the Outlook window. To read new messages later, click No.

Settings For Automatic Processing Of Mail

For other ways to automatically handle messages, see "Outlook Assistants," on page 38.

When you send meeting requests and task requests, you'll eventually receive responses. You can specify the ways Outlook should process these responses when they arrive.

Process Delivery, Read, And Recall Receipts On Arrival. This option directs Outlook to record the response on the message containing your original request. To see the status of responses, open the original message and click the Tracking tab.

Process Requests And Responses On Arrival. With this option turned on, Outlook places on your calendar any meeting requests you receive. When you receive responses to your meeting requests, Outlook records them on your meeting planner.

Delete Receipts And Blank Responses After Processing. Turn on this option to have Outlook automatically delete receipts for the delivery and reading of messages as well as responses to your requests that contain no comments from the responder.

Use Microsoft Word As The E-Mail Editor

Instead of using Outlook message forms and the Outlook text editor for messages, you can choose to use Microsoft Word 97 as your e-mail editor. When you do this, you have at your disposal all of the word processing power of Word for creating a message. You use Word templates as the basis for a message. You can use tables, formulas, fields, and Word's wealth of formatting features when composing a message. You can also attach to your message any object from any Microsoft Windows 95 or Office 97 program.

To use this option, you need to have Microsoft Word 97 installed, and you must turn on the Use Microsoft Word As The E-Mail Editor check box.

You can select a template to use for your messages by clicking the Template button. To choose a Word template, take these steps:

1 Click the Template button.

2 Select the template you want to use.

3 Click the Select button.

Sending Tab

On the Sending tab of the Options dialog box, shown on the following page, you'll find options for the standard font used in new messages, options for standard importance and sensitivity settings, options for tracking the messages you send, and options for saving copies of messages you send.

TIP

> You can format text in individual messages by using the Formatting toolbar or the Format Font command. You can set the importance level of a particular message with the Importance: High and Importance: Low buttons on the Standard toolbar in the message window. You can set the sensitivity level in the message's Properties dialog box. (Choose the File Properties command in the new message window.)
>
> You can also ask for delivery and read receipts for a message by selecting options in the Properties dialog box. If you use these options only rarely, it's better to leave them turned off on the Sending tab in the Options dialog box and instead set them as needed in the message's Properties dialog box or on the message window's Options tab.

When Composing New Messages

For new messages, you can establish standard settings for the text font, for importance and sensitivity levels, for the format of addresses in message headers, and for automatic name checking of e-mail addresses.

Font button. The standard font for new messages is 10-point Arial in autocolor. (Autocolor is the window text color selected in Control Panel. Autocolor is black by default.) If you prefer to use different font options as the standard settings for your new messages, click the Font button. In the Font dialog box, select the font, font style, size, color, and effects (strikeout or underline) that you want to use, and then click OK.

Set Importance.   Most messages you send are of normal importance. That's why Outlook uses Normal as the standard importance setting. If all or most of your messages require top priority, select the High importance option from the drop-down list. On the other hand, if all or most of your messages can be read at any time without compromising your work or your recipients' work, select the Low importance option.

A message that you send with High importance displays a red exclamation mark to the left of its envelope in the message list; a message with Low importance displays a blue downward-pointing arrow. Your e-mail administrator might have set up your e-mail server to deliver messages sent with High importance faster than those sent with Normal or Low importance.

Set Sensitivity.   Most messages you send are not particularly sensitive. That's why Normal is the standard sensitivity setting in Outlook. If a message requires a different level of sensitivity, you have three other choices: Personal, Private, or Confidential.

- The Personal setting displays the word *Personal* in the Sensitivity column of the message list.

- The Private setting displays the word *Private* in the Sensitivity column of the message list. This option prohibits recipients from changing your original message when they reply to it or forward it.

- The Confidential setting displays the word *Confidential* in the Sensitivity column of the message list. Confidential sensitivity notifies the recipient that the message should be treated according to the policies about confidentiality that your organization has set up.

NOTE

The Sensitivity column is not displayed by default. For information about changing the column display, see "Adding Columns from the Field Chooser," on page 455.

Allow Comma As Address Separator. The usual way to separate names in the To, Cc, and Bcc boxes of a message header is with a semicolon. With this check box turned on (as it is initially), you can also separate names with a comma. If you regularly send messages to CompuServe accounts, which have an internal comma in the address, you'll probably want to turn off this check box.

Automatic Name Checking. When this check box is turned on, Outlook checks the names in the To, Cc, and Bcc boxes of a message header against your address books. If a name doesn't appear in at least one of your address books, Outlook marks the name with a sawtooth red underline. You can ignore this underline as long as you're sure that the e-mail address is correct. You can also use the underline as a signal for you to add the name to your personal address book. If you find the underline annoying, you can turn off this check box. You can then ask for name checking in a message window, either by clicking the Check Names button on the Standard toolbar or by pressing Alt+K.

Tracking Options

If it's important that most of your messages be received and read right away—or if you would at least like to have a record of when most of your messages were received and read—you can turn on either or both of the tracking options. If you need this information only for specific messages, you can adjust the tracking options in the Properties dialog box of the message or on the message's Options tab.

Tell Me When All Messages Have Been Delivered. If you like to know when messages have been delivered to the recipients, turn on this check box. When your message arrives in the recipient's mailbox, Outlook delivers a message to your Inbox indicating when the message was received.

Tell Me When All Messages Have Been Read. If you want to know when recipients have opened your messages, turn on this check box. When a recipient opens your message to read it, Outlook sends a notification to your Inbox indicating when the recipient opened your message.

Save Copies Of Messages In Sent Items Folder

For your own record keeping, you might want to have copies of the messages you send. Well, maybe you don't want a copy of every message, but it's safer to keep a copy of all the messages and then later cull out the ones you don't need to save.

By default, Outlook puts a copy of every message you send in your Sent Items folder. If you prefer to be more selective about which messages you keep, turn off this option. If you do, however, remember to add yourself to the Cc box for any messages that you want to keep for your records.

In Folders Other Than The Inbox, Save Replies With Original

Message.   Because you can move or copy messages to other Outlook folders, you might, from time to time, reply to a message while working in a folder other than the Inbox. If you want the reply saved in the folder with the message you're replying to, turn on this check box. If you leave this check box turned off, Outlook saves a copy of your reply in the Sent Items folder.

Save Forwarded Messages.   Outlook is set up to save copies of forwarded messages in your Sent Items folder. If saving forwarded messages isn't important to your work or record keeping, you can turn off this box.

Reading Tab

On the Reading tab of the Options dialog box, shown on the following page, you'll find options for what Outlook should do when you reply to a message, when you forward a message, and after you move or delete a message you're reading. You'll also find options for marking your comments in the text of original messages included in replies and forwards, for closing the window after you reply to or forward a message, and for displaying labels in message headers.

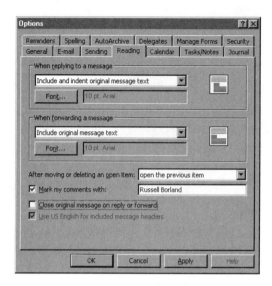

When Replying To A Message

Because replies to messages have a conversational context (the reply takes place as part of a conversation among correspondents), the standard Outlook setup is to include a copy of the original message in the reply. Also, to distinguish the original message from the reply, Outlook indents the original message. You have these additional choices for dealing with the original message in replies:

■ The Do Not Include Original Message option omits the original message from your reply.

■ The Attach Original Message option includes the original message as an attachment, which appears as a message icon. This choice saves space in the message window but requires you and the recipients to double-click the attachment to read it.

■ The Include Original Message Text option includes the original message in the reply but does not indent it.

Font button.   You can choose the font you want Outlook to use for the message text in all your replies. You can, of course, change the font for a specific reply by using the Formatting toolbar or the Format Font command. But if you don't like 10-point Arial in blue as your standard reply font, click the Font button. Then, in the Font dialog box, select the font, font style, size, color, and effects (strikeout or underline) that you want for your standard reply text, and click OK. Outlook will use these settings for all your subsequent replies.

When Forwarding A Message

When you forward a message, you obviously want to include the original message text—that's the idea behind forwarding. Outlook is initially set up to simply include the original message text. You have two other choices for how to do this:

- The Attach Original Message option includes the original message as an attachment, which appears as a message icon that you and the recipients must double-click to read.

- The Include And Indent Original Message Text option indents the original message text.

Font button. For forwarded messages, you can choose the font you want Outlook to use for the comments you include with the original message. If you want to change the standard font for your comments, click the Font button and adjust the settings in the Font dialog box as described in "When Replying To A Message," on the preceding page.

After Moving Or Deleting An Open Item

As part of the process of deleting or moving a message that you've just read, Outlook must close the message window. What should Outlook do after closing the window? You can choose one of the following three options:

- Open The Previous Item is the standard setting. It refers to the usual sorting order in the message list—descending—which places the newest message at the top of the list and the oldest message at the bottom. With this option selected and your message list sorted in descending order, you can start reading the oldest message and move up the list to read the newer arrivals.

- Open The Next Item is the setting to use if you sort your message lists in ascending order (oldest message at the top, newest message at the bottom). With this option turned on and your message list sorted in ascending order, you can start reading the oldest message and move down the list to read the newer arrivals.

- Return To The Inbox is the setting to use if you don't want to jump to the next message in the list. This option is especially handy when you have little time to read your messages and want to select only a message here or there to read.

Mark My Comments With

When you're replying to or forwarding a message with the original message included, you might want to stick comments into the middle of the original message text. When you do, Outlook inserts a label that identifies you as the commentator. The label looks something like this:

[Russell Borland]

You can change the name that appears in the comment label by changing the name in the Mark My Comments With box. If you don't want your comments labeled, turn off this box.

Close Original Message On Reply Or Forward

After you send a reply or forward a message, Outlook by default leaves open the original item's window. This default setting is handy if you like to read through all your messages and dispose of them as you go ("disposing" includes replying to and forwarding messages), continuing to move up or down the message list after you send a reply or forward a message. However, if you're working on a few scattered messages, you might want to turn on the Close Original Message On Reply Or Forward option.

Use US English For Included Message Headers

If you're using a version of Outlook for a language other than English, turning on this check box directs Outlook to translate the labels in the message header (To, Subject, From, and Sent) into English. You'd want to turn on this check box only if you are sure that all the recipients of your messages read English. Turn off this box to keep message header labels in the language of the version of Outlook you're using.

The Use US English For Included Message Headers check box is dimmed and unavailable in the English-language version of Outlook.

Calendar Tab

The Calendar tab of the Options dialog box offers options for setting up the calendar work week, your working hours, the standard reminder time for appointments, the font for dates, and the display of week numbers. You can also designate which calendar file to use, choose a time-zone setup, add holidays to your calendar, and adjust some advanced scheduling options.

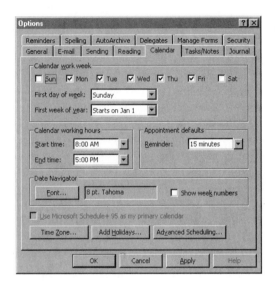

Calendar Work Week

You can specify your standard work week schedule for your Outlook calendar. You can indicate which days of the week you work, the first workday of the week, and the first workday of a new year.

- By default, Outlook's calendar sets up Monday through Friday as standard workdays. If your workdays are different, you can simply turn the appropriate check boxes on and off to reflect your own work week.

- Outlook also initially designates Sunday as the first day of a full week, although you can change this by selecting a day from the First Day Of Week drop-down list. (In some European countries, for example, Monday is considered the first day of the week.)

■ The First Week Of Year option allows you to specify exactly when your work calendar starts in a new year: January 1, the first four-day week in January, or the first full (five-day) week in January.

Calendar Working Hours

A workday can start at various hours. Many people start at 8:00 A.M., others at 9:00 A.M. My father started work at 4:30 A.M. Flextime systems in modern companies can mean that individuals start work at various times during the day. You can set the start time and end time for your own workday so that your calendar can indicate to others the timeframe in which you might be available for meetings. The Start Time and End Time drop-down lists include both hours and half-hours for the entire day. If you need to set different times (for example, 8:45 A.M. or 9:15 P.M.), you can type in the time.

Appointment Defaults

When you've set up an appointment, Outlook sends you a reminder before the appointment's start time. By default, Outlook reminds you fifteen minutes beforehand. You can change this lead time by selecting a different amount of time from the Reminder drop-down list. You have a wide range of choices, from a few minutes to several hours or even two days.

Date Navigator

The Date Navigator is the calendar of months in the upper right corner of the Calendar folder window. The font that Outlook uses to display the dates on the Date Navigator is 8-point Tahoma. You can change the font by clicking the Font button and adjusting the settings in the Font dialog box. If you would like to see the week number (1–52) displayed beside each week in the Date Navigator, turn on the Show Week Numbers option.

Use Microsoft Schedule+ 95 As My Primary Calendar

If you are switching to Outlook from Microsoft Schedule+ 95 (version 7) and you still need to use Schedule+ 95 because some members of your organization haven't yet switched to Outlook, turn on this option. Outlook displays the appointments, tasks, and events that you set up in Schedule+, but it doesn't include your contacts. When this option is turned on, people who are still using Schedule+ can see your appointment schedule when they're trying to arrange a meeting.

If you turn on this option, you cannot use the Outlook Contacts folder as an address book. See the sidebar "Oh, No! The Show This Folder As An E-Mail Address Book Check Box Is Not Available!" on page 449.

Time Zone Button

People travel with their computers all the time. When you're on the road in another time zone, it's convenient to have that time zone's clock visible so that you can set appointments and task times to fit your location. Outlook gives you the means to set your current time zone and to show a second time zone. You can even swap the two zones when you travel from one to the other. Click the Time Zone button on the Calendar tab to open the Time Zone dialog box:

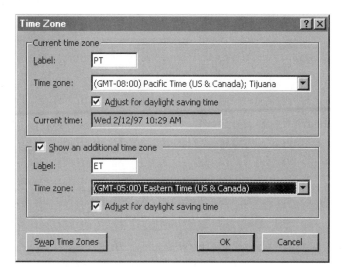

Current Time Zone. In the Time Zone dialog box, select your current time zone from the drop-down list in the Time Zone box. In the Label box, type a label that represents the time zone; for example, you might use PT for Pacific Time. This label will appear above the time slots adjacent to the appointment slots on your calendar. If you want Windows to automatically adjust your computer clock and your calendar when daylight saving time begins and ends, leave the Adjust For Daylight Saving Time check box turned on.

Show An Additional Time Zone.   When you travel to another time zone and plan to use your calendar there, you can set up a second time zone for the calendar. To set it up, turn on the Show An Additional Time Zone check box and complete the Label and Time Zone boxes just as you did for your current time zone. On your calendar, time slots for this second time zone will appear to the left of the time slots for the current time zone.

Swap Time Zones button.   When you move into the second time zone and it becomes your current time zone, you can swap the zones (making your second time zone the current one). To do this, simply click the Swap Time Zones button. When you return home and want to switch back, click the Swap Time Zones button again. When you swap time zones, the time slots for the current time zone move next to the appointment slots on your calendar.

Add Holidays Button

The Outlook calendar is initially set up to indicate the holidays observed in the country for which your computer is set up. If you also observe (or simply want to be informed about) holidays in other countries, click the Add Holidays button on the Calendar tab to add more holidays. In the Add Holidays To Calendar dialog box, turn on the check boxes for those countries whose holidays should appear on your calendar. Adding holidays for other countries makes particularly good sense if you do any business internationally—this way, you'll know when businesses in other nations are closed.

Advanced Scheduling Button

Click the Advanced Scheduling button to set up how Outlook should process meeting requests that are sent to you. You can also specify how you want your free time and busy time information to appear to others.

Tasks/Notes Tab

On the Tasks/Notes tab of the Options dialog box, Outlook provides settings for task reminders and for following the progress of tasks you've assigned to someone else. You can choose display colors for overdue and completed tasks. You can set the number of hours per day and per week that you bill for tasks. And you'll find options for formatting notes.

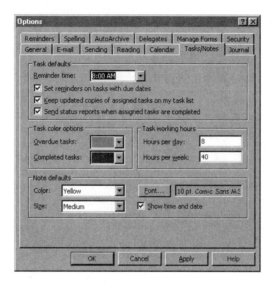

Task Defaults

Set the time of day you want your task reminders to appear, and set the actions you want Outlook to take for tasks.

Reminder Time.   Set the time of day at which Outlook should display your task reminders. The drop-down list displays hours and half-hours throughout the day. If you want your reminders to appear at an in-between time (say, 9:15 A.M.), type that time in the box. If you start Outlook after the time set here, Outlook displays the reminders at startup.

Set Reminders On Tasks With Due Dates.   Leave this option turned on if you want Outlook to automatically set a reminder for a task that has a due date. The reminder appears on the due date at the time you set in the Reminder Time box above. You can change the reminder date and time in the task item window.

Keep Updated Copies Of Assigned Tasks On My Task List. When you assign a task to someone else, you might want to receive updates to the task status as it changes. Leave this check box turned on to keep a copy of the task in your task list so that Outlook can update the task status as it changes.

Send Status Reports When Assigned Tasks Are Completed. When this option is turned on, you will receive a status report when the person to whom you have assigned a task marks the assigned task completed.

Task Color Options

For your task list, you can select a specific color for tasks that are overdue and another color for completed tasks. These colors help you quickly identify which tasks are overdue, which tasks have been completed, and which tasks are not overdue.

Task Working Hours

Part of tracking tasks is setting the number of hours used to calculate the cost of a task. You can set the hours per day and hours per week you use to calculate task-hour costs.

Note Defaults

In the Note Defaults area, you can establish the format you prefer to use for new notes:

- Set the color of new notes in the Color box. Your choices are Blue, Green, Pink, Yellow (the standard color), and White.

- In the Size box, select the standard size for notes (Small, Medium, or Large).

- To change the font for the text of notes, click the Font button to open the Font dialog box, where you can adjust the settings to your preference.

- To omit the time and date display from the text of notes, turn off the Show Time And Date check box. (Outlook will continue to record the creation date and time for notes, however, even if this option is turned off.)

Journal Tab

Outlook is initially set up to record journal entries each time you create, open, close, or save any file in Office 97 (Microsoft Access, Microsoft Excel, Microsoft Office Binder, Microsoft PowerPoint, and Microsoft Word). On the Journal tab of the Options dialog box, you can add Outlook activities that you want to record in your journal.

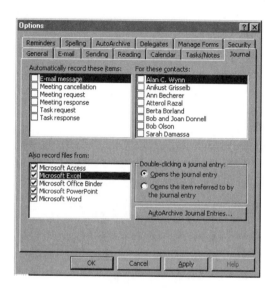

Automatically Record These Items.   Turn on the appropriate check boxes to have Outlook automatically record journal entries for e-mail messages, meeting cancellations, meeting requests, meeting responses, task requests, and task responses that are sent to or received from the contacts you select in the For These Contacts list.

For These Contacts.   For each Outlook action, turn on the check box for the contacts that you want to record. This list includes only the names listed in your Contacts folder. If you have no contacts set up, this list is empty. If a name you want to select is not listed, click OK in the Options dialog box, add the new contact, and then return to this tab.

Also Record Files From.   Turn off the check box for any Office program whose actions you don't want to record. Other programs that are compatible with Office 97 might also appear in this list.

Double-Clicking A Journal Entry. Select what should happen when you double-click a journal entry. Outlook can either open the journal entry form itself or open the item associated with the entry (the e-mail message, the PowerPoint file, and so on). The setting you choose here for the double-click action also determines what is opened when you choose the File Open command in the Journal folder window, when you right-click a journal entry and choose Open from the shortcut menu, and when you press Ctrl+O.

AutoArchive Journal Entries button. Click this button to change AutoArchive settings. For details, see Chapter 15, "Archiving Folder Items."

Reminders Tab

On the Reminders tab of the Options dialog box, you'll find options for how Outlook should notify you when a reminder you've set for a task or an appointment comes due.

Display The Reminder. Turn on this option to have Outlook display a reminder message. In the message window, you can close the reminder if you don't need further reminding, you can reset the reminder to appear again after an interval you specify, or you can edit the task or appointment. For details, see "Setting a Reminder," on page 241, and "Setting a Task Reminder," on page 266.

Play Reminder Sound. Turn on this option to have Outlook play a sound to notify you that a task or an appointment is due. If you don't have a sound card, you'll hear a beep. If you do have a sound card, you can set the reminder sound to any .WAV file by typing its full pathname in this box or by clicking the Browse button to find the file.

Spelling Tab

When you check the spelling of messages, Outlook compares the words in your message text with a dictionary file. If the spelling checker can't find the word in its dictionary, it shows you the word in a dialog box and gives you a chance to correct the spelling, ignore the word (because it's a special word or a word you made up for the nonce), or add the word to the dictionary.

On the Spelling tab of the Options dialog box, you'll find options for checking the spelling of messages and for how (and when) the check should be conducted. By default, Outlook suggests correct spellings for misspelled words. It also checks numbers, words that include numbers, and words that are written in all capital letters, as well as any original text in replies and forwarded messages. You can ask the spelling checker to ignore any or all of these types of information in message text.

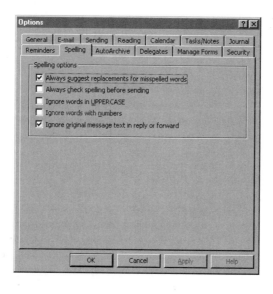

Always Suggest Replacements For Misspelled Words. If you don't want Outlook to automatically suggest correct spellings for words not included in the dictionary file it uses, turn off this check box. When this option is turned off, you must click the Suggest button in the Spelling dialog box to get a suggestion from the spelling checker. If you prefer to always have a suggestion to work from, leave this check box turned on.

Always Check Spelling Before Sending. If you're someone who always likes to check spelling before sending a message, the Always Check Spelling Before Sending option is for you. If you turn on this check box, Outlook checks the spelling in your message text after you click the Send button but before the message is sent.

Ignore Words In UPPERCASE. To tell the spelling checker to ignore words that are written in all capital letters, turn on the Ignore Words In UPPERCASE check box. The spelling checker then ignores words such as FILENAME.

Ignore Words With Numbers. To tell the spelling checker to ignore numbers, turn on the Ignore Words With Numbers check box. The spelling checker will then ignore words that contain a mix of numbers and letters (such as WSJ010846) and words that consist entirely of numbers (such as 123456789, or the 97 in Office 97).

Ignore Original Message Text In Reply Or Forward. The spelling checker is set up to ignore the original text included in replies and forwarded messages. If you want Outlook to check the spelling in the original text, turn off this check box.

AutoArchive Tab

SEE ALSO
You need to take additional steps to set up automatic archiving, especially for folders that don't contain e-mail messages. For details, see Chapter 15.

On the AutoArchive tab of the Options dialog box, shown at the top of the facing page, Outlook offers general settings for automatically archiving folders. You can set the time span between archiving, ask for a prompt when archiving starts, direct Outlook to delete items after they're archived, and set the file that you want Outlook to use for archives.

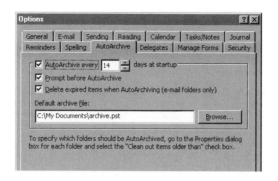

- To specify the time interval at which automatic archiving should take place, choose the number of days (1–60) in the AutoArchive Every [ ] Days At Startup box. Turn off the check box to prevent all automatic archiving.

- Turn off the Prompt Before AutoArchive option if you don't want a prompt before the AutoArchive process begins.

- The AutoArchive process deletes expired items from e-mail folders by default. To prevent this, turn off the Delete Expired Items When AutoArchiving (E-Mail Folders Only) option.

- In the Default Archive File box, you can edit the filename or type a new filename. To locate or create another archive file in your file system, click the Browse button.

Security Tab

? SEE ALSO

For information about installing add-ins, see "Add-In Manager Button," on page 49.

If you are running Outlook with Microsoft Exchange Server and you have the Digital Security add-in installed, you'll see the Security tab on the Options dialog box. On the Security tab, shown at the top of the next page, you'll find options for encrypting your messages, adding your digital signature to messages, setting your security file, changing your security password, setting up advanced security, logging off advanced security, and sending security keys.

Getting Started

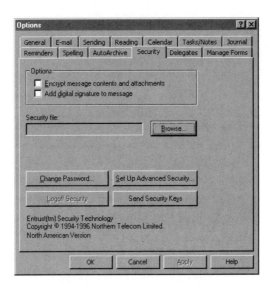

Advanced security provides a layer of protection for your messages. To use encryption and a digital signature, you must have first set up advanced security.

- Encryption ensures that only someone who logs on to the e-mail server as a valid recipient can read your message. Turn on the Encrypt Message Contents And Attachments option to encrypt your messages. Without encryption, your messages are sent as readable text.

- A digital signature assures the recipient that you are really the person who sent the message—in other words, that the message is not some bogus transmission sent by a pernicious computer hacker—and that the message has not been altered along the way. Turn on the Add Digital Signature To Message option to add a digital signature to each message you send.

When advanced security is available to you, you'll probably want to use it most of the time. If some recipients of a particular message don't have advanced security, however, you have to send the message without encryption or a digital signature. To save yourself from having to answer the message that appears each time you send a message to a recipient without advanced security, you might want to turn off the options for using encryption and a digital signature. (For information about using encryption and a digital signature for individual messages, see "Set Up Advanced Security Button," on page 73.)

Security File

This box lists the name of your security file. If the filename isn't listed (but advanced security is set up) or if you have another security file that you want to use, type the filename or click the Browse button to locate the advanced security file.

Change Password Button

You can use the Change Password button to change your advanced security password. Here are the steps:

1   Click the Change Password button.

2   In the Change Security Password dialog box, type your current advanced security password in the Old Password box.

3   In the New Password box, type the new advanced security password.

4   In the Confirm Password box, type *exactly* the same password that you typed in the New Password box.

5   Click OK.

Set Up Advanced Security Button

Before you can use advanced security, you must set it up. To set up advanced security, take these steps:

1   Send a request for advanced security for your account to the Exchange administrator.

2   Your Exchange administrator must set up and turn on advanced security for your account.

3   The Exchange administrator sends you a token, a special keyword assigned by the administrator.

4   Choose the Tools Options command, select the Security tab of the Options dialog box, and then click the Set Up Advanced Security button.

5   In the Set Up Advanced Security dialog box, type your unique token in the Token box. Choose a password to use for Advanced Security, enter it in the Password box and in the Confirm Password box, and then click OK.

6 Click OK in the message box telling you that a message has been sent to your Exchange server. Click OK in the Options dialog box.

7 Your Exchange server verifies your token and notifies you with a message. Open the message from the Exchange server, and enter your password in the dialog box that appears. You'll see a message that security has been set up. Click OK. The message from your server is deleted automatically.

At this point, you should open the Security tab of the Options dialog box and turn on the encryption and digital signature options. From now on, when you send a message, Outlook requires access to your security file, which has its own password (the one you chose in step 5). To open your security file and send the message, type the password and click OK.

If a recipient doesn't have advanced security, you'll see a message box telling you this. You then have two choices for delivering the message:

■ Click the Don't Encrypt Message button to send the message anyway. When encryption is turned on, this is the only way to send a message to a recipient who doesn't have advanced security.

■ Click the Cancel Send button if you decide not to send the message to someone who doesn't have advanced security.

You can, of course, turn off encryption and your digital signature on the Security tab, as explained earlier. If you do so, you can encrypt a single message or add your digital signature to a single message by clicking the Seal Message With Encryption button or the Digitally Sign Message button on the new message window toolbar. You can also use these buttons to turn off security for an individual message.

When you receive a message with a digital signature, click the Verify Digital Signature button on the message window toolbar to verify that the message is authentic:

Your e-mail server requires access to your security file before reading a digital signature.

Logoff Security Button

When you're using advanced security, Outlook requires access to your security file. When Outlook needs this access, it provides a dialog box in which you type your advanced security password. This dialog box also contains the Don't Prompt For Password Again Until Next Microsoft Exchange Logon check box. If you turn on this check box, you don't have to type your advanced security password every time you send a message or read a secured message. However, selecting this option means that your Outlook account is open to anyone who sits down at your computer and sends a message. To prevent unauthorized use of your account while you're away from your computer, you can log off advanced security.

To log off advanced security after you have turned on the Don't Prompt For Password Again Until Next Microsoft Exchange Logon option, choose the Tools Options command, click the Security tab, and then click the Logoff Security button.

This button is active only after you have turned on the Don't Prompt For Password Again Until Next Microsoft Exchange Logon option. When you return to your computer and send a message or read a secure message, you'll once again see the dialog box that asks for your security password.

Send Security Keys Button

Depending on your installation of Outlook, the Security tab might also display the Send Security Keys Button. Before you can send and receive encrypted and digitally signed messages with people outside your organization, you need access to their public encryption key, and they need access to your public encryption key. To send your public encryption key to someone else, click the Send Security Keys button.

If you're not logged on to advanced security, you'll see the Microsoft Exchange Security Logon dialog box. Type your security password and click OK. Then follow these steps in the Security Key Exchange Message dialog box, shown on the next page.

1 Click the To button to select names from your address books, or...

type the names of the message recipients.

2 If necessary, correct your e-mail address.

3 Change your display name if you like.

7 Click Send.

4 Click here to verify you have the public security key.

5 Turn off any check box for information you don't want to send to your recipients.

6 Fill out information you want to send.

Delegates Tab

On the Delegates tab of the Options dialog box, you can give others permission to perform Outlook tasks on your behalf.

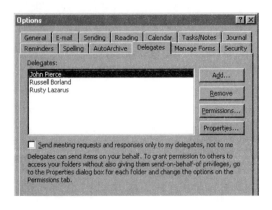

Delegates

The Delegates box lists those people you have designated as your delegates. Use the buttons along the right side of the Delegates box to change the list or to change the types of permission you grant to a delegate.

Add Button

To add a delegate to your list of delegates, follow these steps:

1 Click the Add button on the Delegates tab.

2 In the Type Name Or Select From List box, type a name, or select names from the list below the box.

3 Click the Add button, and then click OK to open the Delegate Permissions dialog box.

5 Turn off this check box if you don't want your delegate to receive copies of meeting requests.

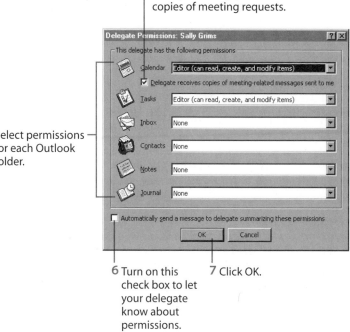

4 Select permissions for each Outlook folder.

6 Turn on this check box to let your delegate know about permissions.

7 Click OK.

If you type or select more than one name as a delegate, the Delegate Permissions dialog box shows the phrase *<Multiple delegates>* in its title bar. The permissions you set apply to all the delegates you selected. To set permissions for individuals, either add them one at a time or add them all at once and then change permissions for each one with the Permissions button. (See "Permissions Button," below.)

Remove Button

To remove a delegate from your delegates list, simply select the name of the delegate in the Delegates box and click the Remove button. Outlook does not ask you to confirm deletion of a delegate.

Permissions Button

When you want to change the level of permissions for a delegate, take these steps:

1 Select the name of the delegate in the Delegates box.

2 Click the Permissions button.

3 Change the permission settings in the Delegate Permissions dialog box (shown on the preceding page).

4 Click OK in the Delegate Permissions dialog box.

Properties Button

The Properties button displays the Properties dialog box for the name you select in the Delegates box. The Properties dialog box shows address book information, such as the delegate's e-mail name, title, and so on.

Send Meeting Requests And Responses Only To My Delegates, Not To Me

If you have arranged for a delegate to keep track of your calendar, you can take yourself off the meeting-request-and-response carousel. To set this up, take these steps:

1 In the Delegate Permissions dialog box, give the delegate you have chosen to take care of your calendar Editor permission for your Calendar folder.

2 Turn on the Delegate Receives Copies Of Meeting-Related Messages Sent To Me option.

3 Click OK in the Delegate Permissions dialog box.

4 On the Delegates tab, turn on the Send Meeting Requests And Responses Only To My Delegates, Not To Me box.

5 Click OK in the Options dialog box.

Manage Forms Tab

? SEE ALSO

For more information about creating and using forms, see Part VI, "According to Form."

Forms are an integral part of Outlook. You use forms to send and read messages, to set and request appointments, and to respond to meeting and task requests. Every folder item window in Outlook is a form. In addition, Outlook provides the tools for creating custom forms. In some cases, these forms are set up by an organizational forms designer. In other cases, you or a colleague might create a special form for your own purposes. To make forms work, you need to set aside some temporary storage space for them on your computer. Also, you can install forms that are included in form libraries to use in your work. For dealing with the necessary aspects of form life in Outlook, you turn to the Manage Forms tab of the Options dialog box. On this tab, you can also change your Microsoft Windows NT network password.

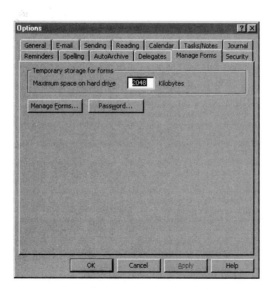

Temporary Storage For Forms

When you read a message or posting or when you create a message or posting with a form that isn't stored on your hard disk, Outlook downloads the form and stores it temporarily. This way, if you read or create an item that uses this form again in the next few days, it's ready at hand, and the process goes more quickly.

To prevent forms from taking up hard disk space that you need for other work, you can limit the amount of space Outlook can use for temporarily storing forms. In the Maximum Space On Hard Drive box, type a number (in kilobytes) for the amount of space you want to set aside for temporary form storage. If you use many different forms frequently and have plenty of free space on your hard disk, you might change this value to a higher number. Otherwise, the default setting of 2048 kilobytes is probably appropriate. When Outlook has filled the space you've set aside, it discards the oldest form stored in temporary storage to make room for the newest form you're using.

Manage Forms Button

Outlook downloads forms for reading messages when you need them. But when you want to use a form to send a message, you'll need to have the form installed. That's where the Manage Forms button comes into play. The Forms Manager dialog box helps you copy, update, and remove forms. To manage forms, do the following:

1 Click the Manage Forms button on the Manage Forms tab.

2 Click the Set button to add more forms.

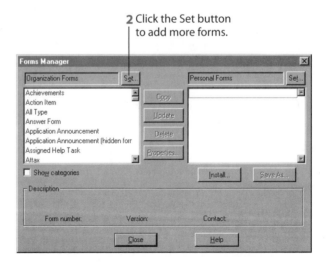

3 Select the library that contains the form, or...

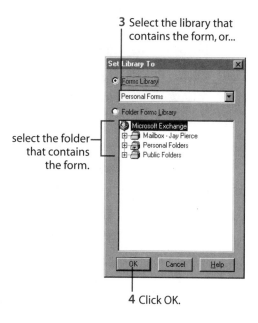

select the folder that contains the form.

4 Click OK.

5 When you've returned to the Forms Manager dialog box, select the forms that you want to add from the list at the left.

6 Click Copy. When Outlook has finished copying the forms, their names appear in the list at the right.

7 To copy forms from other folders, repeat steps 2 through 6.

8 Click the Close button in the Forms Manager dialog box.

Password Button

In some organizations, you might be required to change your password according to a certain schedule. Even if you aren't required to do this, it's a good idea to change your network password regularly, at least once every 60 days or so. Doing so helps maintain network security. The Password button on the Manage Forms tab opens the Change Windows NT Password dialog box.

Here's how to change your Windows NT password:

1 Click the Password button on the Manage Forms tab.

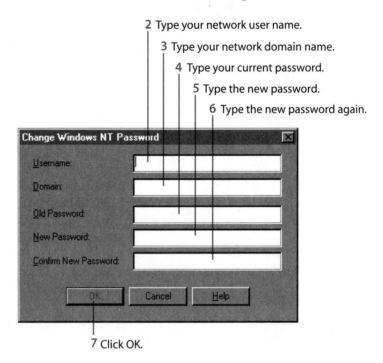

2 Type your network user name.

3 Type your network domain name.

4 Type your current password.

5 Type the new password.

6 Type the new password again.

7 Click OK.

Now that you're acquainted with the Outlook window and the options you can use to help you make Outlook work the way you want it to, in the remainder of this book, you'll see Outlook in action.

Electronic Mail

Messages and Faxes

You have something to say, and you wanna say it. Someone else has something to say, and you wanna hear it. You know something someone else needs to know; someone else knows something you need to know. You want to swap lies (as well as facts). Well, to swap tales with other people, you send them an e-mail message or a fax, or they send you one, through Microsoft Outlook 97.

The process of electronic mail is like a swap meet. You send up a message on a hard disk somewhere (on a computer known as a server) so that the person whom you want to see the message (and only that person) can pull it down and read it. It's the same for everyone who sends a message—send up and read, send up and read. The messages you pull down (receive), someone else sent up to you. (You can also send up messages for yourself.)

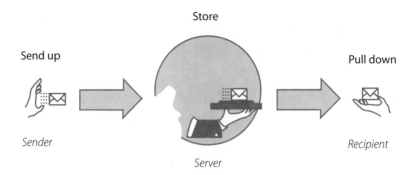

Although the process of sending a fax is usually more direct, it can be very similar: fax services can receive faxes for you and store them on a server from which you can retrieve them. In general, the process of trading information has three important parts: composing the message you want to send, sending the message to the right place, and reading the messages others send to you.

Your message, whether you send it by e-mail or fax, can include words and numbers (text), web page addresses (URLs), pictures, charts and graphs, audio, and video; in fact, it can include any type of information that you can create in a Windows-based application. (See "Adding Text from a File," on page 104, and "Adding 'Other Stuff'," on page 105.) You can also add special effects and decorations to the text—boldface, italic, underlining, color, bullets, and paragraph indention. (See "Adding Text Decorations," on page 95, for information.)

After you compose and decorate (format) a message, you're ready to address the message so that you can send it to the right place for those people who should see it. Key to addressing a message is your address book. To find the right person, you need to use the right address book at the right time, and you need to make your address book as useful as possible. (See Chapter 4, "Mucking About in Address Books.") After you address the message, you push it along, by sending, forwarding, or replying.

And, of course, when someone else stuffs a message in your mailbox, you want to read it (maybe) and then deal with it in some way or other. Because a message can contain any object created by any Windows-based application, some parts of a message might appear as icons. You'll want to know how to make an icon open up and reveal its contents. You might also have more than one place to store mail messages—in various Outlook folders and in files outside Outlook. (See "Gathering Messages from the Beyond," on page 113, and "Moving a Folder Item" on page 358.)

Finally, for those days when nothing but a fax will do, you can find all the details about using Outlook to set up, send, and receive faxes at the end of this chapter—see "Facts About Fax," on page 123.

Message Windows

Messages appear in a message window. In Outlook, you can see messages in several types of windows. Two of the most common are the standard message window and a WordMail window. (You can also see messages in windows designed for meeting and task requests and responses, and in windows for messages based on special forms created by you or someone else.)

Standard Message Form

Unless you've turned on Microsoft Word 97 as your e-mail editor, you'll see the standard message form, shown in Figure 3-1, when you open a message window.

Standard toolbar   Message header boxes

FIGURE 3-1.
Outlook's standard message form.

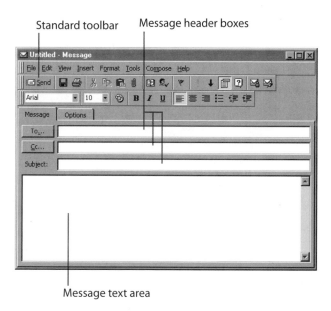

Message text area

We'll look at how to use this standard message form in the sections "Sending a Message," on page 90, "Replying to a Message," on page 114, and "Forwarding a Message," on page 117.

WordMail Messages

Outlook's standard message form is fine for many purposes, and it gives you some useful formatting options such as color, indention, paragraph alignment, and bullets. But, if you prefer, you can use Microsoft Word 97 to compose a new message or to read, reply to, or forward a message. By choosing Word as your electronic mail editor, you use a Word template as the basis for a message, and you can incorporate tables, formulas, and fields in your message and use Word's entire array of formatting features when composing a message.

To set up the WordMail tools, you must have Word 97 installed. Then follow these steps:

1 Choose the Tools Options command to open the Options dialog box.

2 Click the E-Mail tab.

3 Turn on this check box.

4 Click Template.

5 The WordMail Template dialog box displays the contents of the Office folder (which is inside the Microsoft Office folder inside the Program Files folder on your hard disk). This folder contains the WordMail template Email, as well as other templates specifically for e-mail messages: Flame, Hightech, Midnight, Ocean, Rain, and Urgent. (Word templates have the filename extension .DOT.) These WordMail templates include special decorations such as a border along the left edge of the message area. Select the template you want to use, and then click the Select button.

6 Click OK to close the Options dialog box.

After you turn on the WordMail option, each time you compose a new message or read, reply to, or forward a message, you'll see a window like the one shown in Figure 3-2 on the following page, which looks much like your Microsoft Word window.

Keep in mind that you can use any Word template for WordMail. Whether the Word template is supplied by Microsoft or created by you or someone else, Outlook adds the message header when you create a new message. So if you want a special style of e-mail message, you can create a Word template that suits your purposes and then use it with Outlook to create that special message.

FIGURE 3-2.
The WordMail
message window.

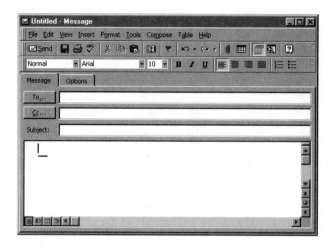

> **NOTE**
>
> If you select as your WordMail template a Word template that contains automatic macros (AutoOpen, AutoNew, AutoStart, and AutoQuit), Word does not run these macros when you start a new message, open a message, or close a message.

Sending a Message

It's easy to create a new e-mail message—and Outlook gives you lots of options for protecting, formatting, delivering, and tracking your message, as well as for drawing attention to the message and adding attachments to it.

Creating a New Message

The fastest and easiest way to send a message is simply to type the text and click the Send button. In this basic case, your message looks tidy but unspectacular, and it also requires the least effort.

To send a simple message, do the following:

New Mail Message

1 Click the New Mail Message button on the Standard toolbar.

2 In the new message window, click the To button to display the Select Names dialog box.

4 Click the To button.

3 Type a name (or part of a name), or...

select a name from the list.

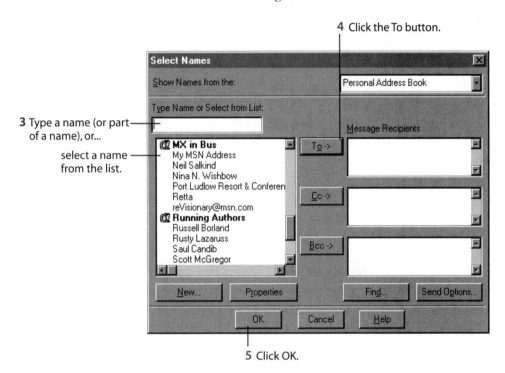

5 Click OK.

6 In the message window, click in the Subject box and type a brief description of the subject of your message.

7 Press the Tab key to move to the message text area, and then type your message.

Send

8 When your message is ready to send, click the Send button.

When you type the beginning of a name in the Select Names dialog box (step 3), Outlook jumps to the first name in the list that matches the letters you've typed. You can then scroll, if you need to, to find

II

Electronic Mail

the name you want. You can also send a message to several recipients at one time. To do this, either select each name and then click the To button for each selection, or hold down the Ctrl key while you click all the names you want and then click the To button.

At the same time as you address your message to the main recipients, you can also designate who should receive copies or "blind carbon copies" of the message. To fill in the Cc and Bcc boxes of the message header at the same time as you fill in the To box, select the names of the recipients for the appropriate header box and click the related button (Cc or Bcc) in the Select Names dialog box.

Instead of clicking the To button in the message window to address your message, you can simply type the names of the recipients. Separate the names either with a semicolon or with a comma. (For commas to work as separators, the Allow Comma As Address Separator option on the Sending tab of the Options dialog box must be turned on. You should avoid using a comma as an address separator if you send e-mail to CompuServe addresses, which contain their own internal commas.)

Sending a Protected Message

When you want privacy for your messages, you can encrypt them. When you want to assure your recipients that you actually sent the messages they received in your name and that the messages weren't tampered with during transit, you can digitally sign them. You can both encrypt and digitally sign a message.

SEE ALSO

For information about reading an encrypted message or checking a digital signature, see "Reading a Protected Message," on page 111.

You can use encryption and digital signatures only if you are running Outlook with Microsoft Exchange Server and have set up advanced security. For details about how to do this, see "Set Up Advanced Security Button," on page 73.

If you want to encrypt or digitally sign all messages that you send, choose the Tools Options command, select the Security tab, and turn on the Encrypt Message Contents And Attachments option and the Add Digital Signature To Message option. If you don't have these options turned on, you can still encrypt or digitally sign a single message by following these steps:

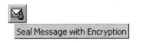

Seal Message with Encryption

Digitally Sign Message

1 Create the message.

2 Click one or both of the Standard toolbar buttons that are shown on the left.

3 Click the Send button. Outlook will display the Microsoft Exchange Security Logon dialog box before it sends the message:

5 Click OK.

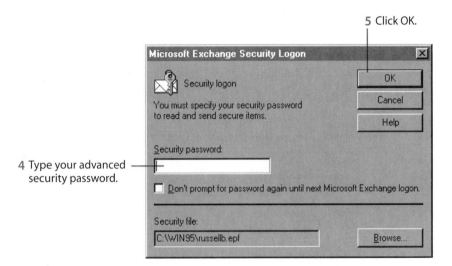

4 Type your advanced security password.

![WARNING]

In the Microsoft Exchange Security Logon dialog box, you can turn on the Don't Prompt For Password Again Until Next Microsoft Exchange Logon check box if you want to send encrypted messages without having to type your password again during the current Outlook session. But watch out! If you turn on this box, anyone can send protected messages in your name (and read your protected messages). To prevent this, log off advanced security when you leave your computer unattended. (For directions, see "Logoff Security Button," on page 75.)

If you decide to save the message in your Inbox for later completion, Outlook still requires you to log on to advanced security when you close and save the message. When you reopen the message to complete it, you'll also have to log on to advanced security.

Electronic Mail

Stamping Your Signature

Have you ever received a message with a few standard closing lines at the end of it? Maybe the sender's name, an e-mail address, a postal address, and some pithy saying? Would you like to add such lines at the end of your messages? Outlook gives you AutoSignature to do just that.

AutoSignature automatically adds whatever closing you want to your new messages. AutoSignature can also add a closing to replies and forwarded messages—you decide.

Here's how to set up an AutoSignature:

1 Choose the Tools AutoSignature command.

2 Turn on this check box.

3 Type your signature lines.

Click here if you want to set the font for selected text in your AutoSignature.

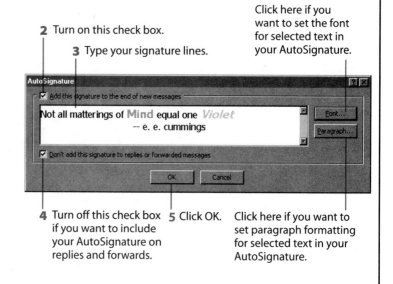

4 Turn off this check box if you want to include your AutoSignature on replies and forwards.

5 Click OK.

Click here if you want to set paragraph formatting for selected text in your AutoSignature.

The next time you send a message, Outlook adds your AutoSignature at the end of the message. For replies and forwards, Outlook adds the AutoSignature above the copy of the message you are responding to or forwarding.

NOTE

If any of your recipients don't have advanced security set up, you'll see a message box telling you that the recipients can't process encrypted messages. To send the message anyway, click the Don't Encrypt Message button. The message then goes out without protection. To send protected messages within your organization, swapping security keys isn't necessary—it's part of setting up Microsoft Exchange Server in your organization. For recipients outside your organization, you'll need to swap keys; for details, see "Send Security Keys Button," on page 75.

Adding Text Decorations

A plain text message is quick and easy, but you might want to decorate the message's text a little, just to make e-mail life more lively. Outlook provides several ways to enhance the appearance of your mail messages. Here's the list of basic text decorations you can use:

- Boldface, italic, and underlining

- Color

- Various fonts and sizes

- Bullets

- Paragraph indention

- Paragraph alignment (left-aligned, right-aligned, and centered)

To apply decorations to the text in a message, you use the buttons and boxes on the Formatting toolbar in the new message window:

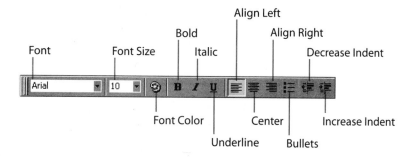

Besides using the toolbar, you can add and remove text decorations with menu commands and key combinations.

Electronic Mail

II

Menu commands. The Format menu in the new message window contains two commands: Font and Paragraph. In the Font dialog box, you can select fonts, font sizes, boldface, italic, underlining, and color. The Paragraph dialog box provides options for adding bullets and for setting paragraph alignment.

Key combinations. To add (or start using) a text decoration from the keyboard, press the corresponding key combination shown in the following table. To remove the decoration (or to stop using it), press the key combination again.

Text Decoration	Key Combination
Boldface	Ctrl+B
Italic	Ctrl+I
Underline	Ctrl+U
Stop (or remove) all text decorations	Ctrl+Spacebar
Bullets	Ctrl+Shift+L
Center	Ctrl+E
Increase indent	Ctrl+T
Decrease indent	Ctrl+Shift+T
Left align	Ctrl+L
Underline	Ctrl+U
Increase font size	Ctrl+]
Decrease font size	Ctrl+[
Clear formatting	Ctrl+Shift+Z or Ctrl+Spacebar

Setting Message Options

SEE ALSO

For information about setting up standard options on the tabs of the Options dialog box, see "Setting Outlook Options," on page 46.

Outlook sets up your new messages according to the options selected on the tabs of the Options dialog box. For a specific message, however, you might want to change the standard settings. To do this, click on the Options tab in the message window. This tab is shown in Figure 3-3.

The settings you choose on the message window's Options tab apply only to the message you're working on. Any changes you make here do not affect the standard settings on the tabs of the Options dialog box.

FIGURE 3-3.

The Options tab in Outlook's message window.

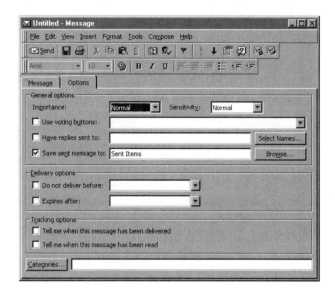

General Options

The first set of options on the message window's Options tab lets you designate how important or sensitive a message is. These options also allow you to include voting buttons in the message or to have replies to your e-mail sent to another e-mail address. When you send a message, Outlook usually saves a copy of it in the Sent Items folder—but if you want to save the copy in another folder, you can specify a different folder on this tab.

Importance

The standard importance level for your messages is set on the Sending tab of the Options dialog box. (See "Set Importance," on page 55.) But sometimes you might want to send a message with a different level of importance. Suppose, for instance, that you need to send an urgent message about a deadline change to members of your project team. It's important that they notice and read the message right away. You can click the Options tab in the message window and select the High importance level in the Importance box. When Outlook delivers that message, it adds a red exclamation mark to the left of the envelope in the recipient's message list, alerting the recipient that this is an important message. (Depending on how your e-mail server is set up, a High importance message might even be delivered faster than messages with Normal or Low importance levels.)

Likewise, if you've just heard a funny story that you'd like to pass along to a friend, but you know that the friend is busily working to complete a project, you can set a Low importance level for your message. When the message arrives, the recipient sees a blue downward-pointing arrow next to the envelope in the message list and knows that this message can wait until the project's work is done.

 TIP

You can click either the Importance: High button (the red exclamation mark) or the Importance: Low button (the blue down arrow) on the Standard toolbar in the message window to set the importance level for an individual message. If you change your mind and want to return the importance level of the message to Normal, click that toolbar button again.

Sensitivity

The standard sensitivity level for your messages is set on the Sending tab of the Options dialog box. (See "Set Sensitivity," on page 55.) If a specific message requires a different level of sensitivity, you can designate this level on the Options tab of the message window. The four levels of sensitivity are Normal, Personal, Private, and Confidential.

 SEE ALSO

For information about changing the column display, see "Setting Up Columns" on page 454.

Outlook shows the corresponding label—*Normal, Personal, Private,* or *Confidential*—in the Sensitivity column of the recipient's message list, provided that the Sensitivity column is displayed. If the Sensitivity column is not displayed, the recipient will see that the message has been marked Personal, Private, or Confidential when she or he opens the message to read it.

The Personal designation is only informational. The Private designation prevents recipients from altering your original message if they reply to it or forward it. The Confidential sensitivity level notifies recipients to treat the message according to your organization's policies about confidentiality.

Use Voting Buttons

Did you ever send a message that asked people to respond to a proposal or an invitation? If you haven't yet, you probably will sometime during your e-mail lifetime. Outlook makes it possible to give your recipients an easy way to send a response to your proposal or invitation: voting buttons. When you turn on the Use Voting Buttons check box on the message window's Options tab, you'll see three choices in the drop-down list—Approve;Reject, Yes;No, and Yes;No;Maybe—which correspond to these three sets of voting buttons:

Select the set of buttons you want to include in your message, and send the message. When Outlook delivers it, the recipients will see the buttons displayed just above the Message tab in the message window, along with the instruction *Please respond using the buttons above.*

⑦ SEE ALSO

To find out how to use a voting button in a message you receive, see "Replying Through Voting Buttons," on page 115.

You can even create your own set of voting buttons. Instead of selecting one of the choices in the drop-down list, delete the text that appears in the list box and type in new text with the voting button names you want to use. Separate the names with semicolons, and don't include any spaces: for example, *Red;Green;Blue* or *Tuesday;Thursday*. When your message is delivered, it will display your set of custom buttons.

Have Replies Sent To

When you send a message that requests replies, you might want the replies to go to an e-mail address other than your own. For example, you might invite staff members to a staff party but want your assistant to receive the replies in order to set up a list of attendees or to supply a proper attendance figure to the caterer.

To have the replies to your message sent to another e-mail address, take these steps:

1 On the Options tab of the message window, turn on the Have Replies Sent To check box.

⑦ SEE ALSO

For another way to let recipients send their responses to a different e-mail address, see "Including a Mailto Response Link," on page 107.

2 Type the e-mail address, or click the Select Names button. Clicking the Select Names button displays the Have Replies Sent To dialog box, where you can select the name or names of those who should receive the replies. (Outlook includes your e-mail name in this box by default. To delete your name, select it and press the Delete key.)

Save Sent Message To

You might want to save an occasional message in a folder other than the Sent Items folder. At other times, you might not want to save a

II

Electronic Mail

particular message at all. You make both of these adjustments with the Save Sent Message To option on the message window's Options tab:

- To tell Outlook not to save the message, turn off the Save Sent Message To check box.

- To save a message in a different folder, click the Browse button, select the folder where you want the message saved, and then click OK in the Select Folder dialog box.

If you want to save your message in a folder that doesn't yet exist, follow these steps:

1 Be sure that the Save Sent Message To check box is turned on, and then click the Browse button.

2 In the Select Folder dialog box, click the New button.

3 In the Create New Folder dialog box, type a name for the new folder, and select the folder in which the new folder should be stored. Optionally, you can also type a description of the new folder.

4 Turn off the Create A Shortcut To This Folder In The Outlook Bar check box if you don't want to display the new folder on the Outlook Bar.

5 Click OK in the Create New Folder dialog box, and then click OK in the Select Folder dialog box.

Delivery Options

Some messages are time-sensitive—either they can't be delivered before a specific date, or they expire after a certain date. You can set options for both of these cases on the Options tab of the message window.

To set up a delayed delivery, turn on the Do Not Deliver Before check box and type or select the earliest date on which the message should be delivered. To set an expiration date for a message, turn on the Expires After check box and type or select an expiration date for the message.

You can use delayed delivery only if you are running Outlook with Microsoft Exchange Server.

Tracking Options

The standard tracking options used for the majority of your messages are set on the Sending tab of the Options dialog box. (See "Tracking Options," on page 56.) But if you want to set a different tracking option for a specific message, you can do so on the Options tab of the message window.

To have Outlook notify you when your message arrives in the recipient's mailbox, turn on the Tell Me When This Message Has Been Delivered check box. To have Outlook notify you when the recipient has opened your message, turn on the check box labeled Tell Me When This Message Has Been Read. You can choose either or both of these options. When your message arrives (or when the recipient opens it), Outlook delivers a message to your Inbox conveying this information.

Bear in mind that even though the label for the Tell Me When This Message Has Been Read check box contains the word *Read*, Outlook can tell you only that the message was opened. You have to assume that the recipient opened the message to read it, not to simply glance at it and move on. You can decide for yourself the worth of this assumption.

Categories

For more information about categories, see "Working with Categories," on page 462.

A handy way to organize messages is to group them into categories. By assigning a message to a category, you can match it up with other messages that belong to a specific project, an activity, a group, or any other designation. This lets you collect similar items for easy review and retrieval. To assign a message to a category by using the message window's Options tab, follow these steps:

1 Click the Categories button on the Options tab of the message window.

You can add new categories
by typing the category
name here and clicking the
Add To List button.

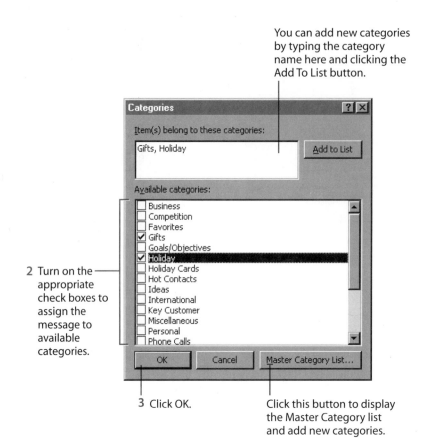

2 Turn on the
appropriate
check boxes to
assign the
message to
available
categories.

3 Click OK.

Click this button to display
the Master Category list
and add new categories.

Flagging a Message

Message Flag

Even though you can make a Subject line informative and can include instructions within message text, you still might find it useful to add a "flag" to a message. A message flag is a line that appears in the message header that has information about the nature of the message or that requests a response to the message. You set a message flag with the Message Flag button on the Standard toolbar in a message window.

Here's how to set a message flag:

1 Click the Message Flag button. Outlook displays the Flag Message dialog box.

2 Select the flag message you want to use, or type your own message.

3 If you want to set a due date, type or select the date here.

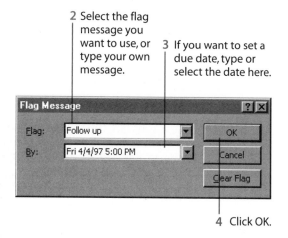

4 Click OK.

A message with a message flag looks like this:

Message flag

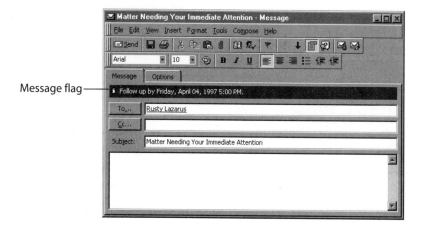

In the recipient's message list, a flagged message displays a flag beside its icon (assuming the Flag Status column is displayed). When the flag is red, the recipient hasn't yet responded. When the flag is white, a response has been made.

To remove a message flag, click the Message Flag button, and then click the Clear Flag button in the Flag Message dialog box.

Adding Text from a File

If you have a plain text file stored on disk (for example, a file saved in Windows Notepad), you can insert the text from the file as part of your message. You can also attach files of any sort to any message you send, whether it is a new message, a forwarded message, or a reply.

Insert File

To insert or attach a file to a message, follow these steps:

1 Click the Insert File button on the message window toolbar. (If the Insert File button isn't visible, choose the View Toolbars command and then choose the Standard toolbar.)

2 Select the disk and folder that contain the file.   **3** Select the file or files you want to attach.

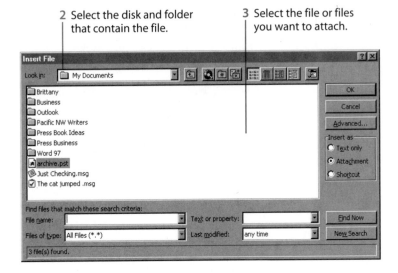

4 In the Insert As box, select the form that the file should have in your message:

- The Text Only option inserts the file as plain text with no formatting. This option is best used with files created in an application such as Notepad.

- The Attachment option inserts the file as an icon, which the recipient opens and reads using the program used to create the file.

- The Shortcut option links the attachment and its original file. This makes the message move through your e-mail system faster because the message is much smaller. To do this, the file must be in a shared folder (a folder that the recipients can connect to in order to read the attached file) on a hard disk.

5 Click OK.

Adding "Other Stuff"

Outlook provides a way to add "other stuff" (items other than text) to your message. What you can add besides existing files depends on which Windows-based applications are available on your computer. If, for example, you have Microsoft Office 97 Professional Edition installed, you can add the following:

- Microsoft Paint pictures and Microsoft Object Packager objects

- Microsoft Word documents, charts from Microsoft Graph, math and scientific equations from Microsoft Equation Editor, and text effects from Microsoft WordArt

- Microsoft Excel spreadsheets and charts

- Microsoft PowerPoint pictures, presentations, and slides

- Microsoft Access database files

- World Wide Web page addresses (URLs)

- Mailto response links

If you and your recipients have sound cards installed, you can add sound objects. If you have Microsoft Video for Windows installed, you can add video clips.

 NOTE

For you technoid readers, "other stuff" is called "attachments"—usually files created by other Windows-based applications. For really technoid readers, "other stuff" can also be any OLE, DirectX, or ActiveX object. Phew!

Electronic Mail

You can attach "other stuff" to new messages, forwarded messages, or replies. To insert a new piece of "other stuff," do the following:

1   Choose the Insert Object command.

3 Select the type of object.   **4** Click OK.

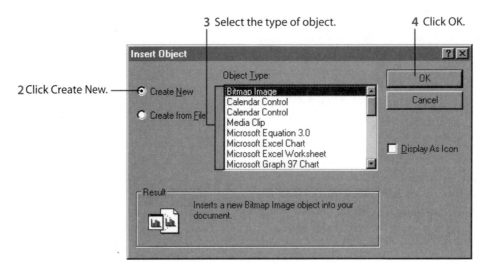

2 Click Create New.

5   In the window that appears, create the object as you usually do in the application associated with the object. Here is an example of a Bitmap Image object window:

6 Click in the message area outside the object window when you've finished creating the objects.

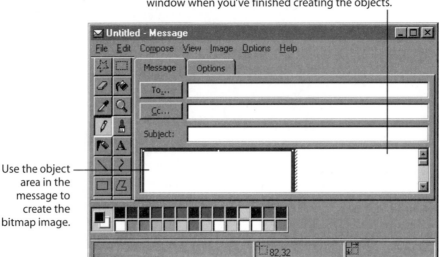

Use the object area in the message to create the bitmap image.

To insert an existing piece of "other stuff" from a file, follow these steps:

1 Choose the Insert Object command, and click Create From File.

2 Click the Browse button to find the file.

3 Select the disk and folder that contain the file, select the file, and then click OK.

4 In the Insert Object dialog box, turn on the Link check box to create a link to the file. If you want to display the file as an icon, turn on the Display As Icon check box.

5 Click OK.

 TIP

Anytime you send a very large or very long file in a message, it's better to send it as an icon. An icon takes up less space in the message window, and usually it's easier for people reading the message to view a large file in the window of the application used to create the file. Also, Microsoft Exchange Server has a 2-MB limit on message size. If you're sending a very large file, it's better to link it, which reduces message size considerably. Remember that a linked file must reside on a disk and in a folder to which the recipient has read access.

Sending a URL in a Message

? SEE ALSO

To find out how to use a URL in a message, see "Following a URL from a Message," on page 113.

Admit it—you've been surfing the World Wide Web, and you've found a web site you want to share with someone. The easiest way to do this is to send the web site address (URL) to your friend. So how do you get the URL into a message? You can either type it or copy it. When you type or paste a URL into message text, Outlook formats the URL as a link to the web page, right before your eyes. In fact, as soon as you type *http:/,* Outlook formats the link, which might look something like this:

http://mspress.microsoft.com

The URL is formatted with an underline and in blue.

Including a Mailto Response Link

From time to time, you might want to send a message that offers your recipients an e-mail address to which they can send questions or comments rather than sending their replies to you. For example, let's say you want to encourage your friends to send a message to the president of the United States at president@whitehouse.gov. One way

? SEE ALSO

For an alternative way to have responses to a message sent to another e-mail address, see "Have Replies Sent To," on page 99. To find out how to use a Mailto response link, see "Replying Through a Mailto Response Link," on page 116.

to set this up is to include a "Mailto" response link in your message. A "Mailto" response link looks like this:

mailto:president@whitehouse.gov

The Mailto is formatted with an underline and in blue.

To add a Mailto to a message, simply type it. As soon as you type *mailto:* and the first letter of an e-mail address, Outlook formats the Mailto response link.

Attaching Messages

Usually, to send a copy of a message to someone—even lots of someones—you just forward the message. That's fine if you want to send only *one* message. But suppose you want to forward several related messages all at one time? For that, you need to attach messages to your new message. You can attach other messages to any message you send, even if the message you're sending is itself a forwarded message or a reply.

To attach an existing message to the message you're working on, take these steps:

1 Choose the Insert Item command in the message window.

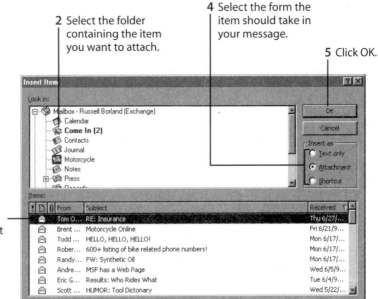

Recalling, Replacing, or Resending a Message

Let's say you sent a message to your project team but inadvertently failed to include the date of the next team meeting. Rather than send a new message, you can recall or replace the message you've already sent. You can recall or replace only those messages you've sent to recipients who are logged on and using Outlook and who have not read the message or moved the message out of their Inboxes. To replace a message, you must send a new one. If you do not send a new message, however, the original message is still recalled.

To recall or replace a message, follow these steps:

1 On the Outlook Bar, open the Mail group, and then open the Sent Items folder.

2 Open the message you want to recall or replace.

3 Choose the Tools Recall This Message option.

4 In the Recall This Message dialog box, do one of the following:

- To recall the message, select the Delete Unread Copies Of This Message option, and then click OK.

- To replace the message with another, select the Delete Unread Copies And Replace With A New Message option, and then click OK. In the new message window that appears, type the new message, and then click the Send button.

5 To receive a notification about the success or failure of recalling or replacing the message for each recipient, select the Tell Me If Recall Succeeds Or Fails For Each Recipient check box.

To simply resend a message (rather than recall or replace the message), follow these steps:

1 On the Outlook Bar, open the Mail group, and then open the Sent Items folder.

2 Open the message you want to resend.

3 Choose Tools Resend This Message.

4 In the message window that appears, click the Send button.

II

Electronic Mail

Reading a Message

Whether you're "Hooked on Phonics" or you learned to read the old-fashioned way—"See Dick. See Jane. See Dick and Jane."—you'll be applying your reading skills to at least some of the messages you receive. (One side effect of having electronic mail is that people tend to read *every* message for a while. Then they become more selective. It's a lot like people who are new to television—in the beginning they watch everything, can't turn it off, and have no powers of discrimination. Eventually people become more discerning about how much television they watch and what they watch—whether you like their taste or not!)

To learn how to automatically dispatch incoming messages that you don't want to read to the dustbin or to other places in Outlook or your file system, see "Inbox Assistant," on page 39.

A mail message can contain text that you read in the message window as well as attachments ("other stuff") that you have to open (as you would open an envelope that contains a paper letter). A message can also contain a link to a World Wide Web page (a URL), a Mailto response link, or voting buttons.

To read mail message text, simply double-click the message line in your Inbox's message list. If parts of a long message fall below the bottom of the window, scroll through the message window to read them.

While reading messages, you can use the Next Item and Previous Item buttons on the Standard toolbar in a message window to move from message to message. Beside each of these buttons is a down arrow that you càn click to see a list of commands that let you move more quickly to the messages you want to read. For example, you can move to the next or previous message from the same sender or to the next or previous unread message.

Reading a Protected Message

? SEE ALSO

For details about setting up advanced security, see "Set Up Advanced Security Button," on page 73. For information about sending an encrypted or digitally signed message, see "Sending a Protected Message," on page 92.

If someone sends you a message that's encrypted or digitally signed, you must be logged on to advanced security before you can read the message or check a digital signature. If you're not logged on when you try to open an encrypted message or check a digital signature, Outlook asks you to log on to advanced security. If you don't do so, Outlook won't open the message. This is how Outlook keeps other people from reading protected messages.

To read a protected message, double-click the message line in your Inbox's message list. When the Microsoft Exchange Security Logon dialog box appears, type your advanced security password, and then click OK.

! WARNING

> In the Microsoft Exchange Security Logon dialog box, you can turn on the Don't Prompt For Password Again Until Next Microsoft Exchange Logon check box if you want to read any encrypted message or check any digital signature on a message without having to type your password again during the current Outlook session. But watch out! If you turn on this box, anyone can read protected messages (and send protected messages in your name). To prevent this, log off advanced security when you leave your computer unattended. (For directions, see "Logoff Security Button," on page 75.)

Checking a Digital Signature

A digital signature assures the recipient that the name of the person in the From line of a message actually sent the message. A digital signature also indicates that the message has not been altered or tampered with while being sent.

To check a digital signature, follow these steps:

1 Double-click the message line of the digitally signed message in your Inbox's message list. (The message might also be encrypted.)

2 In the Microsoft Exchange Security Logon dialog box, type your advanced security password, and then click OK.

3 Click the Verify Digital Signature button on the Standard toolbar.

Verify Digital Signature

II

Electronic Mail

4 In the Verify Digital Signature dialog box, check the information Outlook provides, and then click OK.

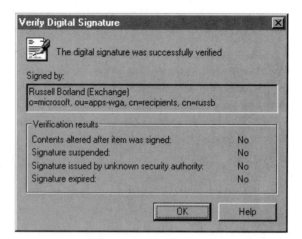

Seeing "Other Stuff"

The "other stuff" in a mail message can be any type of information in any form that's created with a Windows-based application. For example, a message could contain a video clip of your family picnic, complete with Uncle Slim dancing the limbo in his Hawaiian shirt and Jamaican straw hat. Usually, "other stuff" appears in the message as an icon.

To see the "other stuff" stored inside an icon in a mail message, do this:

1 Double-click the icon in the mail message.

2 View the "other stuff" as you would usually view information in the application used to create the file.

3 When you've finished looking at the "other stuff," close the file. (You can also close the application if you wish.)

4 Return to Outlook. (If you close the application that displays the "other stuff," you return to Outlook automatically.)

This point might seem obvious, but it's worth noting: if a fax contains "other stuff," you can see it or use it only if you receive the fax on your computer. On a paper fax, "other stuff" is simply an image on paper.

Following a URL from a Message

When you receive a message that contains a URL (a web site address), you can simply click the URL in the message text to visit the web site. Windows starts your web browser and connects to the web site.

Gathering Messages from the Beyond

Think about receiving e-mail in terms of the way you receive physical mail such as letters, magazines, and packages. You can receive them at home, at a box at a U.S. Post Office, at a package center that has private post boxes, or at a commercial carrier's offices. In a similar fashion, you can receive e-mail from various services in Outlook.

If you are signed up for other electronic mail services, you can use Outlook to read the messages you receive through these services. For example, you could have accounts on MSN, CompuServe, America Online, or AT&T.

Most of your messages will probably come to you through Outlook. Every so often, Outlook checks for new messages. But unless you keep a connection to these other services open all the time, Outlook won't automatically check them for new messages. So you must specifically tell Outlook to deliver your messages.

If you have only one mail service set up, choose the Tools Check For New Mail command to request message delivery.

If you have more than one mail service set up, follow these steps:

1 Choose the Tools Check For New Mail On command.

2 Select the services you want Outlook to check for new mail.

3 Click OK.

TIP

> To get all your messages from all your electronic mail services at once, turn on the check boxes for all the services listed in the Check For New Mail On dialog box.

If the message service you select in the Check For New Mail On dialog box is one that you must sign on to, Outlook starts that service's logon routine. After you log on (if necessary), Outlook collects your messages, and they appear in your Inbox, ready to read, just like any other messages you receive through Outlook.

Replying to a Message

Oftentimes a message provokes you to respond. So what do you do? Send back a reply. You can direct your response only to the person who sent the message, or you can respond to everyone who received it.

To reply to a message, do the following:

1 Select the message line in the message list, or open the message.

2 To reply to the one person who sent the message, click the Reply button on the Standard toolbar. To reply to the entire audience (all those who received the original message), click the Reply To All button (also on the Standard toolbar).

3 Type your response anywhere in the message area. (Outlook positions the insertion point at the top of the message area, above the original message.) You can type your response at the top, at the bottom, or anywhere within the original message. You can format the text and add any "other stuff" just as you can for a new message.

4 Delete any parts of the original message that you don't need to send back.

5 Click the Send button on the message window's Standard toolbar.

TIP

If you modify the original message, Outlook puts your name in square brackets at the leading edge of your changes. For ways to change this behavior, see "Mark My Comments With," on page 60.

You'll notice that Outlook indents the original message when you reply either to the sender or to all those who received the message. Also, Outlook includes the entire original message in the reply. If you'd like to change the way Outlook handles replies, you can choose the Tools Options command and adjust the settings on the Reading tab of the Options dialog box. You can set up Outlook so that original messages are not indented in your replies. You can also choose to exclude the original messages from your replies, or you can opt for including them as attachments rather than text. In addition, you can select different font effects for your replies. For details about these options, see "Reading Tab," on page 57.

 TIP

Too often, people simply add their comments to a message they've received and then reply to everyone who received the original message. After half a dozen replies to everyone, the message gets quite long. Most of this extra baggage isn't really necessary, so it's best to throw away the excess baggage. Keep the message short and crisp for the sake of your hard disk and for the sake of the e-mail system's performance.

Replying Through Voting Buttons

When you receive a message that contains voting buttons, simply click the button that corresponds to your vote. Outlook displays a dialog box like the following:

1 Select your means of response.

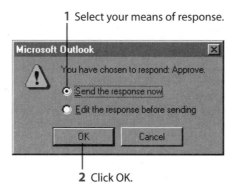

2 Click OK.

If you select Send The Response Now, Outlook immediately sends the message without opening a reply form. The message arrives with your response inserted in front of the original Subject line; for example, *Approve: Special Offer.*

If you select Edit The Response Before Sending, Outlook opens a reply message addressed to the proper e-mail address and with the Subject line and original message text included. You can add additional comments if you like. Then click the Send button to send your reply. The message arrives with your response inserted in front of the original Subject line.

Replying Through a Mailto Response Link

When you receive a message that contains a Mailto response link in the message text, you can send a response, a question, or a comment by clicking the Mailto response link. Outlook opens a new message addressed to the e-mail address in the response link and with the Subject line set up for you to fill in. Simply add your message text, and then click the Send button.

Replying to a Message Flag

When you receive a message with a flag and a due date, you can easily record your response to the flag when you've finished taking the action the flag requests:

1 Click the Message Flag button.

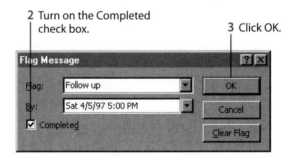

The flag area of the message displays the date on which you marked the action completed. You now have a record that you can store in an Outlook folder.

Forwarding a Message

 SEE ALSO

To set up Outlook to automatically forward messages of interest, see "Inbox Assistant," on page 39.

As Rocky says to Bullwinkle, "And now for something *really* important." Let's say someone has sent you a really important message. You think that other people might want or need the information in the message, even though they weren't originally recipients. In this case, you can forward the message to other interested parties.

To forward a message, follow these steps:

1 Select the message line in the message list, or open the message.

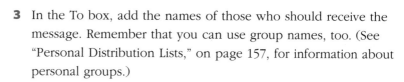

2 Click the Forward button on the message window toolbar.

3 In the To box, add the names of those who should receive the message. Remember that you can use group names, too. (See "Personal Distribution Lists," on page 157, for information about personal groups.)

4 If you want to add your own two cents worth as a preface to the message, type your response anywhere in the message area. You can use text decorations or add any "other stuff" just as you can for a new message.

5 Delete any parts of the original message that you don't need to send on.

6 Click the Send button.

 TIP

> If you modify the original message, Outlook puts your name in square brackets at the leading edge of your changes. For ways to change this, see "Mark My Comments With," on page 60.

Saving Messages in Files

Sometimes a message is so important or useful that you'll want to save it in a file that you can open in another application.

To save a message in a file, do this:

1 Select the message from the message list, or open the message. You can save several messages in the same file by selecting all of them in the message list at the same time.

2 Choose the File Save As command to open the Save As
dialog box:

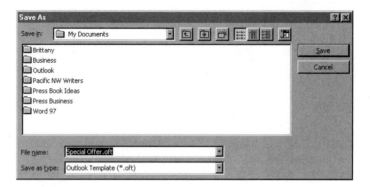

3 If you select a single message, Outlook creates a name for the
file by using the Subject line of the message. If you select more
than one message, you need to enter a name for the file in the
File Name box. You can select a different disk or select a
different folder if you want by using the Save In box.

4 In the Save As Type box, select the format for the file you want
to save. The following types are available:

Text Only	Saves the text of the message but none of the formatting and none of the "other stuff." This is the only format available if you selected more than one message.
Rich Text Format	Saves the text, formatting, and "other stuff" (including attachments) in the message for use in another application.
Outlook Template	Saves the message as a template for other messages you'll create.
Message Format	Saves the message as a message, including information about the sender, the recipients, and the subject. You can import the file into Outlook later.

5 Click the Save button.

Saving Message Attachments

When you receive a message with an attachment that is a file, you might decide that you want to save the attachment. If a message has more than one file attached, you can save one, some, or all of the files.

NOTE

> The following steps work only for attachments that are files. You'll know an attachment is a file because the filename appears below the file icon. If you don't see a filename, the icon represents a linked or embedded object. To save "stuff" other than attached files, use the steps listed in "Saving 'Other Stuff' from a Message," on page 121.

To save a file attachment, do the following:

1 Select the message in the message list. A message with an attachment shows a paper clip icon on its message line.

2 Choose the File Save Attachments command.

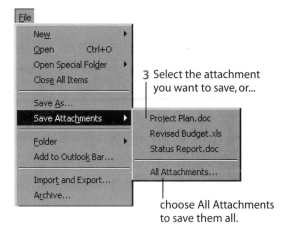

4 If you choose to save all attachments, skip ahead to step 9. If you choose to save only one attachment, you see the dialog box shown at the top of the following page.

5 Select the folder in which you want to save the attachment.

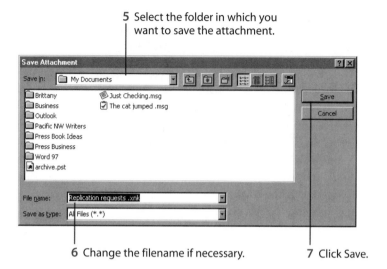

6 Change the filename if necessary.

7 Click Save.

8 If you saved only one attachment and want to save another, repeat steps 1 through 7.

9 If you choose to save all attachments, Outlook first displays the following dialog box:

If you change your mind and decide not to save one of the attachments, hold down the Ctrl key while you click the name.

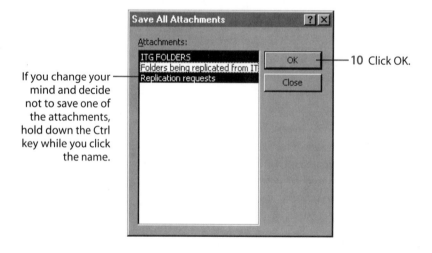

10 Click OK.

12 Click OK.

11 Select the folder in which you want to save the attachments.

If you open the Save Attachments submenu and it displays the word *None*, the attachments in the message are linked or embedded objects rather than files. In this case, see "Saving 'Other Stuff' from a Message," below.

As an alternative to selecting message lines in the message list and choosing the File Save Attachments command, you can save attachments from within a message. When you use this method, you can select more than one attachment to save without saving all of them.

Here's how to save attachments from within a message:

1   Open the message with the attachments.

2   Choose the File Save Attachments command.

3   Follow steps 9 through 12 in the preceding procedure.

Saving "Other Stuff" from a Message

Some kind souls like to insert pictures and other information directly in a mail message without creating a file for the inserted items. Saving this kind of "other stuff" is a little different, but it's not really very difficult.

To save "other stuff" from a message, take the steps listed on the following page.

Electronic Mail

1 Open the message, and double-click the item you want to save.

2 The Outlook window changes to show the menu bar and toolbars of the application that the message sender used to create the item. Select the item that you want to save, and then press Ctrl+C to copy your selection to the Clipboard.

3 Start the appropriate application (the one used to create the item), and then press Ctrl+V to paste the selection into a new document in that application.

4 Save the document with the item you inserted.

5 Close the application.

6 Switch back to your Outlook message, and then click anywhere outside the item to bring back the Outlook menu bar and toolbar.

Saving Orphaned Items

Some types of "other stuff" might have been created with an application that does not save its work in files—for example, Microsoft Draw, Microsoft Graph, Microsoft Equation Editor, or Microsoft WordArt. This "other stuff" is referred to as orphaned items. In these cases, you have to use a more indirect method to save the items in a file.

To save an orphaned item in a file, follow these steps:

1 Select the item in the mail message.

2 Press Ctrl+C or choose the Edit Copy command to copy the item to the Clipboard.

3 Start an application that accepts the item, such as Microsoft Word, Microsoft Excel, or possibly Microsoft Paint.

4 Press Ctrl+V or choose the Edit Paste command to paste the item from the Clipboard.

5 Save the document as you normally save a document in the application.

Facts About Fax

One of the services you can add to your Outlook profiles is the ability to send and receive faxes. You can also set up a separate profile that you use only for faxes. The rest of this chapter describes the following procedures for using the fax service in Outlook:

? SEE ALSO

For details about setting up fax service as part of an existing profile or as a separate profile, see "Adding Fax Service to a Profile," on page 16.

- Setting fax options

- Adding fax addresses to your address book and Contacts folder

- Sending a fax

- Protecting a fax

- Receiving a fax and retrieving a fax from a fax service

Setting Fax Options

Most of the time, the faxes you send will be in a standard setup. (For exceptions, you can change the setup as you prepare a specific fax—see step 8 in "Sending a Fax," on page 137.) Although Outlook's default options for faxes might be just fine for your needs, you might want to review them. In particular, you'll want to check the setup of dialing and modem options.

Here are the general steps for setting standard fax options:

1 Choose the Tools Microsoft Fax Tools command, and choose Options from the submenu.

2 In the Microsoft Fax Properties dialog box, click the tab that contains the options you want to set—Message, Dialing, Modem, or User.

3 Set the options as appropriate on each tab—consult the specific instructions in the following sections.

4 When you've finished setting options, click OK.

II

Electronic Mail

Setting Message Options

On the Message tab of the Microsoft Fax Properties dialog box, shown in Figure 3-4, you can select the time when you want Outlook to send your faxes, you can choose a standard message format, and you can set up a standard cover page. The following sections explain the various options on this tab.

FIGURE 3-4.

The Message tab of the Microsoft Fax Properties dialog box.

Select the time to send faxes.

Turn off the cover page, select a different style, or click Browse to locate a different cover page style.

Select the message format.

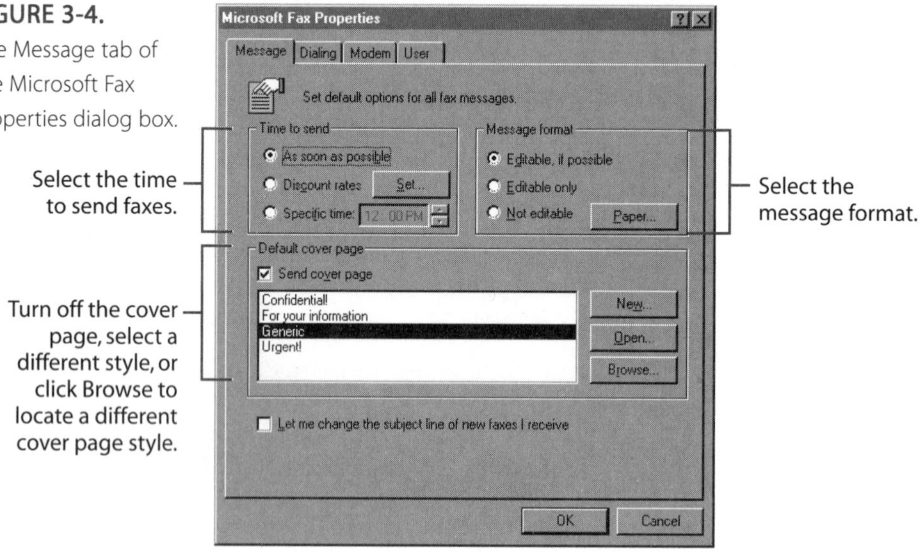

Time To Send.   You can designate a time when Outlook should normally send your faxes.

■ When you select the As Soon As Possible option, Outlook sends the fax right away if you're using a network-connected fax service and you're connected to the network. Outlook also sends the fax right away if you're working offline with a profile that has no online services but you have a fax modem in your computer. If you're working offline with a profile that includes an online service, Outlook sends the fax as soon as you connect to the online service that handles faxes.

■ When you select the Discount Rates option, Outlook sends faxes only during the hours when your telephone rates are discounted. To set the hours of discounted rates, click the Set button.

1 Set the starting time
for discount rates.

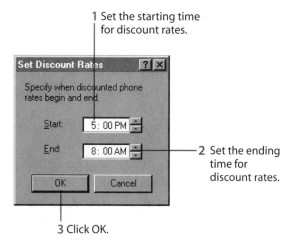

2 Set the ending
time for
discount rates.

3 Click OK.

■ When you select the Specific Time option, Outlook holds faxes until the time you set in the box.

Message Format.   You can decide whether you want recipients to be able to edit most of your faxes. To be editable, your fax must be received on a computer. If most of your faxes are sent to paper fax machines, you'll want to choose the Not Editable option; choose the Editable Only option if you send most faxes to computers. The Editable If Possible option sends the fax in editable format if it goes to a computer but otherwise sends it as not editable.

To set the paper setting for your faxes, follow these steps:

1   Click the Paper button.

2 Select the paper size.

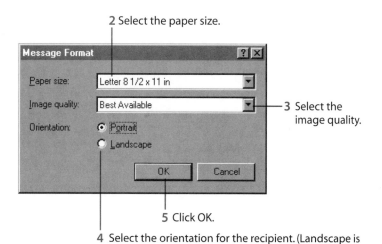

3 Select the
image quality.

5 Click OK.

4 Select the orientation for the recipient. (Landscape is usually chosen only for computer reception.)

Default Cover Page. If you don't want to send cover pages with your faxes, turn off the Send Cover Page check box. If you do want cover pages on your faxes, leave the Send Cover Page check box turned on and select the style of cover page. The Confidential, For Your Information, and Urgent styles add these labels to the fax cover page.

You can create a new cover page (New button), change the design of the four listed cover pages (Open button), or choose a different cover page that's stored on a disk (Browse button):

- When you click the New button, Outlook starts the Fax Cover Page Editor with a blank sheet on which you can design your own cover page. You can add boxes (data fields) to accept information such as the recipient's name, company name, telephone numbers, date, and subject line. You insert these items and others by using the commands on the Insert menu: Recipient, Sender, and Message and the commands on their submenus. With the Formatting toolbar, you can format the text and paragraphs of the cover page. You use the Drawing toolbar to add graphics to your cover page. When you've finished, save the new cover page. When you quit the Fax Cover Page Editor, Outlook adds the new cover page name to the list on the Message tab.

- When you click the Open button, Outlook starts the Fax Cover Page Editor and opens the cover page you selected in the list. You can then rearrange, substitute, edit, change formatting, and add or remove boxes. When you've completed your changes, save the cover page. You can open another cover page from within the Fax Cover Page Editor, just as you open a document in any Windows-based application.

- Click the Browse button to locate and open a cover page file on a disk. You will use this button when your organization has cover page files stored on a network server. After you select the cover page file and click the Open button in the Browse Cover Page dialog box, Outlook adds the name to the list of cover pages on the Message tab.

If someone gives you a fax cover page file, copy it to your Windows folder (or the folder in which Windows is installed). That's where Outlook looks for cover page files when you open the Microsoft Fax Properties dialog box. If you want to remove a fax cover page from the list in this dialog box, move the file to a folder other than the Windows folder.

Let Me Change The Subject Line Of New Faxes I Receive. If you receive faxes on your computer, you might want to change the subject line of an incoming fax to make the subject line more descriptive of an action you must take or a point you want to note. The subject line appears in the folder items list of the folder where you keep the fax. If you want to be able to change the subject line of incoming faxes, turn on the check box labeled Let Me Change The Subject Line Of New Faxes I Receive.

Setting Dialing Options

On the Dialing tab of the Microsoft Fax Properties dialog box, shown in Figure 3-5, you can set up the locations from which you send faxes, create a list of telephone numbers with toll prefixes, and specify how Outlook should handle retries when a fax doesn't go through on the first attempt.

FIGURE 3-5.

The Dialing tab of the Microsoft Fax Properties dialog box.

Set dialing properties.

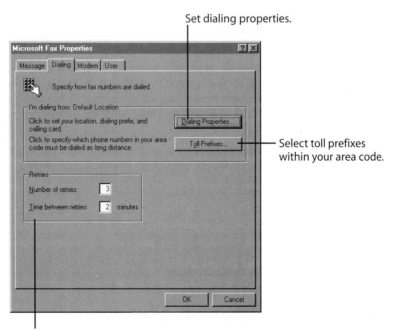

Select toll prefixes within your area code.

Set up Outlook's retry procedures.

Dialing Properties. When you need to set or change the standard dialing properties, click the Dialing Properties button to open the Dialing Properties dialog box:

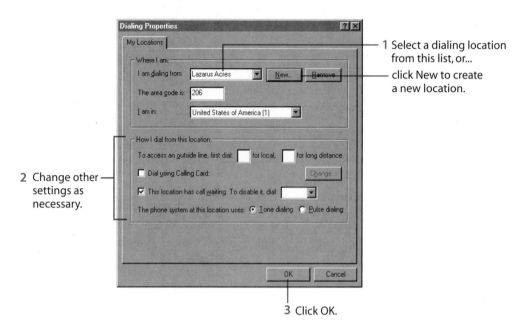

1 Select a dialing location from this list, or...

click New to create a new location.

2 Change other settings as necessary.

3 Click OK.

❓ SEE ALSO

For details about changing your calling card settings from the Dialing Properties dialog box, see "Calling Card Dialing," on page 186.

If you dial a network or other e-mail or fax service from the same telephone all the time, you need to set up only one location. If you dial from several telephones, you need to set up a location for each telephone from which the dialing is different.

To create a new location for dialing, click the New button in the Dialing Properties dialog box. In the Create New Location dialog box, type the location name, and then click OK to return to the Dialing Properties dialog box, where you can set up the properties for the new location.

Toll Prefixes. Some telephone area codes cover a very compact geographical area in which all the prefixes can be called toll free. Other telephone area codes cover a wide geographical area in which only a few prefixes might be toll free. If the area code from which you send your faxes contains prefixes that aren't toll free from your location, you can provide a list of the prefixes that require dialing the area code first.

1 Click the Toll Prefixes button on the Dialing tab of the Microsoft Fax Properties dialog box.

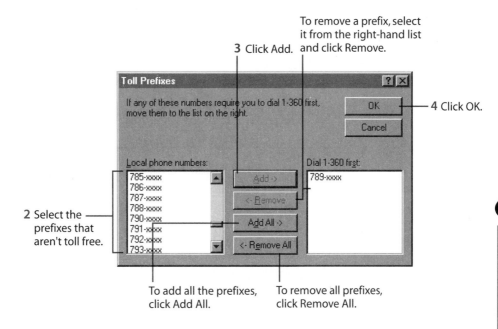

To remove a prefix, select it from the right-hand list **3** Click Add. and click Remove.

4 Click OK.

2 Select the prefixes that aren't toll free.

To add all the prefixes, click Add All.

To remove all prefixes, click Remove All.

 **TIP**

If you can call toll free to only a few prefixes in your area code, click Add All in the Toll Prefixes dialog box, and then remove the few prefixes that you can call toll free.

Retries. For various reasons, a fax doesn't always get to its destination—a busy line, no fax machine answer, a faulty connection, a glitch in the receiving machine. You can decide how many times Outlook should try to get your fax through to the recipient—simply set the number in the Number Of Retries box on the Dialing tab. You can also decide how long you want Outlook to wait between retries. Because the most common problem with sending a fax is probably a busy line, you might want to wait the two minutes initially set up in Outlook. To specify a different waiting period, set the number of minutes in the Time Between Retries box.

Setting Modem Options

The Modem tab of the Microsoft Fax Properties dialog box, shown in Figure 3-6, lets you select the modem Outlook will use for faxes and set the options for that modem.

Select the modem
to use for faxes.

Click here to change
the modem setup.

FIGURE 3-6.
The Modem tab of
the Microsoft Fax
Properties dialog box.

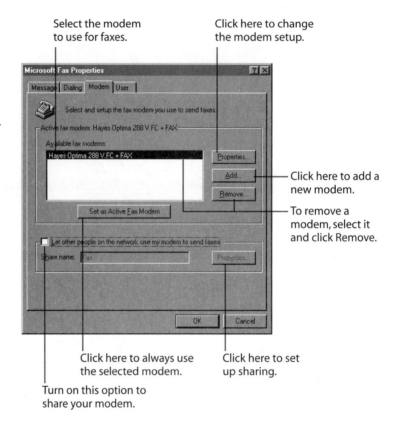

Click here to add a
new modem.

To remove a
modem, select it
and click Remove.

Click here to always use
the selected modem.

Click here to set
up sharing.

Turn on this option to
share your modem.

Adjusting Modem Properties. You can set up your modem to answer incoming calls, and you can adjust the modem speaker volume and set your call preferences. To set modem properties, select the modem from the list on the Modem tab, and click the Properties button. You can then change the settings in the Fax Modem Properties dialog box, shown in Figure 3-7.

Turn off this option if you want
to listen to the speaker during
transmission.

Set the modem
speaker volume.

FIGURE 3-7.

The Fax Modem
Properties dialog box.

Select the type
of answering
you want.

Turn off this
option if you're
using a shared
network modem
that collects and
sends faxes.

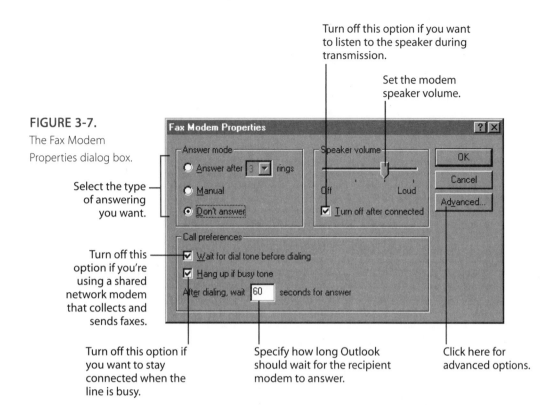

Turn off this option if
you want to stay
connected when the
line is busy.

Specify how long Outlook
should wait for the recipient
modem to answer.

Click here for
advanced options.

In this dialog box, you can specify how your modem should answer
incoming calls:

- If you use your telephone line primarily for fax reception and
  you want your computer fax modem to automatically answer
  every incoming call, select the Answer After option and set the
  number of rings the fax modem should allow before it answers.
  If you use the line only for faxes, you can set the number of
  rings to one. The standard setting of three rings gives you a
  chance to answer in case you occasionally receive voice calls on
  this line. This setting also ensures that you're not receiving a
  single-ring call made in error.

■ If you use your telephone line for both voice and fax and you want to manually switch on fax reception, select the Manual option. When a call comes in and you hear the fax warble, click the Answer Now button in the Microsoft Fax Status window. (See "Receiving a Fax," on page 145.)

■ If you don't want your computer to answer a telephone line at all, select the Don't Answer option. You should select this option if you receive your faxes from a fax service rather than directly.

Clicking the Advanced button in the Fax Modem Properties dialog box displays a dialog box in which you can set more options for fax transmission and reception:

Turn on this option if you can't reliably send or receive faxes at speeds higher than 9600 bits per second (bps).

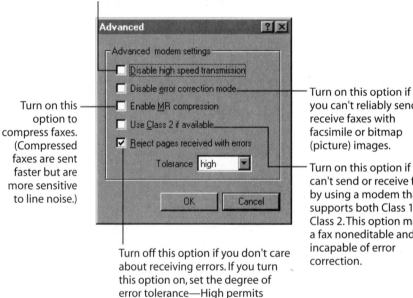

Turn on this option to compress faxes. (Compressed faxes are sent faster but are more sensitive to line noise.)

Turn on this option if you can't reliably send or receive faxes with facsimile or bitmap (picture) images.

Turn on this option if you can't send or receive faxes by using a modem that supports both Class 1 and Class 2. This option makes a fax noneditable and incapable of error correction.

Turn off this option if you don't care about receiving errors. If you turn this option on, set the degree of error tolerance—High permits more errors than Low.

Adding a new modem.   If the modem you want to use is not listed on the Modem tab of the Microsoft Fax Properties dialog box, you can add it. You can add either a local modem (a modem in your computer or attached to it) or a network modem.

To add a modem, take these steps:

1 Click the Add button on the Modem tab.

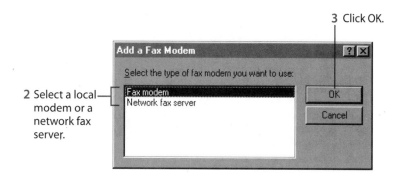

3 Click OK.

2 Select a local modem or a network fax server.

4 If you selected a local fax modem, work through the Install New Modem Wizard. If you selected a network fax server, type the share name of the modem and click OK.

Sharing properties.   If your organization has fewer modems than computers, you might need to share your modem with others. When your modem is shared, the people to whom you give the proper permissions can send their faxes through your modem.

To share your modem, follow these steps:

1 On the Modem tab, turn on the check box labeled Let Other People On The Network Use My Modem To Send Faxes.

2 Click the Properties button to set up sharing. Outlook displays the NetFax dialog box. (The first time you share your modem, Outlook first displays the Select Drive dialog box. In this dialog box, select the drive on which you will share your modem, and then click OK.)

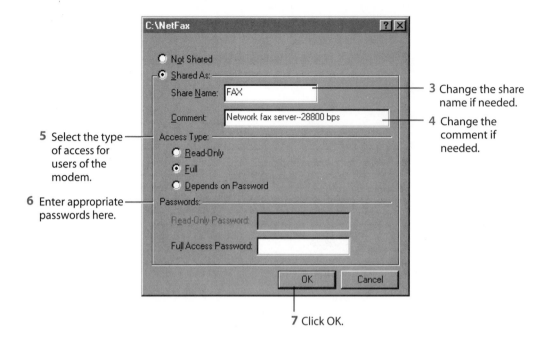

3 Change the share name if needed.

4 Change the comment if needed.

5 Select the type of access for users of the modem.

6 Enter appropriate passwords here.

7 Click OK.

Setting User Options

On the User tab of the Microsoft Fax Properties dialog box, shown in Figure 3-8, you set up your sender information. Note that the entries you supply can appear on your fax cover sheet and can be used by recipients as your return fax address.

FIGURE 3-8.

The User tab of the Microsoft Fax Properties dialog box.

Fax Addresses

In Outlook you have three ways to set up a fax address, two of them in your address book and one on the spot. You can add a fax number to an e-mail address in your Personal Address Book or to a contact entry in your Contacts folder, which becomes an entry in the Outlook Address Book. For information about setting up entries in your address books, see "Adding Someone," on page 153, and "Setting Up Your Contact List," on page 296.

Follow these steps to set up a fax address in your Personal Address Book:

1 Choose Outlook's Tools Address Book command.

2 In the Address Book dialog box, select your Personal Address Book from the Show Names From The box, and then click the New Entry button.

3 In the New Entry dialog box, select Other Address from the list and click OK.

4 Fill out the New - Address tab, following the example of the one shown here:

5 Type the recipient's name.

6 Type the recipient's fax number.

7 Type the word *FAX*.

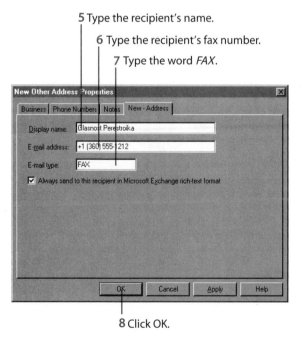

8 Click OK.

To address a fax on the spot, fill in the name and telephone number in the second Compose New Fax Wizard panel, as explained in the section "Sending a Fax," beginning on the following page.

Sending a Fax

? **SEE ALSO**

For details about settings you might want to adjust through the Dialing Properties button and the Options button in the Compose New Fax Wizard, see "Setting Message Options," on page 124, and "Setting Dialing Options," on page 127.

When you've set up your fax service and modem, you're ready to send a fax. You have two ways to do this—by using Outlook's Compose New Fax Wizard or by addressing a message to a fax recipient from your address book and clicking Send. Here are the steps for using the wizard:

1 Choose Outlook's Compose New Fax command. Outlook starts the Compose New Fax Wizard.

2 If you need to change your dialing location or how your call is dialed, click Dialing Properties.

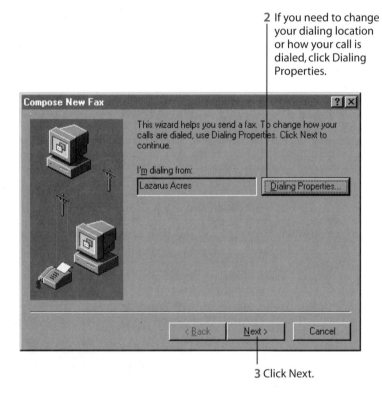

3 Click Next.

4 On the second panel of the wizard, type the recipient's name in the To box, and select the appropriate country from the drop-down list. Type the recipient's fax number, and turn on the Dial Area Code option if needed. Then click the Add To List button. (Note that when you click the Add To List button, Outlook sets up a fax address in your Personal Address Book.) Repeat these steps for each recipient if the fax is being sent to several people. (Alternatively, you can click the Address Book button to select names of recipients.)

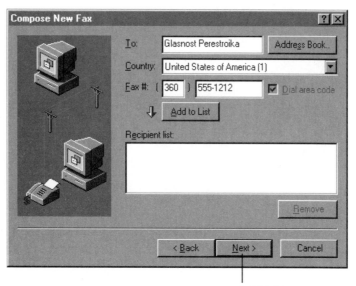

3 Click Next.

6 Choose whether to include a cover page.

7 Select a style for the cover page, if appropriate.

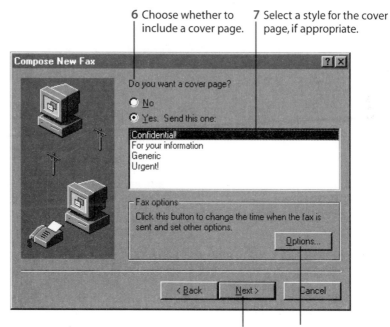

9 Click Next.

8 If necessary, click Options to change the standard fax setup.

Electronic Mail

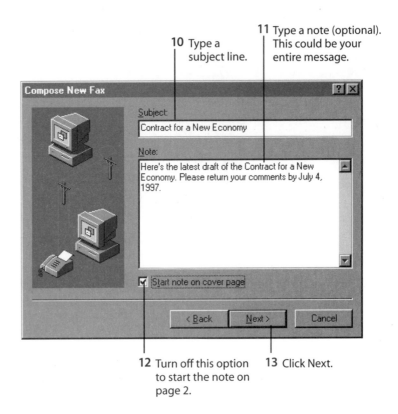

10 Type a subject line.

11 Type a note (optional). This could be your entire message.

12 Turn off this option to start the note on page 2.

13 Click Next.

14 If your fax will be received by a computer, you can add a file to the fax by clicking the Add File button on the next panel of the wizard, shown on the facing page. In the dialog box, select the file you want to include and click Open. Repeat this procedure for each file that you want to send in your fax. The files will appear as icons in your message.

15 If you change your mind and decide not to include a file in your fax, select the file and click Remove.

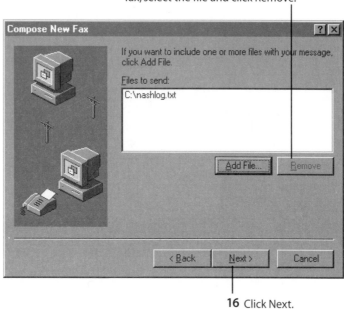

16 Click Next.

17 On the Finish panel of the Compose New Fax Wizard, click the Finish button.

To send a fax using the message window, you must have the recipients set up with a fax address in your address book. (See the sidebar "Fax Addresses," on page 135, for information about how to do this.)

First open a new message, and then follow these steps:

1 Click to To button, select the address book you need from the Show Names From The box, and then select the fax recipient or recipients from the address book. Click OK in the Select Names dialog box.

2 In the message window, enter a subject and a message as you would for a regular e-mail message. You can format the message and add attachments as you can for other messages. When you've finished composing the fax message, click the Send button.

3 You'll see the Microsoft Fax Status dialog box, informing you of the status of the fax as Outlook prepares the fax message, initiates the fax modem, and then sends the fax.

Checking the Status of Outgoing Faxes

If you set up a number of faxes to send, you might want to know which fax is being sent and how many more are in the fax queue. To check the status of outgoing faxes, do the following:

1 Choose the Tools Microsoft Fax Tools command.

2 Choose Show Outgoing Faxes from the submenu to see a list of outgoing faxes. To cancel an outgoing fax, select it from the list and then choose the File Cancel Fax command.

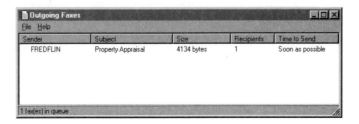

Protecting Your Privacy

If you send a fax to a recipient who receives faxes on a computer, you can protect your fax with either a password or key encryption.

Sending a Password-Protected Fax

1 Choose the Compose New Fax command, and work through the Compose Fax Wizard to its third panel (which contains the Options button), or start a new message and address it to a fax address.

2 Click the Options button on the third panel of the wizard, or, if you are working in the message window, choose the File Send Options command and click the Fax tab.

3 Click the Security button.

4 Choose the Password-
Protected option.

5 Click OK.

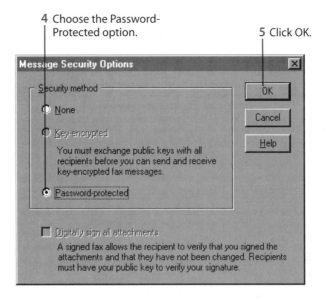

8 Click OK.

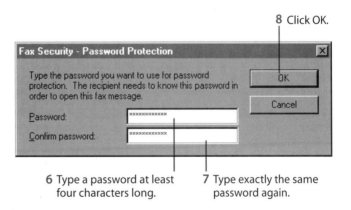

6 Type a password at least
four characters long.

7 Type exactly the same
password again.

9 Click OK in the Send Options dialog box, and then work your
way through the rest of the wizard, or finish the fax message
and send it.

TIP

Before you send a password-protected fax, tell the recipient what the
password is. Remember: passwords are case-sensitive—uppercase and
lowercase letters are recognized as different characters.

Electronic Mail

Protecting Faxes with Encryption

Encryption uses two keys to scramble the contents of a fax before you send it—a public key and a private key. Each encryption key is a unique letter combination of a password that you type into Outlook. The keys become part of your user information. Recipients of an encrypted fax use your public key in conjunction with their own private key to decode the fax.

Before you can send a key-encrypted fax, you need to take these steps:

- Create your public encryption key.

- Send your public key to each fax recipient.

- Ask each recipient to send you his or her public key to add to your address book.

Creating your fax security key set.   Microsoft Fax uses your password and user information to create your unique public key and private key (your key set). Here's how to establish your key set:

1 Choose the Tools Microsoft Fax Tools command, and then choose Advanced Security from the submenu.

2 Click the New Key Set button.

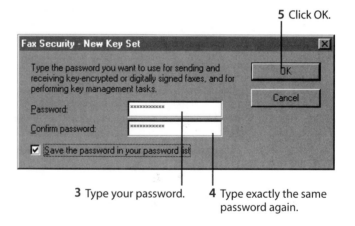

5 Click OK.

3 Type your password.   **4** Type exactly the same password again.

6 Click Close in the Advanced Fax Security dialog box.

 **NOTE**

You usually need to create your public key only once.

Sending your public key to fax recipients. To send your public key to your fax recipients, take these steps:

1 Choose the Tools Microsoft Fax Tools command, and then choose Advanced Security from the submenu.

2 Click the Public Keys button. If the Fax Security-Key Set Password dialog box appears, type your password and click OK.

3 Click the Save button in the Fax Security-Managing Public Keys dialog box. Outlook then opens the Fax Security-Save Public Keys dialog box.

4 Select your name and the names of others whose public keys you want to share, click the To button, and then click OK.

5 In the Fax Security-Save Public Keys dialog box, switch to the disk and folder where you want to save your public keys file. Type a filename, and then click the Save button.

6 Click the Close button in the Fax Security-Managing Public Keys dialog box and then in the Advanced Fax Security dialog box.

7 Send the file as an attachment in an e-mail message, or deliver it on a floppy disk to your recipients.

> **NOTE**
>
> You usually need to send your public key only once to each recipient.

Adding public keys to your address book. To make it possible to receive encrypted faxes, you need to have a record of the sender's public encryption key. The best way to keep this record and make it readily available to Outlook for decoding faxes is to add public keys to your address book.

To add public keys to your address book, do the following:

1 Choose the Tools Microsoft Fax Tools command, and then choose Advanced Security from the submenu.

2 Click the Public Keys button. If the Fax Security-Key Set Password dialog box appears, type your password and click OK.

3 Click the Add button in the Fax Security-Managing Public Keys dialog box.

4 In the Fax Security-Add Public Keys dialog box, locate and select the file that contains the other people's public keys, and then click the Open button.

5 Select the key or keys that you want to add, and click OK.

Public keys you add might not show the name you want. To assign a public key a name in your address book, click Change Name, and then click the name you want to assign to the key.

Sending a key-encrypted fax.   When you send a key-encrypted fax, you can also add a digital signature.

1 Choose the Compose New Fax command, and work through the Compose New Fax Wizard to its third panel (which contains the Options button), or start a new message and address it to a fax address.

2 Click the Options button on the third panel of the wizard, or choose the File Send Options command and click the Fax tab.

3 Click the Security button.

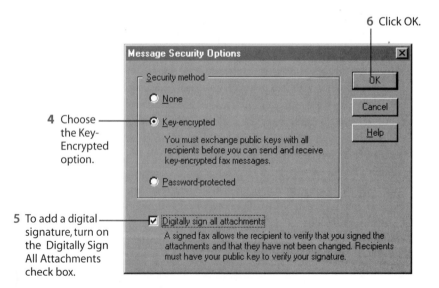

6 Click OK.

4 Choose the Key-Encrypted option.

5 To add a digital signature, turn on the Digitally Sign All Attachments check box.

7 In the Fax Security-Key Set Password dialog box, type your fax security password and click OK. (To avoid performing this step in the future, turn on the Save This Password In Your Password List box in the dialog box.)

8 Click OK in the Send Options dialog box, and then work your way through the rest of the wizard, or finish the fax message and send it.

 NOTE

You cannot forward a key-encrypted message, but multiple people can send a digitally signed fax.

Receiving a Fax

You can set up Outlook to receive faxes in your Inbox. Before you can receive faxes, however, you must perform the following two actions:

- Set up your modem to answer incoming calls by selecting one of the Answer Mode options in the Fax Modem Properties dialog box. (See "Setting Modem Options," on page 130.)

- Decide whether you want to be able to change the subject line of the faxes you receive. On the Message tab of the Microsoft Fax Properties dialog box, turn on (or off) the check box labeled Let Me Change The Subject Line Of New Faxes I Receive. (See "Setting Message Options," on page 124.)

TIP

If you usually have Outlook set up to receive faxes and you want to discontinue doing so, select Don't Answer as your Answer Mode option.

After you complete these two actions, you're ready to receive a fax. How you do this depends on the Answer Mode option you've chosen:

- If you selected the Answer After option, simply let Outlook answer the call and receive the fax.

- If you selected the Manual option, when a call comes in and you hear the fax warble in the handset, click the Answer Now button in the Microsoft Fax Status window and hang up the handset.

II

Electronic Mail

Click here to answer a fax call.

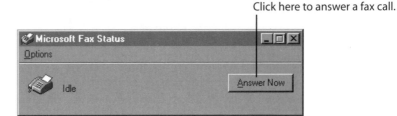

If the Microsoft Fax Status window is not visible when the telephone rings, double-click the Fax icon at the right end of the Windows 95 Taskbar.

Received faxes appear in your Inbox, just as e-mail messages do. You can then treat the faxes just as you treat any folder item in Outlook.

Retrieving a Fax from a Service

If you have your faxes sent to a fax service instead of directly to your computer, you can request that the service send your faxes to you. To request faxes from your fax service, follow these steps:

1 Choose the Tools Microsoft Fax Tools command, and then choose Request A Fax from the submenu. You'll see the first panel of the Request A Fax Wizard.

2 Select this option to retrieve all available faxes, or...

select this option to request a specific fax, and then type the title and password (if applicable).

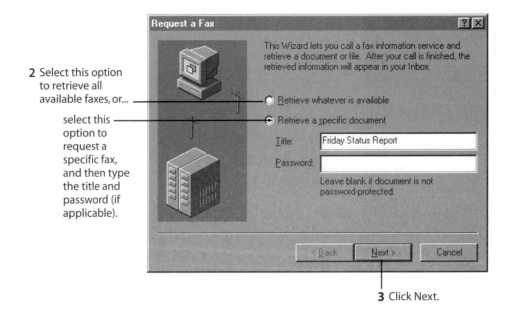

3 Click Next.

4 Type the name of the fax service in the To box, and select the appropriate country from the drop-down list. Type the fax service's fax number, and turn on the Dial Area Code option if needed. Then click the Add button. (Alternatively, you can click the Address Book button to select names.)

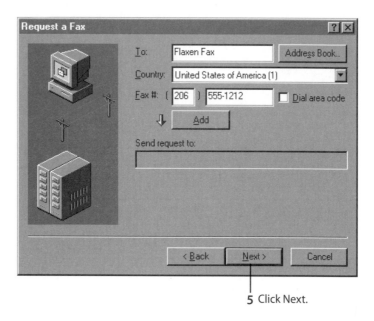

5 Click Next.

6 Select the time you want
  Outlook to send the request.

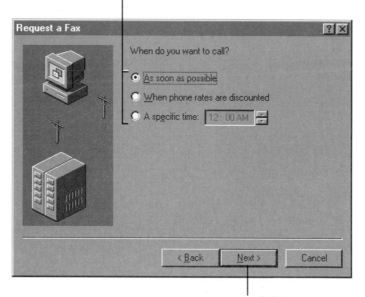

7 Click Next.

8 Click the Finish button.

9 When the faxes arrive, receive the faxes as described in the previous section, "Receiving a Fax," on page 145.

Mucking About in Address Books

I f you're like most users of Microsoft Outlook 97, you have more than one address book. First and foremost, you have organizational address books—one for the entire organization (called the Global Address List), one for your department (your network domain), possibly some for other departments (other network domains), and perhaps an Offline Address Book. Second, you have your Personal Address Book, in which you keep the names and addresses of the groups and people to whom you send e-mail most often. (If your Outlook setup does not include a Personal Address Book, you can add one—see the sidebar "Adding a Personal Address Book to Your Profile," on page 151).

You can also have the Outlook Address Book, which is created automatically from entries in your Contacts folder for which you've included an e-mail address or a fax phone number. And finally, you also have a separate address book for each online service you use to send and receive e-mail. For example, if you use MSN (the Microsoft Network), you have a separate address book for your MSN e-mail account.

What's a network domain? It's a collection of computers and users that share a common database and a common security policy.

Opening an Address Book

Who'd have ever thought that adults would need directions for opening an address book? How hard can it be? Actually, it's not hard at all, once you know where to go and what to do.

To open an address book, simply click the Address Book button on the Standard toolbar. Outlook displays the names that are in your default address book.

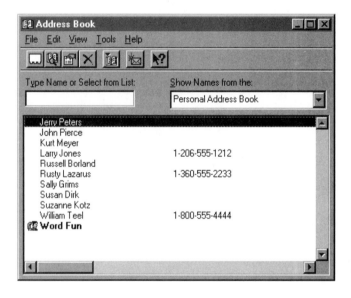

Adding a Personal Address Book to Your Profile

If you want to add a Personal Address Book to the profile you are using, you can add it by following these steps:

1 Choose the Tools Services command.

2 On the Services tab, click the Add button.

3 In the Add Service To Profile dialog box, select Personal Address Book, and then click OK.

4 In the Personal Address Book dialog box, enter a name for the Personal Address Book in the Name box.

5 In the Path box, enter the path of the personal address book file, or click the Browse button to locate a personal address book file that already exists.

6 Click OK in the Personal Address Book dialog box, and then click OK again in the message box that appears.

7 Click OK in the Services dialog box, and then exit and restart Outlook.

To add a Personal Address Book to a profile other than the one you are currently using, double-click the Mail And Fax icon on the Windows Control Panel. On the Services tab, click Show Profiles. On the General tab, click the profile you want in the Profile box, click Properties, and then follow steps 2 through 7 above.

Switching Address Books

When you have more than one address book, some names and addresses might not be included in all of them. You'll sometimes need to switch between address books to find the person you want to contact with e-mail or a fax.

To switch address books, do the following:

1 Click the Address Book button on the Standard toolbar.

2 Click the Show Names From The box. From the drop-down list, select the address book you want to open.

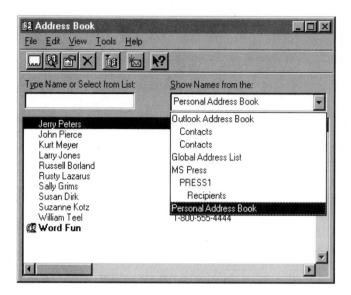

The names contained in the selected address book appear in the window.

Finding People

Even if you have only one or two address books, the number of names an address book can hold can make finding a certain person time-consuming and even tiresome. You need a way to locate a name quickly and efficiently so that you can get on with creating and sending a message and then move on to other tasks. Outlook provides a helpful tool for locating that certain someone easily and quickly.

To find a name in an address book, take these steps:

1 Click the Address Book button on the Standard toolbar.

2 In the Show Names From The box, select the address book you want to look in.

3 Type the beginning of the name in the Type Name Or Select From List box. Outlook jumps to the spot in the list that matches the name you've started to type. You can, of course, simply scroll the list of names in the window to find the name you're looking for.

Adding Someone

When you first start using Outlook, your address books will contain a standard list of people within your organization or members of an online service. Because many people around the country and around the world now use e-mail regularly, you'll develop "pen pals" as well as professional contacts with whom you'll want to exchange messages. You can, of course, simply type an e-mail address in each message you send, but e-mail addresses are singularly weird. It's really hard to remember them. Consider, for example, a CompuServe address: nine numbers with a comma in the middle. And you have no way of knowing who the heck resides behind some random number. On most other online services, people can select their own "handle"—or unique identification—which seldom looks anything like their legal name.

To avoid confusion, to reduce memorization, and to make sure you use the correct e-mail address every time, you should add names and addresses to your Personal Address Book or to your Outlook Contacts folder. (When you add a contact entry with an e-mail address, the entry is added to your Outlook Address Book.)

Think of your Personal Address Book as your "little black book." In your address books, you keep the name and "address"—an e-mail identification, a fax number, or any other electronic identification—of each of your correspondents.

You can add new names, change names, and remove names as often as you want, and an electronic address book is much easier to keep straight than a paper address book. No ugly erasures, no running out of space. And your Personal Address Book—as well as all the other address books you use—can help you find names in many different ways.

 NOTE

> You can add new names only to your Personal Address Book. Only e-mail administrators can add names to organizational address books. To add names to your Outlook Address Book, you must add names to your Contacts folder. For details, see "Setting Up Your Contact List," on page 296.

To add a name and address to your Personal Address Book, do the following:

1 Click the Address Book button on the Standard toolbar.

2 Click the New Entry button on the Address Book toolbar.

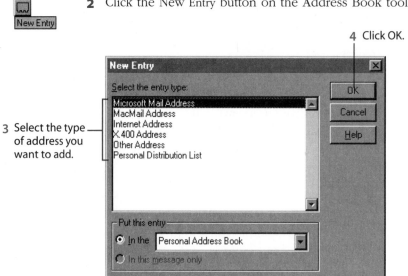

4 Click OK.

3 Select the type of address you want to add.

5 The next dialog box you see depends on the type of entry you selected in the New Entry dialog box. For most new entries, you'll enter information such as the name to display in the address book and the e-mail address. The example on the facing page is based on selecting Other Address.

Note that if you set up a fax number for an entry in your address book, you should type the fax number in the E-Mail Address box (step 7) and type *FAX* in the E-Mail Type box (step 8).

6 Type the name to show in the address book (required).

7 Type the e-mail address (required); for instance, *russb@microsoft.com*.

8 Type the designation for the e-mail system (required if the box is present); for example, *SMTP.* Check with your e-mail administrator if necessary.

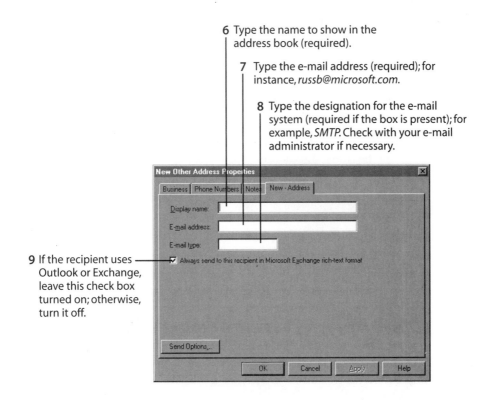

9 If the recipient uses Outlook or Exchange, leave this check box turned on; otherwise, turn it off.

10 Fill in the boxes on the other tabs with as much information as you want. For example, the Business tab provides boxes for addresses and a phone number. The Phone Numbers tab contains boxes for various phone numbers, including a box for the person's fax number. If you want to send a fax to this person, be sure to enter the fax telephone number.

11 When you finish filling out the tabs, click OK.

When you add a name and address, Outlook requires only that you fill in the boxes on the initial tab. You can leave the other tabs blank and fill them in any time later by using the Properties button on the Address Book toolbar. Clicking the Properties button displays the same dialog box that you saw after you clicked OK in the New Entry dialog box.

TIP

You can use the information on the Business tab to fill in mailing labels in Microsoft Word 97.

Internet Encoding Methods

When you add an entry to your Personal Address Book, you will often be adding an address for someone with whom you exchange e-mail over the Internet. Depending on your Outlook setup, you can use the Send Options button in the New Address Properties dialog box to select options for how to send messages and attachments to your Internet correspondents.

Turn on this check box to specify encoding.

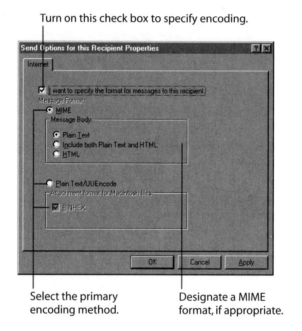

Select the primary encoding method.

Designate a MIME format, if appropriate.

Different e-mail systems use different encoding methods for sending attachments and formatting across the Internet. These methods allow you to send whole documents, as well as files in other formats, through e-mail. The three most commonly used encoding methods are MIME (Multipurpose Internet Mail Extensions), which allows you to send highly formatted documents; uuencode, which converts binary files to text; and (for Macintosh files only) BINHEX (Binary-Hexadecimal). The standard encoding method for Outlook is MIME. If an e-mail address in your address book uses uuencode, select that option for the e-mail address.

For addresses that use MIME, you can select various formats for the body of your messages: Plain Text, HTML (HyperText Markup Language—the encoding for World Wide Web pages), or both.

Personal Distribution Lists

Do you know a bunch of people to whom you want to send e-mail regularly? You probably think you have to remember everybody's name every time. And you have to type or select all those names every time. Too slow. Too prone to errors. Too boring!

Instead, you can create personal groups—also called personal distribution lists. A personal group is a group of e-mail correspondents. You add their names to the personal group, and then, when you want to send e-mail to all the members of the group, you simply select or type the group name. Outlook takes care of sending your message to all those lucky people.

Outlook provides the tools you need to create personal groups, to edit a personal group (to add and delete names), to delete personal groups, and to give a personal group a new name.

Creating a Personal Distribution List

Once you've decided to set up a personal group, the steps are pretty easy. You simply name the group, open the address book or books that contain the names you need, and select the names.

Here's how to create a new personal distribution list:

1 Click the Address Book button on the Standard toolbar.

2 Click the New Entry button on the Address Book toolbar.

3 In the New Entry dialog box, select Personal Distribution List in the Select The Entry Type box, and then click OK.

4 Type a name for your personal group.

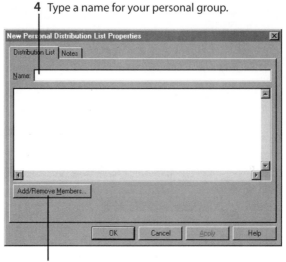

5 Click Add/Remove Members.

6 In the Edit Members Of dialog box, use the Show Names From The box to select the address book containing the names you want to add to this personal group. You can switch to a different address book at any time if you want to add names from several address books. (Note that the title bar of the Edit Members Of dialog box displays the name of the personal distribution list. For example, if the group's name is Gliders, the title bar shows Edit Members Of Gliders.)

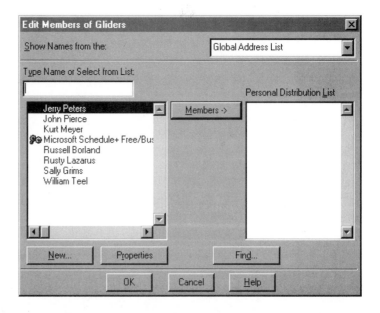

Electronic Mail

7 In the left-hand box of the Edit Members Of dialog box, select the names you want to add to the group. To add more than one name at a time, hold down the Ctrl key and click the names. These names don't have to be listed consecutively. To add several consecutive names, select the first name, hold down the Shift key, and then click the last name. Outlook selects all the names from the first to the last that you clicked.

8 Click the Members button. The selected names now also appear in the Personal Distribution List box.

9 When you've finished adding members to your personal distribution list, click OK in the Edit Members Of dialog box.

10 In the New Personal Distribution List Properties dialog box, you can click the Notes tab and enter any information that you want about this personal group. This information can be handy if someone asks you what this group is about. You can copy this information into a reply and save yourself some time and effort by not having to remember and type a description of this personal group each time you're asked.

11 When the properties for this new personal distribution list are all set, click OK. The new personal distribution list now appears in your Personal Address Book with a "group" icon next to the name, as shown here:

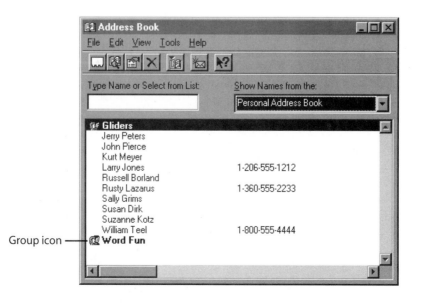

Group icon

You can add new names to your Personal Address Book as you're creating a personal distribution list. To do so, click the New button in the Edit Members Of dialog box and follow the steps for "Adding Someone," on page 153. You can also change the information for a person by selecting the name and clicking the Properties button in the Edit Members Of dialog box.

Editing a Personal Distribution List

People come and people go. From time to time, a personal distribution list changes. New people want to be in your club; others want out. (And there are always a few you just want to throw out!) For your personal distribution list to be fully useful all the time, you need to be able to add and remove names as the need arises.

To add a name to an existing personal distribution list, follow these steps:

1 Click the Address Book button on the Standard toolbar, and then select your Personal Address Book.

2 Select the personal distribution list you want to change.

3 Click the Properties button on the Address Book toolbar.

4 Click the Add/Remove Members button.

5 In the Show Names From The box, select the address book that contains the name you want to add, select the name from the Type Name Or Select From List box, and then click the Members button.

6 Click OK.

To remove a name from a personal distribution list, follow these steps:

1 Repeat steps 1 through 4 in the preceding procedure.

2 In the Edit Members Of dialog box, select the name or names you want to remove in the Personal Distribution List box.

3 Press the Delete key. Be sure to delete the extra semicolon and the space that separates the deleted name from the names surrounding it in the list.

4 When you've finished, click OK in the Edit Members Of dialog box, and then click OK in the Properties dialog box.

Deleting a Personal Distribution List

Sometimes groups disband—not even the Beatles lasted forever, though one fears that the Rolling Stones might. When you no longer want or need a personal distribution list, you can remove it from your Personal Address Book.

To delete a personal distribution list, take these steps:

1 Click the Address Book button on the Standard toolbar, and then select your Personal Address Book.

2 Select the name of the personal distribution list you're removing, and then click the Delete button on the Address Book toolbar.

3 When Outlook asks whether you want to permanently remove the selected users from the address book, click Yes.

4 Close the address book.

 NOTE

> The individual names of the group members you added from other address books remain in your Personal Address Book after you delete a distribution list. If you want to remove individual names as well, select the names, and then click the Delete button on the Address Book toolbar.

Renaming a Personal Distribution List

Maybe a group changes its colors; maybe a group changes its mind; maybe you just want to use a different group name for whatever reason. Outlook provides a way to change the name of a personal distribution list without too much trouble.

To rename a personal distribution list, do the following:

1 Click the Address Book button on the Standard toolbar, and then select your Personal Address Book.

2 Select the group name you want to change.

3 Click the Properties button on the Address Book toolbar.

4 Type the new name of the personal distribution list in the Name box, and then click OK.

Sharing a Personal Distribution List with Others

After you create a personal distribution list name, you'll want others in the group to use it. But it's sometimes a pain in the neck to get an e-mail administrator to set up a public distribution list, especially if it's a "private" or social group rather than a business group. So here's how to send the name of your personal distribution list and a list of its members to others:

1 Click the Address Book button on the Standard toolbar, and then select your Personal Address Book.

2 Select the personal distribution list name, and click the Properties button on the Address Book toolbar.

3 Click the Add/Remove Members button.

4 Select all the names in the Personal Distribution List box.

5 Copy the names to the Clipboard by pressing Ctrl+C.

6 Close all the dialog boxes and the address book.

7 Compose a message to the people to whom you want to send the group names.

8 Paste the names from the Clipboard into the message area by pressing Ctrl+V, and tell the recipients the name of the personal distribution list.

9 Send the message.

When the recipients receive the message with the names, they can use it to create their own version of the personal distribution list, as follows:

1 Select all the names in the message, and copy the names to the Clipboard.

2 Create a new personal group, and give it the same name as the one you copied.

3 Click the Add/Remove Members button.

4 Paste the names from the Clipboard into the Personal Distribution List box.

5 Close all the dialog boxes and the address book.

The recipients will then have a personal distribution list that contains the same members as your original list.

CHAPTER 5

Setting Up Outlook for Remote Work

M any people never need to use Microsoft Outlook 97 beyond their workplace desktop. But for you adventurous types who travel with your computers, you can set up Outlook to dial in to and connect to your e-mail server and work with your e-mail and calendar.

When you're lodged in a hotel, you still might want to see the messages, postings, and meetings that are going on at headquarters. For times such as these, you can send and delete messages, set up appointments and tasks, request meetings, and respond to meeting and task requests. And, with some preliminary setup, you can also see the contents of public folders as well as your server folders.

This chapter introduces the various ways you can use Outlook to work from a remote computer. You'll find detailed instructions for setting up both online and offline work. This chapter focuses on the setup procedures involved in remote use. Chapter 6, "Running Outlook for Remote Work," focuses on how you use Outlook once your setup is complete—making connections, working with folders, sending messages, and so on.

You have three ways to work remotely with your e-mail:

- Work remotely online only (no offline work). See "Setting Up to Work Remotely Online Only," on page 166.

- Work online and offline, sometimes remotely, with offline folders. You can use this offline folders method only if you are running Outlook with Microsoft Exchange Server as your e-mail server. See "Setting Up to Work Online and Offline, Sometimes Remotely," on page 169.

- Use Remote Mail to send and receive messages, but work offline most of the time. See "Setting Up Remote Mail and Offline Work," on page 177.

Before you decide between using offline folders or Remote Mail, consult the sidebar "Offline Folders Vs. Remote Mail," on the facing page.

Offline Folders Vs. Remote Mail

When you use offline folders or Remote Mail, Outlook provides several ways for you to manage messages and other items from remote locations. If you run Outlook with Microsoft Exchange Server, it's probably better to use offline folders. If you don't use Microsoft Exchange Server or if you simply need to download messages from your Inbox (and not use the calendar or other of Outlook's features), it's better to use Remote Mail. Use the following descriptions to determine the method that is best for you.

You'll want to use the offline folders method in these cases:

- You use Outlook with Microsoft Exchange Server.

- You want to update the contents of any folder.

- You want to synchronize the folders between two computers—for instance, you want to have identical folder contents on the server and on your remote computer.

- You want to download your calendar or a task list to a remote computer.

- You don't need to worry about the cost of time on the telephone—for instance, you have an inexpensive local phone connection to your mail delivery service.

Use the Remote Mail method in these cases:

- You use Outlook with a server other than Microsoft Exchange Server.

- You want to retrieve messages for your Inbox only.

- You want to minimize time spent on the telephone—for instance, your computer at home has a slow modem, or you're connecting from a hotel or airport where the cost of telephone access is high.

II

Electronic Mail

> **NOTE**

To work with Outlook remotely, your system administrator must set up your user account with dial-up access rights so that you can dial in to the network. Contact your system administrator for assistance.

Setting Up to Work Remotely Online Only

You can dial in to your organization's network with the Dial-Up Networking feature in Microsoft Windows 95. After you connect to the network over the telephone line, you can then run Outlook just as if you were connected directly to the network. Using this method, you don't work with Outlook offline, so you don't need to make any changes to an Outlook profile. You do, however, need to set up Dial-Up Networking in Windows 95, as explained here:

1 Click the Start button on the Windows 95 Taskbar, and click Programs. Click Accessories, and then, on the submenu, click Dial-Up Networking.

If you have not created a dial-up networking connection before, you'll see the welcoming panel of the Make New Connection Wizard. Otherwise, you'll see the Dial-Up Networking window.

2 Double-click Make New Connection.

3 Type or accept the name for your connection.

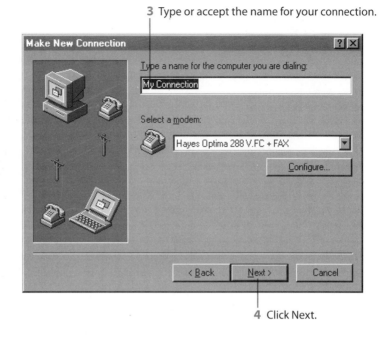

4 Click Next.

 SEE ALSO

See "Calling Card Dial-
ing," on page 186, for
details about setting
up Outlook to dial up
using your telephone
calling card.

5 Type the area code.

6 Type the telephone number
of your network connection.

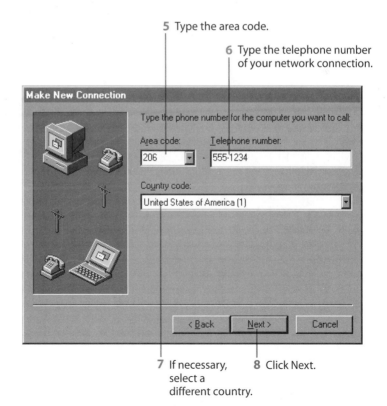

7 If necessary,
select a
different country.

8 Click Next.

II

Electronic Mail

9 On the Finish panel of the Make New Connection Wizard, click Finish.

When you're ready to connect to the network computer, take the steps described in "Running Outlook to Work Remotely Online Only," on page 192. You can use a dial-up networking connection for all the tasks you would usually perform while directly connected to a network.

What About My Connections to Other Online Services?

If you have accounts on other online services, such as MSN (The Microsoft Network), CompuServe, America Online, or AT&T, you can set up these services in a profile. Then Outlook starts that service when you start Outlook. If you want to connect to the service, follow your usual logon procedure. To set up an information service in a profile, follow these steps:

1 In the Windows Control Panel, double-click the Mail And Fax icon.

2 In the Properties dialog box, click the Show Profiles button.

3 In the Mail And Fax dialog box, select the profile to which you want to add an information service, and then click the Properties button.

4 Click the Add button in the Properties dialog box to display the Add Service To Profile dialog box.

5 Select the information service you want to add to this profile, and then click OK. If the service you want to add is not listed, you need a disk that contains the files required to set up the service. Insert the disk in your computer, and then click the Have Disk button. In the Install Other Information Service dialog box, type the drive letter for the disk that contains the files for the information service, or click the Browse button to select the disk and folder that contain the files. Click OK. When the service is installed, click OK in the Add Service To Profile dialog box.

6 Click OK in the Properties dialog box, and then click the Close button in the Mail And Fax dialog box.

Note that typically you can add only one dial-in information service to a profile. Why? Because each dial-in information service requires a modem and a telephone line. When one service is using the modem and telephone line, a second service won't have access to the line. If, however, you have multiple modems connected to your computer and a telephone line for each modem, you can then set up one dial-in information service for each modem and telephone line.

Setting Up to Work Online and Offline, Sometimes Remotely

Wouldn't it be a shame to have to give up the fancy tools you use with Outlook simply because you aren't connected to your Microsoft Exchange Server? You might not be connected either because you are away from your network connection or because the network or your Microsoft Exchange Server is currently not functioning. For these situations, you can use offline folders.

You can use offline folders only if your e-mail server is Microsoft Exchange Server and you are using a profile for which you've indicated that you travel with your computer.

For offline work, you might want to see the contents of various server folders and public folders. When you use offline folders in Outlook, you can work with the items in any offline folder if you have set up other server folders and public folder favorites for offline use. (Personal folders are always available offline because they are stored on the hard disk in your computer.)

This method of working in Outlook parallels the method described in the preceding section, with one difference. For this method, you set up offline folders so that you can work on your messages, appointments, tasks, and other Outlook folder items without being connected to your e-mail server.

You can use a single Outlook profile for both online and offline work. If you do, each time you start Outlook you'll be asked whether you want to connect or work offline. Click the button that fits the situation.

With offline folders, you can synchronize your Inbox folder, Calendar folder, Tasks folder, and any other folder from your remote location to make the contents identical to the contents of these folders on your e-mail server. You can download all the items in all offline folders in one step.

NOTE

If you use offline folders, you cannot use Remote Mail to download messages.

Here are the general steps involved in setting up Outlook for both online and offline work. You'll find the details for all five steps in the following five sections.

1 Set up an offline folder file.

2 Download the Offline Address Book.

3 Set up public folder favorites for public folders you want to open offline.

4 Designate other folders for offline use.

5 Synchronize all offline folders.

Setting Up an Offline Folder File

To set up an offline folder file, take these steps:

1 Connect to your e-mail server for online work, either through a network connection or through Dial-Up Networking.

2 If necessary, switch to your Inbox.

3 Choose the Tools Services command.

TIP

It really is much better to perform the steps for setting up an offline folder file while connected through a network connection than while connected through Dial-Up Networking. Why? Most dial-up networking connections run through modems that have much lower speeds than a network connection. Through a modem connection, the processes Outlook must perform before you can work offline can take a *very* long time. Over a direct network connection, the processes go relatively quickly.

4 Select Microsoft Exchange Server.

5 Click Properties.

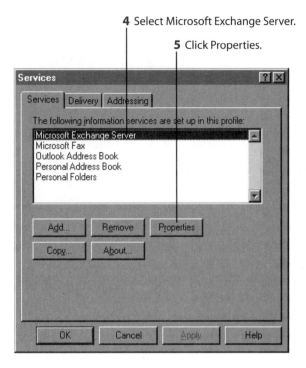

6 In the Microsoft Exchange Server dialog box, click the Advanced tab.

7 Click Offline Folder File Settings.

8 Accept the filename,
type a new name, or...

if you already have an offline
folder file, click Browse to locate it.

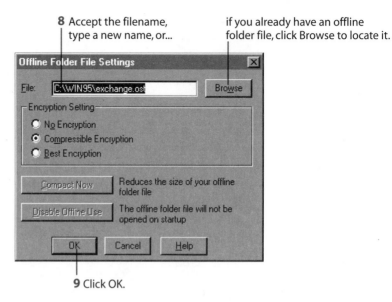

9 Click OK.

10 Click OK in the Microsoft Exchange Server dialog box, and then click OK in the Services dialog box. You're now ready for the next phase of setting up offline folders: downloading the Offline Address Book.

Turning Off Offline Folders

If you later want to discontinue using all offline folders, here's how to do it:

1 Connect to your e-mail server for online work, either through a network connection or through Dial-Up Networking.

2 If necessary, switch to your Inbox.

3 Choose the Tools Services command, select Microsoft Exchange Server, and click the Properties button.

4 In the Microsoft Exchange Server dialog box, click the Advanced tab, and then click the Offline Folder File Settings button.

5 In the Offline Folder File Settings dialog box, click the Disable Offline Use button.

6 Click Yes when Outlook asks whether you want to continue.

7 Click OK first in the Microsoft Exchange Server dialog box and then in the Services dialog box.

Downloading the Offline Address Book

When you're working offline, you'll probably want to compose new messages, reply to messages, and forward messages. Before you can specify the recipients of your message or place the message in your Outbox to be sent later, you need to have the Offline Address Book available. If you don't download the Offline Address Book, Outlook tells you that you can't compose or otherwise work with a message until you download the address book.

To download the Offline Address Book, do the following:

1 Connect to your network and start Outlook.

2 Choose the Tools Synchronize command.

3 Choose Download Address Book from the submenu.

4 In the Download Offline Address Book dialog box, select the level of detail you need in this address book. The first option downloads the address book with all its information. The second option omits details information. This second option is faster, but without details you cannot use encryption or digital signatures.

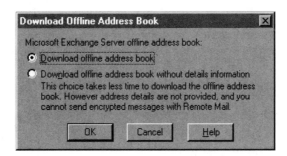

5 Click OK. You'll see a message that shows you how download-ing is progressing. When downloading is complete, you're ready to work with messages offline.

Working Remotely with Public Folders

While you're working offline, you can't open public folders, at least not directly. Outlook helps you get around this restriction through public folder favorites. If you've already set these up, you're in a good position to take advantage of them during offline work. If you haven't yet set up any public folder favorites, you must do so before you can work with the contents of a public folder offline.

Setting up public folder favorites is quite easy; simply follow these steps:

1 Find and open the public folder you want to add to your Public Folders Favorites folder. (You can do this by displaying the Other group on the Outlook Bar and clicking the Public Folders icon.)

2 Choose the File Folder command, and then choose Add To Public Folder Favorites from the submenu.

You'll see a message that the folder was added successfully to your Public Folders Favorites folder. At this point, the folder you added displays the contents of its related public folder, and you can set the folder in the Public Folders Favorites folder to be available offline. (See the next section.)

When you're working offline, the public folder favorite contains the contents of the related public folder as they were the last time you synchronized the folders. You can read items in the folder, post new items, and reply to postings and messages. You can also delete items and add forms if you have permission to do so. Outlook copies the changes you make in the offline favorite folder to its related public folder the next time you connect to your Exchange server.

Designating Folders for Offline Work

Your Inbox, Outbox, Sent Items, and Deleted Items folders on your Exchange server are immediately available offline as well as online when you set up your offline folder file. (See "Setting Up an Offline Folder File," on page 170.) When you work offline, these folders contain all the items that were in the folders when you last exited Outlook. You can open and view these folders as you would while working online. You can send messages, move messages, delete messages, and empty your Deleted Items folder—all while you're working offline.

In addition to these folders, you can set up for offline use any other server folders on your Exchange server as well as any public folder favorites you have set up.

To designate a server folder or a favorite public folder for offline use, take these steps:

1 Right-click the folder you want to set up for offline use, and then choose Properties from the shortcut menu. As an alternative, you can click the folder, choose the File Folder command, and then choose Properties For from the submenu.

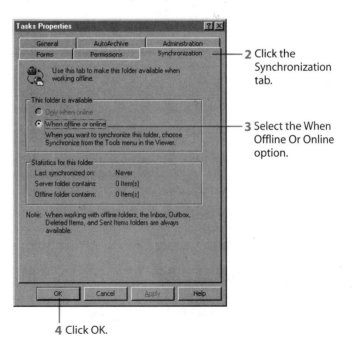

2 Click the Synchronization tab.

3 Select the When Offline Or Online option.

4 Click OK.

This folder is now available for work offline as well as online. If you no longer want a folder to be available for offline work, select the Only When Online option on the Synchronization tab of the Properties dialog box.

You cannot set up your four main server folders—Inbox, Outbox, Sent Items, and Deleted Items—for exclusively online work unless you turn off offline folders. For instructions on how to do this, see "Turning Off Offline Folders," on page 172.

Synchronizing Folders

After you set up folders for offline use, you need to periodically synchronize the offline folders with their related folders on the Exchange server. Outlook synchronizes your offline folders automatically whenever you connect to Microsoft Exchange Server. Before exiting Outlook, and while you're still connected to your Exchange server, you can synchronize any folders that you have set up to be available offline. To synchronize a single folder, do the following:

1   Select the folder that you want to synchronize.

2   Choose the Tools Synchronize command.

3   Choose This Folder from the submenu.

You cannot synchronize a public folder directly. If you want to synchronize a public folder, you must select the copy of the folder in your Public Folders Favorites folder.

To synchronize all folders, choose the Tools Synchronize command, and then choose All Folders from the submenu. In either case—synchronizing a single folder or all folders—Outlook displays a window indicating its progress as it synchronizes the folder or folders.

Automatically Synchronizing All Offline Folders

When you use offline folders, you'll connect to your Microsoft Exchange Server at least occasionally, either over a network or with

Dial-Up Networking. Outlook always synchronizes offline folders when you connect to your Microsoft Exchange Server. After that, you can synchronize any or all offline folders whenever you want while you're connected to the Exchange server. To further help you keep your offline folders synchronized, you can set an option to have Outlook automatically synchronize all offline folders with your online (server) folders when you exit an online Outlook session. To do so, follow these steps:

1 While working online in Outlook, choose the Tools Options command, and click the General tab.

2 Turn on the When Online, Synchronize All Folders Upon Exiting check box, and then click OK.

With this option turned on, your offline folders are consistent with your online folders when you start to work offline. Leave this option turned off only if you prefer to manually synchronize your offline folders (by using the Tools Synchronize command) while you're working online. You can manually synchronize folders at any time you're online, even if you have turned on this option on the General tab.

Setting Up Remote Mail and Offline Work

If you need to work only with the messages in your Inbox, or if you want to spend as little time as possible on the telephone line, you can dial up your e-mail server with Remote Mail. By connecting to your e-mail server with Remote Mail, you get only a list of message headers. Remote Mail then disconnects from the server to save you from expensive phone charges. You mark the messages you want to read and the messages you want to delete and then connect with Remote Mail again to download. When you reconnect to your e-mail server, Outlook downloads only those messages marked for download, deletes those messages marked for deletion, and disconnects again. You can then read the downloaded messages and perform all the actions—reply, delete, forward, move, and save—that you perform with messages when you're connected to your e-mail server through a network. You simply repeat the Remote Mail connection until you've finished receiving and sending messages.

> If you use offline folders, you cannot use Remote Mail to download messages. If you have set up offline folders, either create a new profile without offline folders, or turn off these folders for the profile that you want to use for Remote Mail. See "Turning Off Offline Folders," on page 172.

Before you can connect through Remote Mail, you need to perform the following general steps:

1 Download the Offline Address Book while you're connected to your e-mail server. For details, see "Downloading the Offline Address Book," on page 173.

2 Set up personal folders, either in an existing profile or in a new profile. You can do this either online or offline.

3 Set up Remote Mail connections, providing Outlook with information such as your user name and password.

4 Set up Remote Mail options, which you can do either online or offline.

Adding Personal Folders to a Profile

A personal folder file (which uses the .PST filename extension) is usually located on your computer's hard disk. Your personal folders mirror the set of folders used to store messages and other items on your e-mail server. Personal folders include the Inbox folder, the Calendar folder, and the other Outlook folders available on your server. You can work with items in personal folders even when the network or mail delivery service is unavailable. When you use Remote Mail in Outlook, a copy of your message is downloaded from your server to your Personal Folders Inbox.

The easiest way to set up personal folders in Outlook is during the creation of a profile. When the profile wizard asks whether you travel with this computer, choose Yes. The profile wizard then sets up personal folders for you.

⑦ SEE ALSO

For information about setting up a profile, see "Creating a Profile," on page 8.

To add personal folders to an existing profile, take these steps:

1 Select the Services tab of the Properties dialog box for the profile you want to change. If you're currently using the profile in Outlook, do this by choosing the Tools Services command and clicking the Services tab. If you want to change a profile that you aren't currently using, double-click the Mail And Fax icon on the Windows Control Panel. Click the Show Profiles button, select the profile you want to change, and then click the Properties button.

2 On the Services tab, click the Add button.

3 In the Add Service To Profile dialog box, select Personal Folders, and click OK.

4 In the Create/Open Personal Folders File dialog box, either type a name for a new personal folders file or select an existing personal folders file (one you use for another profile), and then click the Open button.

5 If you created a new personal folders file, you see the Create Microsoft Personal Folders dialog box. In this dialog box, you can use the Name box to change the name for the personal folders. This name appears in the Outlook Folder List. (If you select a personal folders file that is already stored on your computer, you'll see a dialog box in which you can change the name of the personal folders file, the password, and other settings.)

6 Type a password for these personal folders in the Password box. The password can be the same as your network logon password or your regular Outlook password.

7 Type the same password again in the Verify Password box.

8 To avoid typing the password each time you start Outlook, turn on the Save This Password In Your Password List box.

II

Electronic Mail

9 Click OK in the Create Microsoft Personal Folders dialog box.

10 Click OK in the Services dialog box or the Properties dialog box (depending on the method you used to open the Properties dialog box in step 1).

Setting Up Remote Mail Connections

Before you can use Remote Mail, you must provide Outlook with information about your remote connection. To provide Outlook with this information, you need to set Dial-Up Networking options and Remote Mail options. Follow these steps:

1 Choose the Tools Services command, select Microsoft Exchange Server, and then click the Properties button.

2 Click the Dial-Up Networking tab.

3 Select the option for your Remote Mail connection. You have two choices:

- Dial Using The Following Connection. You'll want to select this option when you're working offline and you're going to use Remote Mail over a telephone line only. This option starts the dial-up process for you when you run Remote Mail. The connection names that are listed come from the Windows 95 Dial-Up Networking window.

- Do Not Dial, Use Existing Connection. You'll want to select this option when you're working offline and you're connected directly to your network or you've opened a dial-up connection through Windows 95 Dial-Up Networking. This option simply connects to your Microsoft Exchange Server through the existing connection rather than by dialing up.

4 If you turn on the Dial Using The Following Connection option, you can select an existing connection name from the drop-down list, or you can create a new connection by clicking the New button. If you need to modify a connection, click the Properties button. (For the additional steps involved in creating a new connection or modifying a connection, see "Setting Up to Work Remotely Online Only," on page 166.) To change the location, click the Location button, and follow the instructions in "Setting Dialing Options," on page 127.

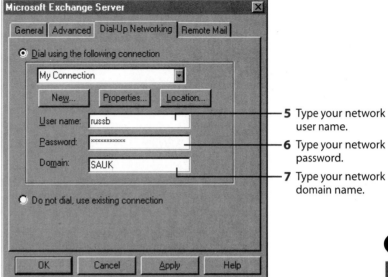

5 Type your network
user name.

6 Type your network
password.

7 Type your network
domain name.

8 Set options on the Remote Mail tab, as explained in "Setting
Remote Mail Options," below, and then click OK.

9 Click OK in the Services dialog box.

Setting Remote Mail Options

Remote Mail makes it possible for you to save time by screening
messages before you download them. Remote Mail first downloads
message headers only, allowing you to mark them for reading or
deletion. You can then download in their entirety the messages that
you have marked for reading.

We'll look at two options that can make Remote Mail work better
for you:

■ Filtering Remote Mail so that you don't have to see messages
you don't care about when you're away from your office

■ Scheduling automatic dial-in times so that you can keep your
folders at home current

To set Remote Mail options, take the following steps. The specific
options are detailed in the next two sections.

1   Choose the Tools Services command, select Microsoft Exchange Server, and then click the Properties button.

2   Click the Remote Mail tab.

3 You can tell Outlook to process all marked items, or...

tell Outlook to process only items that match a filter.

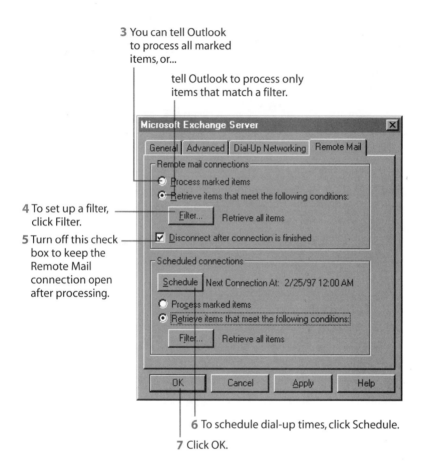

4 To set up a filter, click Filter.

5 Turn off this check box to keep the Remote Mail connection open after processing.

6 To schedule dial-up times, click Schedule.

7 Click OK.

8   Click OK in the Services dialog box.

Filtering Remote Mail

A filter sets up conditions that tell the Remote Mail part of Outlook which message headers to download. A filter can do the following: screen out messages you don't want to deal with and pass through only those message headers that you do want to see; allow shorter connection times while Remote Mail downloads the message headers; provide shorter work sessions for you because you aren't wading through extraneous messages.

Here's how to set up a Remote Mail filter:

1 Choose the Tools Services command, select Microsoft Exchange Server, and then click the Properties button.

2 Click the Remote Mail tab.

3 Select the Retrieve Items That Meet The Following Conditions option, and then click the Filter button.

4 In the Filter dialog box, set up the criteria for the filter you want to use. You can fill in any or all of the four criteria, which are explained in Table 5-1 on the following page.

5 Click Advanced to set more criteria.

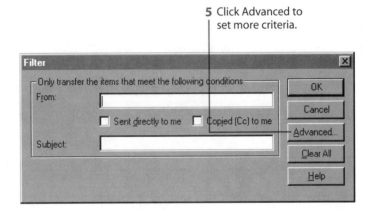

6 Click the Advanced button in the Filter dialog box to open the Advanced dialog box, which you can use to set up any advanced criteria you need. Table 5-2 on the following page describes these advanced settings.

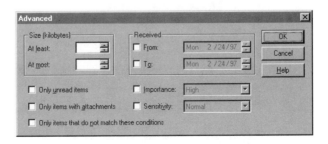

7 Click OK in all the open dialog boxes.

TIP

You don't have to fill out the Filter dialog box at all. You can set up criteria in the Advanced dialog box either in addition to criteria you set up in the Filter dialog box or instead of setting criteria there.

Table 5-1. Settings in the Filter Dialog Box.

Setting	What Is Delivered to You
From	Only items from a particular sender
Sent Directly To Me	Only items with your name in the To box
Copied (Cc) To Me	Only items with your name in the Cc box
Subject	Only items with subjects that include the text you type in the Subject box (Separate multiple entries with semicolons.)

Table 5-2. Settings in the Advanced Dialog Box.

Setting	What Is Delivered to You
Size At Least	Only items that are larger than the size you set (in kilobytes)
Size At Most	Only items that are smaller than the size you set (in kilobytes)
Received From	Only items received after the date you set (To see items between two dates, also set a Received To date.)
Received To	Only items received before the date you set (To see items between two dates, also set a Received From date.)
Only Unread Items	Only items you haven't yet read
Only Items With Attachments	Only items that contain attachments (files or messages)
Importance	Only items set to the specified level of importance—High, Normal, or Low
Sensitivity	Only items with the specified level of sensitivity—Normal, Personal, Private, or Confidential
Only Items That Do Not Match These Conditions	Only items that meet the *reverse* criteria of all the settings in both the Filter dialog box and the Advanced dialog box

TIP

Notice the option in the Advanced dialog box labeled Only Items That Do Not Match These Conditions. Selecting this option reverses all the other conditions you set up in the Filter and Advanced dialog boxes. For example, if you turn on this option and the Only Unread Items box, only items that you have already read will be delivered to you.

It's a simple matter to turn off a Remote Mail filter:

1 Click the Filter button on the Remote Mail tab.

2 In the Filter dialog box, click the Clear All button, and then click OK. The label beside the Filter button on the Remote Mail tab changes to Retrieve All Items. Clicking the Clear All button clears both the Filter and the Advanced dialog box settings.

3 Select the Process Marked Items option on the Remote Mail tab.

Scheduling Remote Mail Connections

When you're away from your network connection, you might want to connect with Remote Mail at a specific time or at specific intervals or both. With Remote Mail scheduling, you can set the time and interval you want Outlook to use to dial in and connect.

To set up a dial-in schedule for Remote Mail, follow these steps:

1 Choose the Tools Services command, select Microsoft Exchange Server, and then click the Properties button.

2 In the Microsoft Exchange Server dialog box, click the Remote Mail tab.

3 On the Remote Mail tab, click the Schedule button.

  NOTE

You can set both a specific time and a time interval for the scheduled connections in the Schedule Remote Mail Connection dialog box (which appears when you click Schedule, and which is shown at the top of the following page). That's because the time interval you specify in the At box functions independently of the time you specify in the Every box. The At check box establishes a single time connection; the Every check box establishes a connection according to a time interval (such as one hour) from the *current system time*—not from the time you enter in the At box. (In the example on the next page, notice that the next connection is at 1:22 P.M.; we can assume, then, that the time interval was established at 12:22 P.M.)

II

Electronic Mail

4 Turn on this check box to connect daily at a specific time.

Set the specific time here.

Set the interval here.

5 Turn on this check box to connect at regular intervals.

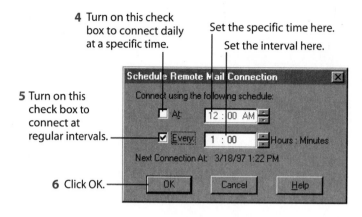

6 Click OK.

7 In the Scheduled Connections area, select the Process Marked Items option to have Outlook process all marked items, or select the Retrieve Items That Meet The Following Conditions option to set up a filter. (See "Filtering Remote Mail," on page 182.)

8 Click OK in all the open dialog boxes.

Calling Card Dialing

For various reasons, you might want to charge your dial-up calls to a telephone calling card. That's easy to set up. Here's what you do:

1 Use one of the following methods to open the Dialing Properties dialog box, which displays the My Locations tab:

- From within Outlook, choose the Tools Services command, select Microsoft Exchange Server, click Properties, click the Dial-Up Networking tab, and then click Location.

- In the Windows 95 Dial-Up Networking window, double-click a connection and then click Dial Properties.

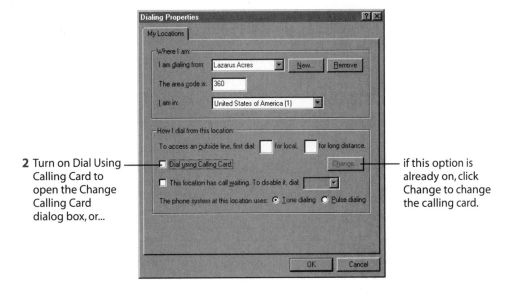

2 Turn on Dial Using Calling Card to open the Change Calling Card dialog box, or...

if this option is already on, click Change to change the calling card.

II

Electronic Mail

3 Select the specific type of calling card you want to use.

4 Type your calling card number and PIN.

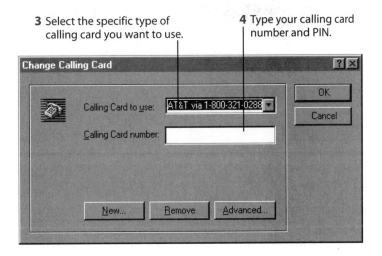

5 To see the dialing rules for your calls, click the Advanced button in the Change Calling Card dialog box. Outlook opens the Dialing Rules dialog box. You can't change the dialing rules for the types of calling cards listed by Outlook. You can set up dialing rules for calling cards you add. For more information, see the next section.

Adding a New Calling Card

If the type of calling card you want to use isn't listed in the Change
Calling Card dialog box, you can add it to the list. To add a new
calling card, take these steps:

1 In the Change Calling Card dialog box, click the New button.

2 Type the name of your calling card.

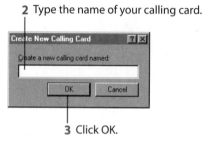

3 Click OK.

4 Enter your calling card number.

5 Click the Advanced button in the Change Calling Card dialog
box to set up dialing rules for your calls.

6 Type dialing rules for local calls.

7 Type dialing rules for long-distance calls within your country.

8 Type dialing rules for international calls.

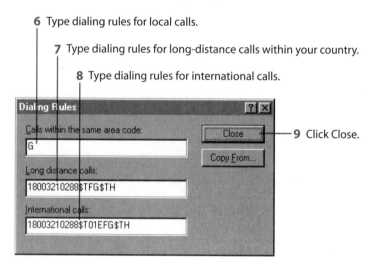

9 Click Close.

The dialing rules for calling cards are based on specific letters
and symbols as well as numbers. To see an on-screen list of
letters and symbols used in dialing rules, click the Help Question

Mark button in the upper right corner of the Dialing Rules dialog box, and then click one of the rules boxes. The list will look something like this:

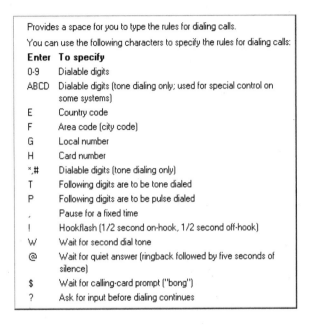

Provides a space for you to type the rules for dialing calls.

You can use the following characters to specify the rules for dialing calls:

Enter	To specify
0-9	Dialable digits
ABCD	Dialable digits (tone dialing only; used for special control on some systems)
E	Country code
F	Area code (city code)
G	Local number
H	Card number
*,#	Dialable digits (tone dialing only)
T	Following digits are to be tone dialed
P	Following digits are to be pulse dialed
,	Pause for a fixed time
!	Hookflash (1/2 second on-hook, 1/2 second off-hook)
W	Wait for second dial tone
@	Wait for quiet answer (ringback followed by five seconds of silence)
$	Wait for calling-card prompt ("bong")
?	Ask for input before dialing continues

10 If the calling card you're setting up can use dialing rules that have been set up for another card, click the Copy From button in the Dialing Rules dialog box. In the Copy Dialing Rules dialog box, select the calling card with the dialing rules you want to copy, and click OK.

Copy Dialing Rules

Select the calling card from which to copy:

AT&T credit card
AT&T Direct Dial via 10ATT1
AT&T via 1-800-321-0288
AT&T via 10ATT0
British Telecom (UK)
Calling Card via 0
Carte France Telecom
CLEAR Communications (New Zealand)
Global Card (Taiwan to USA)

OK   Cancel

Running Outlook for Remote Work

N ow that you've set up Microsoft Outlook 97 for remote work (see Chapter 5, "Setting Up Outlook for Remote Work"), you're ready to work with Outlook remotely. In this chapter, you'll read about the ways you can run Outlook for remote work. The method you use will depend on your Outlook setup and the work you need to do.

You have three ways to run Outlook for remote work:

- Work remotely online only (no offline work). Use this method if you have a non-toll telephone connection to your e-mail server. If you still need to set up Outlook for this option, see "Setting Up to Work Remotely Online Only," on page 166.

■ Work online and offline, sometimes remotely; this way uses offline folders. You can use this offline folders method only if your e-mail server is Microsoft Exchange Server. Use this method when you prefer not to connect to your e-mail server full time. If you still need to set up Outlook for this option, see "Setting Up to Work Online and Offline, Sometimes Remotely," on page 169.

■ Use Remote Mail to send and receive messages but work offline most of the time. Use this method when you're away from a network connection and the telephone call to your e-mail server is a toll call. If you still need to set up Outlook for this option, see "Setting Up Remote Mail and Offline Work," on page 177.

Before you decide whether to use offline folders or Remote Mail, consult the sidebar "Offline Folders Vs. Remote Mail," on page 165.

One of the beauties of working with Outlook remotely is that you can perform a lot of your work without being connected to your e-mail server. You can read new (and old) messages, create new messages, compose replies, and forward messages. You can also delete messages that you no longer need or want. Then, when you connect to your e-mail server, the messages you want to read are downloaded, the messages you want to send are sent to the server for routing, and the messages you want to delete disappear.

Running Outlook to Work Remotely Online Only

When you're ready to connect to the network computer to work with Outlook remotely, take these steps:

1 Click the Start button on the Windows 95 Taskbar, and point to Programs on the Start menu. Click Accessories, and then click Dial-Up Networking on the Accessories submenu.

2 In the Dial-Up Networking window, double-click the connection you set up to connect to your network dial-up computer.

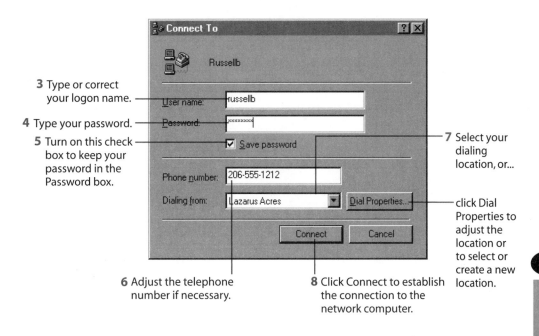

3 Type or correct your logon name.

4 Type your password.

5 Turn on this check box to keep your password in the Password box.

7 Select your dialing location, or...

click Dial Properties to adjust the location or to select or create a new location.

6 Adjust the telephone number if necessary.

8 Click Connect to establish the connection to the network computer.

If you need to click the Dial Properties button to change or set a location (step 7), consult "Dialing Properties," on page 128 for details.

9 When Dial-Up Networking has established the network connection, start Outlook as you do when you're connected directly to the network.

TIP

Turn on the Save Password box in the Connect To dialog box only if your computer is always secure. With this option turned on, anyone can use your dial-up networking connection to connect to the network. If you sometimes leave your computer where it's available to anyone, it's better to turn off the Save Password box. This means you'll have to type your password each time you want to establish a dial-up networking connection, but your computer will be much more secure.

II

Electronic Mail

Running Outlook to Work Online and Offline, Sometimes Remotely

Working in Outlook both online and offline with offline folders is a simple matter of starting Outlook and connecting to your Microsoft Exchange Server.

> You can use the offline folders method only if your e-mail server is Microsoft Exchange Server.

To work in Outlook when you have offline folders set up, take these steps:

1 Start Outlook.

2 In the dialog box that appears, click the button that fits the situation:

- Click the Connect button if your computer is connected to your Microsoft Exchange Server through a network or if you have established a dial-up networking connection. (See "Setting Up to Work Remotely Online Only," on page 166 and "Running Outlook to Work Remotely Online Only," on page 192.)

- Click the Work Offline button if your computer is not connected.

3 Perform your work in Outlook.

4 Choose the File Exit And Log Off command to quit Outlook.

Here are a few important points to keep in mind when you use Outlook for both online and offline remote work:

- If you connect when you start Outlook, Outlook automatically synchronizes your folders.

- If you have turned on the When Online, Synchronize All Folders Upon Exiting option on the General tab of the Options dialog box (see "General Tab," on page 46), Outlook also synchronizes your offline folders when you exit.

- You can direct Outlook to synchronize a single offline folder or all offline folders at once. For directions, see "Synchronizing Folders," on page 176.

- If you start Outlook to work offline, you must exit and log off Outlook and then restart Outlook to connect to your e-mail server.

Moving Items to Different Folders

? SEE ALSO

For information about how to move items to a different folder, see "Moving a Folder Item," on page 358.

While you're working offline, you might want to move an item to a different folder. This is a simple process: You move the item just as you would when you're connected to your Microsoft Exchange Server. The next time you connect to your server, either remotely or through a network connection, the Microsoft Exchange Server moves the items in the server folders to match the moves you made while you were working offline. This movement of items among folders is part of the synchronization process.

Running Remote Mail

To use Remote Mail, follow these steps:

1 Start Outlook.

2 In the dialog box that appears, click the Work Offline button.

3 Choose the Tools Remote Mail command, and then choose Connect from the submenu. Alternatively, you can click the Connect button on the Remote toolbar—see "Checking Out the Remote Toolbar," on page 199. Outlook starts the Remote Connection Wizard.

II

Electronic Mail

4 Turn on the service connections you want to make.

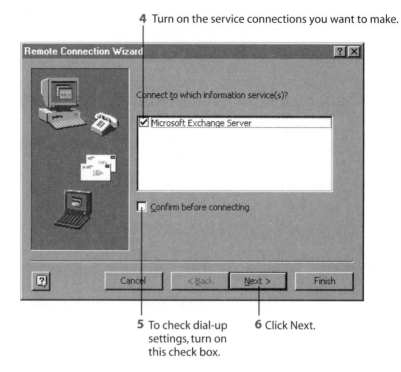

5 To check dial-up settings, turn on this check box.

6 Click Next.

7 Select this option to download all messages, or...

select this option to download message headers only (other choices might be listed); turn off check boxes for actions you don't want.

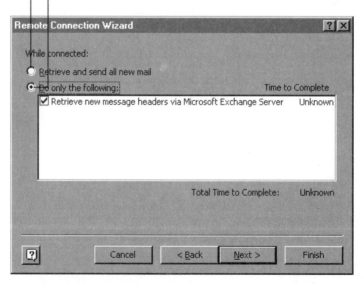

8 Click the Next button as long as it's active. When it's no longer active, click the Finish button. For example, if you turned on the Confirm Before Connecting check box on the first Remote Connection Wizard panel, click the Next button on the second panel. If you turned off the Confirm Before Connecting box, click the Finish button.

9 Outlook shows a message box telling you that your computer is dialing and then that your computer is connecting to your server. When the connection is established, you can work with messages using Remote Mail.

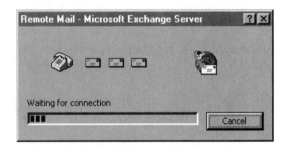

Breaking the Remote Mail Connection

Outlook doesn't keep a persistent Remote Mail connection. Remote Mail does its work and then disconnects in order to save you phone charges.

If you want to break the connection yourself before Remote Mail finishes, click the Disconnect button on the Remote toolbar or choose the Tools Remote Mail command, and then choose Disconnect from the submenu.

If you don't want Remote Mail to disconnect automatically, you can do the following:

1 Choose the Tools Services command, select Microsoft Exchange Server, and click the Properties button.

2 Click the Remote Mail tab.

3 Turn off the Disconnect After Connection Is Finished box.

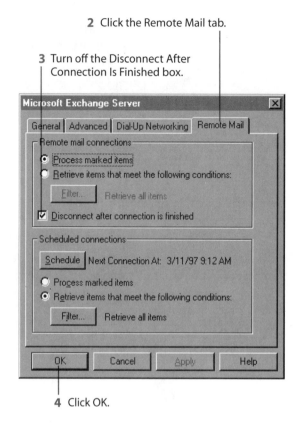

4 Click OK.

5 Click OK in the Services dialog box.

What Happens When You Connect

When the connection is made, Outlook performs the following actions in the order listed:

- Sends any messages you have set up to send—new messages, replies, forwards, and task and appointment responses

- Downloads the complete text of messages for the message headers you've marked for downloading

- Downloads message headers for messages that aren't already in the Inbox in your personal folders

- Deletes messages that you no longer want to keep on the Microsoft Exchange Server

- Disconnects the Remote Mail connection

You can now read and work with the new messages you received, mark new message headers for downloading, or delete messages or message headers.

Big Problem: Can't Download Messages

If the Inbox folder in your personal folders hasn't been synchronized with your Inbox folder on your e-mail server, you'll see a message telling you that Outlook can't download your messages because there's no delivery point. In this case, you need to assign delivery to your personal folders Inbox. Of course, you must first set up personal folders. To do so, follow the steps described in "Adding Personal Folders to a Profile," on page 178.

Checking Out the Remote Toolbar

Outlook provides the Remote toolbar, which contains buttons for Remote Mail commands. Figure 6-1 shows the name of each button on the Remote toolbar.

FIGURE 6-1.

The Remote toolbar.

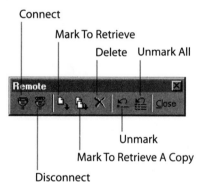

To display the Remote toolbar, use one of the following methods:

- Choose the Tools Remote Mail command, and then choose Remote Tools from the submenu.

- Right-click on a visible toolbar, and then click Remote on the shortcut menu.

- Choose the Tools Remote Mail command, and then drag the band at the top of the submenu into the Outlook window.

II

Electronic Mail

To hide the Remote toolbar, you can use any of these four methods:

- Click the Close button on the Remote toolbar.

- Choose the Tools Remote Mail command, and then choose Remote Tools from the submenu.

- Right-click on a visible toolbar, and then click Remote on the shortcut menu.

- If the Remote toolbar is floating in the Outlook window, click the Close box on the upper right corner of the toolbar.

Marking Messages for Downloading

Marking a message header for retrieval tells Remote Mail that you want to download the complete text of that message so that you can read and respond to it. Here's how to mark a message header for retrieval:

1 In the Inbox message list, select the messages you want to download. To select more than one message, hold down the Ctrl key as you click each message.

2 Click the Mark To Retrieve button on the Remote toolbar. Alternatively, you can choose the Tools Remote Mail command, and then choose Mark To Retrieve from the submenu.

The messages are now marked and ready to download the next time you connect to your Exchange server.

If you accidentally mark a message header for a message that you don't want to download, select it and click the Unmark button to unmark it. If you want to unmark all message headers, click the Unmark All button.

TIP

If you use separate profiles for Remote Mail and for connecting to your e-mail server over a network, use the Mark To Retrieve A Copy toolbar button or command rather than Mark To Retrieve. Mark To Retrieve A Copy puts a copy of the message in your personal folders Inbox and leaves the message in your e-mail server Inbox. If you use Mark To Retrieve, you'll end up with the same message in each of the two inboxes, which can be aggravating or confusing.

Deleting Messages When You Work Remotely

If you no longer want to keep a message, you can mark the message header for deletion. To delete a message header and the message from your e-mail server, simply select the message header, and then click the Delete button on the Remote toolbar. The message moves to your Deleted Items folder.

When you connect to your e-mail server, Outlook completes the deletion.

 NOTE

> To delete the messages in their entirety after they've been downloaded, use the Delete button on the Standard toolbar. As with online messages, deleting offline messages sends them to the Deleted Items folder.

Sending Messages from a Remote Computer

 SEE ALSO

For details about the standard procedures for sending e-mail messages, see "Sending a Message," on page 90.

When you're working offline and want to send a message, you simply compose the message as you would when you're connected to your e-mail server. You can also write replies and set up messages for forwarding. These processes aren't mysterious at all. You use the same commands and steps you use when you're connected. The only true difference is that the messages you set up to send don't go anywhere until you connect to your e-mail server. This connection can be through the network, through Dial-Up Networking, or through Remote Mail.

 NOTE

> You must have a copy of the Offline Address Book in order to set up a message for sending. For more information, see "Downloading the Offline Address Book," on page 173.

After you create a new message, fashion your reply to a message, or set up a message for forwarding, the message lives in your Outbox until the next time you connect. Messages that you set up to send are displayed in your Outbox in italics, as shown on the following page.

PART III

Scheduling Your Time and Tasks

CHAPTER 7

Viewing the Calendar

Your Calendar folder in Microsoft Outlook 97 contains a calendar that shows the appointments you make, the meetings you're scheduled to attend, the events you want to be reminded of, and, usually, a list of the active tasks you have recorded. (In the next chapter, "Scheduling Appointments, Meetings, and Events," you'll learn how Outlook distinguishes among appointments, meetings, and events.)

You can view your calendar in a number of ways, and you can adjust the calendar window (also called the Calendar folder) to suit your work and purposes (and aesthetics). First, however, let's briefly review the various parts of the calendar window.

The Calendar Folder Window

Figure 7-1 shows a typical view of the Calendar folder window. In particular, notice the time slots, the appointment slots, the Date Navigator, and the TaskPad.

Time slots   Appointment slots   Date Navigator

FIGURE 7-1.

The Calendar folder window.

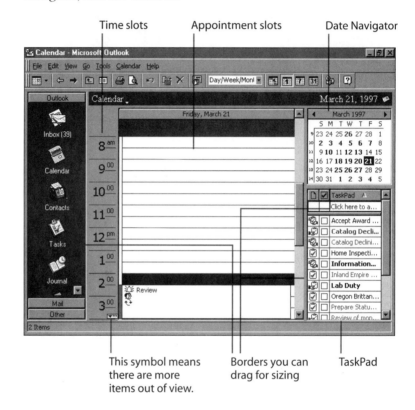

This symbol means there are more items out of view.   Borders you can drag for sizing   TaskPad

Time Slots

 SEE ALSO

To set or change your work hours, see "Calendar Working Hours," on page 62. For other calendar options, see "Calendar Tab," on page 61.

The time slots show the hours of the day, with each full hour numbered. Initially, Outlook is set up with half-hour time slots; a line marks each half-hour increment. The time slots for your working hours appear in light gray, and your nonwork hours appear in dark gray.

Depending on the size of your Outlook window, on the span of time represented by each time slot, and on the resolution of your monitor screen, you can view a range of times that varies from one hour to fifteen or more hours at one glance. If you need to see a time slot that's out of view, use the scroll bar along the right side of the appointment slots to scroll earlier or later times into view. When an appointment or meeting is out of view, you see a yellow rectangle that contains an arrowhead and an ellipsis.

Changing the Bands of Time

You can change the span of time indicated by each time slot to a span that's convenient for your work at the moment. Outlook's initial setup provides half-hour time slots, but you can adjust the time span so that each slot represents an interval as long as sixty minutes or as short as five minutes. To change the time band, take these steps:

1 Right-click anywhere in the time slots.

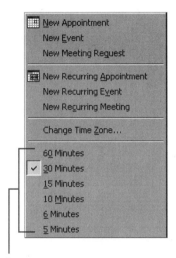

2 Click the time span you want.

Adding a Second Band of Time Slots

You can add a second band of time slots for another time zone, which can help you easily convert the time from one time zone to the other. Typically, you'll use this second band of time slots when you conduct business across times zones. Outlook displays the second band of time slots to the left of the current band. If you travel to a location in the second time zone and want to use your calendar while you're there, you can switch the positions of the time bands so that the band for the second time zone moves next to your appointment slots (becoming the current time band). For information about setting up a band of time slots for a second time zone, see "Time Zone Button," on page 63.

III

Scheduling Your Time and Tasks

SEE ALSO

For information about scheduling appointments and meetings, see Chapter 8.

Appointment Slots

The appointment slots on the calendar show your appointments and meetings for specific dates and times. A calendar item indicates whether the item refers to an appointment or a meeting, whether the appointment or meeting is one-time or recurring, whether the item is private, and whether you've set a reminder. The calendar item also gives you information about the subject, the location, and the duration of the appointment or meeting.

Viewing Details of Appointments and Meetings

No matter what time span you choose for your time slots, you won't be able to see every detail of an appointment or meeting in the appointment slot. To see all the details of an appointment or meeting (and to change any details), you must open the calendar item. To open a calendar item, use one of the following methods:

- Double-click the appointment or meeting item (the calendar item).

- Right-click the calendar item, and then choose Open from the shortcut menu.

- Click the calendar item, and then choose the File Open command (or press Ctrl+O).

TIP

In Day view (the standard view, shown in Figure 7-1, on page 206), you can directly edit the subject and text of an appointment or meeting in the appointment slot. If you set the insertion point in the text of an appointment or meeting, you must then double-click the border of the calendar item or use the right-click or File Open method to open the item.

When you open a calendar item, Outlook displays a window in which you can check or change information about the appointment or meeting. To close this window, use one of the following methods:

- Click the Save And Close button. Be sure to use this method if you made any changes to the appointment or meeting details.

- Click the Close box in the upper right corner of the window. You can use this method if you made no changes to the appointment or meeting details or if you don't want to keep any changes you made.

- Choose the File Close command (or press Alt+F4). Before you choose this command, however, you might want to choose the File Save command (or press Ctrl+S) to save any changes you made.

Date Navigator

 SEE ALSO

For information about how to work with the Date Navigator, see "Using the Date Navigator," on page 213.

You use the Date Navigator to see from one to several months at a glance. (See "Adjusting the Calendar Panes," on page 218, for details about expanding the range of dates visible in the Date Navigator.) Within the month or months shown in the Date Navigator, you can jump to a date simply by clicking it. You can also scroll the Date Navigator to jump months ahead or back. Outlook highlights the dates in the Date Navigator that are visible in the calendar pane.

TaskPad

On the TaskPad, you see a summary of your tasks, as shown here:

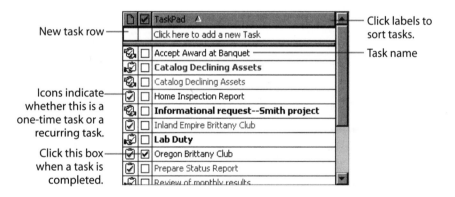

New task row — | Click labels to sort tasks. | Task name

Icons indicate whether this is a one-time task or a recurring task.

Click this box when a task is completed.

 SEE ALSO

For information about working with tasks, see Chapter 9.

Typically, the TaskPad shows your currently active tasks, including tasks that are overdue (shown in red instead of black) and tasks without a specific due date. When you click the Complete box (the check box in the second column), Outlook draws a line through the task. When you've marked a task complete and the due date passes, Outlook removes the completed task from the TaskPad.

Instead of switching to the Tasks folder to set up a new task, you can quickly add a new task to the TaskPad. To do so, follow these steps:

1 Click the subject area of the new task row on the TaskPad.

2 Type the subject of the task.

3 Press the Enter key.

? SEE ALSO

For details about changing the setup of the TaskPad, see "Adjusting the TaskPad," on page 220.

The new task still has no due date. To set or change the properties of the task, you have to edit it. To edit a task on the TaskPad, double-click the task name, make your changes in the task item window, and then click the Save And Close button in the task item window. For more information about task properties, see "Setting Up a Task," on page 258.

How Many Days Do You Want to See?

? SEE ALSO

To learn about other views available in the Calendar folder, see "Other Ways of Viewing the Calendar Folder," on page 225.

The standard calendar view is the Day/Week/Month view. In this view, you can choose between three time spans: one day, one week, and one month. You set the time span by clicking one of these three buttons on the Standard toolbar:

Day   Month

Week

★ TIP

When you select dates in the Date Navigator, your selection affects how many days and which days appear in the appointment slots. For details, see "Selecting Days," on page 216.

Day View

In Day view, you see one day of your calendar, as shown in Figure 7-1 on page 206. The calendar pane includes time slots and appointment slots for a single day. To return to Day view after viewing your calendar in one-week or one-month time spans, click the Day button on the Standard toolbar.

Week View

In Week view, you see one week of your calendar, as shown here:

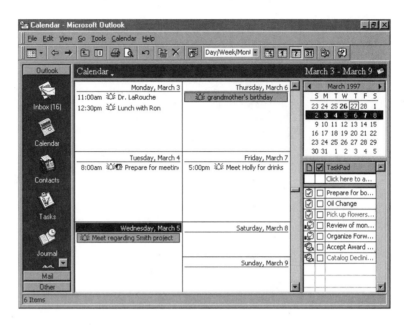

When you choose Week view, the time slots aren't included and the days appear in boxes. Depending on the resolution of your display and on how you've arranged the calendar window, your calendar items show the starting and ending times for appointments and meetings, as well as their characteristics (private, recurring), subjects, and place.

To display your calendar in Week view, click the Week button on the Standard toolbar. To display the appointments and meetings for one day of the week in view, click the date and then click the Day button on the Standard toolbar.

Month View

In Month view, you see an entire month of your calendar, as shown here:

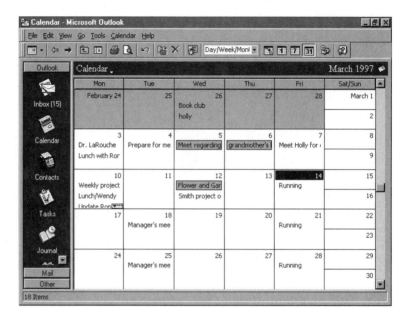

In this view, the days appear in boxes. Again, depending on your display resolution and window arrangement, entries for your appointments and meetings in Month view show the starting time and as much of the subject as fits on one line of the date box.

To display your calendar in Month view, click the Month button on the Standard toolbar. To display the appointments and meetings for one day of the month in view, click the date and then click the Day button on the Standard toolbar.

Getting a Date

Much of your calendar work will usually focus on "today"—after all, today is the day you're living and working through. But setting appointments and scheduling meetings necessarily involves dates and times in the future. Also, when you want to review your schedule for the days, weeks, or months ahead, you need to jump to other dates. And if you want to review past appointments and meetings, you'll need to jump back in time. (Yes, the calendar is a kind of time machine, taking you back and forth in time.)

SEE ALSO

You can use Outlook's Find Items command to find specific appointments, events, and meetings. For details, see "Searching Folder Contents," on page 372.

When you need to jump to another date, you can use the Date Navigator or the Go To Date command. When it's time to jump back to reality—er, the present—Outlook gives you several time tunnels back to today.

Using the Date Navigator

Depending on the size of the Outlook window, the resolution of your monitor screen, and the size of the Date Navigator pane, you can see a single month or several months at a time in the Date Navigator. Figure 7-2 shows the Date Navigator displaying four months at a time.

FIGURE 7-2.

The Date Navigator displaying four months at a time.

 TIP

The Date Navigator is typically visible in Day view and Week view but absent from Month view. You can display the Date Navigator in Month view by placing the mouse pointer on the right window border, where it becomes a double vertical line with horizontal arrows, and dragging the border to the left toward the center of the calendar window.

To jump to another date, use one of the following methods:

- If the date is visible in the Date Navigator, click the date.

- If the date is not in view in the Date Navigator, click the left arrow in the top band of the Date Navigator to move back one month, or click the right arrow to move forward one month. Even if two or more months are visible in the Date Navigator, these arrows change in the Date Navigator display only one month at a time.

■ Click any month label in the Date Navigator to open a list containing the three months before and the three months after the month you've clicked, as shown here:

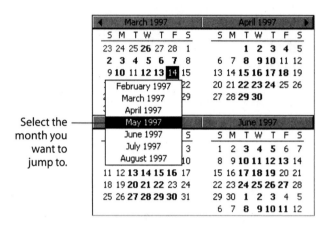

Select the month you want to jump to.

After you've selected a new month and jumped to it, you can repeat this method to move backward or forward beyond the span available in the list.

When you click a month label and open the list of months, you can drag the mouse pointer to the top or bottom border of the list to scroll through an even larger list of months. You must hold the tip of the mouse pointer arrow exactly on the top or bottom border line to scroll.

Using the Go To Date Command

For dates that are farther away than a few months, you'll probably want to use the Go To Date command, which can take you to any date within the Outlook date range.

To jump to any date, follow these steps:

1   From the Go menu, choose the Go To Date command.

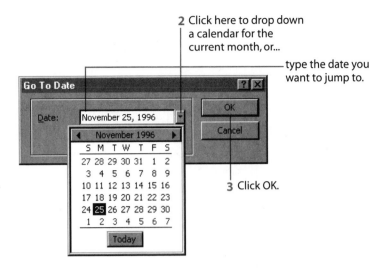

2 Click here to drop down a calendar for the current month, or...

type the date you want to jump to.

3 Click OK.

In the Date box of the Go To dialog box, you can type the date you want to see in any standard date format—for instance, to jump to October 13, 1999, you can type *10-13-99, 10/13/99, Oct-13-99,* or *October 13, 1999.* You should note the following points about typing in dates:

- If you type a two-digit year number in the range 70–99, Outlook assumes that you mean 1970–1999. For the numbers 00–69, Outlook uses 2000–2069.

- If you want a year that's not within the century from 1970 to 2069, you must type the entire year number. The oldest date you can type in the Date box is April 1, 1601. The most future date you can type in the Date box is August 31, 4500. That range should just about cover it for your use of this version of Outlook.

- After you select or enter the date you want to see in the Go To Date dialog box, you can use the Show In list to choose to view the date in Day, Week, or Month view.

TIP

After you type a date in the Date box of the Go To Date dialog box, click the down arrow beside the date to see the month calendar for the date you've typed. You can then refine your date jump if you need to.

III

Scheduling Your Time and Tasks

Jumping Back to Today

When you've moved to a past or future date, you'll often want to jump back to today's date. You can do this quickly in any of the following ways:

- If you're in the Day/Week/Month view of the calendar, click the Go To Today button on the Standard toolbar. This button is available whether you're viewing a day, week, or month time span. Note, however, that on small and lower resolution monitor screens, you might have to widen the Outlook window or even maximize it to see the Go To Today button. If the toolbar isn't large enough to display all the buttons, Outlook hides this button in preference to showing other ("more important") buttons.

- Click today's date in the Date Navigator.

- Right-click any appointment slot or any date label in the calendar pane, and then choose Go To Today from the shortcut menu.

- Choose the Go To Today command from the Go menu.

Selecting Days

As you use the TaskPad and calendar, you might want to check the active or completed tasks for a selected number of days. You might also want to check on appointments or meetings for a set of selected days. You can select days either in the calendar pane or in the Date Navigator pane. You can select a range of consecutive days in the calendar pane, and you can select a range of consecutive days or scattered days in the Date Navigator.

Selecting Days in the Calendar

Here's how to select a range of consecutive days in the calendar pane:

1 Display the calendar in Week view or Month view.

2 Move to the week or month where you want to select days.

3 Use one of these methods to select the days you want:

- Drag over the days you want to select.

- Click the first date of the range, hold down the Shift key, and then click the last date of the range. You can select as many visible days as you like this way, including all the days that are visible in the calendar pane.

If you scroll the calendar after you select a range of days, Outlook moves the selection to the corresponding day boxes currently visible in the calendar pane.

Selecting Days in the Date Navigator

You can select consecutive days or scattered days in the Date Navigator. When you select days in the Date Navigator, Outlook changes the calendar pane to display the days you selected. In this way, you can display ranges and numbers of days that differ from what the Day, Week, and Month views show.

To select a range of consecutive days in the Date Navigator, follow these steps:

1 Adjust the Date Navigator pane to show the months in which you want to select days.

2 Use one of these methods to select the days you want:

- Drag over the days you want to select. You can select as many as eight consecutive days or as many as six consecutive weeks this way. After you select the ninth day, the selection expands to selecting weeks at a time.

- Click at the left end of a week to select that week. Drag down along the left end of weeks to select as many as six weeks.

- Click the first date of the range, hold down the Shift key, and then click the last date of the range. You can select as many as 14 days this way.

III

Scheduling Your Time and Tasks

To select scattered days in the Date Navigator, follow these steps:

1 Adjust the Date Navigator pane to show the months in which you want to select days.

2 Click one of the days you want to select.

3 Hold down the Ctrl key while you click the other days you want to select. You can select as many as 14 days this way.

Adjusting the Calendar Panes

Because the calendar window contains three panes, the amount of space for each pane is limited, especially if you work in an Outlook window that isn't maximized. Also, if you are using a lower resolution display, you'll have less space available for the separate panes than if you are using a display with a higher resolution.

When you need to view or work in one of the panes and you require a more expanded view of the pane's contents, you can adjust the window to give more space to one pane and less space to the other two. (You can also hide the TaskPad and the Date Navigator, but you can't hide the calendar.)

Between each of the panes in the Calendar folder window is a border that you can drag to adjust the size of the panes. (See Figure 7-1, on page 206.) When you position the mouse pointer on one of these borders, the pointer arrow changes to a double line with two arrows (pointing either up and down or left and right).

- Drag the vertical border between the calendar and the Date Navigator and the TaskPad to the left or right to change the width of the calendar pane. This also changes the width of the Date Navigator and the TaskPad.

- Drag the horizontal border between the Date Navigator and the TaskPad up or down to change the height of these two panes.

- Drag the vertical border between the calendar and the Outlook Bar to change the size of the Outlook Bar. This also changes the width of the other panes.

Hiding and Restoring the TaskPad

If you want to use the space the TaskPad occupies for either calendar items or the Date Navigator display, you can hide the TaskPad. To do so, perform one of the following actions:

- Drag the border along the right side of the calendar pane to the right.

- Drag the bottom border of the Date Navigator down.

After you've hidden the TaskPad, you might want to see it again. Take the action that fits the circumstances in your calendar window:

- If the calendar pane extends to the right window border, place the mouse pointer on the right window border and then drag the border to the left toward the center of the window.

- If the Date Navigator covers the TaskPad, place the mouse pointer on the bottom window border, just above the status bar, and then drag the border upward to the middle of the Date Navigator.

Hiding and Restoring the Date Navigator

You can hide the Date Navigator to make extra room for either calendar items or the TaskPad. To do so, use one of these methods:

- Drag the border along the right side of the calendar pane to the right.

- Drag the top border of the TaskPad upward.

To restore the Date Navigator after you've hidden it, take one of the following actions:

- If the calendar pane extends to the right window border, place the mouse pointer on the right window border and then drag the border to the left toward the center of the window.

- If the TaskPad covers the Date Navigator, place the mouse pointer just above the TaskPad label and then drag the border down to the middle of the TaskPad.

III

Scheduling Your Time and Tasks

Adjusting the TaskPad

The TaskPad typically lists your active tasks. Overdue tasks appear in red. You can change the view of your tasks, and you can also change the formatting and arrangement of TaskPad columns.

Selecting a TaskPad View

? SEE ALSO

For more ways to view tasks, see "Viewing Your Tasks," on page 284.

When you choose the TaskPad View command on the View menu, you can select a view of the TaskPad from a submenu. Some of the views you can choose are similar to the views you have in the Tasks folder, but they have been modified to suit the TaskPad, where you have limited space and where you're more likely to be concerned about current tasks rather than tasks that are long past or far in the future.

All Tasks View

In All Tasks view, the TaskPad lists every task you have set up (for all days), including completed tasks, which have a line drawn through the item. If you have many task items, you will have to spend a lot of time scrolling through the list to find what you need. If the TaskPad pane is small, you'll find this view quite useless.

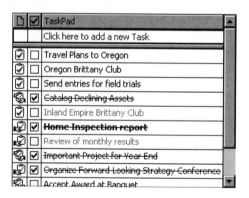

To switch the TaskPad to All Tasks view, choose the View TaskPad View command and click All Tasks on the submenu.

Today's Tasks View

Today's Tasks is the standard view for the TaskPad. In this view, the TaskPad list contains only the tasks that are active for today (including overdue tasks). For the TaskPad and the calendar, "today" means the date indicated by your computer clock.

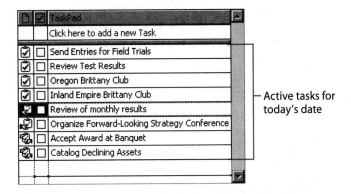

Active tasks for today's date

To return to Today's Tasks view after selecting a different view, choose the View TaskPad View command and click Today's Tasks on the submenu.

Active Tasks For Selected Days View

You can select a range of days, either in the calendar pane or in the Date Navigator pane, to have the TaskPad display tasks that are active during the selected days. You might want to use this view when you are thinking about a vacation, a business trip, or a professional activity (such as a conference, seminar, or trade show) that takes you away from work for several days or weeks. For vacation planning, you need to know which tasks must be completed before you leave and which can be rescheduled with new due dates after you return. For a business trip, the list of tasks might help you determine what preparations you need to make before you leave so that you have all the materials and information you need to take with you. For a professional activity that takes you from the office, you might want to know all this—what to do before you leave, what to take with you, and what you can delay until after you return.

III

Scheduling Your Time and Tasks

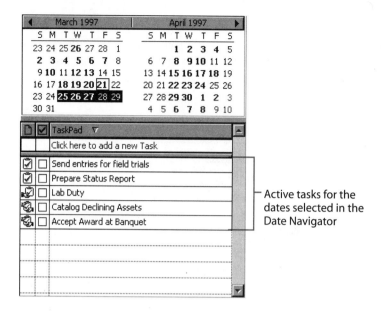

Active tasks for the dates selected in the Date Navigator

To switch the TaskPad to Active Tasks For Selected Days view, first select the dates you want to check. (See "Selecting Days," on page 216.) Then choose the View TaskPad View command, and click Active Tasks For Selected Days on the submenu.

Tasks For Next Seven Days View

Sometimes you want to see all the tasks for the coming week (the next seven days). The Tasks For Next Seven Days view shows tasks with a due date that falls during the next seven days, including today. (If you have the Include Tasks With No Due Date option turned on, the list also includes tasks without a due date. To exclude these tasks so that the list contains only tasks with a due date during the next seven days, follow the steps in "Including Tasks with No Due Date," on page 224.) To determine the seven days included in this view, Outlook counts from today's date as indicated by your computer clock. (See the illustration at the top of the facing page.)

To switch the TaskPad to Tasks For Next Seven Days view, choose the View TaskPad View command and click Tasks For Next Seven Days on the submenu.

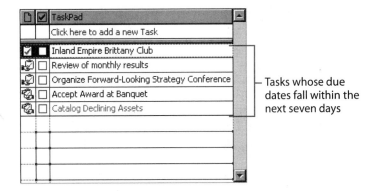

Tasks whose due dates fall within the next seven days

Overdue Tasks View

When you're behind on some of your tasks and want to concentrate on cleaning up tasks that are past due, you can choose the Overdue Tasks view to display only overdue tasks in the TaskPad. (When you choose this view, you'll probably want to exclude tasks without a due date. For details, see "Including Tasks with No Due Date," on the following page.)

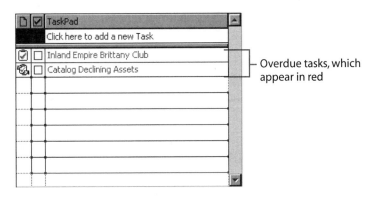

Overdue tasks, which appear in red

To switch the TaskPad to Overdue Tasks view, choose the View TaskPad View command and click Overdue Tasks on the submenu.

Tasks Completed On Selected Days View

From time to time, it's useful to review your accomplishments, especially during performance review time. You can select days, either in the calendar pane or in the Date Navigator pane, to have the TaskPad display tasks that you completed on the selected days.

III

Scheduling Your Time and Tasks

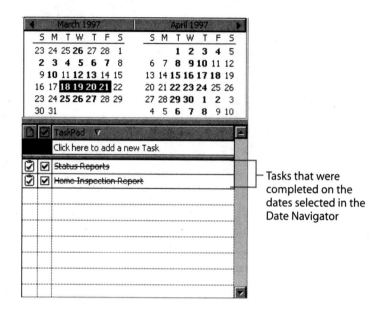

Tasks that were completed on the dates selected in the Date Navigator

To switch the TaskPad to Tasks Completed On Selected Days view, first select the dates you want to check. (See "Selecting Days," on page 216.) Then choose the View TaskPad View command, and click Tasks Completed On Selected Days on the submenu.

Including Tasks with No Due Date

In all the available TaskPad views, the list can either include tasks without a due date or exclude them. Initially, the TaskPad includes these tasks in its list of task items. To exclude tasks without a due date, simply choose the View TaskPad View command, and click Include Tasks With No Due Date on the submenu to turn off this option. If you decide later that you would like to display tasks without a due date again, repeat this procedure to turn on this option.

Setting Up Parts of the TaskPad

You can set up your TaskPad to show additional or different columns or to group tasks. You can sort tasks, and you can format the view you use for the TaskPad. To change TaskPad settings, choose the View TaskPad Settings command. On the submenu, choose the command for the settings you want to change.

You can right-click a TaskPad column label to display a shortcut menu that contains commands related to the commands on the TaskPad Settings submenu, plus five additional commands: Remove This Column, Field Chooser, Alignment (with an additional submenu that contains the Align Left, Align Right, and Center commands), Best Fit, and View Summary.

Information about all the commands on the TaskPad Settings submenu and shortcut menu (except Format View and View Summary) appears in Chapter 17, "Columns, Categories, Grouping, Sorting, Filtering, and Custom Fields." For information about the Format View command, see "Formatting Views," in Chapter 18, on page 509. For information about the View Summary command, see "Modifying a View," on page 507.

Other Ways of Viewing the Calendar Folder

SEE ALSO

You can also set up views to look at your appointments and meetings in various ways. For information, see Chapter 18. For information about grouping, sorting, filtering, and adding custom fields, see Chapter 17.

Day/Week/Month view of the Calendar folder is the standard view and is the view you'll probably use most often. In this view, you have the Date Navigator and the TaskPad available.

Day/Week/Month is not, however, the only view that Outlook provides. The following sections describe five other views you can use for your Calendar folder. All of the views are displayed by choosing the View Current View command and then choosing the view you want from the submenu.

Active Appointments View

To see a list of all your active appointments and meetings—that is, future appointments and meetings—choose Active Appointments view. Active Appointments view displays appointments and meetings in a table arrangement, as shown at the top of the following page.

In this view, the appointments and meetings are grouped by recurrence—nonrecurring, daily, weekly, monthly, yearly, and any other recurrence pattern an appointment or meeting might have.

III

Scheduling Your Time and Tasks

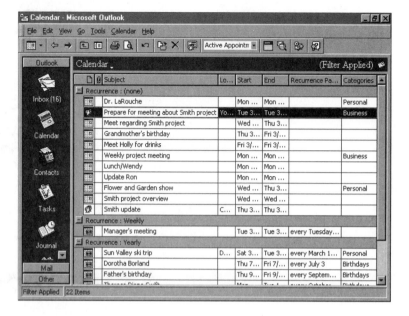

Events View

To see all events (including annual events) that you've added to your calendar, choose Events view, which displays events and annual events in a table, as shown here:

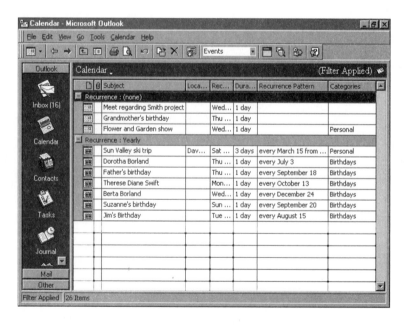

In this view, events are separated into two groups: nonrecurring and yearly recurrence. Yearly recurrence means an annual event.

Annual Events View

If you want a list that contains only the annual events on your calendar, switch to Annual Events view:

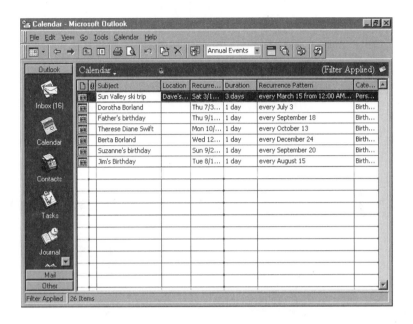

Recurring Appointments View

For a list that contains only recurring appointments and meetings, switch to Recurring Appointments view:

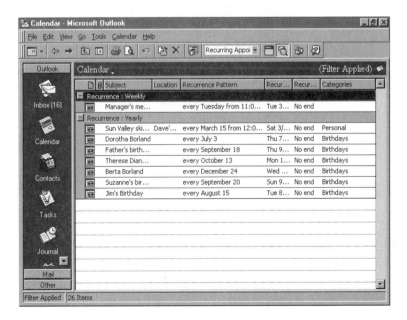

III

Scheduling Your Time and Tasks

In this view, appointments and meetings are grouped by recurrence—daily, weekly, monthly, yearly, and so on. The difference between this view and Active Appointments view is that Recurring Appointments view does not show one-time appointments and meetings.

By Category View

If you assign a category to each appointment and meeting, you can see your calendar items listed by category. If you assign more than one category to an appointment or meeting, Outlook lists it in each category.

To see your appointments and meetings grouped by category, switch to By Category view:

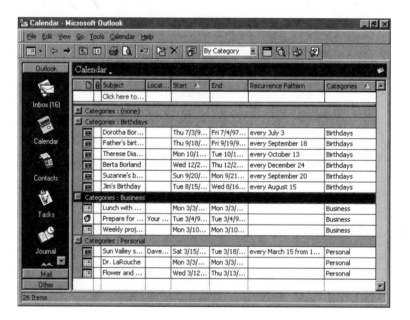

In the next chapter, "Scheduling Appointments, Meetings, and Events," you'll learn how to set up and use calendar items to keep track of where you need to be and when you need to be there.

Scheduling Appointments, Meetings, and Events

In your Microsoft Outlook 97 Calendar folder, you can set up calendar items—appointments, meetings, and events. An appointment is an occasion with specific beginning and end times to which you don't invite others through Outlook. A meeting is an occasion with specific beginning and end times to which you do invite others through Outlook. An event is an all-day affair to which you might or might not invite others. All three kinds of calendar items can be one-time occasions or affairs that recur at specific intervals (daily, weekly, monthly, or yearly).

In this chapter, you'll learn how to set up calendar items and how to change them—how to change the start and end times, how to set up recurring items, how to deal with reminders when they appear, how to adjust other properties of calendar items, and how to copy an item.

Setting Up a Calendar Item

Outlook offers numerous types of calendar items. Three elements determine the type of a specific calendar item: time span (all-day or a specific time span), invitations (whether or not others are invited), and recurrence (one-time or recurring). Table 8-1 shows the types of calendar items and the various combinations of elements that determine an item's type.

TABLE 8-1. Calendar Item Types and Elements Determining Type.

Item Type	Time Span	Invitations	Recurrence
Appointment	Specific	No	No
Recurring appointment	Specific	No	Yes
Meeting	Specific	Yes	No
Recurring meeting	Specific	Yes	Yes
Event	All day	No	No
Recurring event	All day	No	Yes
Invited event	All day	Yes	No
Recurring invited event	All day	Yes	Yes

To set up a calendar item, first open the Calendar folder and then move to the date of the affair. (See "Getting a Date," on page 212.) You can then use one of the following methods to create a new calendar item of the type you want:

- An appointment

New Appointment

  - Click the New Appointment button on the Standard toolbar.

  - Choose the Calendar New Appointment command.

  - Press Ctrl+N.

  - Right-click in the calendar pane (the time slots, the appointment slots, or the date above the appointment slots), and then choose New Appointment from the shortcut menu.

  - Choose the File New command, and then choose Appointment from the submenu.

- A recurring appointment

  - Choose the Calendar New Recurring Appointment command.

  - Right-click in the calendar pane, and then choose New Recurring Appointment from the shortcut menu.

- A meeting

  - Choose the Calendar New Meeting Request command.

  - Press Ctrl+Shift+Q.

  - Right-click in the calendar pane, and then choose New Meeting Request from the shortcut menu.

  - Choose the File New command, and then choose Meeting Request from the submenu.

  - Click the Plan A Meeting button on the Standard toolbar.

  - Choose the Calendar Plan A Meeting command.

- A recurring meeting

  - Choose the Calendar New Recurring Meeting command.

  - Right-click in the calendar pane, and then choose New Recurring Meeting from the shortcut menu.

- An event

  - Choose the Calendar New Event command.

  - Right-click in the calendar pane, and then choose New Event from the shortcut menu.

  - Double-click the dark gray band that appears between the date and the appointment slots in the calendar pane.

- A recurring event

  - Choose the Calendar New Recurring Event command.

  - Right-click in the calendar pane, and then choose New Recurring Event from the shortcut menu.

III

Scheduling Your Time and Tasks

- An invited event or a recurring invited event

  - Create a meeting or a recurring meeting, and then turn on the All Day Event option in the calendar item window (as explained in "Changing the Type of Calendar Item," on page 242).

  - Create an event or a recurring event, click the Meeting Planner tab, and then send invitations to the event (as explained in "Inviting Others," on page 244).

Creating a New Calendar Item from a Different Folder

If you're working in an Outlook folder other than the Calendar folder, you can set up a new meeting or appointment by using one of the following methods. Later you can change the item as necessary.

- Click the down arrow at the right side of the New button on the Standard toolbar, and then choose Appointment or Meeting Request from the menu.

- Choose the File New command, and then select Appointment or Meeting Request from the submenu.

- Press Ctrl+Shift+A for a new appointment; press Ctrl+Shift+Q for a meeting request.

You can also drag other Outlook items to the Calendar folder icon on the Outlook Bar to create appointments. For example, if you are working in the Contacts folder, you can select a contact card and drag it to the Calendar folder icon. Outlook opens a meeting request window addressed to the contact. Modify the meeting information—subject, location, start time, and end time—and then send the meeting request.

When you create a calendar item, by whatever method, Outlook opens a calendar item window similar to the one shown in Figure 8-1. The title bar indicates what type of item you're creating. Figure 8-1 points out various features of this window; you'll find information about these features throughout this chapter.

FIGURE 8-1.
A calendar item window for an appointment.

You can type a location for the appointment, or...

click the down arrow to select a previous location.

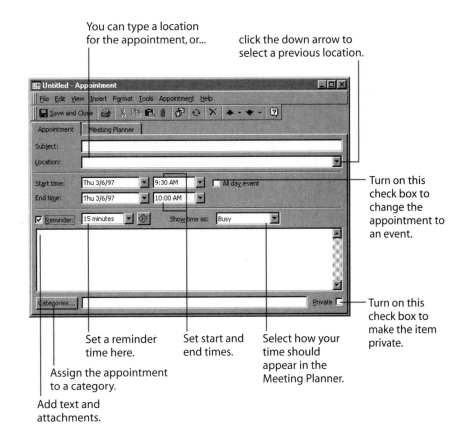

Turn on this check box to change the appointment to an event.

Turn on this check box to make the item private.

Set a reminder time here.

Set start and end times.

Select how your time should appear in the Meeting Planner.

Assign the appointment to a category.

Add text and attachments.

⭐ **TIP**

The calendar item window changes slightly for each type of item. Besides the difference in the title bar, items with invitations (meetings and invited events) have a To button and a box for the names of those you want to invite. Items with invitations also have a colored band at the top of the Appointment tab that shows the status of the invitations.

III

Scheduling Your Time and Tasks

Quickly Setting Up a Calendar Item

To quickly set up a calendar item without worrying about the finer points of settings such as location or invitations, take these steps:

1 Go to the date for the new item. (See "Getting a Date," on page 212.)

2 Click the starting time, either in the time band or the appointment slots, and drag down to the ending time.

3 Type a name for the item. Outlook inserts the typed text in an appointment box in the appointment slots.

4 Press Enter or click outside the appointment box. An appointment now appears on your calendar. It displays a reminder icon (set to the standard reminder time) but has no location, notes, or categories. To learn how to change the appointment setup, see "Changing a Calendar Item," on page 238.

Planning a Meeting

SEE ALSO

For more information about extending invitations, see "Inviting Others," on page 244.

The main difference between scheduling a meeting and planning a meeting is the approach you take. Schedule a meeting when you know that the time you select is convenient for all those you invite to the meeting—you know they'll be there. Plan a meeting when you want to find a time that fits the schedules of those you invite.

You can, of course, start the process of scheduling a meeting and then use the Meeting Planner tab in the meeting request window to check the schedules of the invitees. Planning a meeting merely reverses this course, tackling the issue of others' schedules before setting up the meeting details. In visual terms, when you schedule a meeting by creating a new meeting request, you see the Appointment tab when the meeting request window appears. When you plan a meeting, you see the Plan A Meeting dialog box first, and then you see the Appointment tab. The Plan A Meeting dialog box serves the same function as the Meeting Planner tab in the meeting request window.

To plan a meeting, take these steps:

1 Click the Plan A Meeting button on the Standard toolbar or choose the Calendar Plan A Meeting command.

2 In the Plan A Meeting dialog box, click the Invite Others button. You'll see the Select Attendees And Resources dialog box.

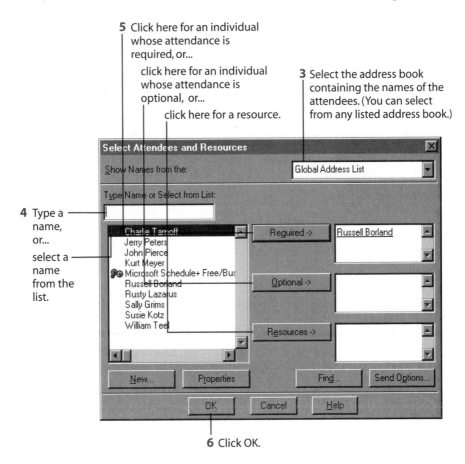

5 Click here for an individual whose attendance is required, or...

click here for an individual whose attendance is optional, or...

click here for a resource.

3 Select the address book containing the names of the attendees. (You can select from any listed address book.)

4 Type a name, or...

select a name from the list.

6 Click OK.

7 In the Plan A Meeting dialog box, you can now review the schedules for attendees, select the time for the meeting, and set other details for the meeting.

III

Scheduling Your Time and Tasks

These bars mark times when
attendees are not available.

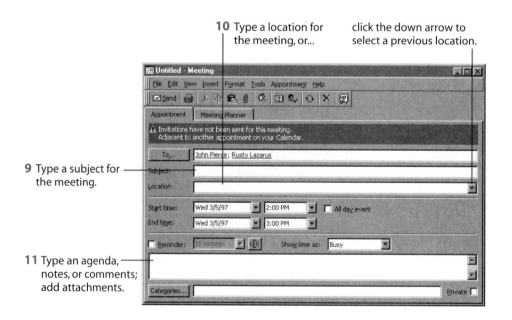

Drag these
bars to set
the meeting
time, based
on the
attendees'
schedules.

Click AutoPick
to select the
next available
time for all
attendees.
Repeat as
needed.

If necessary, adjust the start
and end dates and times.

Click here to move
backward in time.

8 Click Make
Meeting.

10 Type a location for
the meeting, or...

click the down arrow to
select a previous location.

9 Type a subject for
the meeting.

11 Type an agenda,
notes, or comments;
add attachments.

12 If you want to check meeting details again, click the Meeting
Planner tab in the meeting request window. As mentioned
earlier, this tab displays information you set up in the Plan A
Meeting dialog box. On this tab, you can review and change the

details of the meeting, review the schedules of the invited attendees, adjust the display of the schedule, and invite other attendees if necessary.

This section shows invitees
and their free and busy times.

These bars show
the start and end
of the meeting.

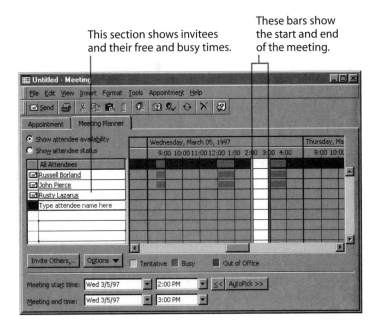

13 When you've finished reviewing the meeting details, click the Send button in the meeting request window. Outlook sends messages to the people and resources you invited.

Meeting resources include conference rooms, audio/visual equipment, and other equipment or material you need for a meeting. If your server administrator has set up rooms and equipment in the Global Address List, you can "invite" the resources to a meeting. When you invite a resource to a meeting, a message is delivered to the Inbox for the resource, which is (usually) handled by a living person. If you are in charge of monitoring the Inbox for a resource, you can set options for processing meeting requests automatically. Choose the Tools Option command, click the Calendar tab, and then click the Advanced Scheduling button. In the Advanced Scheduling dialog box, you can set up options so that Outlook will automatically accept meeting requests and process cancellations, automatically decline (or accept) conflicting meeting requests, and automatically decline (or accept) recurring meeting requests.

III

Scheduling Your Time and Tasks

Handling a Meeting Request When You're Working Remotely

You can request meetings and respond to meeting requests you receive while you're working offsite—either working offline or working through a remote connection to your e-mail server. This is possible because meeting requests are sent as e-mail messages.

Before you can deal with meeting requests offline, you must take these steps:

1 Download the Offline Address Book. For information about how to do this, see "Downloading the Offline Address Book," on page 173.

2 Be sure that you're using Outlook for your scheduling. If you set up Outlook to use Microsoft Schedule+ 95 as your primary calendar, you won't be able to request or plan meetings. For more about this setup, see "Use Microsoft Schedule+ 95 As My Primary Calendar," on page 62.

3 If you're working remotely in a time zone different from that of your office, you might want to set up a time band for the time zone in which you're working. For details, see "Time Zone Button," on page 63.

Changing a Calendar Item

Appointments, meetings, and events change. Sometimes the time changes, or perhaps the place. For some calendar items, you might want to add more notes and comments or insert files, messages, or other objects that pertain to the occasion you're scheduling. You might decide to alter the reminder setting, designate a calendar item as private, or adjust other properties. You might need to fine-tune appointments you set up quickly.

The general steps for changing a calendar item are as follows:

1 Open the calendar item in one of the following ways:

- Double-click the calendar item.

- Right-click the calendar item, and then choose Open from the shortcut menu.

- Click the calendar item, and then choose the File Open command (or press Ctrl+O).

2 Change the calendar item as directed in the following sections. (You might want to refer to Figure 8-1, on page 233.)

3 Save and close the calendar item window in one of the following ways:

- Click the Save And Close button. Be sure to use this method if you made any changes to the calendar item details.

- Choose the File Close command (or press Alt+F4). If you made changes to the calendar item, Outlook asks whether you want to save the changes before closing the item. Click Yes to save the changes. Click No if you don't want to save the changes. You can also choose the File Save command (or press Ctrl+S) to save any changes you made to the calendar item details.

When your calendar is displayed in Day view, you can directly edit the subject and text of an appointment or a meeting in the appointment slots. If you set the insertion point in the text of an appointment or a meeting, you must double-click the border of the calendar item or use the right-click or File Open method to open the item.

Changing Times

After you set up a calendar item, you might need to change the beginning or end time of the item—perhaps a meeting must run longer because of added agenda items, or perhaps an appointment must be shortened or postponed because of your travel schedule. To change the times, first locate and open the calendar item. Then, in either the Start Time box or the End Time box (or both), select the new time. If the new time is other than on the hour or half-hour, select the nearest time and then edit the minutes. For example, if the new time is 11:45, select 11:30 and then edit 30 to 45. (Notice that the list of times in the End Time box shows the length of the calendar item.) If you change the time for a meeting, click the Send Update button to send a message to attendees informing them of the new time.

III

Scheduling Your Time and Tasks

Dragging a Calendar Item to a New Time

Instead of opening a calendar item and setting the start time and end time, you can drag a calendar item to new times, as follows:

- To change the start time of a calendar item, drag the top border of the item up for an earlier time or down for a later time. The bottom border stays put, which means that you are also lengthening or shortening the calendar item time.

- To change the end time of a calendar item, drag the bottom border of the item up for an earlier time or down for a later time. The top border stays put, which means that you are also shortening or lengthening the calendar item time.

- To change the calendar item start time without changing the block of time for the item, drag the left or right border of the item up for an earlier time or down for a later time. Both the top and bottom borders move together.

If you change the start or end time for a meeting by dragging the calendar item, Outlook displays a message asking whether you want to update the meeting attendees about the change in time. To send a message to attendees alerting them of the change, click Yes in the message box. Outlook opens the calendar item, which displays the new time. Click the Send Update button to send a message to the meeting attendees.

 TIP

When you drag a calendar item, the box moves in increments reflecting the time span you have set up in the time band. If you change the time span interval in the time band, the amount of time you can drag the calendar item changes to match the new interval. To change the time span, see "Changing the Bands of Time," on page 207.

Dragging Invitation Times

On the Meeting Planner tab in the meeting request window, two vertical bars on the time grid show the start (the green bar) and end (the red bar) times of the meeting you are planning. (You can see the bars in the illustration on page 237; this view is displayed when the Show Attendee Availability option is selected.) You can drag these bars to change the start and end times. When you do, the start and end times change in the time boxes at the bottom of the dialog box.

 TIP

If you want to move a calendar item to a different date but keep the start and end time, select the calendar item and drag it to the appropriate date in the Date Navigator.

Setting a Reminder

Outlook is initially set up to remind you of a calendar item 15 minutes before the item's start time. In many cases, the 15-minute warning is sufficient. For some calendar items, however, you might want a reminder with a longer lead time; for other items, you might need less.

To change the reminder time for a specific calendar item, follow these steps:

1 Locate and open the calendar item.

2 Click the down arrow at the right end of the Reminder box, and select the new reminder time from the drop-down list. You can also type the reminder time you want in the Reminder box.

3 Save and close the calendar item window.

 NOTE

If you inadvertently set the reminder for a time before the current time (for example, your meeting is at 3:00, and you set a reminder for one hour—but it's already 2:15), Outlook displays a message that the time has passed and that the reminder can't be set. Click Yes if you don't want to set any reminder; click No to return to the calendar item and set the reminder to a shorter time interval.

 SEE ALSO

You can change the default reminder time for all of your calendar items; see "Appointment Defaults," on page 62.

If you don't want a reminder for a calendar item, turn off the check box to the left of the Reminder box in the calendar item window. You can also eliminate the reminder by right-clicking the calendar item in the appointment slots, and then choosing Reminder from the shortcut menu.

Categorizing Your Calendar Items

 SEE ALSO

For information about working with categories in Outlook, see "Categories" in Chapter 3, on page 102.

As with other Outlook items, you can assign calendar items to categories so that organizing your items is easier. By assigning a calendar item to a category, you can then view your appointments, meetings, and events grouped by category. To assign a calendar item to a category, open the item and click the Categories button in the calendar item window. (You can also enter a category name in the text box to the right of the Categories button.) In the Categories dialog box, select the category or categories to which you want to assign the item and then click OK.

Changing the Type of Calendar Item

If you set up a calendar item and then later decide that you need to change it to a different type of calendar item, you don't have to delete the item and insert a new one. Instead, in many cases, you can simply turn on the All Day Event check box in the calendar item window.

When you turn on All Day Event, Outlook converts the calendar item to an event and sets the start and end times to midnight. Table 8-2 shows how turning the All Day Event option on and off affects a calendar item.

TABLE 8-2. Effects of the All Day Event Option.

All Day Event On	All Day Event Off
Event	Appointment
Invited event	Meeting
Recurring event	Recurring appointment
Recurring invited event	Recurring meeting

Describing Your Time

When others are planning meetings, they can check the Meeting Planner to see when you have other engagements. The Meeting Planner usually shows that you are "busy" during the times of your appointments. Sometimes, however, even though you have an engagement, you might want your calendar to reflect that you are something other than "busy" during that time. That's where the Show Time As box in the calendar item window comes into play.

The Show Time As box (which is located on the Appointment tab) gives you four options to choose from, described below: Free, Busy, Tentative, and Out Of Office.

- Even though you have an engagement scheduled, you might want to be available for an important meeting—your engagement can be moved or canceled. In this case, select the Free option.

- The standard selection for new engagements is the Busy option.

- Sometimes you pencil in an engagement, either because you're not sure it will happen or because you want to be available for other engagements that might be more important. In this case, select the Tentative option.

- If you're going to be away from the office for an engagement, you might want to make that clear to anyone planning a meeting, to let them know that you can't be reached. In this case, select the Out Of Office option.

On the Meeting Planner tab, Outlook displays a legend of the color and pattern it uses to mark your time according to your choice.

Adding Attachments to an Item

In the box at the bottom of the calendar item window, you can type any text that you want to keep with the item. Because this box works the same as the message area in an e-mail message, you can attach files, messages, and any other Microsoft Windows 95 or Microsoft Office 97 objects to any calendar item. For example, if you're sending a meeting request, you can type the agenda and include attachments for any background or preparatory material related to the meeting.

For information about attachments, see "Adding Text from a File," on page 104, "Adding 'Other Stuff'," on page 105, and "Attaching Messages," on page 108.

Keeping Items Private

SEE ALSO

For information about granting permissions and assigning delegates, see "Delegates Tab," on page 76.

When you give others permission to view your Calendar folder, or when you assign a delegate who can perform actions such as responding to meeting requests on your behalf, these people can see the subject of a calendar item. If you have private calendar items that should not be seen by authorized users of your Calendar folder, turn on the Private check box in the calendar item window of each item.

TIP

You can also turn the Private setting on or off by right-clicking the calendar item in the appointment slots and then choosing Private from the shortcut menu.

Changing Invitations

You change invitations any time you add a name to the invitation list for a meeting or an invited event. You can also change the invitation list by including the names of people and resources but not sending them an invitation. Or you can cancel all invitations, which converts a meeting to an appointment and an invited event to an event.

Inviting Others

To select the additional attendees and resources you want to invite, open the calendar item and click the To button in the meeting request or invited event window. You can also click the Meeting Planner tab and then click the Invite Others button. In either case, you see the Select Attendees And Resources dialog box, shown earlier on page 235. Select the people and resources you want to invite, and then click OK.

Including But Not Inviting Others

For each attendee you invite, you can click the envelope icon to the left of the name to see a menu like this:

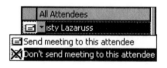

You'll probably use this menu most often with resources, which might not have e-mail addresses, even though you can type the resource's name in the Select Attendees And Resources dialog box. If you have a resource without an e-mail address, you can simply choose not to "send the meeting" to this "attendee." This prevents you from receiving a message that your message can't be delivered. You want others to know, however, that the people and resources you've invited will be available for the meeting—the room, any A/V equipment, a computer, and so on.

TIP

If you want to remove a name entirely from an invitation list, select the name on the Meeting Planner tab of the meeting request window and then press the Delete key.

Canceling Invitations

You can convert a meeting to an appointment or an invited event to an event by canceling all invitations (after you've set up the invitations but before you've actually sent them). To cancel the sending of invitations, you can either click the Cancel Invitation button on the Standard toolbar in the calendar item window or choose the Appointment Cancel Invitation command.

If you later change your mind and decide to issue the invitations after all, you can either click the Invite Attendees button on the Standard toolbar in the calendar item window or choose the Appointment Invite Attendees command. Outlook uses the original invitation list on the Meeting Planner tab in the calendar item window.

Changing Recurrence

After you create a calendar item, you might need to change its recurrence status, either by altering the existing recurrence pattern, by changing the details of a single occurrence, or by converting a one-time calendar item to a recurring item (or vice versa).

To set or change the recurrence of a calendar item, you must first open the item. If the item you open is already part of a recurring series of items, you'll see the Open Recurring Item dialog box before the item itself opens. In this dialog box, choose whether you want to open this occurrence of the item or the full series of recurring items and then click OK.

If you open a single occurrence of a recurring series of items, you can change the location, subject, or reminder time for that occurrence in the calendar item window. You can also change the start or end time for that occurrence (but not for the series). If you want to change the subject, location, or reminder for the entire series while working in the calendar item window for a particular occurrence, click the Edit Series button on the Standard toolbar or choose the Appointment Edit Series command. Doing so opens a separate calendar item window that pertains to the entire series.

III

Scheduling Your Time and Tasks

After making any changes you want in the calendar item window, take one of the following actions to work with the recurrence pattern and series:

- Choose the Appointment Recurrence command.

- Click the Recurrence button on the Standard toolbar.

- Press Ctrl+G.

Outlook displays the Appointment Recurrence dialog box, shown in Figure 8-2. In this dialog box, you can adjust the start and end times and the duration of the calendar item, specify the recurrence pattern, adjust the range of a recurring series of items, or remove recurrence (converting the calendar item to a one-time occurrence). After you click OK in this dialog box, any changes you have made—such as new meeting times or a new recurrence pattern—appear in the calendar item window, which you can now save and close.

Select one of the four recurrence patterns, and specify the details.

Change the start time or the end time.

Change the duration (which also changes the end time).

FIGURE 8-2.

The Appointment Recurrence dialog box

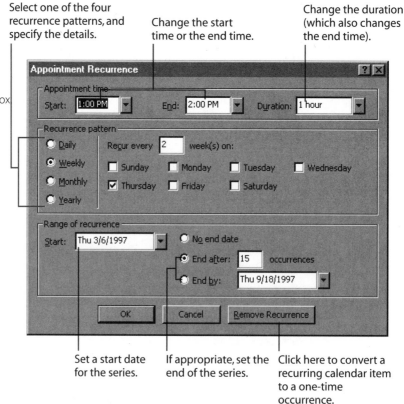

Set a start date for the series.

If appropriate, set the end of the series.

Click here to convert a recurring calendar item to a one-time occurrence.

The following sections take a closer look at two parts of the Appointment Recurrence dialog box: the Recurrence Pattern area and the Range Of Recurrence area.

Recurrence Pattern

The recurrence pattern you select in the Appointment Recurrence dialog box tells Outlook how to set up your calendar for each engagement in the recurring series. Each recurrence pattern—Daily, Weekly, Monthly, and Yearly—has its own set of options, which appear to the right of the list of patterns.

Daily recurrence pattern.   When an engagement recurs every day or recurs with a specific number of days between occurrences, you should select the Daily recurrence pattern. This recurrence pattern is your choice if you have an engagement that recurs every 30 days, for example. You can select a daily pattern that includes weekdays only (Monday through Friday), or you can specify a certain number of days between engagements by selecting the Every [ ] Days option in the Recurrence Pattern area and typing the number of days in the box— from 1 day (daily, including weekends) to 999 days (about 2 years and 9 months).

Click here to set a day interval
that includes weekend days.

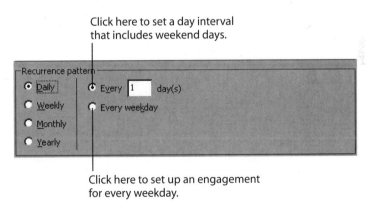

Click here to set up an engagement
for every weekday.

 TIP

If the number of days between engagements is divisible by seven, you might prefer to use the Weekly recurrence pattern. You'll also want the Weekly pattern if an engagement recurs two or more days each week.

Weekly recurrence pattern. You'll want to select the Weekly recurrence pattern when an engagement recurs weekly on the same day, recurs with a specific number of weeks between occurrences, or recurs two or more days each week. Type in a number to set the number of weeks between engagements—from 1 week to 99 weeks (just under 2 years). You can also specify the day (or days) of the week.

Set the number of weeks between engagements.

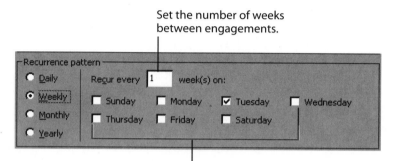

Turn on the check boxes for the days of the week on which the engagement occurs.

Monthly recurrence pattern. When an engagement recurs monthly on the same day or recurs with a specific number of months between occurrences, the Monthly recurrence pattern is your best choice.

Click here to designate a specific date.

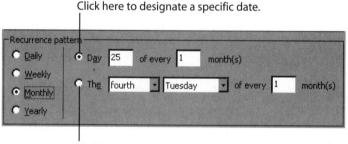

Click here to designate a relative date.

When your engagement recurs on a specific date each month (or every so many months), select the first option on the right side of the Monthly Recurrence Pattern area. In the first box, type a number to set the specific date of the month. If the number you type for the date is greater than 28 (or 29 in leap years), Outlook notifies you that for months with fewer days than you specified, the engagement is set for the last day of the month. In the second box, type the number of months between engagements—from 1 month through 99 months (8 years, 3 months).

When your engagement recurs in a specific pattern but not necessarily on the same date each time, select the second option on the right side of the Recurrence Pattern area, which specifies a relative day. For example, some organizations hold a meeting on the second Tuesday of each month. From month to month, the actual date changes— March 11 and April 8 are second Tuesdays in 1997, for instance. After you select this option, do the following:

1 Select the occurrence of the day during the month—first, second, third, fourth, or last.

2 Select the day pattern. In addition to the named days of the week, you can select Day, Weekday, or Weekend Day.

3 Set the number of months between engagements—from 1 month to 99 months (8 years and 3 months).

Yearly recurrence pattern. Select the Yearly recurrence pattern when an engagement recurs annually on the same day every year.

Click here to designate a specific date.

Click here to designate a relative date.

Select the first option on the right side of the Yearly Recurrence Pattern area when your engagement recurs on the same date each year. Choose a month from the drop-down list, and type in a number to set the specific date. If the number you type is greater than 28 (or 29 in leap years), Outlook sets the engagement for the last day of the month for any month with fewer days than you specified.

Select the second option on the Yearly Recurrence Pattern area, which specifies a relative day, when your engagement recurs in a specific pattern but not necessarily on the same date each time. If, for example, your club holds its annual party each year on the second Tuesday of December, the actual date was December 10 in 1996—but it will be December 9 in 1997. After you select this option, follow the steps on the next page.

1 Select the occurrence of the day during the month—first, second, third, fourth, or last.

2 Select the day pattern—Day, Weekday, Weekend Day, or the named days of the week.

3 Select the month.

Range Of Recurrence

When you create a new series of recurring engagements, Outlook doesn't set an end date for the series. That's fine for recurring engagements that you expect to continue for many years or for those times when you don't know if a series is ever going to end. But sometimes, as if by magic, you do know when a series of engagements will end. In such a case, you can set the end of the series.

In the Range Of Recurrence area of the Appointment Recurrence dialog box, you have three choices for ending a series: No End Date, End After, and End By. The No End Date option is pretty obvious. Use one of the other options under the following circumstances:

End After.   If you know the number of engagements in the series, select the End After option and type the number in the box. Although the End After box shows 10 occurrences as its standard entry, you can set the number of occurrences to any number from 1 through 999. (Setting the number of occurrences to 1 is the same as setting up a one-time engagement.) If your recurring engagements add up to more than 999, you need to set an End By date instead of setting the number of occurrences.

TIP

If you set an End After number, Outlook sets the End By date to match the number of occurrences. You might not see this change until after you close the Appointment Recurrence dialog box and then reopen it. You can force Outlook to display the change, however, by setting the End After number and then clicking the End By option. You can then select either option to get the same result. Note, however, that this doesn't work in reverse—if you select a date in the End By box, Outlook does not change the number of occurrences. If you set a date past 999 occurrences, don't click the End After option. If you do, Outlook resets the End By date to the date of the last occurrence.

End By.   If you know the date of the last engagement in the series, select the End By option. The End By box initially shows a date that matches the 10 occurrences in the End After box. In the End By box, you can type a date, or you can click the down arrow to display a calendar from which you can select the end date. For more information about using this calendar, refer to the techniques described in "Using the Date Navigator," on page 213.

Adjusting Other Calendar Item Properties

? SEE ALSO

For information about the AutoArchive feature, see Chapter 15.

In the area at the bottom of the calendar item window, you can type notes and comments that pertain to the item. You can format the text of your notes and comments with buttons on the Formatting toolbar. (To turn on this toolbar, choose the View Toolbars command and choose Formatting from the submenu.) In addition, your notes can include inserted files and folder items from any Outlook folder.

You can also set other properties for a calendar item. In the calendar item window, choose the File Properties command to display the Properties dialog box for the calendar item, shown in Figure 8-3.

Select the level of importance:
High, Normal, or Low.

FIGURE 8-3.

A Properties dialog
box for a calendar item.

Turn on this check
box to block
automatic
archiving of this
calendar item.

Turn on this check
box to get a
receipt when your
item is read.

Turn on this
check box to get
a receipt when
your item is
delivered.

Turn off this
check box if you
don't want to
save a copy of
this item.

Select the level of
sensitivity: Normal,
Personal, Private, or
Confidential.

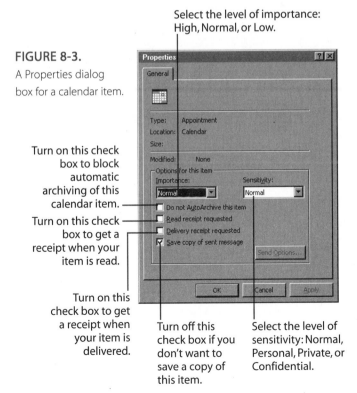

III

Scheduling Your Time and Tasks

Canceling a Calendar Item

When you need to cancel a calendar item, first click the item to select it. Then use one of the following methods to cancel (delete) the item:

- Click the Delete button on the Standard toolbar.

- Press Ctrl+D.

- Choose the Edit Delete command.

- Right-click the calendar item, and then choose Delete from the shortcut menu.

- Open the calendar item, and then click the Delete button on the Standard toolbar in the calendar item window.

Outlook moves deleted calendar items to the Deleted Items folder.

If you delete a calendar item that is part of a series, you see the message in the following dialog box:

Click here to delete the entire series.

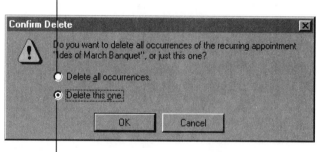

Click here to delete only the selected calendar item.

If you delete an item to which others have been invited, Outlook displays a dialog box in which you can choose to send a cancellation or delete the item without sending a cancellation.

 NOTE

> If you open the series of a recurring item and delete the item, you don't see the Confirm Delete dialog box. However, if the recurring item is a meeting or an invited event, you'll see a message asking whether you want to send a meeting cancellation before deleting the item.

You can also use the Appointment Cancel Meeting command in the calendar item window to cancel a meeting and delete the item. Open the calendar item window, and choose the Appointment Cancel Meeting command. Outlook displays a dialog box in which you can choose to send a cancellation to attendees and delete the item or simply delete the item without sending a cancellation.

Copying a Calendar Item

If you need to set up a calendar item that is similar to an existing item, you can copy the original calendar item. The steps for copying a calendar item are as follows:

1 Locate the calendar item, and click its left border.

2 Choose the Edit Copy command (or press Ctrl+C).

3 Go to the date where you want to set up the new calendar item.

4 Click the appointment slot for the beginning time of the new calendar item.

5 Choose the Edit Paste command (or press Ctrl+V).

6 Fine-tune the copy of the calendar item to fit the new circumstances.

Dealing with a Reminder

As you've learned, Outlook helps you remember your scheduled engagements by displaying a reminder on the date and at the time you set for the reminder. Here's a picture of a reminder:

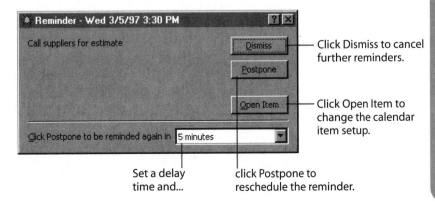

Click Dismiss to cancel further reminders.

Click Open Item to change the calendar item setup.

Set a delay time and...

click Postpone to reschedule the reminder.

III

Scheduling Your Time and Tasks

If you need to reschedule (postpone) the reminder, select one of the listed delay times. (You can't type a delay time.) Your choices range from five minutes to a week. If you postpone the reminder past the start time of the calendar item, the Reminder message displays the word *Overdue* in its title bar when it reappears. If you need to reschedule the entire calendar item, click the Open Item button and make the necessary changes in the calendar item window.

 NOTE

> You can postpone a reminder only in the Reminder message box (although you can change the initial reminder time in the calendar item window).

Receiving and Responding to a Meeting Request

When someone invites you to a meeting or an event, you receive an e-mail message that looks like the illustration shown here:

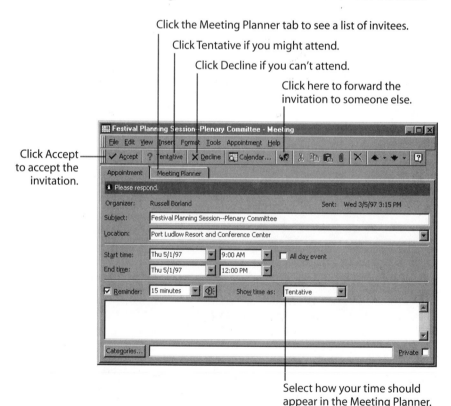

After you click one of the toolbar buttons to send your response, Outlook asks whether you want to send a response and whether you want to add comments to your response:

Click here to send no response.

Click here to send a response without comment.

Click here to add a comment to your response.

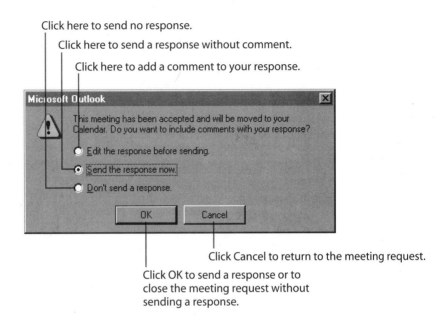

Click Cancel to return to the meeting request.

Click OK to send a response or to close the meeting request without sending a response.

> **NOTE**

If you want Outlook to process meeting requests automatically, you can use settings in the Options dialog box. Choose the Tools Options command, click the Calendar tab, and then click the Advanced Scheduling button. In the Advanced Scheduling dialog box, you can select options for Outlook to automatically accept meeting requests, decline meeting requests that conflict with your existing schedule, and decline requests for recurring meetings. For more information, see "Advanced Scheduling Button," on page 64.

Who's Coming and Who's Not?

When you receive a meeting request message, you can click the Meeting Planner tab to see a list of all the people and resources that are invited, as shown on the following page. Notice that the Meeting Planner tab for invitees does not include either the status of responses or an Invite Others button. You can turn on the Show Attendee Availability option to see the schedules for the other attendees.

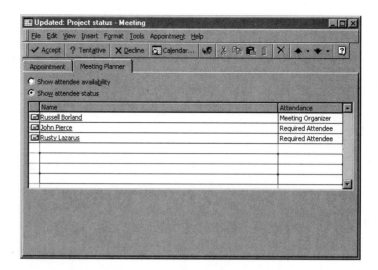

When you open a calendar item for a meeting you requested, you see a slightly different version of the Meeting Planner tab. This organizer's version indicates the responses you've received so far to your meeting request and allows you to expand the list of invitees:

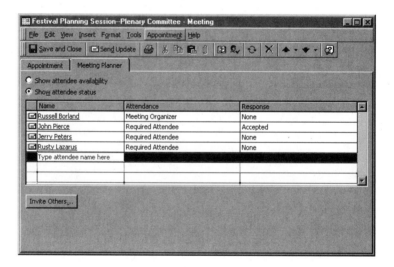

Controlling Your Tasks

We all have tasks to perform, every day. Two characters from the movie *Local Hero* summed it up pretty well:

"A lot of money, Ben. You'd never have to work again."

"We all have to work, Gordon. I mean, the beach has to be worked. Think of the state it'd get to if it wasn't worked."

For many daily tasks, we need a list to remind us. At home we have "Honey, do" lists and "job jars"; at work we have goals and projects. For tasks with deadlines, for large tasks that continue for a long time, and for tasks that can be started at a future date but that we dare not forget to perform, having a task list can help remind us what needs doing and when that doing must be done.

In your Microsoft Outlook 97 Tasks folder, you can set up tasks, describe them, specify start and end dates, set reminders, track the progress of your work on the task, estimate and track how much effort is expended, record costs, and note contacts and billing information. In Outlook you can assign a task to someone else (send them a task request), and someone else can assign a task to you (send you a task request). Outlook also provides tools that make it easy to report the status of an assigned task, both during work on the task and at its completion.

Here's a typical Tasks folder, with the task list displayed in Simple List view:

One-time task —
Recurring task —

Completed task —
Assigned task —

 **NOTE**

The TaskPad in the Calendar folder window is tied directly to entries you make in the Tasks folder. The TaskPad displays active tasks and tasks completed on the date showing on the calendar. You can open a task from the TaskPad and enter and change the details about a task, the same as you can by opening a task in the Tasks folder. You can also edit the information about a task that is displayed in the TaskPad. For more information about the TaskPad, see "Adjusting the TaskPad," on page 220.

Setting Up a Task

Tasks in Outlook involve three elements: the task description and settings, recurrence, and ownership. Although the first element is common to all tasks, the details of a task's description and settings can vary greatly from one task to another. The second element, recurrence, determines whether the task is a one-time occurrence or a task that recurs from time to time. The third element, ownership, designates the task as a job you do yourself or as a job you ask someone else to perform.

When you need to set up a new task, you can open the Tasks folder and use one of the following methods:

New Task

- Click the New Task button at the left end of the Standard toolbar.

- Choose the Tasks New Task command.

- Choose the File New command, and then select Task from the submenu.

- Press Ctrl+N.

Outlook opens a task window, which initially displays the Task tab. On this tab, you can name the task, set due dates, assign a priority, and set up various other features that will help you accomplish the task. Figure 9-1 shows an example of a task window and highlights some of the options you'll find on the Task tab. We'll discuss these options and settings throughout this chapter.

FIGURE 9-1.
The Task tab of a task window.

Set a reminder
here.

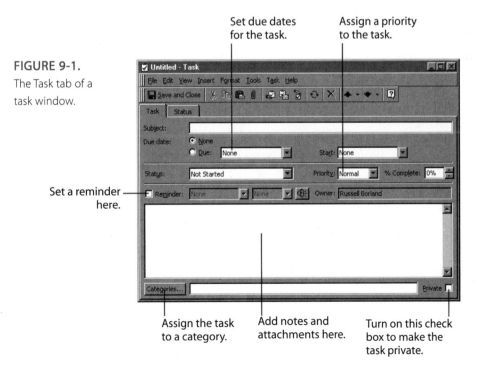

Set due dates
for the task.

Assign a priority
to the task.

Assign the task
to a category.

Add notes and
attachments here.

Turn on this check
box to make the
task private.

Scheduling Your Time and Tasks

After you enter information for a task in the task window, click the Save And Close button to add the task to your task list. If you want to close the window without saving the information you've entered, click the Close button in the upper right corner of the window (or choose the File Close command) and then click No when Outlook asks whether you want to save your changes.

Creating a New Task from a Different Folder

If you're working in an Outlook folder other than the Tasks folder when you need to set up a new task, use one of the following methods to create the task. Later you can fine-tune or change it as necessary.

- Click the down arrow at the right side of the New button on the Standard toolbar, and then choose Task or Task Request from the menu.

- Choose the File New command, and then select Task or Task Request from the submenu.

- Press Ctrl+Shift+K for a new task; press Ctrl+Shift+U for a new task request.

Quickly Setting Up a Task

? SEE ALSO

In the Contacts folder, you can set up a new task that you will perform for a contact. For details, see "Setting Up a Task for a Contact," on page 314.

When you need to set up a task quickly without worrying about the fine points of the settings, you can simply open the Tasks folder and do the following:

1 Click the top row of the task list (which reads *Click here to add a new task*).

2 Type the name of the task.

3 If applicable, type a due date for the task in the Due Date column to the right.

4 To quickly add another task, press the Enter key. To finish adding new tasks this way, press the Tab key and then press the down arrow key.

The new tasks now appear in the task list. Later, if you want to add more information about a task or make any other changes, you can open the task item (by double-clicking it, for example, or by right-clicking the task item and choosing Open from the shortcut menu), make your changes in the task window, and then click the Save And Close button on the Standard toolbar.

If you'd prefer to select a due date rather than type one, click the Due Date box and then click the down arrow that appears. Select a date from the calendar that Outlook displays. For more information about using this calendar, see "Using the Date Navigator," on page 213.

Setting Up a Recurring Task

If you have a task that must be repeated at a regular interval, you can set up a recurrence pattern for the task. This way, an occurrence of the task appears on your task list at the proper intervals so that you have an ongoing reminder of the work you need to do.

If you want to establish a recurrence pattern for a task that you assign to someone else, you must set up the recurrence when you create the task. You can't add recurrence or change the recurrence pattern after you send a task request. For more details about task requests, see "Sending a Task Request," on page 269.

You can establish a recurrence pattern for a task when you first set up the task, or you can open one of your existing tasks and change it from one-time to recurring (or vice versa) or adjust its recurrence pattern. To do so, open the task item you want to work with and then take one of the following actions in the task window:

- Click the Recurrence button on the Standard toolbar.

- Choose the Task Recurrence command.

- Press Ctrl+G.

In the Task Recurrence dialog box, shown in Figure 9-2 on the next page, you can set the intervals at which the task should recur, and you can designate the start and end dates for the series of recurring tasks. You can also change a recurring task to a one-time task by clicking Remove Recurrence. Setting up a recurring task is very similar to the process of setting up a recurring calendar item, discussed in Chapter 8, "Scheduling Appointments, Meetings, and Events." In fact, the two areas of the Task Recurrence dialog box—Recurrence Pattern and Range Of Recurrence—also appear in the Appointment Recurrence dialog box, shown in Figure 8-2, on page 246.)

FIGURE 9-2.

The Task Recurrence dialog box.

Select one of the four recurrence patterns, and specify the details.

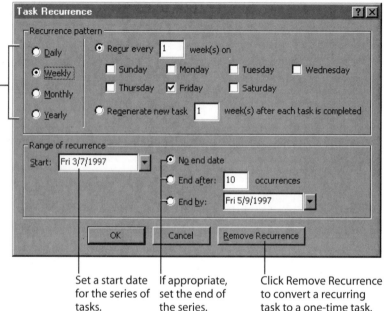

Set a start date for the series of tasks.

If appropriate, set the end of the series.

Click Remove Recurrence to convert a recurring task to a one-time task.

The recurrence pattern you set up in the Task Recurrence dialog box tells Outlook when each occurrence in the series of tasks is active and due. When you select one of the four recurrence patterns—Daily, Weekly, Monthly, or Yearly—a corresponding set of options appears on the righthand side of the Recurrence Pattern area. These options allow you to specify how Outlook should calculate the intervals between occurrences of a recurring task. When you complete an occurrence of the task, Outlook creates the next occurrence on the basis of the recurrence pattern you set and adds the next occurrence to your task list. The recurrence pattern options for tasks are nearly the same as those in the Appointment Recurrence dialog box; consult "Recurrence Pattern," on page 247, for details about how to set them.

The one difference between setting recurrence patterns for a task and for a calendar item is the Regenerate New Task option in the Task Recurrence dialog box. This option is valuable when a task must recur a specified number of days (or weeks, months, or years) after the previous completion of the task (rather than at a specific interval). For example, you could set up the recurring task of changing your security password every 60 days. Then, for one reason or another, you might change your password in fewer than 60 days. If you have turned on the Regenerate New Task option, Outlook will create a new occurrence of the task, resetting the due date to 60 days after the date you mark the previous occurrence of the task complete.

The second area of the Task Recurrence dialog box, Range Of Recurrence, is identical to the area of the same name in the Appointment Recurrence dialog box. It's easy to see how to set a start date; for details about setting end dates, see "Range of Recurrence," on page 250.

When you click OK in the Task Recurrence dialog box, you return to the task window. If you have set up a recurrence pattern, the colored band at the top of the Task tab now displays information about the intervals at which the task will recur. Notice also that if you have changed the recurring task's start date in the Task Recurrence dialog box, Outlook changes the due date in the task window (and in the task list) accordingly.

If you open a recurring task and change the due date or start date for the task in the task window, Outlook displays a message telling you that you have changed the date for only one occurrence of the task and that to change all future occurrences you need to open the Task Recurrence dialog box. If you click OK in the message box to accept the changes you've made to the single occurrence of the task, Outlook lists that occurrence of the task in the task list separately. The start date and due date for the recurring task are updated according to the existing recurrence pattern.

Skipping a Task in a Series

When a recurring task comes due, you might find that you don't need to perform the task this time, although you will need to do so for future due dates. When you want to skip one occurrence of a recurring task, open the task and choose the Task Skip Occurrence command. Outlook resets the due date to the next occurrence of the recurring task.

You cannot undo skipping an occurrence, so if you skip an occurrence in error, you need to reset the start date on the Task tab. If you've made other changes that should be saved, but you also want to undo skipping an occurrence, be sure to reset the start date on the Task tab.

NOTE

The Skip Occurrence command is not available for recurring tasks you've set up with the Regenerate New Task option in the Task Recurrence dialog box.

Creating a Task from a Calendar Item (and Vice Versa)

If you have set up an item on your Outlook calendar (a meeting, an appointment, or an event) that involves a task, you can easily use the calendar item to create a task. Follow these steps:

1 Select the calendar item in your Calendar folder.

2 Choose the Edit Copy To Folder command.

3 In the Copy Items dialog box, select the Tasks folder, and then click OK.

4 When a task window appears, set up the task as you usually would. Notice that Outlook displays information about the calendar item in the message area of the task window.

5 Click the Save And Close button to save the task and add it to your task list.

You can also use a task to quickly create a calendar item such as an appointment. This is useful when you want to schedule time to work on or complete the task. The process is similar to the one just described: select the task in the Tasks folder, and use the Edit Copy To Folder command to copy the task to your Calendar folder. When a calendar item window appears, set up the item and save it. (For help with setting up calendar items, see Chapter 8, "Scheduling Appointments, Meetings, and Events.")

Setting Task Dates

Outlook sets up new tasks without a due date. If your task needs a due date, you can specify this date, and you can also specify the date on which you should start the task in order to complete it.

As mentioned earlier, you can add a due date in the task list itself by entering it in the Due Date box. (See "Quickly Setting Up a Task," on page 260.) Alternatively, you can specify the due date in the task window by clicking the Due option and then setting a date in the date box. Outlook also lets you set a start date in the task window, in the Start box.

To enter any of these dates, you can either type a date in the appropriate box or click the down arrow at the right end of the box and select a date from the calendar that appears. For information about handy techniques for using this calendar, see "Using the Date Navigator," on page 213.

Ranking Tasks

Most tasks that you perform are routine, at least within the context of your daily chores. From time to time, however, you'll have very important tasks that require your immediate attention, or at least a large portion of your fund of attention. Other tasks are less important than your routine tasks. These tasks of lower importance can be deferred or delayed without affecting your life or your work.

When you create a task, Outlook assigns an importance level (or priority) of Normal to the new task. You can change the importance level to either High or Low. (And later you can change it back to Normal.)

To change the importance level of a task, use one of the following methods:

- Select the level of importance in the Priority box on the Task tab of the task window.

- In the task window, choose the File Properties command. In the Properties dialog box for the task item, select the level of importance in the Importance box.

- Select the task in the task list, and click the Priority column (the column with an exclamation mark as its label). Then select the level of importance from the list that appears. (The Priority column appears in all views of the Tasks folder window except Simple List view and Task Timeline view. To change the view, see "Viewing Your Tasks," on page 284.)

III

Scheduling Your Time and Tasks

When you set an importance level using any one of these methods, Outlook changes the priority setting in the other two locations that show the level of importance.

In the Tasks folder window, a red exclamation mark in the Priority column indicates a task with a High importance level. A task with Low importance is marked by a blue downward-pointing arrow. The Priority column is blank for a task with a Normal level of importance.

Setting a Task Reminder

When you create a new task with a due date, Outlook sets up a reminder for 8:00 A.M. on the due date. If this doesn't suit your work habits—perhaps you'd prefer to be reminded at 3:00 P.M. the day before the due date for a particular task—you can, of course, change the reminder date and time. If your task does not have a due date, Outlook does not automatically set up a reminder; you must set it up yourself.

It's an easy matter to set up or change a reminder:

1   On the Task tab in the task window, click the Reminder check box to turn on this option (if it is not already turned on).

2   In the first Reminder box, set the date on which Outlook should display the reminder. If your task has a due date, you'll see that date in the box initially. To change the date, you can type a new date or click the down arrow beside the box and select a date from the calendar. (For information about using this calendar, see "Using the Date Navigator," on page 213.)

For information about changing the default reminder time (8:00 A.M.) for all tasks with due dates, see "Task Defaults," on page 65.

3   In the second box, you'll see 8:00 A.M. as the default reminder time if your task has a due date. To change the time at which the reminder should appear, type a new time, or select a time from the drop-down list.

4   Save and close the task window.

If you inadvertently set the task reminder for a time that has already passed, Outlook displays a message telling you that the time has passed and that a reminder won't be set. If that's all right with you, click OK to dispense with the reminder. To reset the reminder time, click No. Outlook returns you to the task window, where you can set a new reminder time.

Adding Task Notes

SEE ALSO

For information about attachments, see "Adding Text from a File," on page 104, "Adding 'Other Stuff'," on page 105, and "Attaching Messages," on page 108.

The box at the bottom of a task window provides a space in which you can type any text that should accompany the task. This box is like the message area in an e-mail message, which means that you can attach files, messages, and any other Microsoft Windows 95 or Microsoft Office 97 objects to a task. For example, if you're sending a task request to someone else, you can type directions, goals, concerns, restrictions, and guidance for the task. You can also include attachments for any background or preparatory material related to the task.

Keeping a Task Private

You might want to designate a task as private when it's personal or otherwise sensitive or confidential in nature. When you give others permission to view your Tasks folder, or when you assign a delegate who can perform actions such as responding to task requests on your behalf (see "Delegates Tab," on page 76), these people can see the subject of a task. If you have set up a task that should not be seen by authorized users of your Tasks folder, turn on the Private check box on the Task tab of the task window to keep the task private.

Setting Up a Task Estimate

SEE ALSO

For more information about the Status tab, see "Recording Other Task Information," on page 282.

On the Status tab in the task window, you can record your estimate of the number of hours that a task is likely to take. You might want to use this number as you estimate the cost and billing for a task. You could also use it to test your estimating skills or tools, by later comparing it to the actual hours worked. (See "Actual Work," on page 279.)

To set a time estimate for a task, simply click the Status tab in the task window and type the estimated number of hours in the Total Work box. Outlook converts the number of hours you type to days or weeks. The conversion is based on the number of hours per day and hours per week that you set as your standard on the Tasks/Notes tab of the Options dialog box (which you can display by choosing the Tools Options command).

NOTE

The number of hours you enter in the Total Work box is not connected to the due date you set on the Task tab. You must set the due date yourself.

III

Scheduling Your Time and Tasks

Adjusting Other Task Properties

 SEE ALSO

For information about the AutoArchive feature, see "AutoArchive Tab," on page 70. For information about level of importance, see "Ranking Tasks," on page 265.

In each task window, you can set additional properties for the task item by using the Properties dialog box. As you can see in Figures 9-3 and 9-4, the options available and the information displayed in the Properties dialog box for a new task (Figure 9-3) differ from the options available and information displayed in the Properties dialog box for an existing task (Figure 9-4). In the Properties dialog boxes for both a new task and an existing task, you can adjust task properties such as the level of importance and automatic archiving. Several other options pertain to task requests you send to someone else—for example, the options for requesting a read or a delivery receipt or the option for setting a sensitivity level. Notice in Figure 9-4 that you cannot change the sensitivity level for a task once it's been set up. The sensitivity level can only be set before a task is entered on your task list or before you send a task request.

To set or change task item properties, you create a task or open an existing task and choose the File Properties command to display the Properties dialog box.

Select the level of importance: High, Normal, or Low.

Select the level of sensitivity: Normal, Personal, Private, or Confidential.

FIGURE 9-3.

The Properties dialog box for a new task.

Turn on this check box to block automatic archiving of this task.

Turn off this check box if you don't want to save a copy of your task request.

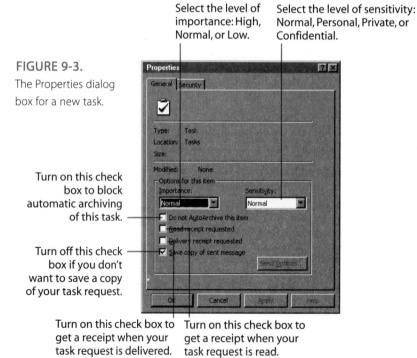

Turn on this check box to get a receipt when your task request is delivered.

Turn on this check box to get a receipt when your task request is read.

Select the level of
importance: High,
Normal, or Low.

FIGURE 9-4.

The Properties dialog
box for an existing
task.

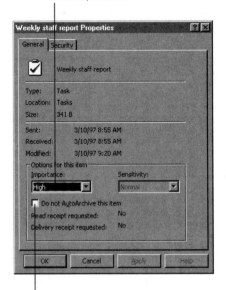

Turn on this check box
to block automatic
archiving of this task.

Categorizing Your Tasks

As with other Outlook items, you can assign tasks to categories so that
organizing your tasks is easier. By assigning a task to a category, you
can view them by category. To assign a task to a category, open the
task and click the Categories button in the task window. (You can also
enter a category name in the text box to the right of the Categories
button.) In the Categories dialog box, select the category or categories
to which you want to assign the task and then click OK. For more
information about working with categories in Outlook, see "Categories,"
in Chapter 3, on page 101, and also "By Category View," in Chapter 7,
on page 228.

Sending a Task Request

You might have a task that you need to pass along to someone else to
perform. (If you're a manager or a project team leader, that's part of
your job.) Or you might be in charge of a project and want some help
with parts of the project. In these cases, you can set up a task and send
a task request to someone else in order to enlist their aid.

III

Scheduling Your Time and Tasks

When you send a task request and receive an acceptance, the ownership of the task passes to the person who accepts your request. At that point, you can receive updates to track the progress of the task, but you can no longer make any changes to the task record.

Once a task is assigned, Outlook keeps track of who owns the task and when it gets updated. When the task owner updates the task, Outlook updates all copies of that task in the task lists of others who kept a copy of the task. (A task can appear on task lists of several people because the person you assign a task to might assign that task to someone else. For information, see "Forwarding a Task Request," on page 275.) When the task is complete, Outlook sends a status report to those who were assigned the task and requested one. You can see the names of people who will receive updates and status reports about the task by viewing the Update List box on the Status tab in the task window.

If you assign the same task to two or more people, you do not receive automatic updates as the task progresses. To keep your finger on the pulse of an assigned task, divide the task into smaller parts and send each part to an individual assignee. That way, you'll receive updates of task status.

The steps for assigning a task to another person are as follows:

1 Open the Tasks folder, and create a task request in one of the following ways:

- Click the down arrow to the right of the New Task button on the Standard toolbar, and choose Task Request from the menu.

- Choose the Tasks New Task Request command.

- Choose the File New command, and then select Task Request from the submenu.

- Press Ctrl+Shift+U.

Assign Task

- After creating a new task, click the Assign Task button on the Standard toolbar in the task window.

- Create a new task, and then, in the task window, choose the Task Assign Task command.

2 Outlook displays a task request window, shown here. Fill out as much of the information on the tabs as you need to—you can set a due date and a start date, prioritize the task, add notes, and so on. The Keep An Updated Copy Of This Task On My Task List option retains a copy of this task on your task list in order to receive periodic status reports. The Send Me A Status Report When This Task Is Complete option provides you with a status report when the assignee marks the task complete.

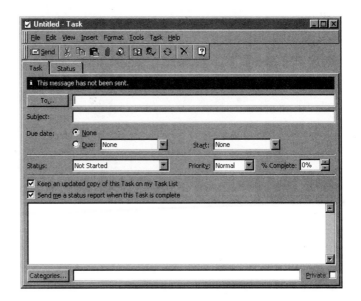

3 In the To box of the task request window, type the name of the person or persons to whom you're assigning the task. If you'd prefer to select the name (or names), click the To button to open the Select Task Recipient dialog box (a variation of the Address Book dialog box you use for e-mail messages). You can select as many names as necessary.

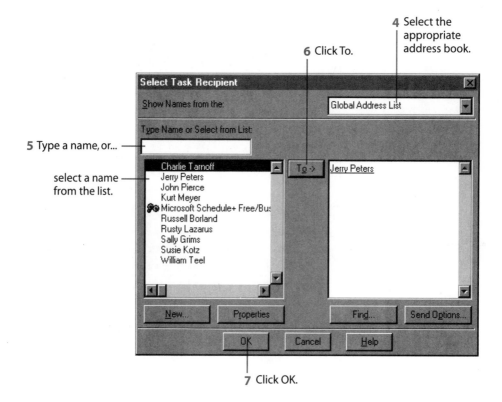

4 Select the appropriate address book.

6 Click To.

5 Type a name, or...

select a name from the list.

7 Click OK.

8 Click the Send button in the task request window to send the task request to the person or persons you've assigned to the task.

After you send a task request, you can't change the names of the assignees unless one of them declines the task.

Reassigning a Task

You've assigned a task to someone and that someone has accepted the task, but now you change your mind about who should complete the assignment. In such a case, you can create an unassigned copy of the task and assign the copy to someone else. To do this, you must have turned on the Keep An Updated Copy Of This Task On My Task List option on the Task tab of the original task request.

When you create an unassigned copy of a task, everyone who formerly received task updates or status reports will not receive them for the re-assigned task. The original task you assigned stays on the task list of the person you assigned it to, but an updated copy of the original task will not appear on your task list. If you or anyone else who was assigned the original task requested a status report for that task, you and the people who requested it will receive the status report when the owner of the original task marks the task complete.

To create an unassigned copy of a task and reassign the task, you take the following steps. Remember, you must have selected the Keep An Updated Copy Of This Task On My Task List option in the original task request you sent.

1 In your task list, open your copy of the task you want to reassign.

2 Click the Status tab.

3 On the Status tab, click the Create Unassigned Copy button and then click OK. Outlook makes a copy of the task and displays it in the task window.

4 In the task window, click the Assign Task button on the Standard toolbar.

5 In the To box, enter the name of the person you now want to assign the task to, and then click Send.

Receiving and Responding to a Task Request

When you receive a task request, you can accept it, in which case it becomes your task and appears on your task list. You can decline the request, in which case the task is returned to the sender and reappears on the sender's task list. You can assign the task to someone else who has more time or more expertise. Or you can simply delete the task request message.

When you receive a task request, you see a message like the one shown on the Task tab in the illustration below:

Click here to accept the task request.

Click here to decline the task request.

Click here to assign the task to someone else.

Click here to delete the task request.

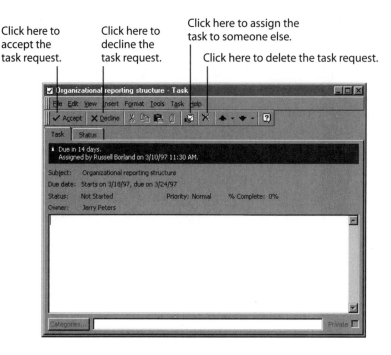

After you've clicked the Accept or Decline button, Outlook displays a message asking whether you want to edit your response or send your reply without a response. If you choose not to edit your response, Outlook sends the message without displaying any further windows. If you choose to edit the response, Outlook provides a typical message window with a colored band showing your response. Your response also appears in the Subject box when the task request is returned. Type any message you want to include, and, when your response is ready, click the Send button.

If you decide to assign the task request to someone else and click the Assign Task button, Outlook displays a task request window that you can use to forward the task request along. See "Forwarding a Task Request," on the facing page.

Accepting a Task

When you accept a task request, you take over ownership of the task. You can then make any changes to the task setup that suit the circumstances.

Once you've accepted a task request, you'll probably want (or be required) to send status reports to the person who assigned the task to you. In some cases, Outlook will send a status report automatically; in other cases, you must prepare and send the report yourself. For more information, see "Sending a Status Report," on page 279.

Declining a Task

When you click the Decline button for a task request, you can send your response with or without comment. Outlook returns the ownership of the task to the sender.

If you are the person who assigned the task, you receive a message telling you that the person to whom you assigned the task has declined to accept it. You then have three choices:

- Return the task to your own task list. You can then try to assign it again, or you can perform the task yourself. To return the task to your task list, open the message that declines the task and choose the Task Return To Task List command.

- If you simply close the window, the task stays on your task list as a declined task. You can open the task response window in your Tasks folder and choose the Task Return To Task List command to make the task active on your own task list.

- Delete the task. Outlook does not ask you to confirm the deletion.

Forwarding a Task Request

If you receive a task request but don't have time to perform the task, you can forward the request to another person who might be able to carry out the task. To forward a task request to someone else, you simply assign the task to that person. The recipient is then in the same boat you were in when you received the task request. If the recipient accepts the task, you're off the hook; the task ownership passes to the recipient. You and the person who originally sent the task request will receive status reports about the task.

III

Scheduling Your Time and Tasks

Do *not* forward a task request as a message unless you're only keeping someone else informed about your workload. Forwarding a task request as a message (rather than assigning the task to another person) does not carry with it an assignment mechanism.

You have two ways to forward a task:

- When you open the task request message, click the Assign Task button on the Standard toolbar in the message window. Follow the steps listed in "Sending a Task Request," on page 269, to assign the task. With this method, you don't actually accept the task. You're likely to use this method when you know right away that you need to assign the task to someone else.

- You can accept the task and then assign it to someone else. Use this method after you've accepted a task and later decide to assign it to someone else.

Deleting a Task Request

(?) **SEE ALSO**

For more about deleting tasks, see "Canceling a Task," on page 283.

If you delete a task request instead of answering it, Outlook asks whether you want to send a message to the sender declining the task request. (It's the polite thing to do.)

Click here to send a reply declining the request and then delete the task request.

Click here to mark the task completed and then delete the task request.

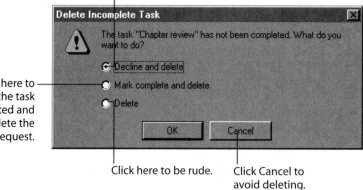

Click here to be rude.   Click Cancel to avoid deleting.

Working with Your Tasks

Outlook's task feature can help you develop efficiency and accountability in your work and your projects. As due dates approach, you can receive timely reminders. You'll be able to track the progress of a task during the course of a project. You'll be able to record certain additional information about a task—mileage, billing information, contacts, and names of companies—to help with wrapping up a task. You'll send or receive periodic status reports. And, you can keep a list of completed tasks.

Receiving a Reminder

As the due date for a task approaches, Outlook displays a reminder on the date and at the time you set for the reminder. Your reminder will look something like this:

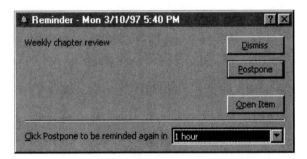

In the Reminder message box, click the Dismiss button to cancel any further reminders. If the reminder makes you realize that you need to change the due date for the task, or if the reminder makes you remember that circumstances have changed and should be reflected in the task setup, click the Open Item button to open the task window, where you can make any necessary adjustments.

If you want Outlook to remind you of the task again, you can postpone the reminder by selecting a delay time from the drop-down list at the bottom of the message box. (You cannot type a delay time in this box.) The list contains choices ranging from 5 minutes to a week. After you select a delay time, click the Postpone button.

If you postpone the reminder until after the task's due date and time (not a very useful thing to do), Outlook will display the Reminder message box nonetheless, with the word *Overdue* in the title bar.

> **NOTE**
>
> The Reminder message box is the only place where you can postpone a reminder, although you can change the reminder time in the task window.

Tracking the Progress of a Task

The tabs of the task window provide three boxes in which you can track the progress of a task: Status, Percent Complete (% Complete), and Actual Work.

Status

In the Status box on the Task tab, you can record the current status of a task by selecting one of these choices from the drop-down list:

- Not Started. Outlook assigns this description to all new tasks.

- In Progress. Select this description after you've started a task. If you set the Percent Complete box to a number other than 0, Outlook sets the Status box to In Progress (except when the current status is set to Waiting On Someone Else or Deferred—see below).

- Completed. Select this description when you finish the task. When you mark a task completed in one of the other ways available to you (see "Marking Tasks Completed," on page 281), Outlook sets the Status box to Completed.

- Waiting On Someone Else. If your task requires that someone else complete a prerequisite task before you can continue work on yours, select this description.

- Deferred. Select this description when you defer a task until a later time.

Percent Complete

SEE ALSO
For additional ways to mark a task completed, see "Marking Tasks Completed," on page 281.

In the Percent Complete box on the Task tab, you can record the percentage of the task that you've completed so far. You can use the scroll arrows to set 0%, 25%, 50%, 75%, or 100%, or you can type any number from 0 through 100.

Note the following points about the Percent Complete box:

- When you set the percentage to any number other than 0 or 100, Outlook changes the Status box setting from Not Started to In Progress. (If the Status box is set to Waiting On Someone Else or Deferred, changing the Percent Complete box doesn't change the Status box setting.)

■ If you set the percentage to 100%, Outlook changes the Status box setting to Completed. Likewise, if you set the Status box to Completed, Outlook sets the Percent Complete box to 100%.

■ If you reduce the percentage in the Percent Complete box to 0%, Outlook changes the Status box setting from In Progress to Not Started. (If the Status box is set to Waiting On Someone Else or Deferred, changing the Percent Complete box doesn't change the Status box setting.)

■ If you reduce the percentage in the Percent Complete box below 100%, Outlook changes the Status box setting from Completed to In Progress, Waiting On Someone Else, or Deferred, depending on what the Status box setting was before the task was set to 100% completed.

Actual Work

In the Actual Work box on the Status tab, you can record the number of hours that a task has taken so far. You can use this number to estimate the percentage of a task that has been completed. You can also use it to check the accuracy of your early estimates, by comparing it to the figure you entered in the Total Work box when you set up the task. (See "Setting Up a Task Estimate," on page 267.)

When you type the number of hours worked so far in the Actual Work box, Outlook converts that number to days or weeks. The conversion is based on the number of work hours per day and per week that you set as your standard on the Tasks/Notes tab of the Options dialog box (which you can display by choosing the Tools Options command).

> **NOTE**
>
> The number in the Actual Work box is not connected to the settings in the Status box or the Percent Complete box on the Task tab. You have to set the values in those boxes yourself.

Sending a Status Report

Whether you're working on a task that you set up yourself or a task that someone assigned to you, you might need to send periodic status reports. Sending a status report is a pretty simple matter.

To send a status report, take these steps:

1 Open the task whose status you're going to report.

2 Update the status of the task, ensuring that the information in the Subject, Priority, Due Date, Status, Percent Complete, Total Work, and Actual Work boxes of the task window is accurate. Outlook adds this information to the text of the status report message.

3 Choose the Task Send Status Report command, or click the Send Status Report button on the Standard toolbar.

4 You'll see a message window like the one shown here. Outlook has already supplied the status information and has filled in the information in the message header boxes.

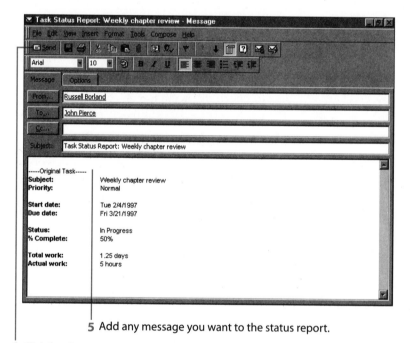

5 Add any message you want to the status report.

6 Click Send.

Sending an Automatic Status Report

If you have been assigned and have accepted a one-time (nonrecurring) task, Outlook automatically creates and sends a status report to the person who assigned the task when you mark the task completed.

For recurring tasks that have been assigned to you, Outlook sends an automatic status report only at the end of the series. For a series without an end date, Outlook does not send a status report.

 **TIP**

> To prevent Outlook from automatically sending a status report at the completion of an assigned task, turn off the Send Status Reports When Assigned Tasks Are Completed option on the Tasks/Notes tab of the Options dialog box (displayed when you choose the Tools Options command).

Marking Tasks Completed

When you've finished a task, you'll want to cross it off your task list by marking it completed. Marking a task completed draws a line through the task in the task list, removes the task from your list of active tasks, sets up the next task in a series, shuts off reminders for the task, and (for assigned tasks) sends a status report to the person who assigned the task to you.

To mark a task completed, use one of the following methods:

- In the task window, choose the Task Mark Complete command.

Mark Complete

- In the task window, click the Mark Complete button on the Standard toolbar.

- Select Completed in the Status box on the Task tab of the task window.

- Set the Percent Complete box on the Task tab of the task window to 100%.

- Set the Date Completed box on the Status tab of the task window to today or a date before today. Type the date, or click the down arrow beside the box to select a date from the calendar. (This method is especially useful if you actually finished the task earlier than the date you marked it completed. If you used another method to mark it completed on the later day, Outlook inserts that date in the Date Completed box. In this case, you'll want to reset the completion date to the actual date you finished the task.)

III

Scheduling Your Time and Tasks

- Click the Complete box in the TaskPad of the Calendar folder when it's in Day/Week/Month view. (See "TaskPad," on page 209.)

All these methods of marking a task completed affect the other places where task status is displayed. As you'll learn later in this chapter (see "Viewing Your Tasks," on page 284), Outlook gives you numerous ways to set up and view the task list in the Tasks folder window. In certain views, you can use these additional methods of marking a task completed:

- If you have selected Simple List view, click the Complete column in the Tasks folder window.

- If you have selected a view that displays the Status column in the Tasks folder window, click the task's entry in that column and select Completed from the list that appears.

- If you have selected a view that displays the Percent Complete column in the Tasks folder window, set the task's entry in that column to 100%.

- If you have selected a view that displays the Date Completed column in the Tasks folder window, set the task's entry in that column to today's date or to a date before today.

Recording Other Task Information

? SEE ALSO

For information about the Total Work and Actual Work boxes on the Status tab, see "Setting Up a Task Estimate," on page 267, and "Actual Work," on page 279.

In addition to task status and particulars, you might want to record other information about a task, such as mileage, billing information, contact names, or client and company names. You can record this information on the Status tab of the task window, shown in Figure 9-5.

On the Status tab, you can record valuable information that can help you perform your ongoing work, evaluate your efforts on this task, and plan for future tasks. For instance, you can type the number of miles you've logged for this task in the Mileage box. In the Billing Information box, enter any particulars about billing for this project. In the Contacts box, type the names of people you've contacted while carrying out the work, either as clients or as resources. Type the names of the companies for whom you are performing the task in the Companies box.

FIGURE 9-5.

The Status tab of a task window.

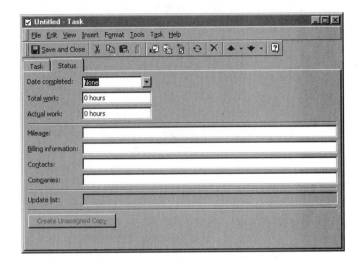

Canceling a Task

When you want to cancel a task, locate it in the Tasks folder window and select the task. Then use one of the following methods to delete it:

- Click the Delete button on the Standard toolbar.

- Press the Ctrl+D shortcut key.

- Choose the Edit Delete command.

- Right-click the task item, and then choose Delete from the shortcut menu.

- Open the task, and then click the Delete button on the Standard toolbar in the item window.

Outlook moves deleted tasks to the Deleted Items folder.

If you delete a recurring task, you see this message:

Click here if you want to delete all occurrences of the recurring task.

Click here if you want to delete only the current occurrence.

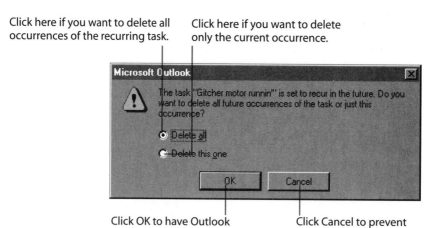

Click OK to have Outlook perform the deletion.

Click Cancel to prevent the deletion.

Viewing Your Tasks

Outlook provides several ways to view your tasks. Initially, Outlook displays the Tasks folder window in Simple List view. To select a different view, use one of these methods:

■ Open the drop-down list of views on the Standard toolbar, and select a view from the list.

■ Choose the View Current View command, and then select a view from the submenu.

SEE ALSO
You can also view tasks on the TaskPad in the Calendar folder. The TaskPad has its own set of views; for details, see "Selecting a TaskPad View," on page 220.

All of Outlook's built-in views for the Tasks folder (except the Task Timeline view) are table views. A table view displays task information in columns. (The number of columns varies with the view you select.) In two of the table views (By Category and By Person Responsible), the tasks are also grouped. The Task Timeline view shows tasks along a calendar. (You can find instructions for changing the format of both a table view and a timeline view in "Formatting Views," on page 509.)

In addition to Outlook's built-in views for tasks, you can set up your own views to look at folder contents in various ways. For information about views, see Chapter 18, "Setting Up Views." For details about grouping, sorting, and filtering items in a folder, see Chapter 17, "Columns, Categories, Grouping, Sorting, Filtering, and Custom Fields."

Simple List View

Simple List view shows all the tasks in your Tasks folder in a table that has four columns: the Icon column (in which different icons indicate the type of task—one-time, recurring, or assigned), the Complete column (in which a check mark indicates a completed task), the Subject column, and the Due Date column.

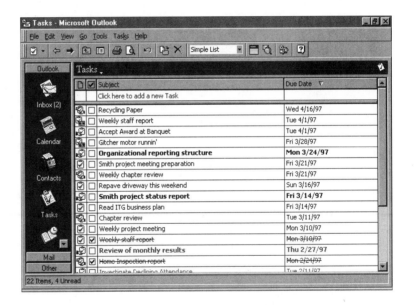

Detailed List View

Detailed List view (shown on the following page) displays all your tasks in a table with eight columns: Icon, Priority, Attachment, Subject, Status, Due Date, Percent Complete, and Categories.

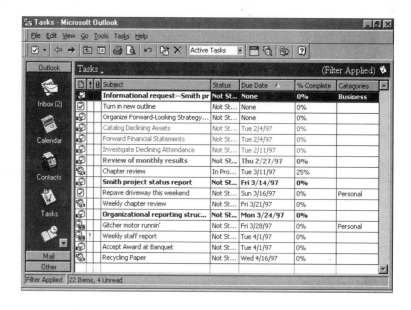

Active Tasks View

Active Tasks view lets you see all active tasks in your Tasks folder. In this view, tasks are ordered by due date by default. The tasks are listed in a table with the same eight columns used in Detailed List view. Completed tasks are not displayed.

Next Seven Days View

Next Seven Days view lists only the tasks that are due in the next seven days. The table's eight columns are the same as those found in Detailed List view. All tasks that are due later than seven days from today are not displayed.

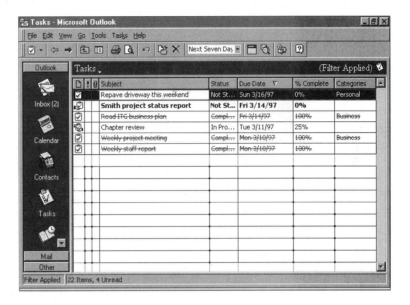

Overdue Tasks View

Overdue Tasks view (shown on the following page) displays only those tasks that are currently overdue. The table columns in this view are the standard eight used in Detailed List view. All completed tasks as well as tasks that are not overdue as of today are hidden.

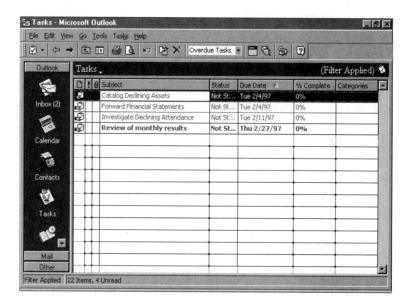

By Category View

If you assign your tasks to categories, you can view the tasks grouped by category. By Category view lists the tasks in a table with the eight columns of Detailed List view. The groups of tasks are separated by category headers. If you assign a task to more than one category, Outlook lists that task in each of the assigned category groups.

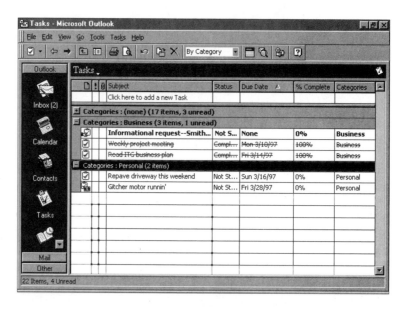

Assignment View

Assignment view shows only those tasks that you have assigned to someone else (tasks for which you sent a task request). The assigned tasks appear in a table with seven columns: Icon, Priority, Attachment, Subject, Owner (the person to whom you sent the task request), Due Date, and Status. Tasks are listed if the recipient of your task request has accepted the task or has not yet replied to your request.

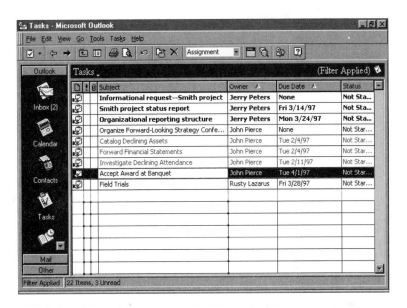

By Person Responsible View

By Person Responsible view (shown on the following page) displays all the tasks in your Tasks folder grouped according to who owns the tasks (you and those to whom you've assigned tasks). If you assigned a task to more than one person, the task appears in the group for each owner. This view shows tasks in a table with eight columns: Icon, Priority, Attachment, Subject, Requested By (for tasks that were assigned to you), Owner, Due Date, and Status. The groups are separated by headers indicating the name of each owner.

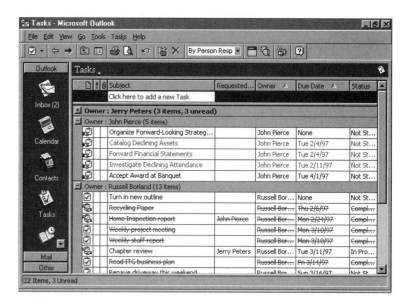

Completed Tasks View

Completed Tasks view displays only those tasks that you have completed. This view's table contains seven columns: Icon, Priority, Attachment, Subject, Due Date, Date Completed, and Categories. All active tasks (tasks that have not yet been completed) are hidden.

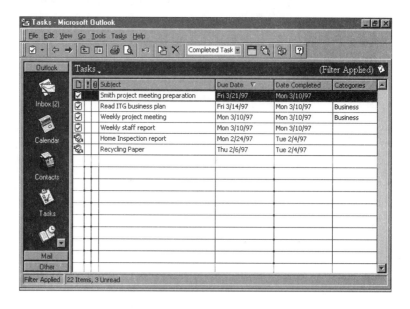

Task Timeline View

Task Timeline view arranges all the tasks in your Tasks folder on a timeline that shows the dates in a band across the top of the window. Tasks are listed below the dates. A task bar delineates the date range for each task.

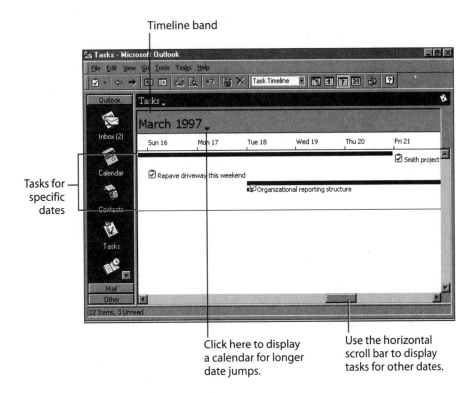

Timeline band

Tasks for specific dates

Click here to display a calendar for longer date jumps.

Use the horizontal scroll bar to display tasks for other dates.

You can change Task Timeline view in the following ways:

- Click the Day button on the Standard toolbar to see tasks for a single date, listed by the hour.

- Click the Week button on the Standard toolbar to see tasks for a single week, listed by the day.

- Click the Month button on the Standard toolbar to see tasks for a month, listed by the day of the year. When you're viewing tasks for a month, you see only task icons, not the subjects of the tasks. Place the mouse pointer on a task icon or on the bar marking the duration of the task to see the task subject pop up.

After you use Outlook for a while, you'll have task entries so far away from today's date that you can't easily or quickly scroll to them in Task Timeline view. When you want to jump to a date far away from today's date, you have two choices: clicking the down arrow beside the month name or choosing the Go To Date command from the Go menu.

To jump to a date within the current year, click the down arrow beside the month name in the Tasks folder window, and use the drop-down calendar:

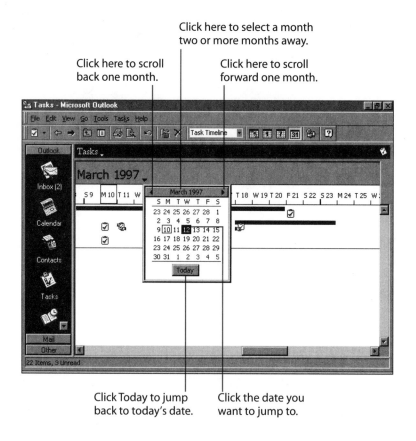

Click here to select a month two or more months away.

Click here to scroll back one month.

Click here to scroll forward one month.

Click Today to jump back to today's date.

Click the date you want to jump to.

To jump to any date, you can use the Go To Date command on the Go menu in the Tasks folder window. For detailed information about how to do this, see "Using the Go To Date Command," on page 214.

PART IV

Keeping Track of People and Things

CHAPTER 10

Contacts

I n Hollywood in particular, and in Los Angeles in general, people believe that their Filofax is their most valuable possession. (Well, at least that's what movies and television shows lead us to believe.) Most people who deal with other people keep some kind of list of names, addresses, phone numbers, and fax numbers. In some cases, this is a rotary file; in other cases, it's a box, a pouch of business cards, or an address book (the infamous "little black book"); and in still other cases, it's a calendar or a personal secretary or an electronic personal information device.

Microsoft Outlook 97 provides the Contacts folder, in which you can keep a list of your contacts, along with all the information you want to record about each one (or at least all the information you *have* about each one). You can see your contact list by clicking the Contacts folder on the Outlook Bar to open the folder. Once you've set it up, your list might look something like the one shown in Figure 10-1.

FIGURE 10-1.

A contact list in the Contacts folder window.

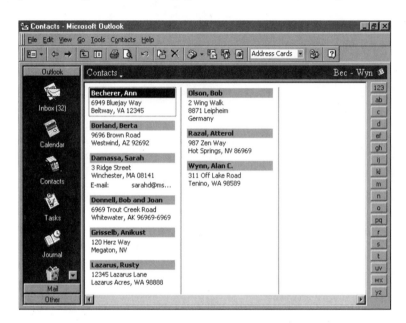

 **TIP**

You can set up your address books—which you use for sending messages in Outlook and for addressing letters and envelopes in Microsoft Word—to include your Contacts folder as an address book. For details, see the sidebar "Oh, No! The Show This Folder As An E-Mail Address Book Check Box Is Not Available!," on page 449.

Setting Up Your Contact List

The first task in compiling a useful list of contacts is to set up entries for the people with whom you work and socialize regularly. You can (and probably will want to) add information for all your friends and family members, too.

Using the Contact Window

To add a new entry to your contact list, use one of the following methods:

- Click the New Contact button on the Standard toolbar.

- Choose the Contacts New Contact command.

- Choose the File New command, and then choose Contact from the submenu.

- Press Ctrl+N.

Outlook opens the contact window, in which you supply the information for the new contact. Each of the four tabs in this window—the General tab, the Details tab, the Journal tab, and the All Fields tab—has a specific function, explained in the following sections.

When you've entered all the information, click the Save And Close button to close the contact window and add the new contact entry to your contact list. Notice, however, that all four tabs in this window contain a variation of the standard Save And Close button.

When you want to add several new contacts, click the Save And New button, which appears on the right, instead of Save And Close. Clicking Save And New saves the information you've just entered, adds the new entry to your contact list, and displays an empty contact window, ready for you to enter information for another new contact.

Adding a New Contact from a Different Folder

If you're working in an Outlook folder other than the Contacts folder when you need to set up a new contact entry, use one of the following methods to create the entry. Later you can change it as necessary.

- Click the down arrow beside the New button on the Standard toolbar, and then choose Contact from the menu.

- Choose the File New command, and then select Contact from the submenu.

- Press Ctrl+Shift+C for a new contact.

General Tab

On the General tab of the contact window, you can enter the name, address, phone numbers, and other basic information for a contact. In this section, we'll look at each option.

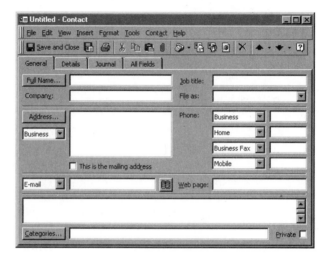

If you have a low-resolution display, be sure to maximize the contact window when you use the General tab. Because this tab doesn't have scroll bars, you might not be able to see the full extent of some of the boxes at a low resolution unless you maximize the window.

Full Name. Type the contact's name in this box. You can enter a contact's complete name—first, middle, and last—in the Full Name box (and include a title, such as Ms., or a suffix, such as Jr.). Outlook recognizes the distinct parts of the name (the name fields) and saves the information appropriately. Notice that the name you enter in the Full Name box appears by default in the File As box as well.

A field is a container for a specific type of information. In Outlook, for example, there are separate fields for a person's last name and first name. On a form, a field appears as a blank box that you fill in or in which you select a choice. In a table, a field is a column.

If you enter only part of a name—for example, only a contact's first name—and then press the Tab key (or if you click the Full Name button), Outlook displays the Check Full Name dialog box, which you can use to check whether Outlook has correctly recognized the name you entered or to enter the other parts of the contact's name.

1 Select a name prefix (Dr., Mr., Mrs., Miss, Ms., or Prof.), or type a name prefix (such as Herr, Frau, Monsieur, or Mademoiselle) if necessary.

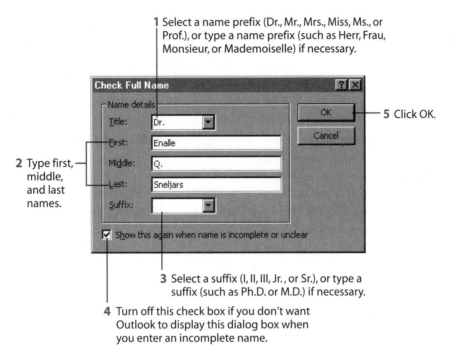

2 Type first, middle, and last names.

5 Click OK.

3 Select a suffix (I, II, III, Jr., or Sr.), or type a suffix (such as Ph.D. or M.D.) if necessary.

4 Turn off this check box if you don't want Outlook to display this dialog box when you enter an incomplete name.

File As. In the File As box, you can select or type the name that should appear as the title of the contact card. Outlook uses the entry in this box to sort the cards in Address Cards, Detailed Address Cards, and Phone List views. (See "Sorting Contacts," on page 323.)

Assuming that you have entered both an individual's name and a company name, the drop-down list in the File As box includes these selections:

■ Last name, First name

■ First name Last name

■ Company name

- Last name, First name (Company name)

- Company name (Last name, First name)

If you don't fill in a company name, the drop-down list provides only the first two selections. You can also type in a different title for the contact card if none of these selections is quite right.

 NOTE

> Company names that start with articles (A, An, or The) are displayed under the next word in the name. For example, "The Microsoft Network" is displayed as "Microsoft Network, The."

Address.   Click the down arrow below the Address button, and select the appropriate description of the address you want to enter (Home, Business, or Other) from the drop-down list. (You can't type your own description in this box.) Then type the address in the Address box, pressing the Enter key at the end of each line. To enter another address for this contact, select a different description from the drop-down list, and type the address in the now-blank Address box.

To designate one of several addresses as a contact's mailing address, select the address from the list to display it. Then turn on the check box labeled This Is The Mailing Address. (If you've entered only one address for a contact, Outlook considers it the mailing address.)

As with the parts of a name, Outlook stores contact addresses in separate fields—street, city, and so on. When you enter a complete address (street, city, state or province, zip or postal code, and country—if that's necessary), Outlook recognizes the pattern of the address and stores the information appropriately. If you enter only part of an address and press the Tab key, Outlook displays the Check Address dialog box, which you can use to complete and correct the address entry. You can also click the Address button to display the Check Address dialog box. Do this to check that Outlook has recognized the address correctly, or to enter the contact's address field by field.

IV

Keeping Track of People and Things

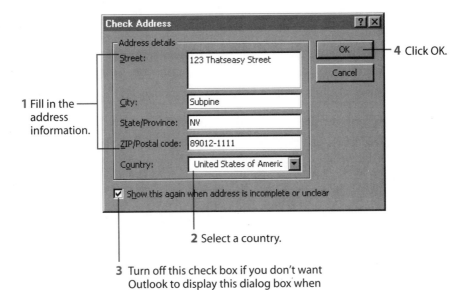

1 Fill in the address information.

2 Select a country.

3 Turn off this check box if you don't want Outlook to display this dialog box when you enter an incomplete address.

4 Click OK.

Phone.   You can record as many as four phone numbers for any one contact. For each number, click the down arrow in the first box, and select a description of the number from the drop-down list. (You can't type your own description, but the list is quite extensive and includes an Other category.) Then type the phone number in the second box. Repeat this process for each of the contact's phone numbers.

When entering phone numbers for a contact, use the following format for international phone numbers and for automatic phone dialing: + *country code (area code) local number.* If you don't enter the country code or area code for a phone number, Outlook adds that information using settings from the Dialing Properties dialog box (which you can open by choosing the Tools Options command, clicking the General tab, clicking the Dialing Options button, and then clicking Dialing Properties).

> **NOTE**

Outlook does not recognize letters in a phone number. You can, however, include notes after the phone number—for example, an extension for the contact.

E-Mail. You can enter as many as three e-mail addresses for your contact. If you want to enter only one e-mail address, simply type it in the empty box. To enter additional e-mail addresses, click the down arrow to select a designation for the address (E-Mail 2, E-Mail 3), and then type the address.

If you want to retrieve an e-mail address from one of your address books, click the Address Book button to the right of the box. Select the contact's name in the Select Name dialog box, and click OK.

Web Page. In this box, you can type the URL for a contact's site on the World Wide Web. Outlook uses this information when you want to visit the web page; see "Connecting to a Contact's Web Page," on page 314.

Notes. In the large unlabeled box near the bottom of the contact window, you can type any text, comments, or notes about the contact. Also, if you have entered dates for the contact's birthday and anniversary on the Details tab of the contact window (see "Details Tab," next), you'll see small calendar icons in the notes section of the General tab, representing the dates. When you double-click one of these icons, Outlook opens a calendar item window, setting up a recurring event for the birthday or anniversary on that date. Click the Save And Close button in that window to add the event to your Outlook calendar. (Later, when you set up a birthday party or an anniversary dinner, you can change the calendar item to a specific appointment; see "Changing the Type of Calendar Item," on page 242.)

Categories. You can assign a contact to any number of categories. Make up your own categories by typing them in the box, or click the Categories button to select from Outlook's list of categories—for example, Holiday Cards, Key Customer, Personal, Suppliers, or VIP. You can have Outlook display your contact list grouped according to the categories you've specified; for details, see "By Category View," on page 321.

Private. When you give others permission to view your Contacts folder, or when you assign a delegate who can perform actions on your behalf that involve using your Contacts folder (see "Delegates Tab," on page 76), you might prefer that these people not have access to all your contact information. If you want to designate a contact as private because the information is personal or otherwise sensitive or confidential in nature, turn on the Private check box.

Details Tab

To add details to a contact entry, fill out the Details tab of the contact window, shown here:

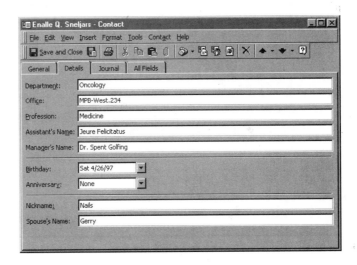

For birthday and anniversary information, you can either type a date in the box or click the down arrow to display a drop-down calendar from which you can select a date.

Journal Tab

SEE ALSO

For information about recording activities for contacts, see "Journal Tab," on page 67. For information about Outlook's journal feature, see Chapter 11.

On the Journal tab of the contact window, you can view the journal entries for the activities you perform with or for the contact—a log of your interactions with this contact, in other words. You might have journal entries for activities such as e-mail messages, faxes, meeting requests, phone calls, and letters.

Turn on this check box to
record journal entries for
activities with this contact.

Select the types of activities you want
to see in the list of journal entries.

Click AutoPreview to see
the beginning of each
listed journal entry.

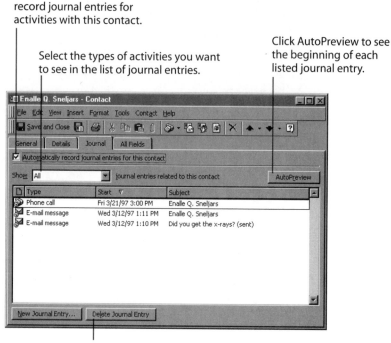

To remove a journal entry, select it
and click Delete Journal Entry.

You can create a journal entry manually by clicking the New Journal
Entry button, which opens a journal entry window. (See "Adding a
New Journal Entry by Hand," on page 327.) You can click a column
heading—Type, Start, or Subject—to quickly sort the list of journal
entries. Click a column heading a second time to change the sort
order—from ascending to descending (alphabetically) or vice versa.

All Fields Tab

The General tab and the Details tab provide a number of fields that
you can use to record information about a contact. However, Outlook
includes many other fields related to contacts that you might find
useful. You'll find these fields on the All Fields tab in the contact
window. You can use these fields to set up each contact entry to fit
the circumstances and traits of the individual contact.

IV

Keeping Track of People and Things

Select All Contact Fields to see
all the types of information
you can add for a contact.

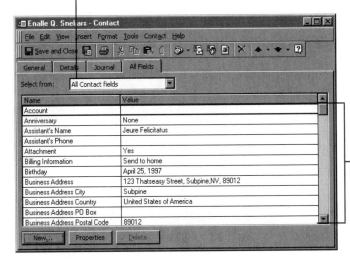

Add or change
information for
fields not shown
on other tabs.

If you find that among all the contact fields provided by Outlook, you
still can't find the field you need, you can use the New button on the All
Fields tab to create your own field. For information about using custom
fields in Outlook, see "Working in Your Own Fields," on page 489.

Adding Another Contact for a Listed Company

It's not uncommon to know more than one person who works for the same
company. Often, all of the people from one company share some of the same
contact information—address, business phone, fax. When you already have
one contact on your list from a particular organization, you can set up an
entry for another person in that organization as follows:

1 Click the card of the existing contact.

2 Choose the Contacts New Contact From Same Company command.

3 When the contact window appears, type the contact's name in the Full
Name box.

4 Add or change information for the contact on the tabs of the contact
window, as necessary.

5 Click the Save And Close button.

Changing Contact Information

To change information about a contact, use one of the following methods:

- Open the Contacts folder, and double-click the contact entry. In the contact window, click the appropriate tab (or tabs), update the information, and click Save And Close.

- On the contact's card in the Contacts folder window, simply click the information you want to change, and update it directly on the card. You can then press the Enter key to move to the next piece of information on the card, or you can click anywhere outside the card. When you change information directly on the card, Outlook updates the tabs of the contact window accordingly. (Keep in mind, however, that you cannot change every piece of information about a contact directly on the card. You cannot, for example, change a contact's name when editing on the card. To change a contact's name or other fields not available for editing on the contact card, open the contact window.)

Removing a Contact

To remove a contact from your list, open the Contacts folder and select the contact entry. Then click the Delete button on the Standard toolbar or choose the Edit Delete command.

Outlook moves the deleted contact entry to the Deleted Items folder.

Working with Your Contacts Folder

The Contacts folder is not simply a convenient place to keep a record of names and addresses. Outlook uses the information in the contact entries to help you carry out activities with your contacts, such as the following:

- Dialing a contact's telephone number
- Sending an e-mail message to a contact
- Sending a letter to a contact
- Connecting to a contact's World Wide Web page

- Setting up a meeting with a contact

- Setting up a task that you need to perform for a contact

Phoning a Contact

If you have a modem set up, you can use your computer to dial any of the telephone numbers listed on any folder item in Outlook. The Contacts folder offers an especially rich variety of ways to dial phone numbers from Outlook.

When you use Outlook to make a phone call, you must do so from the New Call dialog box. To open this dialog box, take one of the following actions:

- In any Outlook folder, choose the Tools Dial command, and select New Call from the submenu.

- In any Outlook folder, press Ctrl+Shift+D.

- If the currently selected folder item contains the phone number you want to call, choose the Tools Dial command, and click the phone number, which appears on the submenu:

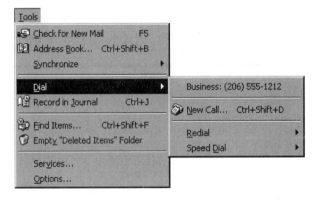

- In the Contacts folder, click the AutoDialer button.

- In the Contacts folder, click the down arrow beside the AutoDialer button to display the same submenu you see when you choose the Tools Dial command. Select New Call from the submenu (shown on the following page), or click the phone number you want to call if it appears.

- Right-click a contact card in the Contacts folder, and choose AutoDialer from the shortcut menu.

After you take any of these actions, Outlook opens the New Call dialog box, shown in Figure 10-2. If the action you took involved a specific phone number—for example, you selected a contact's card containing a phone number before you clicked the AutoDialer button or chose the Tools Dial command—the New Call dialog box will display the phone number (and the contact's name, if you are working in the Contacts folder). Otherwise, the dialog box will be empty, allowing you to type in the contact's name and the telephone number that you want Outlook to dial. This is handy if you don't yet have an entry recorded in your address books or Contacts folder for the person you want to call.

FIGURE 10-2.

The New Call dialog box.

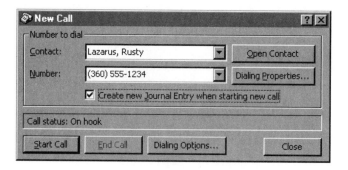

To place a telephone call from the New Call dialog box, follow these steps:

1 If the name of the person you want to call doesn't already appear in the Contact box, you can type it there. (Note, however, that including the name is optional.)

2 If the Number box is empty, type the phone number. If the box already contains a phone number but the contact has several numbers recorded in your address books or Contacts folder, click the down arrow in the Number box and select the appropriate phone number from the drop-down list.

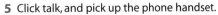

3 Click the Start Call button to have Outlook dial the number.

4 Outlook displays the Call Status dialog box:

5 Click talk, and pick up the phone handset.

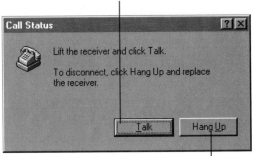

If the line is busy or the call isn't answered, click Hang Up to end the call, and then click Close in the New Call dialog box.

6 When you've finished your conversation, click the End Call button in the New Call dialog box, and then click the Close button.

If the name (or part of a name) that you type in the Contact box of the New Call dialog box is already recorded in one of your address books or in your Contacts folder, Outlook completes the name and fills in the phone number for you when you move the insertion point to the Number box.

SEE ALSO

For information about setting up dialing properties, see "Setting Dialing Options," on page 127 and "Calling Card Dialing," on page 186.

Notice the Open Contact button in the New Call dialog box. When this button is active, you can click it to review or change contact information in the contact window. You can also use the New Call dialog box to review or change information about the location you're dialing from, about how you dial from this location, or about your calling card. Click the Dialing Properties button to display the My Locations tab of the Dialing Properties dialog box.

Speed Dialing

Many modern telephones provide a memory system that allows you to store several telephone numbers that you call frequently. You can assign each number to a specific button and then call the number simply by pressing the button. In Outlook, you can store a great many frequently called numbers by using the Speed Dial feature.

To set up or change speed-dial entries, you need to open the Dialing Options dialog box. The most common way to find this dialog box is to open the New Call dialog box, as explained in the preceding section, and click the Dialing Options button. (Basically, any dialog box that displays a Dialing Options button can get you to the Dialing Options dialog box.)

If you haven't set up any speed-dial numbers, clicking None on the Speed Dial submenu opens the New Call dialog box, in which you can click the Dialing Options button to set up speed dialing.

To set up or change a speed-dial entry, take these steps in the Dialing Options dialog box:

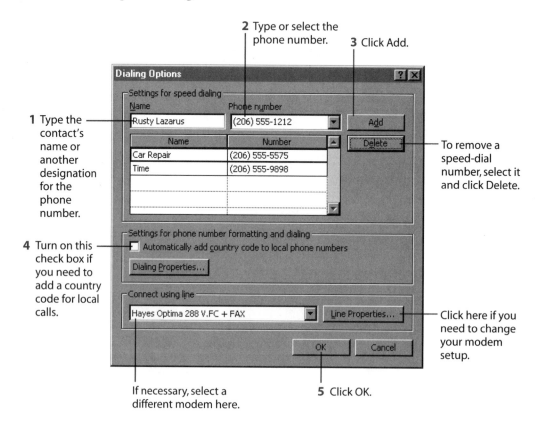

2 Type or select the phone number.

3 Click Add.

1 Type the contact's name or another designation for the phone number.

To remove a speed-dial number, select it and click Delete.

4 Turn on this check box if you need to add a country code for local calls.

Click here if you need to change your modem setup.

If necessary, select a different modem here.

5 Click OK.

If you type a name or part of a name that appears in one of your address books or your Contacts folder, Outlook automatically completes the entry for you. You can, of course, modify the results of the automatic completion. If the name you type has more than one telephone number (for example, a voice number or two and a fax number), you can select from the Phone Number list the number you want to set up for speed dialing.

At any time, you can return to the Dialing Options dialog box to change a speed-dial name or number. To change the name or number, simply click it, edit the entry, and click OK.

Redialing

Outlook keeps a list of recent phone numbers you've dialed from Outlook. When you want to redial a number you've called previously, take these steps:

1 Choose the Tools Dial command, or click the down arrow beside the AutoDialer button.

2 On the submenu, point to the Redial command. Then click the number on the Redial submenu that you want to dial again.

3 In the New Call dialog box, click the Start Call button to dial as usual.

⭐ **TIP**

> If you have not yet placed a call from Outlook, you can click None on the Redial submenu to open the New Call dialog box.

Recording a Call in a Journal Entry

Although Outlook's Journal folder can keep an automatic record of some of your activities with your contacts (see Chapter 11, "Journal," as well as "Journal Tab," on page 67 in Chapter 2, for more information), it does not include an option for automatically keeping track of phone calls. The New Call dialog box, however, does give you an option for recording telephone calls and for keeping notes of your conversation during the call.

In the New Call dialog box (see Figure 10-2, on page 308), turn on the check box labeled Create New Journal Entry When Starting New Call. Then, when you click the Start Call button, a journal entry window appears, as shown here:

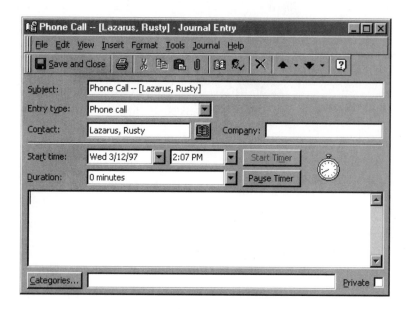

As Outlook dials the number, the window remains on your screen, and the timer immediately begins to time the call. If you don't want to time the call, click the Pause Timer button to stop the timing. (To resume timing, click Start Timer.) During the call, you can type notes, reminders, comments, and so on in the text area at the bottom of the dialog box. At the end of the call, click the Save And Close button to save the record of the call in your Journal folder.

Sending an E-Mail Message to a Contact

Here's an easy way to quickly set up and send a message to a contact:

1   Click the contact's entry in your contact list.

2   Choose the Contacts New Message To Contact command. Outlook opens a new message window and addresses the message to your contact.

5 Make any necessary changes to the message setup.

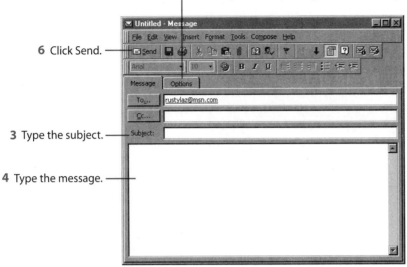

6 Click Send.

3 Type the subject.

4 Type the message.

And here's an even easier way to send a message to a contact:

1 Click the contact's card, and drag it onto the Inbox icon on the Outlook Bar.

2 When a message window appears (addressed to the contact), type the subject of the message in the Subject box, and then type the message.

3 Click the Send button.

Sending a Letter to a Contact

As you work with a contact, you'll no doubt need to send him or her a paper letter from time to time. You can easily set up and print a paper letter from an entry in your Contacts folder.

 NOTE

To create a letter from your Contacts folder, you must have Microsoft Word 97 installed on your computer.

When you select the contact's entry in your Contacts folder and choose the Contacts New Letter To Contact command, Outlook calls on Microsoft Word 97. Word starts up, and Word's Letter Wizard opens. You can then work through the Letter Wizard to create the letter, and you can print both the letter and an envelope in Word. When you've finished, exit Word if you don't need it for other purposes.

Connecting to a Contact's Web Page

If you entered a contact's World Wide Web page address (URL) in the contact window, you can use that URL to quickly connect to the contact's web page. To do so, switch to your Contacts folder, select the contact entry, and then use one of the following methods:

- Choose the Contacts Explore Web Page command.

- Click the Explore Web Page button on the Standard toolbar.

- Press Ctrl+Shift+X.

Setting Up a Meeting with a Contact

When you need to set up a meeting with a contact, you can do so from the contact's entry in your Contacts folder. Simply open your Contacts folder, select the contact's entry, and take one of the following actions:

- Choose the Contacts New Meeting With Contact command.

- Choose the Contacts Plan A Meeting command.

- Press Ctrl+Shift+G.

With the first and third methods, Outlook displays a meeting request window. With the second method, Outlook displays the Plan A Meeting dialog box. For more information, see "Planning a Meeting," on page 234.

Setting Up a Task for a Contact

When you have a task to perform for or on behalf of a contact, you can use the contact's entry in your Contacts folder as the starting point for setting up the task.

When you open your Contacts folder, select the contact's entry, and choose the Contacts New Task For Contact command, Outlook opens a task window, like the one shown on the facing page.

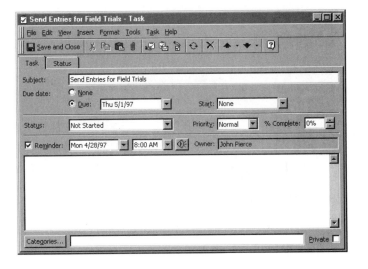

SEE ALSO

For complete information about setting up tasks and working on them, see Chapter 9.

You can fill in the subject of the task and as much other information as you need, on both the Task and Status tabs. Outlook fills in the Contacts box on the Status tab with the name of the contact you selected. When you've finished, click the Save And Close button to add the task to the task list in your Tasks folder.

Sending Contact Information to Others

People change positions—as a result of promotions, retirements, resignations, or lateral moves. When you change your position within your organization, you might need to turn over at least some of your contacts to your replacement. It's easy to do this in Outlook: you simply forward the contacts to your replacement.

To send contact information to someone else, take these steps:

1 Open the Contacts folder, and select the contact entry you want to provide to someone else. To select more than one contact entry, hold down the Ctrl key as you click each entry. To select several consecutive entries, click the first entry, and then hold down the Shift key while you click the last one. To select all the contacts, choose the Edit Select All command or press Ctrl+A.

2 Choose the Contacts Forward command. Outlook opens a message window. The message area contains an icon representing the contact information, as shown on the following page.

3 Fill in the To box.

4 Type any message you want to send with the contact information.

5 Click Send.

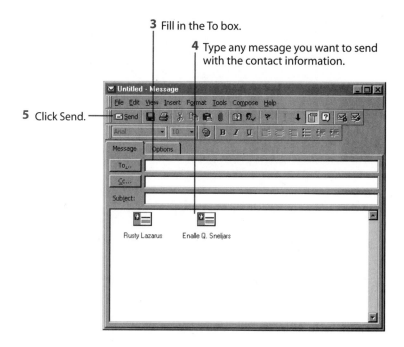

When the recipient receives the message with the contact icons, he or she can select the contact icon in the message area and drag it to the Contacts folder icon on the Outlook Bar to add the contact information to the contact list.

Viewing Your Contacts

SEE ALSO

You can set up custom views for looking at folder contents; for information, see Chapter 18. You can also group, sort, filter, and add custom fields to folder items; for details, see Chapter 17.

Outlook gives you six standard views of your contacts. The following sections explain each view. A drop-down list box on the Standard toolbar displays the name of the current view; initially, you're likely to be in Address Cards view. To switch from one view to another, use one of these methods:

- On the Standard toolbar, click the down arrow to display the drop-down list of views and then select the view you want from the list.

- Choose the View Current View command, and then select the view you want from the submenu.

IV

Card Views of the Contacts Folder

In two views of the Contacts folder—Address Cards view and Detailed Address Cards view—Outlook displays the contact information in a "card" format, almost as if you were looking at rotary file cards laid out on a desk.

The cards are arranged alphabetically by the first word in the card title. You can move to a specific alphabetical section of your contact list by clicking the corresponding alphabetical tab along the right side of the folder window, just as you might use tabs to thumb to various sections of a paper address book.

 TIP

> If some items on a contact card are incomplete and end with an ellipsis (...), you can widen the card to see the complete information. When you place the mouse pointer on the vertical dividing line in the folder window, the pointer becomes a double vertical line with a two-headed arrow. Drag the line to widen the card until you can see all the information you need.

If you left a box blank on the General tab of the contact window when you entered information about the contact—that is, you entered no data in that field—Address Cards view and Detailed Address Cards view do not initially include that field in their display. (If you want to see all the fields that a contact card can display in these two views, turn on the Show Empty Fields check box in the Format Card View dialog box. For details, see "Card Views," on page 516.)

Address Cards View

Address Cards view displays your contacts as small cards that contain some of the basic information from the General tab of the contact window, such as the contact's name, address, phone numbers, and e-mail address. Because the cards are small, Outlook can display a number of them on your screen at one time. This view helps you scroll quickly through a section of your contact list when you are looking for an entry. The illustration on the following page shows an example of Address Cards view.

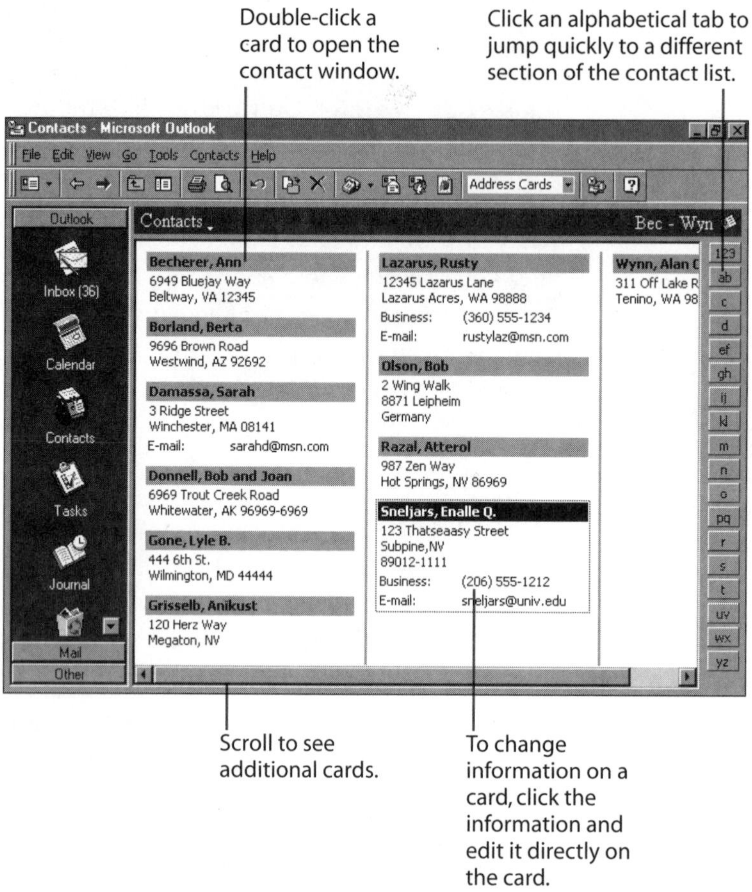

Double-click a
card to open the
contact window.

Click an alphabetical tab to
jump quickly to a different
section of the contact list.

Scroll to see
additional cards.

To change
information on a
card, click the
information and
edit it directly on
the card.

Detailed Address Cards View

When you need to see more of the information from the General tab
of the contact window, use Detailed Address Cards view. Because the
cards are larger and contain more data in this view, you'll see fewer
of them on the screen than you would see in Address Cards view, as
illustrated on the facing page.

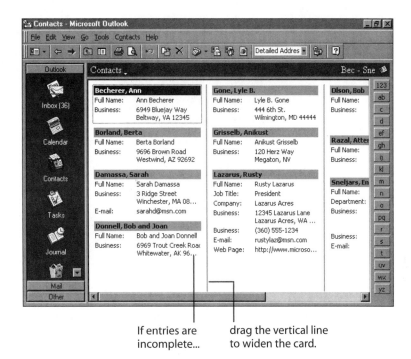

If entries are incomplete...

drag the vertical line to widen the card.

Table Views of the Contacts Folder

? SEE ALSO

You can change the format of a view. For details about formatting table views, see "Formatting Views," on page 509.

The card views of the Contacts folder display your contact list succinctly and attractively, but the cards take up a lot of space in the window. To see more contacts at one time, and to sort the list in different ways, switch to one of the table views of the Contacts folder: Phone List view, By Category view, By Company view, or By Location view.

These views display your contact information in a table arrangement. The names are listed down the left side of the screen, and various pieces of information (depending on the view) appear in columns to the right. You'll usually need to scroll horizontally to see all the columns.

Icons in Contact Lists

In the various table views of your contacts list, you'll see several icons that act as column headings or that indicate information about the contact entry. The following table explains the meaning of each icon.

Icon	Meaning
🗋	This icon appears at the top of the column that shows the item type.
📎	This icon appears at the top of the column that indicates whether the item has an attachment.
📇	This icon indicates that the item is a contact.
📇	This icon indicates that Outlook will automatically record interactions with this contact in the Journal folder.
📎	This icon indicates that this contact entry has an attachment.
✖	This icon indicates that a conflict exists with the contact information in the offline folder for this contact.

Phone List View

In Phone List view, you see a simple tabular list of your contacts, with columns for Full Name, Company, File As (the title of a contact card), and numerous telephone and fax numbers. You'll also find a Categories column listing the categories to which you've assigned the contact, and a Journal column, where a check mark indicates that you've chosen to record interactions with this contact in your Journal folder. Like the card views, Phone List view alphabetizes your contact list by the title you entered in the File As box on the General tab of the contact window.

Your Contacts folder in Phone List view will be similar to the illustration on the following page.

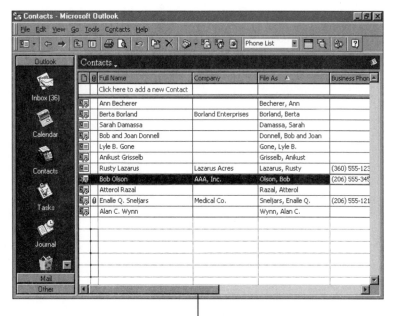

Scroll to see more columns.

By Category View

If you assign contacts to categories, you can see your contact list grouped by category. If you assign a contact to more than one category, Outlook lists that contact in each category. An example of By Category view is shown here:

This heading designates contacts that have not been assigned a category.

Click the minus sign to hide the contacts for a category.

Click the plus sign to display the contacts for a category.

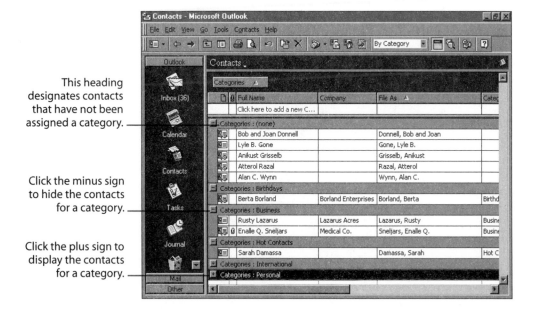

By Company View

Because you might have several contacts at a single company, you might find it handy to view your contacts grouped by company name. This way, you can quickly find the contact you need for a particular company. Here's an example of a Contacts folder in By Company view:

Click the minus sign to hide the contacts for a company.

This heading designates contacts that are not listed with a specific company.

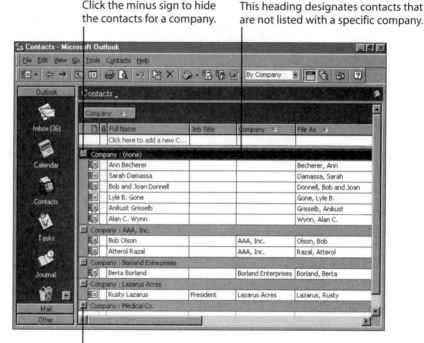

Click the plus sign to display the contacts for a company.

By Location View

Many organizations now conduct business internationally. If your Contacts folder lists contacts in a variety of countries, you might find that using By Location view (shown on the facing page) is a quick way to locate a contact in a specific country. (In this view, the term "location" refers to a country rather than to a city, state, province, or region.)

In By Location view, your contact list might look something like this:

Click the plus sign to display
the contacts for a country.

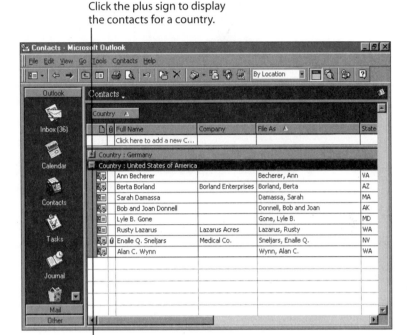

Click the minus sign to hide
the contacts for a country.

Sorting Contacts

SEE ALSO

In the table views of the Contacts folder (except Phone List view), Outlook sorts the entries alphabetically by the Full Name entry. For details about sorting in table views, see "Sorting," on page 468.

In the card views of the Contacts folder and in Phone List view, contacts are sorted alphabetically by the text that appears in the File As box on the General tab of the contact window. To change the order in which the contacts appear, you have to change the File As information in the contact window. To do so, take these steps:

1 Double-click the contact card to open the contact window.

3 Click Save And Close.

2 Select or type a new entry for the sorting order.

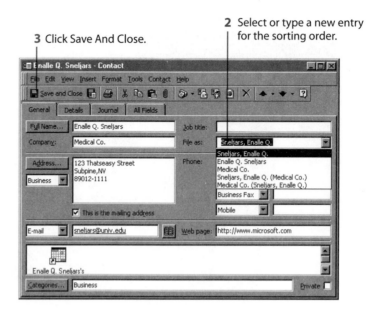

4 Repeat steps 1 through 3 for each card that should appear at a different place in the alphabetical order.

Journal

Remembering everything you've done during a day can be difficult. You probably remember the big events pretty easily—especially if they were very pleasant or very unpleasant. But can you honestly remember every e-mail message you sent, every appointment you made, every document you worked on, every note you took, every person you contacted? I can't, and I'm not *that* unusual (or so I believe).

Microsoft Outlook 97 can keep a journal of Outlook activities such as e-mail messages, task and meeting requests, and task and meeting responses as well as your work with any Microsoft Office 97 document. In the Journal folder, you can direct Outlook to insert journal entries for your interactions with selected contacts automatically. The journal entry identifies the action and records the date and time you performed it.

By assigning each journal entry to a category, you can then group the entries by category so that you can review the actions you've taken for an individual project or task. At the end of the day, the end of the week, the end of the month, or the end of a performance review period, you can review the work you've done and more readily compile a list of activities and accomplishments.

In addition to having Outlook record activities, you can manually add journal entries for activities that you've already performed and for activities that Outlook cannot record automatically. You can even add entries that act as shortcuts to files on your hard disk or to files on another computer on your network so that you can open those files from your Journal folder.

Recording Events in Your Journal

Outlook is initially set up to record a journal entry each time you create, open, close, or save a file in an Office 97 application (Microsoft Access, Microsoft Excel, Microsoft Office Binder, Microsoft PowerPoint, or Microsoft Word). Outlook creates a shortcut to the Office 97 file in the journal entry, even if Outlook isn't running. You can also record Outlook activities in your Journal folder.

To begin setting up your Journal folder, open the folder, and choose the Tools Options command to display the Journal tab of the Options dialog box, shown in Figure 11-1, on the facing page.

? SEE ALSO
You can have Outlook record journal entries for selected activities for any contact in your Contacts folder. See "Journal Tab," on page 303.

The For These Contacts box on the Journal tab includes only the names listed in your Contacts folder. If you haven't set up any contact entries, this box is empty. If a name you want to select is not listed, click OK to close the Options dialog box, add the new contact to the Contacts folder, and then reopen the Journal tab of the Options dialog box, where the name now appears on the list.

For details about double-clicking a journal entry and the specific settings on the Journal tab, see "Changing the Double-Click Action," on page 332. On the Journal tab, you'll also see a button called AutoArchive Journal Entries; for information about the AutoArchive feature, see Chapter 15.

FIGURE 11-1.

The Journal tab of the Options dialog box.

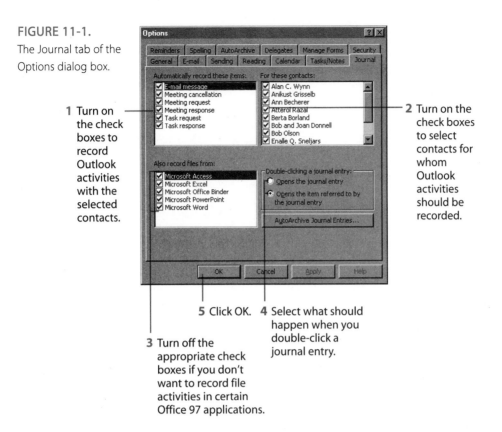

1 Turn on the check boxes to record Outlook activities with the selected contacts.

2 Turn on the check boxes to select contacts for whom Outlook activities should be recorded.

5 Click OK.

4 Select what should happen when you double-click a journal entry.

3 Turn off the appropriate check boxes if you don't want to record file activities in certain Office 97 applications.

Adding Entries to Your Journal

In addition to journal entries for Office 97 application activities, e-mail messages, task and meeting requests, and task and meeting responses, you might also want to record journal entries for appointments and notes, for phone calls, for Office 97 files and documents that you haven't opened, or for files and documents you create with applications that aren't part of Office 97. In these cases, you can add journal entries manually.

Adding a New Journal Entry by Hand

You can add any type of journal entry by hand. Doing so does not create a related Outlook item, but you can copy the journal entry to the proper Outlook folder to create an item. For example, if you manually add a journal entry concerning a task, Outlook doesn't automatically create a new task item in your Tasks folder. But if you copy the journal entry to the Tasks folder, Outlook opens a new task window for the item, where you can set up the task and add it to your task list. (For more information, see "Moving and Copying Folder Items," on page 358).

To add a new journal entry by hand, you need to open a new journal entry window. After you've opened the Journal folder, you can use any of the following methods to open the window:

- Choose the Journal New Journal Entry command.

- Choose the File New command, and then select Journal Entry from the submenu.

- Click the New Journal button on the Standard toolbar.

- Click the down arrow beside the New Journal button, and choose Journal Entry from the menu.

- Press Ctrl+N.

In the new journal entry window, follow these steps:

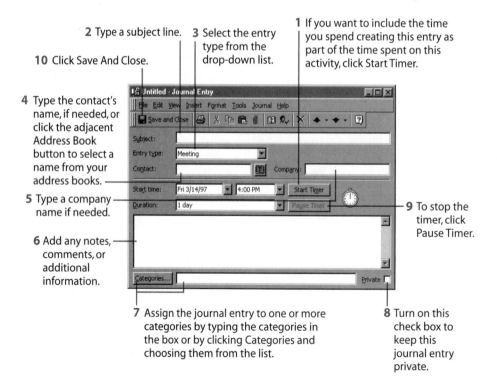

2 Type a subject line.

3 Select the entry type from the drop-down list.

1 If you want to include the time you spend creating this entry as part of the time spent on this activity, click Start Timer.

10 Click Save And Close.

4 Type the contact's name, if needed, or click the adjacent Address Book button to select a name from your address books.

5 Type a company name if needed.

6 Add any notes, comments, or additional information.

9 To stop the timer, click Pause Timer.

7 Assign the journal entry to one or more categories by typing the categories in the box or by clicking Categories and choosing them from the list.

8 Turn on this check box to keep this journal entry private.

> **Adding a New Journal Entry from a Different Folder**
>
> If you're working in an Outlook folder other than the Journal folder when you need to set up a new journal entry, use one of these methods to open the new journal entry window:
>
> ■ Click the down arrow beside the New button on the Standard toolbar, and then choose Journal Entry from the menu.
>
> ■ Choose the File New command, and then select Journal Entry from the submenu.
>
> ■ Press Ctrl+Shift+J.

Using the Timer

A journal entry's timer can give you a record of how much time you spend on activities such as completing a task, making a phone call, or meeting with a contact. To use the timer, simply open the journal entry window, and click the Start Timer button. As you work, leave the journal entry window open. (Minimize the window if you need to see more of the screen.) You can pause the timer so that you're not recording "empty time," such as answering a phone call or being interrupted by a visit that isn't related to the matter at hand.

When you finish the activity, click the Save And Close button in the journal entry window. Outlook stops the timer for you.

Adding Existing Outlook Items to Your Journal

When you've worked on a task, held a meeting, or e-mailed a contact, for example, and have not recorded a journal entry for the activity, you might want to add an entry afterward. Here's how to add a journal entry for an existing Outlook item:

1 Open the Outlook folder containing the item for which you want to add a journal entry.

2 Select the item.

3 Drag the selected item to the Journal folder icon on the Outlook Bar.

4 Outlook opens a journal entry window for the item, as shown. You can add or change information for the entry as needed. Outlook sets the entry type on the basis of the type of item you added. For example, if you add a contact to your journal, Outlook sets the entry type to Phone Call. If necessary, you can select a more accurate description from the Entry Type drop-down list.

5 Click Save And Close. ──

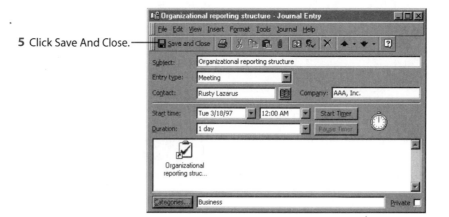

When you add an existing Outlook item to your journal, the icon that appears in the lower portion of the journal entry window (a contact card, a small calendar, a task checklist, or an envelope, for example) represents the Outlook activity or document. If you double-click the icon, Outlook opens the window in which you set up the item—the contact window, the calendar item window, the task window, or the message window, for instance—allowing you to review details about the item or make any necessary changes.

Adding Existing Documents to Your Journal

You've probably already created documents and files in other applications that you might want to add to your Journal folder. Adding existing files and documents to your journal allows you to organize a list of entries that all relate to a single project or task. Also, a journal entry makes it possible for you to open the file or document from Outlook rather than searching with other tools—such as the Windows Explorer or My Computer.

To add a journal entry for an existing file or document from another application, take these steps:

1 Open the My Computer window or Windows Explorer.

2 Open the folder containing the file or document you want to add as a journal entry, and select the file or document.

3 Arrange the My Computer or Explorer window and the Outlook window so that you can see both windows on screen at the same time.

4 Drag the selected file or document to the Journal folder icon on the Outlook Bar.

5 Outlook opens a journal entry window for the file or document. A shortcut icon for the file or document appears in the message area of the window, and the name of the file or document appears in the Subject box. You can change the entry name or the entry type and add other information that you want to record with the journal entry.

6 Click the Save And Close button.

 TIP

You can also open disk file folders from the Outlook Bar. For details, see "Opening a Folder from the Outlook Bar," on page 426.

Opening and Changing Journal Entries

To open a journal entry to see its details, perform one of the following actions in the Journal folder:

■ Right-click the entry, and then select Open from the shortcut menu.

■ Double-click the entry.

■ Select the entry, and then choose the File Open command.

■ Select the entry, and then press Ctrl+O.

When you open a journal entry, you'll see a window like the one shown here:

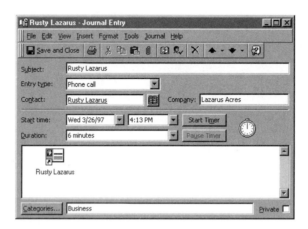

In this window, you can review, add, or change information. If you make additions or changes, be sure to click the Save And Close button when you want to close the window.

Changing the Double-Click Action

By default, Outlook opens the journal entry window when you double-click an entry in the Journal folder window. But, if you prefer, you can change this behavior and instead have Outlook open the item referred to by the journal entry—that is, you could double-click a journal entry for a meeting and have Outlook open the calendar item window for the meeting rather than the journal entry window.

As you saw in Figure 11-1, on page 327, the Journal tab of the Options dialog box contains a section labeled Double-Clicking A Journal Entry. If you want to open the journal entry window when you double-click a journal entry, keep the Opens The Journal Entry option turned on. If you'd rather open the item associated with the journal entry when you double-click the entry, select the option Opens The Item Referred To By The Journal Entry.

IV

Keeping Track of People and Things

This setting affects not only the double-click action but also the following actions:

- Choosing the File Open command

- Right-clicking the journal entry and choosing Open from the shortcut menu

- Pressing Ctrl+O

In other words, if you set a double-click action to open the related item rather than the journal entry, these three actions will also result in opening the related item rather than the journal entry.

 TIP

If you set the double-click action to open the related item rather than the journal entry, you can open the journal entry by right-clicking it and choosing Open Journal Entry from the shortcut menu. If there is no related item for a particular entry (it's a simple journal entry), double-clicking opens the journal entry, regardless of the setting on the Journal tab.

Opening Other Items from Journal Entries

You can use a journal entry to open the file or document associated with the journal entry. For example, if you have a journal entry for a Microsoft Excel worksheet, you can both start Excel and open the worksheet from that entry. How you do this can be affected by the option you set in the Double-Clicking A Journal Entry area on the Journal tab of the Options dialog box. The following list describes the three ways you can open the journal entry item. (See the preceding section, "Changing the Double-Click Action." Also see Figure 11-1, on page 327.)

- If you set double-clicking to open the item referred to by a journal entry, simply double-click the journal entry to open the associated item.

- Right-click the journal entry, and choose Open Item Referred To from the shortcut menu.

- Open the journal entry, and double-click the shortcut for the associated item, which appears in the lower portion of the journal entry window (in the Notes section).

Removing a Journal Entry

You can archive journal entries before deleting them. For details, see Chapter 15.

When you no longer want or need a journal entry, you can remove it from your Journal folder. To remove a journal entry, simply open the Journal folder, select the entry you want to remove, and click the Delete button on the Standard toolbar. Deleting a journal entry does not affect any associated file, document, or Outlook item.

When you delete a journal entry, Outlook moves the entry to the Deleted Items folder. To permanently delete the journal entry from Outlook, you have to empty the Deleted Items folder by choosing the Tools Empty "Deleted Items" Folder command.

Viewing Journal Entries

For details about formatting views or setting up custom views, See Chapter 18. For details about grouping journal entries as well as specifying sorting procedures, setting up special filters, and adding custom fields, see Chapter 17.

Outlook provides several ways to view a listing of your journal entries. The next several sections explain each view.

To switch to a different view, use one of the following methods:

- On the Standard toolbar, click the down arrow in the Current View list box to display the drop-down list of views and then select a view from the list.

- Choose the View Current View command, and then select the view you want from the submenu.

By Type View

The first time you look into your Journal folder, you'll see journal entries listed in By Type view, as shown on the facing page.

Click the minus sign to hide the journal entries for a category.

Click here to display a calendar for longer date jumps.

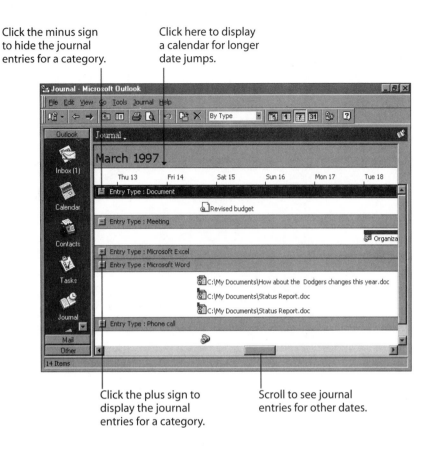

Click the plus sign to display the journal entries for a category.

Scroll to see journal entries for other dates.

When you've used Outlook for a while, your journal entries might range over a long period of time, and you won't be able to scroll to them easily or quickly. Also, you might want to create a journal entry for activities that took place before you started using Outlook. When you want to jump to a date far away from today's date, you can either click the down arrow beside the month name or choose the Go To Date command from the Go menu.

? SEE ALSO

For information about timeline views, see "Timeline Views," on page 512.

To jump to a date within a few months of the current date, click the down arrow beside the month name in the Journal folder window, and use the drop-down calendar, shown in the illustration on the following page.

Click here to scroll
back by month.

Click the date you want to jump to.

Click here to scroll
forward by month.

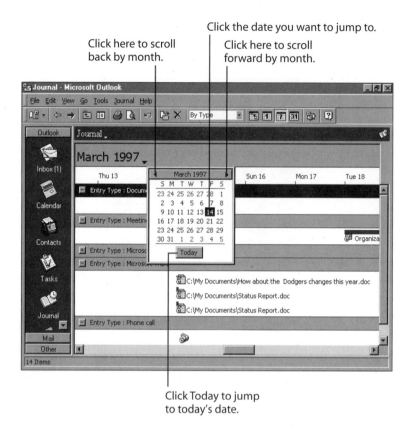

Click Today to jump
to today's date.

To jump to any date, use the Go To Date command on the Go menu in the Journal folder window. For detailed information about how to do this, see "Using the Go To Date Command," on page 214.

By Contact View

If you include contacts in your journal entries, you can see the entries listed by contact. If you assign more than one contact to a journal entry, Outlook lists that journal entry under each contact name. An example of a Journal folder window in By Contact view is shown on the facing page.

IV

Keeping Track of People and Things

Click the plus sign to display the journal entries for a contact.

This heading contains journal entries without a contact.

Click here to display a calendar for longer date jumps.

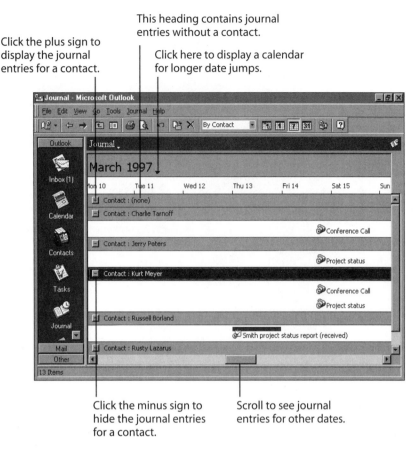

Click the minus sign to hide the journal entries for a contact.

Scroll to see journal entries for other dates.

By Category View

When you assign your journal entries to categories, you can see the entries listed by category. If you assign a journal entry to more than one category, Outlook lists that entry in each category. Your Journal folder window in By Category view will be similar to the illustration on the following page.

1 Click the plus sign to display the journal entries for a category.

4 Click here to display a calendar for longer date jumps.

3 This heading contains journal entries that have not been assigned to a category.

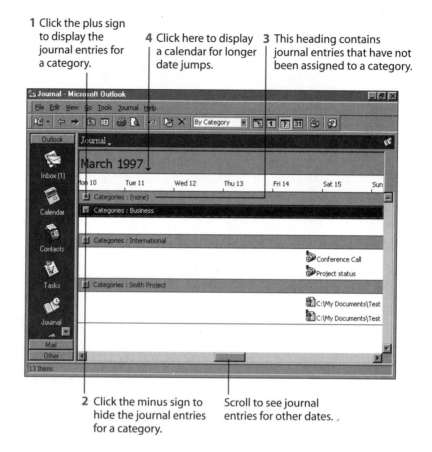

2 Click the minus sign to hide the journal entries for a category.

Scroll to see journal entries for other dates.

Entry List View

The views that display entries on a time scale are useful in their own way, but when you are using one of these views, you can't see all the information Outlook can display for a journal entry unless you open the entry window. To display more information about all your journal entries at one time, switch to Entry List view. In this view, your journal entries are listed in a table arrangement, with columns for the following items: icons for entry types, attachments, descriptions of the entry types, subjects, start dates and times, times spent so far on the journal entries (duration), contact names for each entry, and categories to which each entry has been assigned. On the facing page, you'll see a typical Journal folder displayed in Entry List view.

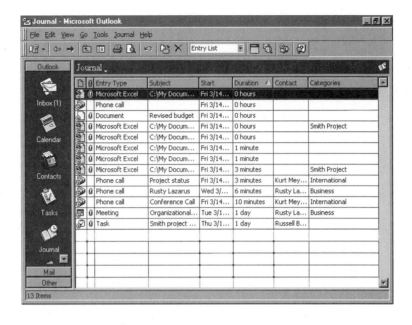

? SEE ALSO

For details about changing the columns you see in Entry List view, see "Setting Up Columns," on page 454. You can group your journal entries by some of the columns you set up in Entry List view; for details, see "Grouping," on page 465.

Journal entries are initially sorted with the most recent start date and time at the top of the list and the oldest start date and time at the bottom of the list. To sort the journal entries a different way in Entry List view, click the column heading for the column you want to use to sort the journal entries. The first click sorts either alphabetically (A–Z) or newest to oldest. A second click sorts either reverse alphabetically (Z–A) or oldest to newest. You can sort the list of journal entries in the following ways:

- Oldest start date and time at the top of the list and most recent start date and time at the bottom of the list

- Alphabetically or reverse alphabetically by Entry Type. (These sortings also apply if you sort by the entry type icon.)

- Entries with attachments alphabetically at the top of the list and without attachments alphabetically at the bottom of the list

- Entries without attachments alphabetically at the top of the list and entries with attachments alphabetically at the bottom of the list

- Alphabetically or reverse alphabetically by subject

- Longest duration at the top and shortest duration at the bottom

- Shortest duration at the top and longest duration at the bottom

SEE ALSO

If you choose the *same* view a second time, the Save View Settings dialog box offers different options. For details, see Chapter 18.

NOTE

If Outlook displays the Save View Settings dialog box when you switch to another view, you have three choices: you can discard the current view settings, save the current view settings with a name you give the view, or revise the current view with the changes you've made to the view. For more information about views and this dialog box, see "Defining a View," on page 502.

> You cannot sort journal entries by category or by contact in Entry List view. To sort your journal entries by category or contact, choose By Category view or By Contact view.

Last Seven Days View

Over time you'll collect a lot of journal entries. Even though you might be conscientious about deleting old journal entries that you no longer need, you'll undoubtedly keep some entries around for a very long time. In your daily work, however, you might find that you are interested only in the recent past. That's where Last Seven Days view can help out. In this view, Outlook displays your journal entries for the past seven days only, in a table arrangement similar to Entry List view:

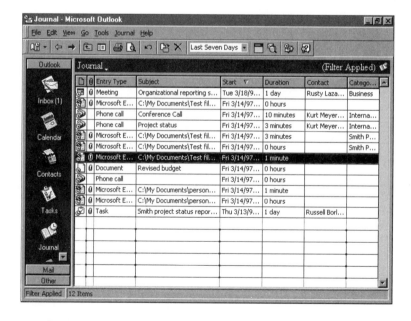

You can sort the entries in all the same ways you can sort in Entry List view; see "Entry List View," on page 338.

Phone Calls View

When you select Phone Calls view, Outlook displays only those journal entries for phone calls you made from the Contacts folder and journal entries you've created yourself by adding a contact to your journal. Phone Calls view displays journal entries as shown here:

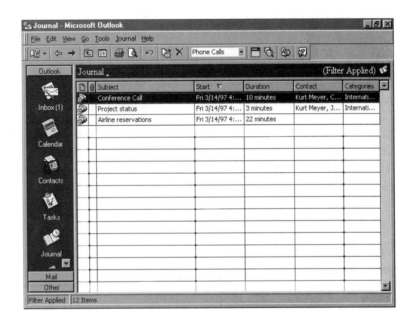

You can sort the entries in all the same ways you can sort in Entry List view; see "Entry List View," on page 338.

CHAPTER 12

Notes

Taking notes, posting notes, sticking notes on everything—from writing notes to classmates in school, notes to ourselves, and notes to family and roommates, to taking notes in meetings—jotting down points that we want to remember or communicate to others seems to be one of the major jobs we do just about every day.

Microsoft Outlook 97 comes with a folder for notes—a place where you can type notes and keep track of them. You can even print your notes (explained in Chapter 14), and you can forward a note to anyone with an e-mail address.

Adding a Note

To create a new note, open the Notes folder, and use one of the following methods:

- Click the New Note button on the Standard toolbar.

- Choose the File New command, and then select Note from the submenu.

- Press Ctrl+N.

- Double-click an empty space in the Notes folder window.

- Click the down arrow beside the New button on the Standard toolbar, and select Note from the menu.

When you use any one of these methods, Outlook opens a new note window, shown here:

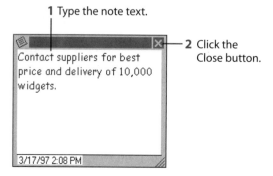

1 Type the note text.

2 Click the Close button.

After you click the Close button, Outlook displays the note text and a note icon in your Notes folder window.

Adding a New Note from a Different Folder

If you're working in an Outlook folder other than the Notes folder when you need to create a note, use one of the following methods:

- Click the down arrow beside the New button on the Standard toolbar, and then choose Note from the menu.

- Choose the File New command, and then select Note from the submenu.

- Press Ctrl+Shift+N.

If you want to add several notes at one time, create the first one, and then click the icon in the upper left corner of the note window and choose New Note from the menu, shown here:

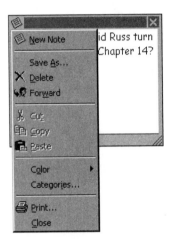

Outlook opens a second note window, in which you can type the second note. You can repeat this for multiple notes, opening as many windows as you need. When you finish typing the last note, click the Close button in each window, and Outlook will add all the notes to the Notes folder.

Working with Notes

? SEE ALSO

For details about printing options, see Chapter 14.

You can edit the text of a note, change the note's color, assign the note to various categories, forward the note to someone else, and copy or move the note to another folder. You can also adjust the default settings for all your notes, changing the default color, size, font, and time and date display.

Editing Note Text

When you want to change the text of a note, simply open the Notes folder, and double-click the note you want to edit. Then type your text changes, and click the Close button.

You can also open a note for editing in the following ways:

- Right-click the note, and choose Open from the shortcut menu.

- Select the note, and choose the File Open command.

- Select the note, and press Ctrl+O.

Giving a Note Some (Other) Color

By default, Outlook's notes have a yellow background and a yellow icon. But you can easily change a note's color to one of four other colors: blue, green, pink, or white. (You can also change the default note color, as explained in "Changing Default Note Settings," on the facing page.) Keeping notes of different colors is a handy way to organize your notes. You might make personal notes one color and notes related to your job another color.

Here's how to change the color of a note:

1 Open the Notes folder, and select the note you want to color differently.

2 Right-click the note, choose Color from the shortcut menu, and then select the new color from the Color submenu.

If you have a note open, you can click the icon in the upper left corner of the note window, choose Color from the menu, and then select the new color from the Color submenu. If the note is closed, right-click it and choose a color from the Color submenu.

Assigning a Note to a Category

As with other Outlook items, such as e-mail messages, meetings, or tasks, you can organize notes by assigning a note to one or more categories. To assign a note to a category, open the note and click the icon in the upper left corner of the note window. Then choose Categories from the menu. (You can also right-click the note in the Notes folder window and choose Categories from the shortcut menu.) You can use one of Outlook's built-in categories or enter a category of your own. For more information about using categories with Outlook items, see "Working with Categories," on page 462.

Sending a Note to Someone Else

If you want someone else to benefit from your careful note taking, you can forward a note. To send a note to someone else, open the note, click the icon in the upper left corner of the note window, and then choose Forward from the menu.

In the message window that Outlook displays, the note appears as an icon in the message area. Type the name of the recipient to whom you want to forward the note, or click the To button to select a name. If you selected only one note to forward, the Subject line will show the note text. If you selected more than one note to forward, the Subject line will be blank. Add any text you want to send with the note and message. When you're ready to send the message with the note attached, click the Send button on the Standard toolbar.

 NOTE

You use the same method for forwarding notes as you use for forwarding all other Outlook folder items. For details, see "Sending Folder Items Elsewhere," on page 382.

Copying or Moving a Note to Another Folder

You can move a note to another folder the same way you move any Outlook item. You can drag a note and drop it on a folder icon on the Outlook Bar to move the note to another folder. For example, if you want to use a note to create a task, open the Notes folder window, select the note you want to use to set up the task, and drag it to the Tasks icon on the Outlook Bar. Outlook opens a task item window, which you can use to enter more details about the task. For more details about moving items from one folder to another, see "Moving a Folder Item," on page 358.

Changing Default Note Settings

Outlook's default note settings display a note in a medium-size yellow window, with the note text in a 10-point Comic Sans MS font. (The note icons are also yellow.) Outlook also displays the time and date you created the note at the bottom of the note window.

If you want to change the default settings for all your notes, open the Notes folder, and choose the Tools Options command to display the Tasks/Notes tab of the Options dialog box:

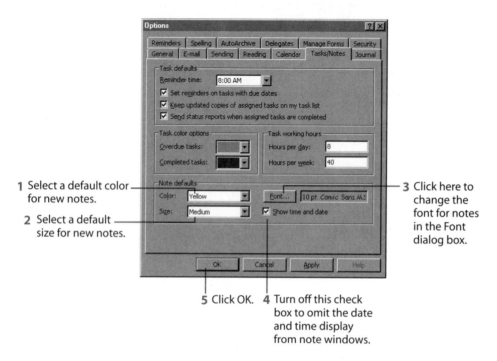

1 Select a default color for new notes.

2 Select a default size for new notes.

3 Click here to change the font for notes in the Font dialog box.

5 Click OK.

4 Turn off this check box to omit the date and time display from note windows.

NOTE

Changes you make to default note color and size in the Options dialog box do not change the color or size of existing notes. Changes you make to the default note font and to the display of the date and time do affect existing notes. Turning off the Show Date And Time check box merely omits the date and time from the note window; Outlook still records the date and time you created the note and displays the information in a column in certain views.

Viewing Your Notes

The views available for the Notes folder include views based on displaying icons as well as views that use a list format. When you first begin to work in your Notes folder, you'll see the window in Icons view, which is the default setting.

To switch to a different view of your Notes folder, use one of the following methods:

- On the Standard toolbar, click the down arrow in the Current View drop-down list, and then select the view you want from the list.

- Choose the View Current View command, and then select the view you want from the submenu.

NOTE

You can also resize a note. To do so, right-click the blue title bar at the top of the note and select Size from the menu. Place the sizing tool that appears on any border of the note, and drag the border to make the note the desired size. To access the Size command from a maximized note, right-click the title bar and choose Restore, then use the sizing tool (as just described) to resize the note.

Icons View

SEE ALSO

You can set up custom views for looking at your notes. For information, see Chapter 18. You can also set up special filters and sorting procedures for your notes; for details, see "Filtering," on page 477, and "Sorting," on page 468.

Icons view displays your notes with an icon and the note text. In Icons view, you can choose how to display the icons: as large icons, as small icons, or as an icon list.

To select one of these icon displays, click one of the three icon buttons on the Standard toolbar, as shown here:

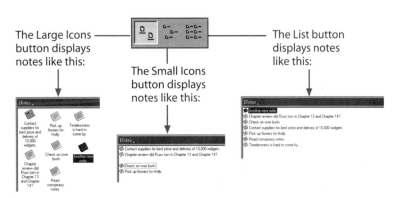

The Large Icons button displays notes like this:

The Small Icons button displays notes like this:

The List button displays notes like this:

If you click the Large Icons button or the Small Icons button, Outlook gives you several ways to arrange the icons in the Notes folder window. The easiest way is to simply drag the icons where you want them to appear in the window. (If you display the icons as a list, however, you can't arrange the icons in the window.)

Another alternative for displaying the icons involves using a dialog box to arrange them:

1 Open the Notes folder, and select Icons view.

2 Choose the View Format View command. Outlook opens the Format Icon View dialog box.

3 Select the view type. These options have the same effect as the similarly named buttons on the Standard toolbar.

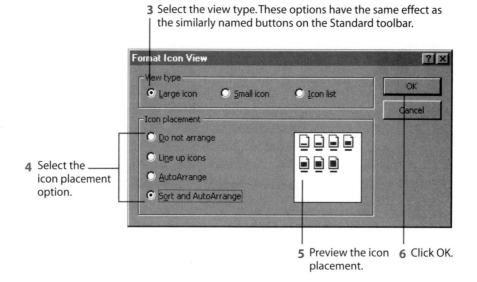

4 Select the icon placement option.

5 Preview the icon placement.

6 Click OK.

The Format Icon View dialog box provides four choices for arranging the icons in the Notes folder window:

- The Do Not Arrange option lets you drag the icons to any spot in the Notes folder window, giving you the freedom to arrange the icons yourself.

- The Line Up Icons option arranges the icons according to a preset grid in the Notes folder window but leaves them close to their original positions. It does not close up gaps between icons.

- The AutoArrange option lines up the icons in rows and columns, closing any gaps.

- The Sort And AutoArrange option sorts the icons alphabetically by the first word of the note and then lines up the icons in rows and columns, closing any gaps.

Notes List View

To see more information about your notes than Icons view can display, switch to Notes List view. In this view, Outlook lists your notes with columns for icons, subjects, creation dates and times, and categories, as in the following illustration:

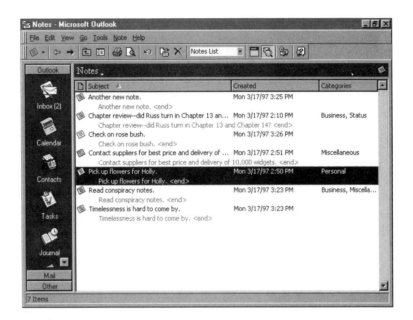

Notes List view initially sorts notes alphabetically by subject. To sort the notes differently in this view, click the column heading for the column you want to use to sort the notes. The first click sorts alphabetically or newest to oldest. A second click sorts reverse alphabetically or oldest to newest. In addition to clicking column headings, you can sort the list by right-clicking a heading, choosing View Summary from the shortcut menu, and then clicking Sort. You can sort the list of notes in the following ways:

- Alphabetically (A–Z) by subject

- Reverse alphabetically (Z–A) by subject

- By color, in this order: blue, green, pink, yellow, white

- By color in reverse order (white, yellow, pink, green, blue)

For details about changing the columns in Notes List view, see "Setting Up Columns," on page 454. You can group your notes by some of the columns you set up in Notes List view; for details, see "Grouping," on page 465.

- Oldest creation date and time at the top of the list and most recent date and time at the bottom of the list

- Most recent creation date and time at the top of the list and oldest date and time at the bottom of the list

If Outlook displays the Save View Settings dialog box when you switch to another view, you have three choices: discard the current view settings, save the current view settings with a name you give the view, or revise the current view by saving the changes you've made to the view. For more information about views and this dialog box, see "Defining a View," on page 502.

> You cannot sort notes by category in Notes List view. To sort your notes by category, choose By Category view; see "By Category View," on the facing page.

Last Seven Days View

If, for some reason, you need to focus your attention only on notes from the current time period, Last Seven Days view can be useful. You see your notes for the past seven days listed in a format similar to that of Notes List view, as shown here:

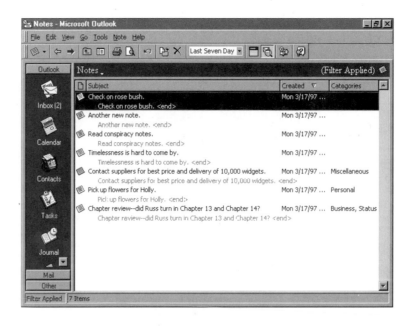

By Category View

If you have assigned at least some of your notes to categories, you can switch to By Category view to see the notes listed by category. A single note can appear in as many categories as you have assigned it to. Your notes folder window in this view will be similar to the following illustration:

This heading designates notes that have not been assigned to a category.

Click the plus sign to display the notes for a category.

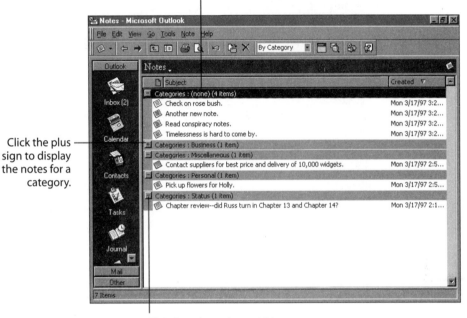

Click the minus sign to hide the notes for a category.

 **TIP**

To assign a note to an additional category in By Category view, drag that note's icon to the new category. The note then appears in both categories.

By Color View

If you use different colors for different types of notes, you can see your notes listed by color when you choose By Color view:

Click the minus sign to hide the notes of that color.

Click the plus sign to display the notes of that color.

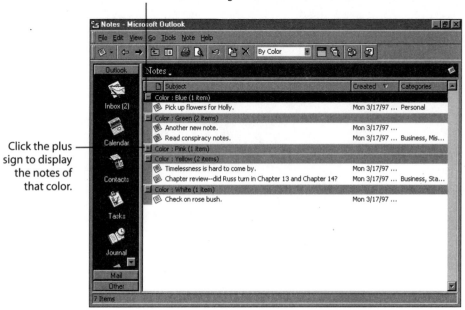

To change a note's color, drag that note's icon to the section that lists the new color. The note then appears with the new color.

PART V

Bending Folders
to Your Will

Managing
Folder Contents

You send and receive messages. You clutter your calendar with appointments and meetings. You set up tasks, send task requests, and respond to task requests. You record activities in your journal. You keep notes. Your Outlook folders are bursting with folder items.

Some of these folder items are in the wrong folder. Some folder items clutter the folders, making it difficult to concentrate and find the items that are most important. Some folder items need to appear in several folders.

To get the most from Microsoft Outlook 97, you need to manage folder contents, to straighten up the messes that simply using Outlook day to day inevitably creates. Can't you just hear your parents telling you, "Straighten up your room—it's a pigsty"? Well, this chapter describes the tools you need to straighten up the messes in your Outlook folders. Your room is your own business.

Moving and Copying Folder Items

You can move or copy folder items to any other Outlook folder or to any folder in your file system. (The term "file system" means anywhere on any disk connected to your computer or to any computer you can connect to through your network.) Outlook generously provides several ways to move and copy folder items. Use whichever method you find convenient.

Before you move or copy a folder item to another folder, you might want to delete parts of the item that you don't want or need to save (extraneous parts of an e-mail message, for instance). This keeps your Outlook folders smaller. Conversely, you can add your own notes and comments to a folder item before you move or copy it. (You can add comments after you move or copy the folder item, too.)

Moving a Folder Item

You can move a folder item either while it's open or while it's closed. To move a folder item to another folder, follow these steps:

1   Open the folder in which the item is currently located, and select the folder item or open it.

2   Take one of the following actions to open the Move Items dialog box:

- Click the Move To Folder button on the Standard toolbar, and choose Move To Folder from the menu.

- If you are in the folder window, choose the Edit Move To Folder command.

- If you are in the folder item window (that is, you have opened the item), choose the File Move To Folder command.

- Press Ctrl+Shift+V.

- Right-click the item in the folder window, and choose Move To Folder from the shortcut menu.

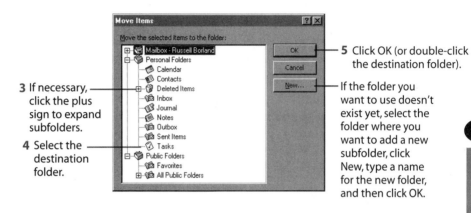

3 If necessary, click the plus sign to expand subfolders.

4 Select the destination folder.

5 Click OK (or double-click the destination folder).

If the folder you want to use doesn't exist yet, select the folder where you want to add a new subfolder, click New, type a name for the new folder, and then click OK.

If you are moving an item to a folder that you use to create items of another type (for example, moving a contact item to your Journal folder), after you click OK in the Move Items dialog box Outlook opens a folder item window in the destination folder, displaying the item that you moved as an attachment. In most cases, Outlook also fills in at least part of the information in the folder item window; you can change any of this information and fill in the rest before clicking the Save And Close button.

You can move multiple folder items at the same time by selecting them all before you begin the process of moving them to another folder. To select more than one item at a time, hold down the Shift key to select adjacent items or hold down the Ctrl key to select nonadjacent multiple items.

V

Bending Folders to Your Will

You can also use one of the following alternatives to move a folder item to another folder more quickly. Both of these methods bypass the Move Items dialog box and immediately open the folder item window in the destination folder.

- Select or open the folder item, click the Move To Folder button on the Standard toolbar, and click the name of the destination folder on the menu.

- Select the folder item, and drag it to the destination folder on the Outlook Bar or in the Folder List.

After you move at least one folder item to a folder, that folder name appears on the menu displayed by the Move To Folder button on the Standard toolbar. To move an item to a listed folder, click the item, click the Move To Folder button, and then select the folder name from the menu.

Copying a Folder Item

You can copy a folder item either while it's open or while it's closed. Here's how to copy a folder item to another folder:

1 Open the folder containing the item, and select the item or open it.

2 Choose the Edit Copy To Folder command (in the folder window) or the File Copy To Folder command (in the folder item window).

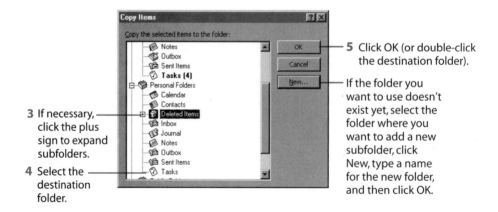

3 If necessary, click the plus sign to expand subfolders.

4 Select the destination folder.

5 Click OK (or double-click the destination folder).

If the folder you want to use doesn't exist yet, select the folder where you want to add a new subfolder, click New, type a name for the new folder, and then click OK.

A faster alternative, which bypasses the Copy Items dialog box, is to select the item and hold down the Ctrl key while you drag the item to the destination folder on the Outlook Bar or in the Folder List.

 TIP

> You can copy multiple folder items at the same time by selecting them all before you begin the process of copying them to another folder. See the tip on page 359 for more information about selecting items.

Copying a Folder Item to an Office 97 Application

You can copy messages, contact information, or notes to other Office 97 applications and use them as a basis for a new project. For example, if you create a folder item in Outlook for a Microsoft Office 97 application document that doesn't exist yet, you can copy the folder item to that application in one of two ways: you can copy the folder item as a package (embedded in the application), or you can add the folder item's text to a document in the application.

To copy a folder item to an Office 97 application as a package, take these steps:

1 Select the folder item you want to copy.

2 Start the Office 97 application to which you want to copy the folder item, and create or open the document to which you'll copy the item.

3 Arrange the Outlook window and the Office 97 document window on your screen so that you can see both at the same time.

4 Drag the folder item into the document window.

The folder item is displayed as an icon in the document. You can double-click the icon to see the folder item.

If you want to copy the text of the folder item into the Office 97 document, take these steps:

1 Select the folder item you want to copy.

V

Bending Folders to Your Will

2 Choose Outlook's File Save As command to save the item as a file you can open in an Office 97 application.

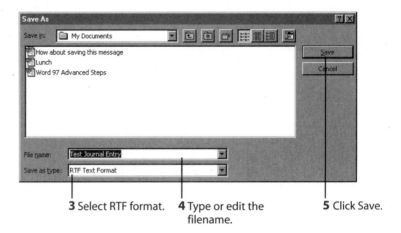

3 Select RTF format.　**4** Type or edit the filename.　**5** Click Save.

6 Switch to the Office 97 application, and open the Rich Text Format (RTF) file for the folder item. You see the text in the appropriate format for the Office 97 application. Here is an example of a Rich Text Format journal entry opened in Microsoft Word:

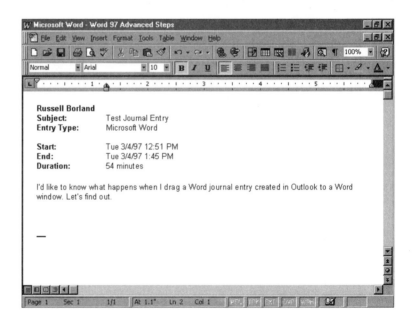

7 Save the Office 97 document.

Posting Your Ideas in a Folder

As another way to add new information to a folder—especially to a public folder that is shared by members of a group—you can post a notice, or you can post a response to a previous posting. Many public folders are designed for posting information that is of interest to specific groups of people. These folders are different from e-mail folders because they're designed for public rather than private use. Although you can compose new postings only in e-mail folders and in public folders, posting in an e-mail folder is less common. You can post a reply to any folder item in any Outlook folder except the Notes folder. You cannot compose new postings or post replies in file system folders.

To post a new notice in an e-mail or public folder, follow these steps:

1 Open the e-mail or public folder where you want to add a new posting.

2 Choose the Compose New Post In This Folder command, or press Ctrl+Shift+S.

5 Click Post.   **3** Type the topic of your posting.

4 Type your note.

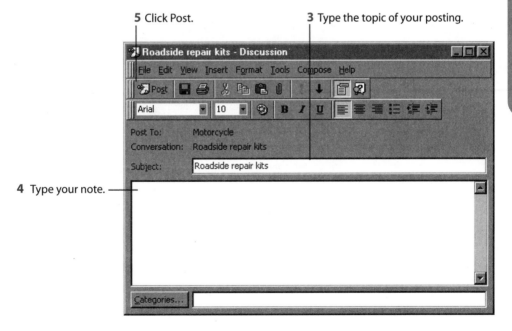

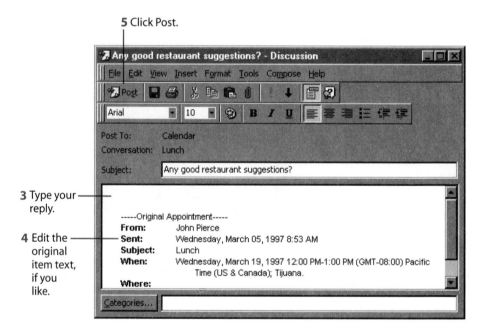

After you click the Post button, Outlook adds the new notice to the folder, marking it with the icon shown at the left.

To reply to a posted notice, double-click it to open a discussion window containing the notice. Click the Post Reply button to open yet another discussion window, in which you can type your reply. Click the Post button in that window, and close the first discussion window by clicking the Close button in the upper right corner of the window.

To post a reply to a folder item, do this:

1 Open the folder containing the item to which you want to post a reply, and select the item.

2 Choose the Post Reply To This Folder command from the Compose menu in e-mail folders and public folders. In other folders, this command appears on the menu named for the folder (Tasks, Contacts, and so on).

Adding Files to a Folder

Every Outlook folder can contain files, but in order to add a file to a folder, Outlook has to create an item that is appropriate for the folder, with the file as an attachment. You use the file system and Outlook folders together to do this.

 NOTE

This procedure copies a file to a folder; it does not remove the file from the file system.

To put a file from your file system in an Outlook folder, follow these steps:

1 Display the Folder List by choosing the View Folder List command.

2 Open the file system folder by opening a My Computer window or a Windows Explorer window outside of Outlook. If you open a My Computer or a Windows Explorer window outside Outlook, arrange that window and the Outlook window so that you can see both on your screen at the same time.

3 In the window showing your file system, select the file you want to put in an Outlook folder.

4 Drag the selected file to the Outlook folder in the Folder List. Outlook creates an item that is appropriate for the folder. In the example shown on the following page, the file has been dragged to the Journal window, and Outlook has opened a journal entry window.

V

Bending Folders to Your Will

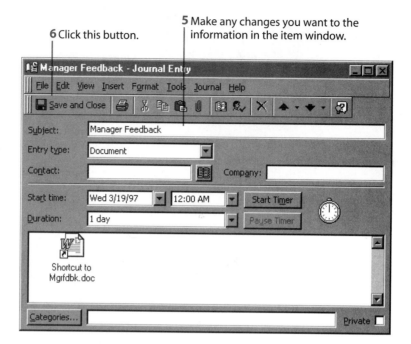

6 Click this button.

5 Make any changes you want to the information in the item window.

The new folder item contains a shortcut to the file. For details about using the shortcut, see "Viewing File Attachments and Shortcuts Stored in Outlook Folder Items," on page 368.

The button you click in step 6 depends on the type of folder item Outlook creates and on what you want to do with it. For example, if you want to send the shortcut in a new message, click the Send button. If you don't want to send a message but do want to keep the item in an e-mail folder, click the Save button and then close the message. For other folder item types, click the Save And Close button as shown in the illustration of the Journal folder, above.

You also have an alternative method for adding a file to an Outlook folder. Instead of dragging the file to the Folder List, you can use this procedure:

1 Open the Outlook folder in which you want to place the file.

2 Create a new item in the Outlook folder.

3 In the folder item window, choose the Insert File command.

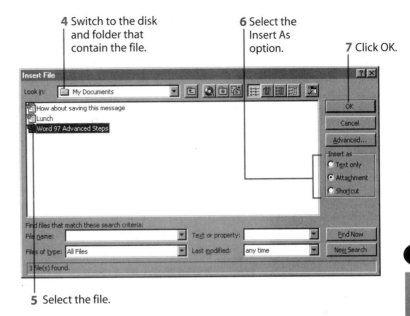

4 Switch to the disk and folder that contain the file.

6 Select the Insert As option.

7 Click OK.

5 Select the file.

8 Fill in the folder item window with the information you want. You might, for example, want to enter a description of the file on the Subject line.

9 If you are working in an e-mail folder, click the Save button, and then click the Close button in the folder item window. For other folder item types, click the Save And Close button.

Notice the Insert As section of the Insert File dialog box (step 6). Which option you choose here depends on what you plan to do with the folder item and on the type of file you're inserting.

- The Text Only option inserts the file as standard text. Typically, you'll select this option when you want to insert plain (unformatted) text files in order to send the file in a message across the Internet. This option makes sense only for simple text files. Art files and files containing formatted text appear as gibberish.

- The Attachment option inserts a complete copy of the data from the file, represented as an icon. Select this option if you will need to readily access the file from the folder item. Because the entire file is stored as part of the folder item, you should select the Shortcut option instead if the file is extremely large.

- The Shortcut option inserts a pointer to the original file, represented as a shortcut icon. Select this option to include a large file. Note, however, that anyone else whom you want to view the file must have access to the disk, folder, and file. For the Shortcut option, it's a good idea to store the file on a network server or in a public folder to which others who must view the file have access.

Viewing File Attachments and Shortcuts Stored in Outlook Folder Items

Whether you copied a file to an Outlook folder as an attachment or as a shortcut, you can easily view the contents of the file. In the folder window, right-click the folder item, and choose View Attachments from the shortcut menu. Then select the attachment name from the submenu.

NOTE

What's the difference between a file attachment and a shortcut? A file attachment sends the entire file within the message. If you have a large file that you'd like to share, you might want to attach a shortcut instead. A shortcut sends the location of the file within the message and is much faster to send and open than a file attachment.

If you open the item, you can use any of these methods in the folder item window to view the file:

- Double-click an attachment or shortcut icon.

- Right-click an attachment or shortcut icon, and choose Open from the shortcut menu.

- Right-click an attachment or shortcut icon, and choose Quick View from the shortcut menu. (Microsoft Windows 95 Quick View must be installed on your computer for this method to work.)

Adding Items to the Favorites Folder

The Favorites folder contains shortcuts to items, documents, and other folders that you use frequently. You can add items to the Favorites folder in several ways:

- You can drag folder items to the Outlook Favorites folder. (This operation takes place within Outlook.)

- You can add icons to the Favorites toolbar on the Office 97 shortcut bar.

- You can add the address of a World Wide Web page (a URL) to the Favorites list in Microsoft Internet Explorer.

If you add a favorite to your Favorites folder (either in Outlook or in the Favorites folder inside the Windows folder), to the Favorites list in Microsoft Internet Explorer, or to the Favorites toolbar of the Office 97 Shortcut Bar, the new favorite automatically appears in all of these places.

Dragging a Folder Item to the Favorites Folder

You can drag any Outlook folder item (or any file) to the Outlook Favorites folder. Depending on how you drag the item, you either move it to the Favorites folder or copy it (which sets up a shortcut to the original).

To move an item to your Outlook Favorites folder, take these steps:

1 Open the Outlook folder (or disk folder) that contains the item you want to move.

2 Click the Other label on the Outlook Bar to display the Favorites folder icon. (The Favorites folder is part of the Other group on the Outlook bar.) Do *not* click the Favorites folder icon.

3 Hold down the Shift key and drag the folder item to the Favorites folder icon.

To set up a shortcut to an item (copy it) in your Outlook Favorites folder, take these steps:

1 Open the Outlook folder (or disk folder) that contains the item.

2 Click the Other label on the Outlook Bar to display the Other group, which includes the Favorites folder icon. Do *not* click the Favorites folder icon.

3 Hold down the Ctrl key while you drag the folder item to the Favorites folder icon.

4 When you see a shortcut menu with the commands Copy Here and Cancel, choose Copy Here.

Adding to Favorites on the Office 97 Shortcut Bar

The Office 97 Shortcut Bar starts out with one toolbar—the Office toolbar—which contains buttons for Outlook items and Office 97 applications. You can add more toolbars to the shortcut bar, including a toolbar for Favorites, which contains buttons for all the entries in your Favorites folder.

If your Office 97 Shortcut Bar doesn't yet display a Favorites toolbar, you'll have to set it up before you can add items to it. To do this, simply right-click a blank area of the shortcut bar, and choose Favorites from the shortcut menu.

 TIP

> When you add toolbars to the Office 97 Shortcut Bar, each toolbar has its own button. To display a different toolbar on the shortcut bar, click the button for that toolbar. The toolbar then slides into place.

You can add an Outlook folder item to the Favorites toolbar on the Office 97 Shortcut Bar as follows:

1 Right-click a blank area of the Office 97 Shortcut Bar.

2 Choose Customize from the shortcut menu to display the Customize dialog box.

3 Select Favorites.

4 Click the Buttons tab.

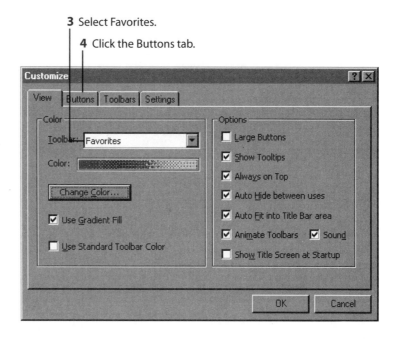

5 Click Add File to add a file (document or program), or...

click Add Folder to add a folder.

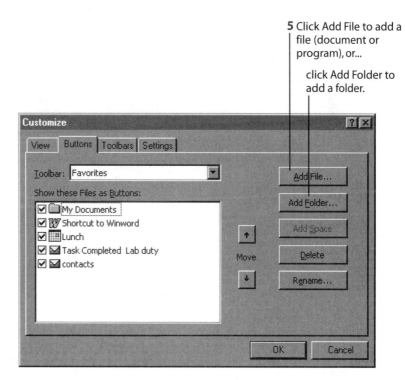

V

Bending Folders to Your Will

6 When you click the Add File or Add Folder buttons, you'll see a standard dialog box in which you can locate the file or folder you want to add. After selecting the file or folder, click the Add button.

7 Click OK in the Customize dialog box.

Adding to Favorites in Microsoft Internet Explorer

In Microsoft Internet Explorer, you can add World Wide Web sites to your Favorites folder as follows:

1 Start Microsoft Internet Explorer.

2 Locate the web page (URL) you want to add to your Favorites folder.

3 Click the Favorites button on the Internet Explorer toolbar, and choose Add To Favorites from the menu, or choose the Favorites Add To Favorites command.

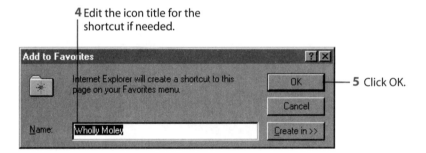

4 Edit the icon title for the shortcut if needed.

5 Click OK.

These web pages are now available in Outlook through your Favorites folder in the Other group on the Outlook bar.

Searching Folder Contents

On its Tool menu, Outlook provides a Find Items command to help you locate items in a folder. This command works for any Outlook folder, including public folders.

Conducting a Search

To locate specific items in a folder, you need to use the Find dialog box, shown in Figure 13-1. Open this dialog box in any one of these ways:

- Choose the Tools Find Items command.

- Right-click the folder you want to search, and choose Find Items from the shortcut menu.

- Press Ctrl+Shift+F.

FIGURE 13-1.

The Find dialog box

Specify the type of folder item.

This tab changes to match the setting in the Look For box.

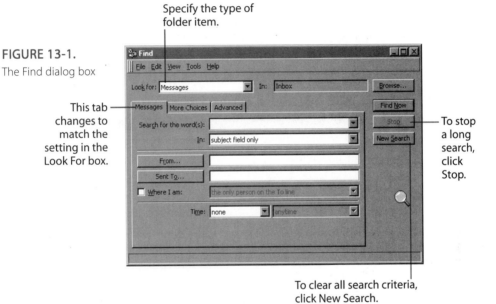

To stop a long search, click Stop.

To clear all search criteria, click New Search.

? SEE ALSO

To see a list of the folders Outlook searches by default and to find out how to expand a search beyond them, see "More on the Find Dialog Box," on page 375.

In the Look For box of the Find dialog box, you'll see the type of folder item that corresponds to the Outlook folder that is currently open (messages for the Inbox folder, journal entries for the Journal folder, and so on). To search for a different type of item, choose another type from the drop-down list. The In box beside the Look For box shows the default folder in which Outlook searches for the items.

The first of the three tabs in the Find dialog box corresponds to the type of folder item you're looking for. As you change the setting in the Look For box, this tab changes, becoming, for instance, the Messages tab or the Journal Entries tab. This tab contains options that you can set or fill out to structure your search.

Although the tabs for different types of folder items vary somewhat, you set them up in similar ways. For instance, on the Messages tab, shown in Figure 13-1 (on the preceding page), you specify search criteria as follows:

- In the Search For The Word(s) box, type a word or phrase that appears in all the messages you're searching for. (If you want to choose words you used in past searches, you can select them from the drop-down list, where Outlook stores them.)

- In the tab's In box, tell Outlook whether to look for the specified word or phrase only in the Subject line of messages (the subject field), in both the Subject line and the body of messages, or in other text fields.

The term "field" simply refers to a location that shows data or to an empty box that you can fill in with details about an item.

To narrow the search even further, you can also set up the following optional criteria:

- Specify messages that were received from or sent to certain people. Type the names of these people in the appropriate boxes, or click the From button or the Sent To button to display the Select Names dialog box, where you can choose names from your address books.

- Tell Outlook to search for messages in which you are the only addressee, messages with multiple addressees, or messages for which you received copies. To do this, turn on the Where I Am check box and select an option from the drop-down list.

- Specify a time. By selecting options in both the Time boxes, you can narrow the search to messages that were, for instance, received or sent within a certain timeframe.

When you've set as many search criteria as you need, click the Find Now button to begin the search.

When Outlook completes the search, the Find dialog box expands downward and displays the folder items that match the criteria you set up. If the list includes folder items you don't want, you can add additional criteria to search the list only and then click the Find Now button again. This way, you can pare the list down to the items you really want to find. If none of the folder items shown fits your needs, click the New Search button and set up different criteria.

When you change your selection in the Look For box after a search, Outlook notifies you that the previous search will be cleared. If you want to start a fresh search, click OK. If you want to keep the previous search, click Cancel.

You can open any found item directly from the Find dialog box by double-clicking the item.

More on the Find Dialog Box

The next several sections take a closer look at some of the features of the Find dialog box.

Look For. As mentioned earlier, the setting in the Look For box of the Find dialog box determines which tab you see in the dialog box. This setting also affects where Outlook will go to find the items you're seeking. The In box next to the Look For box indicates the folder that Outlook will automatically search for the folder items you've specified. Table 13-1 summarizes how the setting in the Look For box determines which folder is searched by default and which tab you see in the Find dialog box.

TABLE 13-1. Effects of Settings in the Look For Box.

Setting in Look For Box	Default Folder Searched (Item in In Box)	Tab Shown
Any Type Of Outlook Item	Personal folders or server folders	Any Items tab
Appointments And Meetings	Calendar folder	Appointments And Meetings tab
Contacts	Contacts folder	Contacts tab
Files	My Documents folder	Files tab
Files (Outlook/Exchange)	Inbox folder	Files tab
Journal Entries	Journal folder	Journal Entries tab
Messages	Inbox folder	Messages tab
Notes	Notes folder	Notes tab
Tasks	Tasks folder	Tasks tab

Browse button. If you need to expand Outlook's search beyond the folder indicated in the In box, you can specify additional folders that Outlook should search. You can't type directly in the In box, but you can click the Browse button to open the Select Folder(s) dialog box, shown on the facing page.

3 Click OK.

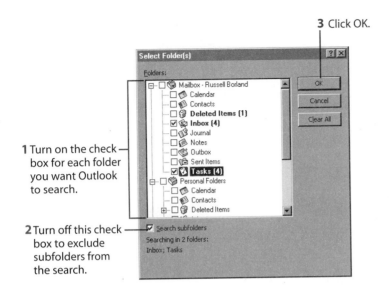

1 Turn on the check box for each folder you want Outlook to search.

2 Turn off this check box to exclude subfolders from the search.

After you click OK in the Select Folder(s) dialog box, Outlook adds the folder names you selected to the In box and includes those folders in the search.

> If you select Files in the Look For box and then click the Browse button, you'll see a Select Folder(s) dialog box that contains a list of all the folders in your file system rather than a list of Outlook's folders.

Files tab. If you're searching for a file with the Find dialog box, you'll notice that the tab Outlook displays when you select Files in the Look For box is a little different from the tabs displayed for other items. In particular, the Named box on the Files tab lets you enter either a filename or a file specification.

To enter a filename, type the complete filename and filename extension. For a file specification, use one of the methods on the following page.

- Type an asterisk (*) to substitute for all filenames or extensions—for example, type *.*pst* to specify all files that have the .PST filename extension.

- Type *word*.** to find all files of any type (any extension) whose filenames start with *word*.

- Type a question mark (?) to substitute for a single character in a filename.

If you've looked for files before by typing a filename or a file specification in the Named box, you can find these entries by clicking the down arrow in the Named box; Outlook stores them in the drop-down list.

If you want to search for all the files of a certain type—for example, all Microsoft Excel workbooks—choose the file type from the Of Type box.

> **NOTE**
>
> When you type a filename or a file specification in the Named box on the Files tab, Outlook's search ignores the selection in the Of Type box.

More Choices tab and Advanced tab. The other two tabs in the Find dialog box, More Choices and Advanced, offer still more options for structuring your search. These two tabs are the same as the More Choices tab and the Advanced tab in the Filter dialog box, discussed in Chapter 17. For information about setting up these tabs, see "Setting Up the More Choices Tab," on page 485, and "Setting Up Advanced Criteria," on page 487. The following section, "Searching for Items by Fields on a Form," also provides an example of using the Advanced tab.

Searching for Items by Fields on a Form

When you're looking for specific folder items, you might consider searching for the individual fields that appear on the various types of forms (dialog boxes and windows) in Outlook. To use a field as a search criteria, follow these steps:

1 Choose the Tools Find Items command to display the Find dialog box.

2 In the Look For box, select the type of folder item you want to find, or select Any Type Of Outlook Item to include all item types in the search.

3 If the folder you want to search does not appear in the In box to the right, or if you want to search more than one folder, click Browse to select from a list. In the Select Folder(s) dialog box, turn on the check boxes next to the folders you want to search, and turn off the boxes next to the folders you don't want to search. Click OK.

4 Click the Advanced tab in the Find dialog box.

5 Click the Field button to display the list of fields.

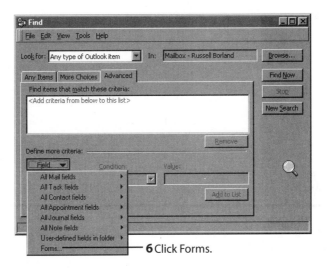

6 Click Forms.

What's a Forms Library?

A forms library is where Outlook stores published forms and where Outlook searches for the forms you select in the illustration above. If you have a custom form that you've designed and you want to share it with others, you publish it in one of the three types of forms libraries: a Personal Forms library, a Folder Forms library, or an Organizational Forms library. These libraries are discussed in detail in Chapter 20, on page 578.

9 Click Add to display the selected
form in the righthand box.

7 Select the forms
library you want
to use.

8 Click the form
containing the
field that you
want to use in the
search criteria.

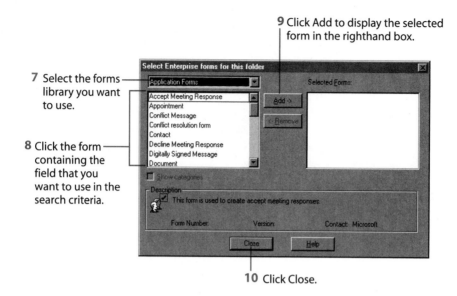

10 Click Close.

11 In the Find dialog box, click the Field button again to display the
list, and point to the name of the form you selected. On the submenu, click the specific field you want to use in the search criteria.
Outlook displays the name of the field in the box under the
Field button.

NOTE

> The key to this search is targeting forms that have been created—either
> standard or custom—for use with a folder. For example, if you select Docu-
> ment as the form type in the Select Enterprise Forms For This Folder dialog
> box, you will have many fields available in step 11. If you select Contact in that
> dialog box, you will not have any fields available in step 11 unless someone
> has created a custom form for the Contacts folder. This is because Outlook
> doesn't provide forms for the Contacts folder.

12 In the Condition box, you can select a condition to use with the
field to set up a specific search criterion.

13 If the condition you select requires a value in order to make sense, Outlook activates the Value box, in which you can enter a value to complete the criterion.

14 Click the Add To List button.

15 To use additional fields from the selected form as search criteria, repeat steps 11 through 14.

16 Click the Find Now button to conduct the search with the new criteria.

> When setting search criteria, if you select more than one search criterion, Outlook finds only the items that meet all the search criteria. However, if you use the same field to set multiple criteria, Outlook finds items that meet any one of the multiple criteria within that field.

Finding All Similar Messages

In e-mail folders, you might want to find all messages about a specific topic or all messages sent by a specific person. Outlook provides a special tool for these purposes.

To find all messages related to a specific topic, take these steps:

1 Open the e-mail folder that you want Outlook to search.

2 Select a message with the topic you're interested in.

3 Choose the Tools Find All command, and then choose Related Messages from the submenu.

Outlook opens the Find dialog box and automatically searches the open folder for messages that have the same topic as the selected message. When the search is finished, the list of matching messages appears in the lower portion of the Find dialog box.

To find all messages from a specific person, you follow the same basic procedure, selecting a message from this person, choosing Tools Find All, and then selecting Messages From Sender from the submenu.

Opening Documents or Starting Programs from Outlook

Because you can show any disk folder on the Outlook Bar and, more important, because you can display the Folder List, which can show all the folders on all the disks connected to your computer, it's relatively easy to open any document or start any program from within Outlook.

All you need to do is switch to the Other group on the Outlook Bar and open the folder that contains the document you want to open or the program you want to start. (If the folder does not have an icon on the Outlook Bar, display the Folder List, and click the icon for the folder there.) Then simply double-click the icon for the document or program file.

Sending Folder Items Elsewhere

SEE ALSO
You can also set up Outlook to automatically send new messages to another person or to any other folder, which is especially useful when you're out of the office. For details, see "Outlook Assistants," on page 38.

You can send any folder item in Outlook to someone else—you simply forward the item. Here's how to send a folder item to someone else:

1   Open the folder, and select the folder item you want to send to someone else. (To select more than one item, hold down the Ctrl key as you click each item. To select several consecutive folder items, click the first item, and then hold down the Shift key while you click the last item. To select all the folder items, choose the Edit Select All command or press Ctrl+A.)

2   In an e-mail folder or a public folder, choose the Forward command from the Compose menu. In other folders, choose Forward from the menu with the same name as the folder.

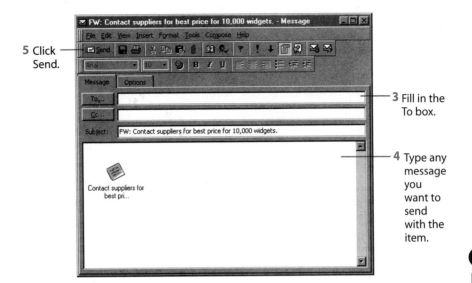

5 Click Send.

3 Fill in the To box.

4 Type any message you want to send with the item.

Removing Items from a Folder

Clutter, clutter, clutter! What a mess! You'll find that you receive many messages that you don't need and don't want to keep. Just as you can quickly dump unwanted postal deliveries in the recycling bin, you can dump folder items in the Deleted Items folder.

To delete a folder item, simply select the item in the folder window or open the item, and then click the Delete button on the Standard toolbar. As an alternative, you can move the folder item to the Deleted Items folder. (See "Moving a Folder Item," on page 358.)

Retrieving Deleted Items

How many times have you thrown something away only to want to retrieve it later? This is especially likely to happen on a computer, where the discarded item isn't physically lying around waiting for you to take it back. Outlook gives you some grace when you delete folder items; you can retrieve a deleted item from the Deleted Items folder by moving the item to another folder. See "Moving a Folder Item," on page 358. You must retrieve the folder item *before* you purge (empty) the Deleted Items folder. After you empty that folder, the folder item is gone for good. Your only recourse then is to have someone send you a copy of the folder item, which, of course, isn't always possible.

Purging Deleted Items

Well, like all good citizens, you've been putting your litter (unwanted folder items and folders) in the Deleted Items folder—that is, you've been deleting folder items and folders right and left to keep your folders tidy. Now your Deleted Items folder is stuffed. (Well, there's really no danger of overflowing the Deleted Items folder; it's just a turn of phrase.) So now you want to purge your Deleted Items folder and just get rid of all those discarded folder items and folders once and for all.

- When you want to completely empty the Deleted Items folder, choose the Tools Empty "Deleted Items" Folder command. When Outlook asks whether you want to permanently delete all the items and subfolders in this folder, click the Yes button.

⚠ WARNING

Unlike deleting folder items and folders from other folders (which sends the item or folder to the Deleted Items folder), deleting folder items and folders from the Deleted Items folder wipes out the items and folders forever.

- When you want to purge only certain folder items and folders from the Deleted Items folder, open the Deleted Items folder, and select the items and folders you want to delete. Click the Delete button on the Standard toolbar, choose the File Delete command, or press Ctrl+D. When Outlook asks whether you want to permanently delete the selected items, click the Yes button.

You can set up Outlook to automatically purge your Deleted Items folder when you quit an Outlook session. To do this, choose the Tools Options command, click the General tab, turn on the Empty The Deleted Items Folder Upon Exiting box, and then click OK. From now on, when you quit Outlook, you'll see a message asking whether you want to empty the Deleted Items folder.

Viewing Files in the Other Group Folders

SEE ALSO

For more information about folders in the Outlook Bar's Other group, see "Other Group," on page 28.

You can use the miscellaneous group of folders, labeled Other, on the Outlook Bar to view files and folders throughout your file system. The My Computer folder, for instance, displays the same icons you see in the My Computer window on your desktop. By clicking one of these icons, you can see a list of all the folders on a disk drive. The My Documents folder, also part of the Other group, is a shortcut to the My Documents folder on your hard drive and can be used to find or open documents.

Outlook provides a number of options for viewing the files in these folders, as shown in the following sections. One view displays icons; other options include table views and a timeline view. (You can change the format of a view; for details about formatting both table views and timeline views, see "Formatting Views," on page 509.)

SEE ALSO

You can set up custom views for looking at your files; for information, see Chapter 18. You can also group your files, specify sorting procedures, set up special filters, and add custom fields to file properties; for details, see Chapter 17.

When you open one of the folders in the Other group, the drop-down list on the Standard toolbar displays the name of the current view. To switch to a different view of the folder, use one of the following methods:

- On the Standard toolbar, click the down arrow to display the drop-down list and then select the view you want from the list.

- Choose the View Current View command, and then select the view you want from the submenu.

V

Bending Folders to Your Will

Icons View

In Icons view, disk drives, folders, and files are displayed with an icon and their name. When you select Icons view, Outlook adds three buttons to the Standard toolbar: Large Icons, Small Icons, and List. Clicking one of these buttons varies Icons view, to display either large or small icons or an icon list. You can also decide how to arrange the file icons in the window.

For all the details about varying this view and arranging the icons, see "Icons View," on page 349.

The following illustration shows files displayed in Icons view with small icons:

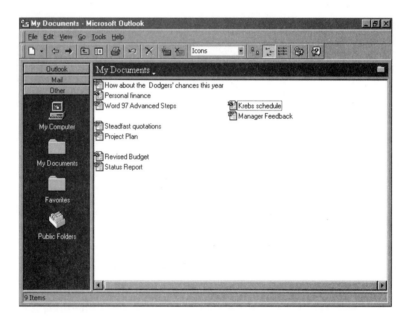

Details View

To see more information about your files, switch to Details view, which is similar to Details view in a My Computer or a Windows Explorer window. You see your files listed with columns for icons, filename, author, type, size, date and time of the last modification, and keywords, as in the illustration on the facing page.

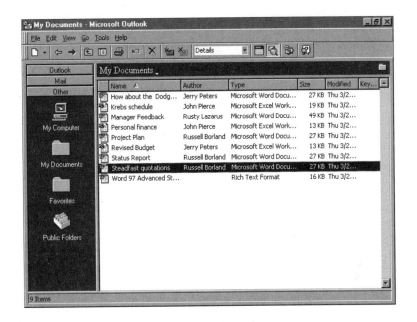

? SEE ALSO

For details about changing the columns in Details view, see "Setting Up Columns," on page 454. You can group your files by some of the columns you set up in Details view; for details, see "Grouping," on page 465.

Files in this view are initially sorted alphabetically by filename. To arrange the files a different way in Details view, click the column heading for the column you want to use to rearrange the files. The first click sorts alphabetically, smallest to largest, or newest to oldest. A second click sorts reverse alphabetically, largest to smallest, or oldest to newest. You can sort the list of files in these ways:

- Reverse alphabetically (Z–A) by filename, author, or keywords

- Alphabetically by filename, author, or keywords

- Largest file at the top of the list and smallest file at the bottom of the list

- Smallest file at the top of the list and largest file at the bottom of the list

- Oldest modification date and time at the top of the list and most recent modification date and time at the bottom of the list

- Most recent modification date and time at the top of the list and oldest modification date and time at the bottom of the list

By Author View

By Author view groups files by their author, making it easier to find files created by a specific person. You see the files grouped by author name, as shown on the following page.

This heading designates
files without an author.

Click the plus
sign to display
files written by a
specific author.

Click the minus
sign to hide the
files written by a
specific author.

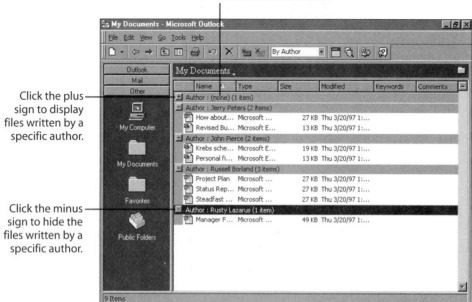

By File Type View

By File Type view groups files by their file type, making it easier to find files created by a specific program. Here is an example of By File Type view:

Click the plus sign
to display the files
for a program.

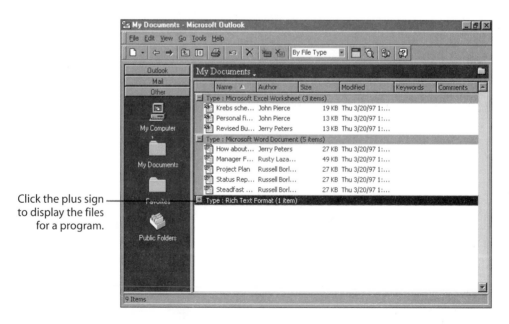

Document Timeline View

Document Timeline view arranges all the documents in the folder on a timeline that shows the dates in a band across the top of the window. Each file (represented by its filename and an icon) appears below the date on which it was last modified, as shown here in a timeline for a week:

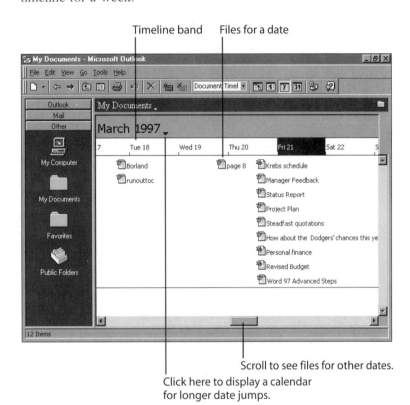

Timeline band   Files for a date

Scroll to see files for other dates.

Click here to display a calendar
for longer date jumps.

You can change Document Timeline view in the following ways:

- Click the Day button on the Standard toolbar to see documents for a single date, listed by the time.

- Click the Week button on the Standard toolbar to see documents for a single week, listed by the day of the week.

- Click the Month button on the Standard toolbar to see documents for a month, listed by the date.

When you have files so far away from today's date that you can't scroll to them quickly in Document Timeline view, you can to jump to a date in one of two ways:

- Click the down arrow beside the month name in the files folder window, and use the drop-down calendar.

- Choose the Go To Date command from the Go menu. For details about how to use this command, see "Using the Go To Date Command," on page 214.

Programs View

Programs view is the standard view you see the first time you look at the files in one of the folders in the Other group. Programs view is a filter that permits only program files (a file that starts an application, for example) and folders to appear in a files folder window, as illustrated here:

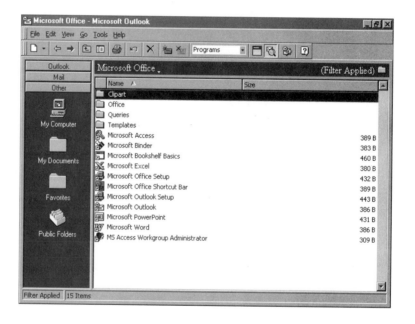

CHAPTER 14

Printing Folder Items

Printing a copy of an item from a Microsoft Outlook 97 folder is a simple matter. If you want to use Outlook's standard print style, it's merely a question of selecting an item and clicking a toolbar button. But if the standard print style doesn't meet your needs, you can select a different print style—Outlook offers several built-in styles for various folders. You can also print a view of an entire folder rather than an individual item, and you can adjust the printing options for either items or views. And if you can't find a built-in print style that suits your purposes, you can modify one of the built-in styles or even create your own print style.

Printing with Outlook's Standard Style

For each Outlook folder—and for each view of that folder—Outlook has a default print style set up. To print folder items using that standard print style, follow these steps:

1 Select the folder item or items that you want to print. (To select more than one item, hold down the Ctrl key as you click each item. To select several consecutive items, click the first item and then hold down the Shift key while you click the last item you want to select. To select all the items in a folder, choose the Edit Select All command or press Ctrl+A.)

2 Click the Print button on the Standard toolbar.

You can preview the printed copy before you actually print it. Select the folder item, and choose the File Print Preview command (or click the Print Preview toolbar button). See "Previewing Printing," on page 400.

Choosing an Alternative Built-In Print Style

Outlook comes to you with certain print styles that are set up for each view in each folder, as listed in Table 14-1. The print styles available for the current folder and view appear in the Print dialog box and on the submenu of the File Page Setup command.

> **NOTE**
>
> For views that you have created, you can use the built-in print styles that are available for other views of the same type. For example, if you create a new card view in the Contacts folder, the print styles are the same as those for Address Cards view.

TABLE 14-1. Outlook's Built-In Print Styles, by Folder and View.

Folder	View	Print Style
Inbox	All views except Message Timeline	Table, Memo
	Message Timeline	Memo
Calendar	All views except Day/Week/Month	Table, Memo
	Day/Week/Month	Daily, Weekly, Monthly, Tri-Fold, Memo
Contacts	Address Cards, Detailed Address Cards	Card, Small Booklet, Medium Booklet, Memo, Phone Directory
	Phone List, By Category, By Company, By Location	Table, Memo, Phone Directory
Tasks	All views except Task Timeline	Table, Memo
	Task Timeline	Memo
Journal	By Type, By Contact, By Category	Memo
	Entry List, Last Seven Days, Phone Calls	Table, Memo
Notes	All views except Icons	Table, Memo
	Icons	Memo

As you can see in Table 14-1, Memo style, which lets you print one or more individual folder items, is the most commonly available print style. When you print an open Outlook item, Memo style is the only print style available. With other built-in print styles, you can print an entire view (as well as individual items, in some cases).

 NOTE

When a view is based on displaying a timeline or icons, you cannot print the entire view. In this case, Outlook offers only the Memo print style, and you can print only individual items.

V

Bending Folders to Your Will

Here's a brief description of what Outlook's built-in print styles do by default:

- **Memo.** Prints one or more selected folder items in a standard memo format. For instance, a printout of an appointment on your calendar might look like this:

Subject:	Lunch with Mark
Start:	Tuesday 3/18/97 12:30 PM
End:	Tuesday 3/18/97 2:00 PM
Recurrence:	(none)

- **Table.** Prints either selected folder items or an entire view. The information appears in a table arrangement with the column headings that are included in that view.

- **Daily.** Prints your calendar for the selected day, 7 A.M. to 7 P.M., and includes the TaskPad and a Notes section.

- **Weekly.** Prints your weekly calendar on one page. This style does not include the TaskPad or a Notes section.

- **Monthly.** Prints your monthly calendar on one page. Like Weekly style, this style does not include the TaskPad or a Notes section.

- **Tri-Fold.** Prints your daily calendar, weekly calendar, and TaskPad in three equal sections, using landscape orientation.

- **Card.** Prints either selected contact cards or an entire view of your Contacts folder. Contact cards appear in alphabetical order, marked by letter tabs, from top to bottom on the page in two columns. Outlook prints two blank cards at the end.

- **Small Booklet.** Prints either selected contact cards or an entire view of your Contacts folder. This style is designed for printing on both sides of a sheet of paper, with eight pages per sheet. You can cut, fold, and assemble the pages to form a booklet.

- **Medium Booklet.** Prints either selected contact cards or an entire view of your Contacts folder. This style is designed for printing on both sides of a sheet of paper, with four pages per sheet. You can cut, fold, and assemble the pages to form a booklet.

- **Phone Directory.** Prints names and telephone numbers for all your contacts or for selected contacts. The list is in alphabetical order, marked by letter tabs. Other contact information is omitted.

The Print button on the toolbar prints the items immediately, using the current Page Setup configuration. The File Print command opens the Print dialog box, in which you can select different print options.

If you want to use one of the alternative print styles that are available, follow these steps:

1 Open the folder that contains the folder items you want to print.

2 Check the current view on the Standard toolbar, and change the view setting if necessary. If you want to print one or more individual folder items, select the item or items.

3 Choose the File Print command to open the Print dialog box.

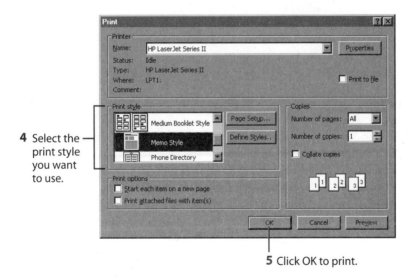

4 Select the print style you want to use.

5 Click OK to print.

Alternatively, you can use this method:

1 Open the folder that contains the folder items you want to print.

2 Check the current view on the Standard toolbar, and change the view setting if necessary. If you want to print one or more individual folder items, select the item or items.

V

Bending Folders to Your Will

3 Choose the File Page Setup command, and select the print style you want to use from the submenu. (The submenu lists the available built-in styles as well as any print styles you have created that apply to the view—see "Creating a Print Style," on page 412.)

4 In the Page Setup dialog box, you can review the settings for the selected print style and make any adjustments you like. (See "Modifying a Print Style," on page 402.)

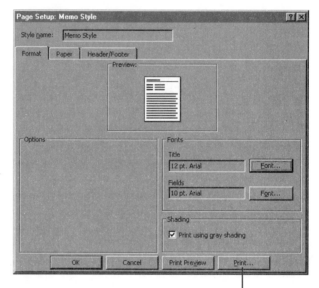

5 Click Print to open the Print dialog box.

6 In the Print dialog box, click OK to have Outlook start printing.

When you want to simply select a different print style, it's easiest to choose the File Print command and choose the print style in the Print dialog box (the first method described on page 395). If you want to adjust a print style before printing, it's more convenient to select the print style from the File Page Setup submenu (the second method described on page 395). This opens the Page Setup dialog box, where you can make the adjustments. Even if you use the first method, however, you can still adjust the style: click the Page Setup button in the Print dialog box to open the Page Setup dialog box.

Printing and Assembling a Booklet

The booklet print styles are designed so that you can print pages on both sides of a sheet of paper and then cut and staple the pages to create a booklet. (In Outlook, *paper* refers to a physical sheet of paper. *Page* refers to the area of the paper that is actually printed.) The layout and page numbering for the booklet are arranged automatically by Outlook.

You can print a booklet on either a duplex printer (a printer that can print on both sides of the paper) or a printer that prints on only one side of the paper at a time. When using a duplex printer, be sure it is set up for duplex printing. You do this in the printer's Properties dialog box (choose the File Print command, and then click the Properties button in the Print dialog box). If you are using a printer that prints on only one side of the paper at a time, print odd-numbered pages first (by selecting Odd in the Number Of Pages box in the Print dialog box), load the paper in the printer again so that the blank side prints, and then print even-numbered pages. (Select Even in the Number Of Pages box.)

To start printing a booklet, choose the File Print command and then select the print style you want to use. For a non-duplex printer, choose Odd in the Number Of Pages box. For a duplex printer, click the Properties button to open your printer's Properties dialog box, and then click the More Options button and select the Flip option you prefer. (Note that None is the default and is for one-sided printing only.) Click the Page Setup button, and then click the Paper tab. In the Page Size box, select ½ Sheet Booklet, ¼ Sheet Booklet, or ⅛ Sheet Booklet. Click Print Preview to see how the pages will appear when printed.

After printing the booklet's pages, cut the paper into the number of sections you specified. For example, if you specified a ⅛ Sheet Booklet, cut the paper into four sections. Each section will show two pages (the odd numbered page on the left or right side and the even numbered page on the opposite side). Stack the sheets of paper in the order of the page numbering, and fold along a ruler or straight edge. You can then staple the sheets of paper together.

Choosing Your Print Options

Whether you choose a built-in style or adjust or create a print style, you can still set various options before you print in Outlook. To set print options, open the Print dialog box in one of the following ways:

■ Choose the File Print command.

V

Bending Folders to Your Will

- Choose the File Page Setup command. Choose a style (or define a new style and select it), and then click the Print button in the Page Setup dialog box.

- Choose the File Print Preview command, and then click the Print button on the Print Preview toolbar. (See "Previewing Printing," on page 400.)

Figure 14-1 shows the Print dialog box and points out some of the print options you can set.

FIGURE 14-1.

The Print dialog box.

If necessary, you can select a different printer.

Click Properties if you need to adjust the printer setup.

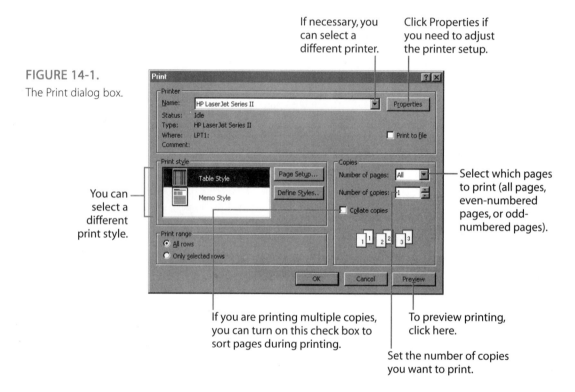

You can select a different print style.

Select which pages to print (all pages, even-numbered pages, or odd-numbered pages).

If you are printing multiple copies, you can turn on this check box to sort pages during printing.

To preview printing, click here.

Set the number of copies you want to print.

The options displayed in the Print Range area of the Print dialog box vary, depending on the type of print style you select. Table 14-2 lists the print styles and the Print Range options available for each style.

TABLE 14-2.   Print Range Options Available for Each Print Style.

Print Style	Print Range Options	Description
Table	All Rows; Only Selected Rows	Choose All Rows to print all items in a folder view; choose Only Selected Rows to print only the folder items you selected before opening the Print dialog box.
Phone Directory, Card, Small Booklet, Medium Booklet	All Items; Only Selected Items	Choose All Items to print all items in a folder view; choose Only Selected Items to print only the folder items you selected before opening the Print dialog box.
Memo	Start Each Item On A New Page; Print Attached Files With Item(s)	Choose this option to print each folder item on a separate page. Choose this option to print the contents of attachments with the text of each folder item.
Daily, Weekly, Monthly, Tri-Fold	Start; End	Select or type the earliest date (Start) and the latest date (End) of the items you want to print.

Most of the time, you'll want to select All in the Number Of Pages box in the Print dialog box to print all the pages of folder items in a printing job. But when you need to collate the pages in a special way, you can select Odd or Even to print only the odd-numbered or even-numbered pages. For information about printing odd-numbered and even-numbered pages to form a booklet, see the sidebar, "Printing and Assembling a Booklet," on page 397.

Printing to a File

If you need to send a file to someone else who will be printing folder items for you, or if you need to print from a different computer, you can "print" folder items to a file. Then you (or the other person) can print the file using the MS-DOS Copy command.

V

Bending Folders to Your Will

To print to a file, take these steps:

1 Choose the File Print command.

2 Turn on the Print To File check box in the Print dialog box.

3 Click OK in the Print dialog box.

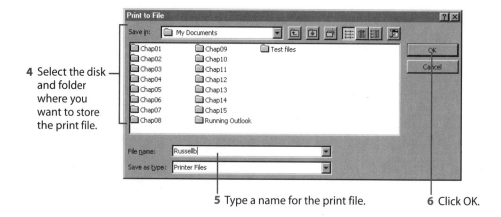

4 Select the disk and folder where you want to store the print file.

5 Type a name for the print file.

6 Click OK.

To print the printer file, click the Start button on the Microsoft Windows 95 Taskbar, click Programs, and then click MS-DOS Prompt. Switch to the directory in which the printer file is stored. At the MS-DOS prompt, type *copy <filename.prn> <printer port:>*, where *filename* is the name of the printer file you want to print, and *printer port* is the port to which your printer is connected (for example, LPT1:). For more information on how to capture a printer port, see Windows 95 Help.

Previewing Printing

Before you print an item or a view, you can preview it to see what it will look like on paper. Print Preview uses the settings for the currently selected print style in the Print and Page Setup dialog boxes.

To preview a selected item or a view before printing, take one of the following actions:

- Click the Print Preview button on the Standard toolbar.

- Choose the File Print Preview command.

- Choose the File Page Setup command, select the print style you want to preview, and then click the Preview button in the Page Setup dialog box.

- Choose the File Print command, and then click the Preview button in the Print dialog box.

Figure 14-2 shows a preview of several notes in the Memo print style and points out useful buttons on the Print Preview toolbar.

Page Up

Page Down

Actual Size   Page Setup

One Page   Print

Multiple
Pages   Close Preview

FIGURE 14-2.

Notes in Print Preview, using the Memo print style.

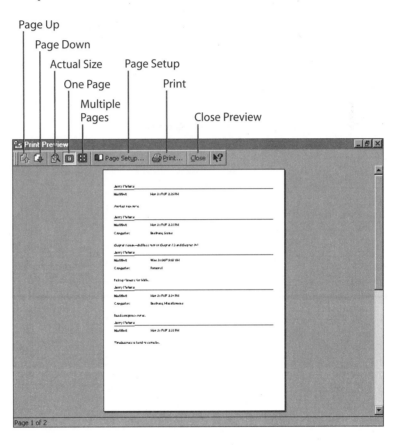

Print Preview displays the full page layout of the items to be printed, reducing the size of the folder item text in order to display an entire page on screen at one time. It's an extremely useful feature when you want to check how the various print styles look on the page, how columns line up, whether the print style needs adjustment, and so on.

If you don't like what you see in Print Preview, you can click the Page Setup button on the Print Preview toolbar to open the Page Setup dialog box. You can then adjust the current print style as explained in "Modifying a Print Style," below, returning to Print Preview whenever you want to check the results of your changes. Or, if you decide to try a different print style, you can click the Print button either on the Print Preview toolbar or in the Page Setup dialog box to open the Print dialog box and select a new style.

If you need to see the text in actual size while you are in Print Preview, you can either click the Actual Size button on the Print Preview toolbar or click anywhere inside the page area. To switch the view back to full page, click again inside the page area.

When you're ready to print, click the Print button on the Print Preview toolbar, and then click OK in the Print dialog box.

Modifying a Print Style

Ⓧ CAUTION

Changes you make to a built-in print style affect that print style in all folders and views where you can use it. For example, if you change the Table style to print with a landscape orientation instead of portrait, all printing you do using this style will be in landscape. If you change a built-in print style, you can return it to its original settings—see "Resetting a Print Style," on page 411.

You can make a number of changes to a print style, including changes to its format, to its standard paper settings, and to the information included in headers or footers.

The general steps for changing a print style are as follows:

1 Choose the File Page Setup command, and choose Define Print Styles from the submenu. As an alternative, you can choose the File Print command, select the print style in the Print Style list, and then click the Define Styles button.

2 Select the print style you want to change.

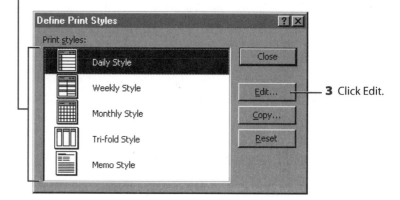

3 Click Edit.

4 Make your changes on any of the three tabs of the Page Setup dialog box, as explained in the next three sections.

5 Click OK in the Page Setup dialog box.

6 Click the Close button in the Define Print Styles dialog box. (To change another print style, repeat steps 2 through 5 instead of clicking the Close button.)

You can also use the Print Preview feature in this process. As you make your changes (step 4), you can click the Print Preview button at any time to see how your adjustments affect the printed page. If you're dissatisfied with the results, click the Page Setup button on the Print Preview toolbar to return to the Page Setup dialog box so that you can continue refining the print style.

When you're satisfied with what you see in Print Preview (and if you don't want to change another print style), click the Close Preview button on the Print Preview toolbar to return to Outlook, or click the Print button on the same toolbar to open the Print dialog box, where you can begin printing as soon as you click OK.

Changing the Format

The Format tab of the Page Setup dialog box always provides a small preview picture of the print style as well as the three standard options indicated in Figure 14-3 on the following page. (This figure shows the Format tab for the Table print style; the tab for the Memo style is very similar.) For all print styles, you can change the fonts used in headings and in the body of the folder items, and you have the option of printing with or without gray shading.

You can also change the format of the Daily, Weekly, Monthly, and Tri-Fold print styles, which are used to print calendar items. Again, you can use different fonts for date headings and for appointments, and you can print with or without gray shading. But you also have some additional layout options, as shown in Figure 14-4 on the following page. (This figure shows the Format tab for the Daily print style.) In the Layout box, you can tell Outlook to print the day's calendar on two pages rather than one, giving you more room to write in information about your appointments and meetings. You can specify the range of time to be printed for the day (in the Print From and Print To boxes), and you can choose to include or omit the TaskPad (which is lined) and the Notes section (which is lined or unlined).

FIGURE 14-3.

The Format tab for the Table print style.

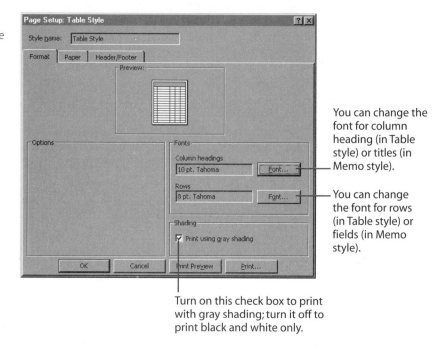

You can change the font for column heading (in Table style) or titles (in Memo style).

You can change the font for rows (in Table style) or fields (in Memo style).

Turn on this check box to print with gray shading; turn it off to print black and white only.

Choose whether to print one day on a single page or on two pages.

Turn on this check box to print a Notes section with lines.

Turn on this check box to print a Notes section without lines.

Turn on this check box to print the TaskPad.

FIGURE 14-4.

The Format tab for the Daily print style.

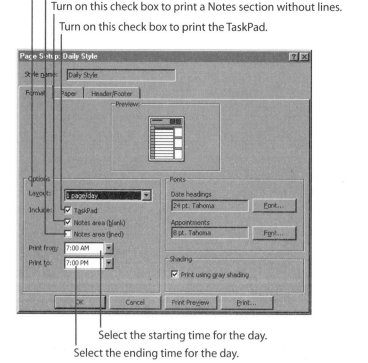

Select the starting time for the day.

Select the ending time for the day.

The Format tabs for the Weekly and Monthly print styles are similar to the tab shown in Figure 14-4, with the following variations:

- The Format tab for the Weekly print style offers the same options you find for the Daily print style. (In this case, of course, you choose whether to print a week—rather than a day—on one page or two.) In addition, this tab contains two Arrange options: click Top To Bottom to have Outlook arrange the seven days down two columns on the page (omitting hour markers), or click Left To Right to have Outlook set up seven columns across the page, one for each day, including hour markers. (If you choose Top To Bottom, Outlook turns off the Print From and Print To boxes—there's no need to specify a range of hours when the hour markers are omitted.)

- The Format tab for the Monthly print style provides the Layout option (which prints a month on one page or two) and the Include options (which print the TaskPad and the Notes section) but omits the Arrange options and the Print From and Print To boxes.

The Format tab for the Tri-Fold print style is a little different. It contains only three options: Left Section, Middle Section, and Right Section. For each section (fold) of a tri-fold printing, you can specify one of the following items to print in that section:

- Daily calendar

- Weekly calendar

- Monthly calendar

- TaskPad

- Notes (blank)

- Notes (lined)

The Format tabs for the Card, Small Booklet, and Medium Booklet print styles, used for printing contact items, are identical. You can see the tab for the Card style in Figure 14-5 on the following page.

V

Bending Folders to Your Will

FIGURE 14-5.

The Format tab for the Card print style.

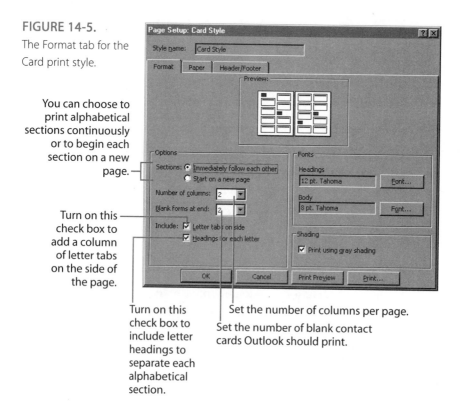

You can choose to print alphabetical sections continuously or to begin each section on a new page.

Turn on this check box to add a column of letter tabs on the side of the page.

Turn on this check box to include letter headings to separate each alphabetical section.

Set the number of columns per page.

Set the number of blank contact cards Outlook should print.

The Sections options on this tab refer to the alphabetical sections of your contact list. You can print alphabetical sections one after another in continuous columns, or you can begin each section on a new page. You can also specify the number of columns per page, and you can tell Outlook to include blank contact cards (forms) at the end of the printing—these are useful if you need to hand-write contact information, to be entered in your contact list in Outlook later. In addition, you can include or omit headings for each alphabetical section as well as letter tabs on the side of the page. When you include letter tabs, they appear on the right-hand side of the page in a shaded column, as shown in Figure 14-6 on the facing page.

FIGURE 14-6.

A page of contact information, previewed using the Card print style with letter tabs on the side.

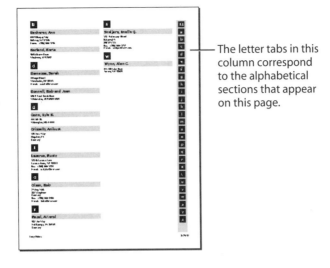

The letter tabs in this column correspond to the alphabetical sections that appear on this page.

Finally, the Format tab for the Phone Directory print style is fairly simple. You can specify the number of columns to print, and you can include or omit headings for each alphabetical section and letter tabs on the side of the page.

Changing Paper Settings

The various print styles have their own paper settings—paper size (or type), page size, orientation, paper source (the tray in your printer), and margins. You can adjust these settings on the Paper tab of the Page Setup dialog box, shown in Figure 14-7. The Paper tab displays the same information for all print styles.

FIGURE 14-7.

The Paper tab for the Memo print style.

Select a paper type (paper size) here.

You can set a custom width and height for paper.

Select the appropriate paper feed for your printer.

You can set different margins.

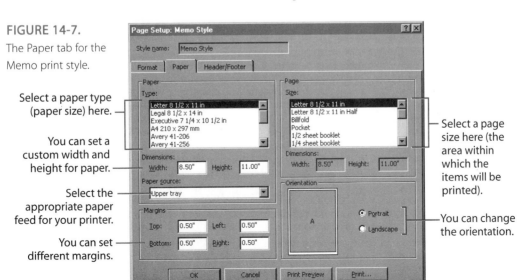

Select a page size here (the area within which the items will be printed).

You can change the orientation.

When printing Outlook items and views, it's important to understand how Outlook distinguishes between paper and page. In Outlook, paper refers to the physical sheet of paper you put in the printer. Page refers to the area of the paper that will be printed on. You can print several pages on a single sheet of paper. For example, in the Small Booklet print style, you can print eight pages of a booklet on a single sheet of paper.

Each print style uses a particular paper type and page size. You can modify the paper type and page size for a print style on the Paper tab of the Page Setup dialog box. When you select a paper type, the list of page sizes available for use with that paper type is displayed in the Page Size list. Settings for paper type and page size in the Page Setup dialog box take precedence over any paper settings you select in the Properties dialog box for your printer (which you open by clicking the Properties button in the Print dialog box). Settings you make in the Orientation area of the Paper tab apply to pages, not to paper type.

Let's say you want to use the Daily print style to print four days worth of calendar items. By default, Outlook prints the items for each day on a separate sheet of 8½-x-11-inch paper. If you want to have all four days appear on one sheet of paper (in effect, changing the page size), select Pocket from the Size list on the Paper tab.

Setting a Custom Paper Size

You can set up any custom paper size you want. To specify a custom paper size, simply select Custom in the Paper Type list, and then set the width and height of the paper in the Dimensions boxes in the Paper Type section.

> If you change the width or height of a listed paper type, Outlook automatically selects Custom in the Paper Type list.

When you set up a custom paper size, the Page Size list includes the appropriate page size choices for that paper size. Outlook also adds Custom and Custom Half as the first two items in the Page Size list.

Setting Margins

When you change the margin settings, you're changing the width and height of the blank space at the borders of the paper. Keep margins small unless you like lots of blank space around the printed information. The larger the margins, the more cramped the information appears because it must fit into a smaller space. You'll often need to print on more sheets of paper if you use large margins.

Outlook's default margins are .50 inch for the top, bottom, left, and right borders of the paper. You can click the Print Preview button in the Page Setup dialog box to see the effect of changes you make to margins.

Setting Up Headers and Footers

For all print styles, the process of setting up headers and footers is the same. The Header/Footer tab of the Page Setup dialog box provides six boxes in which you can insert the text and fields that you want Outlook to print in headers and footers, as shown in Figure 14-8. For some print styles, Outlook presets parts of the header or footer, but you can change any section of the header or footer as you like.

FIGURE 14-8.
The Header/Footer tab of the Page Setup dialog box.

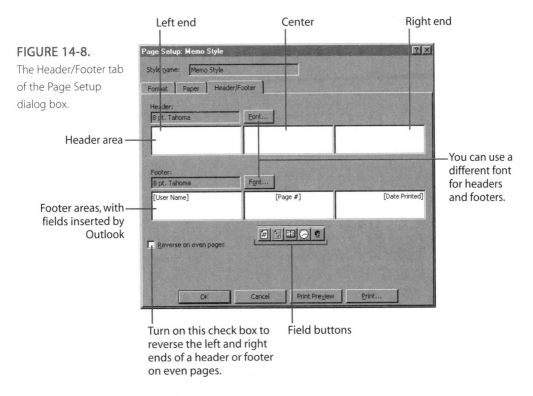

Left end Center Right end

Header area

You can use a different font for headers and footers.

Footer areas, with fields inserted by Outlook

Turn on this check box to reverse the left and right ends of a header or footer on even pages.

Field buttons

Bending Folders to Your Will

You can use only text, only fields, or a combination of text and fields in your headers and footers. The header and footer boxes (left, center, and right) correspond to the location on the page—if you enter text only in the center header box, for instance, Outlook prints a centered header on each page. For the footer set up in Figure 14-8 (on the previous page), Outlook will print the user's name on the left, the page number in the center, and the date of printing on the right.

NOTE

The term "field" refers to a location that shows data or to an empty box that you (or Outlook) can fill in with information.

To insert a field into a header or footer, click one of the Field buttons on the Header/Footer tab:

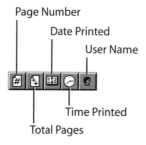

Outlook displays an inserted field as words inside square brackets: *[Page #]*, for example. (You can type the field in the header or footer box instead of clicking a button if you type it in this format.) During printing, Outlook replaces the field with the proper information—the page number, the date of printing, and so on.

You can type any text in any of the header and footer areas. The text might be some special information about the printed items, such as the date range of appointments, meetings, or tasks. You might want to type the word *Page* before the Page Number field. Or you might type the word *of* between a Page Number field and a Total Pages field and then type the word *pages* after the Total Pages field—this way, on each page Outlook prints a header or footer such as *5 of 10 pages*.

If you want the same headers and footers to print on every page, leave the Reverse On Even Pages check box turned off. But if you're printing on both sides of the paper or if you're going to photocopy single-sided printed pages back to back to assemble a booklet, you might want to have Outlook always print the text in the left-most area of the header or footer on the outside of all pages. This would, for instance, allow page numbers to appear on the outside edge of each of two facing pages (both odd and even pages). In this case, turn on the Reverse On Even Pages check box.

Resetting a Print Style

After you make changes to a built-in print style, you might want to restore the original settings. To reset a built-in print style, take these steps:

1   Choose the File Page Setup command, and choose Define Print Styles from the submenu.

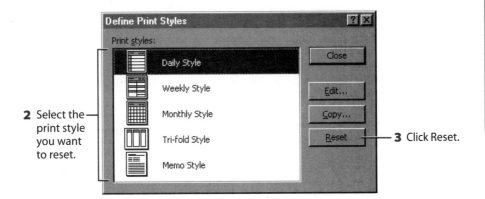

2 Select the print style you want to reset.

3 Click Reset.

4   When Outlook asks you to confirm resetting the print style, click OK.

5   Repeat steps 2 through 4 for each built-in style you want to reset.

6   When you've finished, click the Close button in the Define Print Styles dialog box.

V

Bending Folders to Your Will

NOTE

You can't reset a print style that you have created. You can only modify it or delete it.

Creating a Print Style

Rather than changing a built-in print style and having those changes affect the printing of all folder items for which you use the print style, you can create a print style of your own. You create a print style as a copy of a built-in print style (or as a copy of a print style you've already created). This method gives you some advantages. First, you start from an existing batch of settings, which means that you need to modify only the specific settings that you want to change rather than having to set all the options yourself. Second, in any instance in which the print style you copied applies, your custom style also appears on the File Page Setup submenu (after you exit and restart Outlook) and in the Print dialog box for easy selection. You don't have to re-create your special print style for every view or folder.

Here's how to create a print style:

1 Choose the File Page Setup command, and choose Define Print Styles from the submenu. As an alternative, you can choose the File Print command, select the print style in the Print Style list, and then click the Define Styles button.

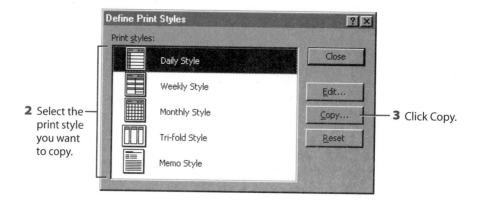

2 Select the print style you want to copy.

3 Click Copy.

4 Type a name for the new print style.

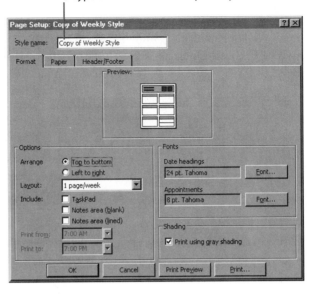

5 Change any settings on any (or all) of the three tabs in the Page Setup dialog box. (For details, see "Changing the Format," on page 403, "Changing Paper Settings," on page 407, and "Setting Up Headers and Footers," on page 409.)

6 Click OK in the Page Setup dialog box.

7 Click the Close button in the Define Print Styles dialog box.

> **TIP**
>
> You can also use the Print Preview feature in this process. As you make your changes (step 5), you can click the Print Preview button at any time to see how your style will appear on the printed page. If you're dissatisfied with the results, click the Page Setup button on the Print Preview toolbar to return to the Page Setup dialog box and continue creating the print style.

Deleting a Print Style You Created

If you no longer want or need a print style that you created, you can delete it. To do so, take these steps:

1   Choose the File Page Setup command, and choose Define Print Styles from the submenu. As an alternative, you can choose the File Print command, select the print style in the Print Style list, and then click the Define Styles button.

2   In the Define Print Styles dialog box, select the print style you want to delete and then click the Delete button.

3   When Outlook asks you to confirm that you want to delete the print style, click OK. Repeat steps 2 and 3 for each custom style that you want to delete.

4   When you've finished, click the Close button in the Define Print Styles dialog box.

Archiving Folder Items

As you use Microsoft Outlook 97, your folders can eventually become cluttered with items that you no longer need on a day-to-day basis—tasks that were long since completed, e-mail messages about a project that has been canceled, appointments from the past, and so on. You can, of course, simply delete these folder items if you're sure that you'll never need them again. But if the items might be important in the future—perhaps that canceled project comes back to life, for instance—you can put them into storage.

Outlook lets you transfer old items to an archive (storage) file on your hard disk. Outlook removes the items from your current folders, reducing the number of folder items so that the folders are easier to use. If you need the archived items in the future, you can retrieve them from the archive file.

You can archive folder items in two ways:

■ Allow Outlook's AutoArchive feature to automatically archive folder items of specified ages on a regular basis.

■ Manually archive folder items yourself as the need arises.

 NOTE

> When you archive Outlook folder items, your existing folder structure is maintained in the archive file. For example, if you choose to archive the items in a subfolder, the main folder is also created in the archive file, but the items in the main folder are not necessarily archived. By doing this, Outlook creates the same folder structure in your archive file as in your mailbox. Even if folders are emptied during archiving, Outlook leaves the folders in place. To remove an empty folder, right-click the folder name in the Folder List and choose Delete from the shortcut menu.

Using the AutoArchive Feature

Outlook is initially set up to automatically archive old items in certain folders every 14 days. Outlook lets you know when it's preparing to run the AutoArchive feature and gives you a chance to cancel it. Every 14 days when you start Outlook, you'll see the following prompt shortly after startup:

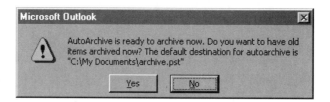

You can vary the 14-day time span, and you can specify additional folders to be archived. You can also change the definition of an "old" (expired) item, and you can use AutoArchive for both archiving and deleting. To set up automatic archiving the way you like, you first need to review or adjust the AutoArchive settings in the Options dialog box. Then you need to set the AutoArchive properties for each folder that you want Outlook to archive automatically.

Setting General AutoArchive Options

As you might recall from Chapter 2, the Options dialog box contains tabs whose settings govern Outlook's default behavior in various areas. To review or change Outlook's default AutoArchive settings, choose the Tools Options command, and click the AutoArchive tab of the Options dialog box, shown in Figure 15-1.

Turn off this check box if you want to prevent all automatic archiving.

FIGURE 15-1.

The AutoArchive tab of the Options dialog box.

Turn off this check box if you don't want to see a prompt before automatic archiving begins.

Turn off this check box to prevent deletion of expired items from e-mail folders.

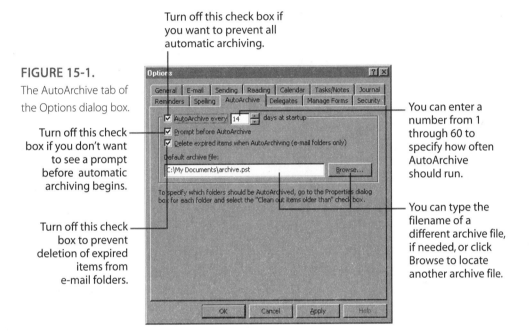

You can enter a number from 1 through 60 to specify how often AutoArchive should run.

You can type the filename of a different archive file, if needed, or click Browse to locate another archive file.

As you see in Figure 15-1, you can change the number of days in the AutoArchive Every [ ] Days At Startup box to tell Outlook how often to run AutoArchive. This option also allows you to completely disable the AutoArchive feature (by turning off the check box) if you prefer to always archive folder items manually.

> AutoArchive runs only when you start up Outlook. If you want to run automatic archiving in the middle of an Outlook session, change the number of days in the AutoArchive Every [ ] Days At Startup option to 1, choose the File Exit And Log Off command, and then restart Outlook.

When the option called Delete Expired Items When AutoArchiving is turned on, Outlook moves expired e-mail messages to the Deleted Items folder rather than adding them to the archive file. Turn off this option to prevent deletion of the items. Also, when AutoArchive runs, items in the Deleted Items folder are not moved to the archive file. Instead they are deleted.

Figure 15-1, on the previous page, shows the name of Outlook's default archive file, ARCHIVE.PST, in the My Documents folder. The .PST file-name extension indicates a personal folders file, which Outlook uses for archiving. You can create more than one archive file. For example, you could create an archive file for the items related to a particular project.

 NOTE

The settings on the AutoArchive tab of the Options dialog box affect both automatic archiving and manual archiving (explained in "Archiving Folder Items Manually," on page 421).

Archiving Vs. Exporting Outlook Folder Items

When thinking about archiving Outlook folder items, it's helpful to keep in mind some differences between archiving items and exporting items. You can only archive Outlook items by using a personal folder file (a file with a .PST extension), but you can export Outlook items to many file types, such as text. Although Outlook can archive all types of items, Outlook archives only files (such as an attached Microsoft Excel spreadsheet or Microsoft Word document) that are stored in an e-mail folder. A file that is not stored in an e-mail folder cannot be archived. When you archive, the original items are copied to the archive file and then removed from the folder that is currently open. When you export, the original items are copied to the export file but are not removed from the current folder.

Setting a Folder's AutoArchive Properties

Once AutoArchive is turned on and the settings adjusted (if necessary) on the AutoArchive tab of the Options dialog box, you need to specify which folders Outlook should automatically archive. By default, the AutoArchive feature is turned on for the Calendar, Journal, Tasks, Sent Items, and Deleted Items folders. To turn on automatic archiving for the Inbox folder, the Notes folder, or any folder that you have created (or to turn it off for the default folders), you need to change the folder's properties, as explained on the facing page.

1 Right-click the folder icon on the Outlook Bar, and choose Properties from the shortcut menu. (If the folder icon does not appear on the Outlook Bar, click the Folder List button on the Standard toolbar, right-click the folder in the Folder List, and choose Properties from the shortcut menu.)

2 In the Notes Properties dialog box, click the AutoArchive tab.

3 Turn on this check box to archive this folder.

4 Specify how old an item must be before it is considered expired.

5 Click here to move folder items to the archive file, or...

click here to delete folder items permanently instead of archiving them.

6 You can type the filename of a different archive file, if necessary, or click Browse to locate another archive file.

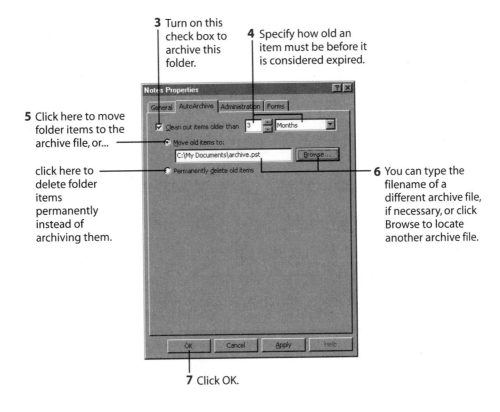

7 Click OK.

V

Bending Folders to Your Will

You'll need to repeat this procedure for each folder that you want to set up for automatic archiving. The AutoArchive choices you select for a folder take effect the next time Outlook automatically archives the folder's items or when you manually archive them.

For each folder, you can choose whether the AutoArchive feature should move expired items to the archive file or should permanently delete them. Choosing the Permanently Delete Old Items option means that expired items are permanently removed. They are not moved to the Deleted Items folder, from which you could retrieve them.

Also, for each folder, you can use the Clean Out Items Older Than option to define the number of days, weeks, or months that Outlook should use to consider an item expired. If you enter 60 days, for example, Outlook will consider items expired as follows:

- An e-mail message will expire 60 days after the date it was sent, received, or last modified.

- An appointment or meeting will expire 60 days after the date of the appointment or meeting or 60 days after the date the item was last modified.

- A task will expire 60 days after the date it was marked completed or 60 days after the date it was last modified.

- A note will expire 60 days after the date it was created or last modified.

- A journal entry will expire 60 days after the date it was created or last modified.

> **NOTE**

Outlook does not archive items from the Contacts folder. Task items from the Tasks folder (both your own tasks and tasks that you have assigned to someone else) are not archived unless they have been marked completed.

Preventing the Automatic Archiving of a Folder Item

Somewhere, in at least one Outlook folder, you're likely to have an item that you don't want Outlook to archive automatically. Maybe it's an item that you want to keep as a reminder. Or perhaps you've set up AutoArchive to permanently delete expired items from the folder, but you don't want to lose this one particular item. In such cases, you can designate the folder item as "Do Not AutoArchive."

To prevent a single folder item from being automatically archived (or deleted by AutoArchive), take these steps:

1 Open the folder that contains the item, and select the item.

2 Choose the File Properties command, and click the General tab in the Properties dialog box.

The item title appears here in addition to the dialog box name (Properties).

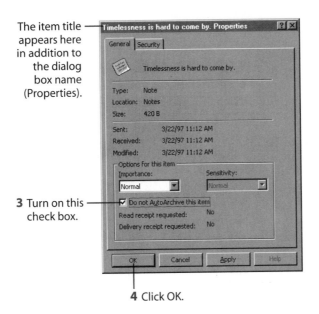

3 Turn on this check box.

4 Click OK.

You must repeat this procedure for each folder item that you want to designate as "Do Not AutoArchive." If a folder contains a number of items you do not want to archive automatically, consider turning off AutoArchive for that *folder* and archive the individual items manually.

 NOTE

You can manually archive a folder item that you've designated as "Do Not AutoArchive." This designation simply prevents AutoArchive from taking any action with the folder item.

Archiving Folder Items Manually

Even though you set up AutoArchive to archive folder items on a regular basis, you still might want to manually archive items from time to time. Perhaps you've finished a project and want to archive the related items sooner than the next scheduled AutoArchive. Maybe you've turned off AutoArchive for a certain folder but nevertheless want to archive a few items from that folder. Or maybe you're finally ready to archive an item that has previously been designated as "Do Not AutoArchive."

V

Bending Folders to Your Will

To manually archive folder items, follow these steps:

1 Choose the File Archive command to open the Archive dialog box.

2 If you select the first option in the dialog box, Archive All Folders According To Their AutoArchive Settings, the rest of the options become unavailable and you should move to step 7.

If you select the second option, Archive This Folder And All Subfolders, proceed to step 3.

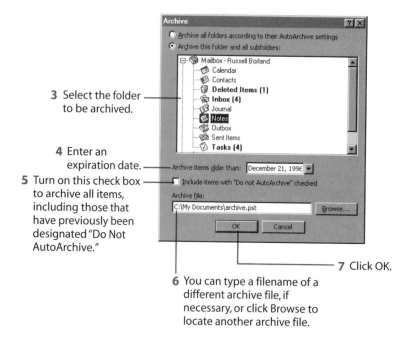

3 Select the folder to be archived.

4 Enter an expiration date.

5 Turn on this check box to archive all items, including those that have previously been designated "Do Not AutoArchive."

6 You can type a filename of a different archive file, if necessary, or click Browse to locate another archive file.

7 Click OK.

You must repeat this procedure for each folder that you want to archive manually.

TIP

To type a date in the Archive Items Older Than box, you can use any standard date format: 10-13-96, 10/13/96, Oct-13-96, October 13, 1996, and so on. Alternatively, you can click the down arrow beside the date to display a drop-down calendar from which you can select the date.

Retrieving Archived Folder Items

You can retrieve items from an archive file either by adding the archive file to your user profile or by importing the archive file. To add the archive file to your user profile, you add it as a personal folders file. In this way, the archive file is attached to your mailbox and remains a separate file that contains all the archived items. If you import the archive file, Outlook moves the archived items back into your mailbox.

To add the archive file to your user profile, follow these steps:

1 Choose the Tools Services command.

2 On the Services tab, click the Add button.

3 In the Add Service To Profile dialog box, select Personal Folders from the Available Information Services box and click OK.

4 In the Create/Open Personal Folders File dialog box, locate the archive file you want to add and then click Open.

5 In the Personal Folders dialog box, name the file. You might want to give the file a name such as Archived Items or name it after a particular project.

6 Click OK in the Personal Folders dialog box, and then click OK in the Services dialog box.

You now have access to the items in the archive file—just display the Folder List and open the folder you need.

To retrieve items from an archive file by importing the file, choose the File Import And Export command to start the Import And Export Wizard. In the wizard's first panel, select Import From A Personal Folder File, and then click the Next button. From there, you can follow the instructions in the Import And Export Wizard.

V

Bending Folders to Your Will

CHAPTER 16

Managing Folders

F olders are an important and integral part of
Microsoft Outlook 97. Outlook stores all items
in folders. Outlook can also display the folders
and files on any disk that's connected to your computer,
whether it's an internal disk drive (hard or floppy) or
a network drive.

Chapter 13, "Managing Folder Contents," described how
to manage the contents of folders. But to make Outlook
work more effectively and efficiently, you also need to
be able to manage the folders themselves. That's what
this chapter describes.

Opening a Folder

Outlook gives you several ways to open a folder. As you know, icons for most Outlook folders appear on the Outlook Bar, on one of the bar's three group panels: Outlook, Mail, or Other. Opening a folder from the Outlook Bar is usually quick and convenient, especially if you display the Outlook Bar most of the time. In addition to the Outlook Bar, you can use the Folder List, the Go menu, and several buttons on the Standard toolbar to open folders.

Opening a Folder from the Outlook Bar

 SEE ALSO

If you want to add a folder icon to the Outlook Bar (or otherwise modify the bar), see "Modifying the Outlook Bar," on page 29.

Just for review, here's how to open a folder that appears on the Outlook Bar:

1 Click the label for the shortcut that contains the folder icon.

2 If necessary, click the small up or down arrow on the Outlook bar to scroll to the folder you want.

3 Click the folder icon.

If the folder you open contains only other folders, you'll see a message in the folder items area of the Outlook window that tells you to select a subfolder. To do this, you must use the steps described in one of the next two sections, "Opening a Folder from the Folder List," or "Opening a Folder from the Go Menu."

Opening a Folder from the Folder List

If you create a folder or if you need to use a folder that's not listed on the Outlook Bar, you can open the folder from the Folder List.

To open a folder that's not on the Outlook Bar (or to open subfolders of a folder that is not on the Outlook Bar), follow these steps:

Folder List

1 Click the Folder List button on the Standard toolbar.

Folder List

2 If necessary, click the plus sign to expand the folder containing the subfolder you want to open.

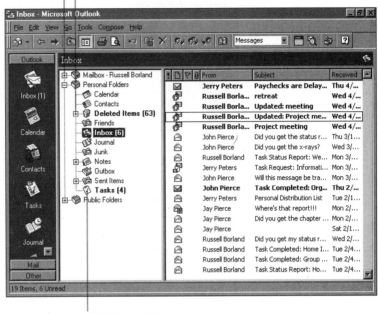

3 Click the folder you want to open.

Opening a Folder from the Go Menu

The Go menu contains a list of the main Outlook folders plus the My Computer folder. This menu also contains four commands for opening folders: Back, Forward, Up One Level, and Go To Folder. (We'll discuss the first three commands in the next section.)

To open a folder listed on the Go menu, click the folder name on the menu. To open a folder that is not listed on the Go menu, do the following:

1 Choose the Go To Folder command from the Go menu.

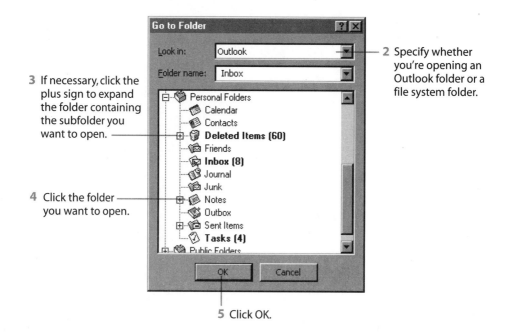

3 If necessary, click the plus sign to expand the folder containing the subfolder you want to open.

2 Specify whether you're opening an Outlook folder or a file system folder.

4 Click the folder you want to open.

5 Click OK.

Opening a Folder from the Standard Toolbar

Outlook's Standard toolbar contains three buttons (in addition to the Folder List button), called Back, Forward, and Up One Level, that you can use to open folders.

Clicking one of these buttons has the same effect as choosing the command of the same name from the Go menu. Here's how they work:

■ Click the Back button to reopen the folder that was open before the currently open folder. The Back button becomes available as soon as you move from the folder that was open when you started Outlook. When you reach the folder that was open when you started Outlook, this button becomes unavailable.

- Click the Forward button to reopen the folder that you opened after the currently open folder. The Forward button becomes available after you move back to a folder you opened previously. When you reopen the latest open folder, the Forward button becomes unavailable.

- Click the Up One Level button to open the folder containing the folder that's currently open. When you open the highest-level folder and click this button, Outlook displays a message telling you that you are at the highest level and that there are no folders above the current one.

> The Back and Forward buttons work the same as the Back and Forward buttons in Microsoft Internet Explorer. The Up One Level button works the same as the Up One Level button in the My Computer and Explorer windows in Microsoft Windows 95.

Opening a Folder in a Separate Window

If you want to see the contents of two folders at the same time, you can open the second folder in a separate window. Sometimes this arrangement can be convenient for quickly switching from one folder to another.

To open a folder in a separate window, right-click the folder, either on the Outlook Bar or in the Folder List. Then choose Open In New Window from the shortcut menu.

Outlook displays a new Outlook window with the selected folder open. You can set up this Outlook window in all the same ways you set up the first Outlook window. Of course, having a separate window gives you the opportunity to set up each window differently.

Opening a Special Folder

On the File menu, you'll find the Open Special Folder command. This command has a submenu you can use to open other folders on a server (for example, Exchange Server Folder) or a set of personal folders. You'll often use the Open Special Folder command if you've been assigned delegate access to another person's Inbox or Calendar folder.

You can open a set of personal folders as follows:

1 Choose the File Open Special Folder command, and then choose Personal Folder from the submenu.

2 Switch to the disk and folder that contain the personal folder file.

4 Click OK.

3 Select the file.

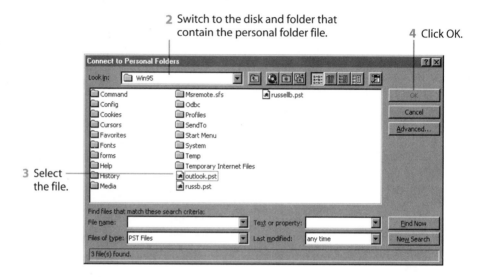

If the personal folders file you open has been assigned a password, Outlook displays the Personal Folders Password dialog box. Enter the password for the personal folders file, and then click OK. Outlook opens the folders in a separate window.

If you're working online, you can open a special folder located on a server as follows. (If you're working offline, the server command on the File Open Special Folder submenu is dimmed and unavailable). To open another person's Inbox or any other of his or her Outlook folders, you must have permission to do so.

1 Choose the File Open Special Folder command, and then choose the server command from the submenu. (The following illustration assumes that this command is Exchange Server Folder.)

2 Type the name of the person whose Inbox or other server folder you want to open, or...

click Name to select the name.

4 Click OK.

3 Select the folder you want to open.

Outlook opens the folder you selected in a new Outlook window.

Creating a Folder

Creating a new folder is a pretty simple task. You can add a new folder inside any existing folder or subfolder.

To create a new folder, follow these steps:

1 Open the folder in which you want the new subfolder to reside.

2 Choose the File Folder command, and then choose Create Subfolder from the submenu.

5 If necessary, select the folder in which the new folder will reside.

3 Type a name for the new folder.

4 Select the type of folder item that the new folder will contain. Use the drop-down list to view the different types of folder items available.

7 Click OK.

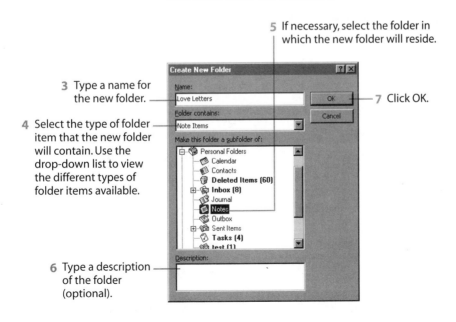

6 Type a description of the folder (optional).

V

Bending Folders to Your Will

Most of the folder management commands on the File Folder submenu can also be accessed from the Folder List. You can expand the Folder List to display the folder you want to work with, right-click the folder, and then choose a command from the shortcut menu.

Copying an Existing Folder

If you have a folder that might prove to be useful in more than one location, you can copy it as a subfolder of another folder (rather than move it). For example, you might copy a server folder to your personal folders. You can even copy an existing folder to a new folder you create during copying.

Here's the way to copy an existing folder as a subfolder of another folder:

1 Open the folder you want to copy.

2 Choose the File Folder command, and then choose the Copy command from the submenu. The Copy command shows the name of the open folder. Alternatively, you can right-click the folder in the Folder List and then choose Copy from the shortcut menu.

3 Select the folder in which the copy will reside, or...
   click New to create a new folder for the copy.

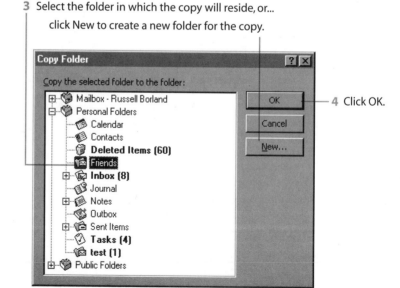

4 Click OK.

For a faster way to copy a folder, hold down the Ctrl key while you drag the folder being copied to the folder in which the copy will reside.

Copying a Folder Design

You can sometimes put a lot of effort into designing a folder—setting up views, grouping items, adding filters, sorting, designing forms, and even granting permissions. After you set up the design of a folder, you might realize that another Outlook folder could benefit from having the same design, or at least a very similar design. Fortunately, rather than going through a laborious setup for each folder, you can simply copy a folder design from one folder to another.

The following procedure describes how to copy a folder design:

1   Open the Folder List, and select the folder to which you will be copying the design of another folder.

2   Choose the File Folder command, and then choose Copy Folder Design from the submenu.

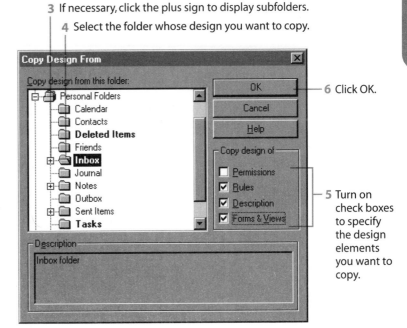

3 If necessary, click the plus sign to display subfolders.

4 Select the folder whose design you want to copy.

6 Click OK.

5 Turn on check boxes to specify the design elements you want to copy.

Bending Folders to Your Will

After you copy a folder design, you can tweak it to suit the folder. For information about folder design, see Chapter 17, "Columns, Categories, Grouping, Sorting, Filtering, and Custom Fields," and Chapter 20, "Designing Personal Forms."

Moving a Folder

Sometimes you just don't get it right the first time (or the second or third time, either). You've got a folder stuck somewhere in your mail system, and you want to stick it somewhere else. What to do, what to do? Move that folder!

You can move a folder into another folder in several ways. Simply display the Folder List and expand it as needed so that both folders are visible. Then drag the folder you want to move to the folder where it will be stored (the destination folder).

Alternatively, instead of dragging the folder, you can choose the File Folder command, and then choose Move from the submenu. Or you can right-click the folder in the Folder List, and then choose Move from the shortcut menu. Either way, when you use the Move command, Outlook displays the Move Folder dialog box, shown here:

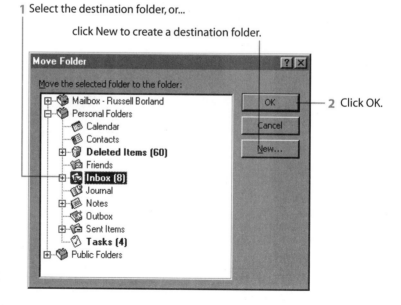

You can move a folder to a server folder, to the Personal Folders folder, or to any other folder within these two folders, where it becomes a subfolder.

> **NOTE**
>
> You can move only the folders that you have created. You can't move the standard (built-in) Outlook folders. You also cannot move a standard server or personal folder. In addition, unless you have permission from the system administrator, Microsoft Exchange won't let you move a folder to the Public Folders folder.

Renaming a Folder

If you didn't get the name right when you created a folder, you can change it. To rename a folder that you created, follow these steps:

1 Open the folder you want to rename.

2 Choose the File Folder command, and then choose Rename from the submenu. The Rename command shows the name of the open folder. Alternatively, you can right-click the folder in the Folder List and then choose Rename from the shortcut menu. If the Folder List is not displayed, you'll see the Rename dialog box.

3 Type the new folder name.   4 Click OK.

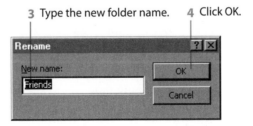

If you choose the Rename command while the Folder List is displayed, Outlook activates the folder name in the Folder List, allowing you to rename the folder simply by typing the new name and pressing the Enter key. This is the same method that you use for renaming folders in the My Computer and Windows Explorer windows.

V

Bending Folders to Your Will

> You can rename only the folders that you have created. You can't rename the standard (built-in) Outlook folders themselves (although you can rename the shortcuts to these folders—the folder icons—on the Outlook Bar). Renaming a folder does not change the name of the corresponding folder icon on the Outlook Bar. To change the name of a folder icon on the Outlook Bar (whether the icon represents a standard Outlook folder or a folder that you created and renamed), see the directions in "Renaming a Folder Icon on the Outlook Bar," on page 32.

Removing a Folder

Some days are just like that—you wake up one morning and realize that you've got a folder that you no longer need. And if you don't need it, you certainly don't want it, do you? So here's what you do to rid yourself (well, OK, rid Outlook) of those unwanted folders.

NOTE

> You can delete only the folders that you have created. You can't delete the standard (built-in) Outlook folders. If the folder you delete has an icon on the Outlook Bar, deleting the folder does not remove the corresponding folder icon from the Outlook Bar. To remove the folder icon from the Outlook Bar, see the directions in "Removing a Folder Icon from the Outlook Bar," on page 31.

CAUTION

Outlook gives you no warning that deleting a folder also deletes all items and subfolders in the folder. So, if you want to keep any of a folder's subfolders or items, move them before you delete the folder. (See "Moving and Copying Folder Items," on page 358, and "Moving a Folder," on page 434.)

When you delete a folder, Outlook moves the folder and its contents to the Deleted Items folder. (The folder becomes a subfolder of the Deleted Items folder.) From there, you can retrieve the folder and its contents if necessary before you permanently delete them. (To retrieve a folder, move it to some other folder.) To completely delete folders and their contents from Outlook, you must delete them from the Deleted Items folder—see "Purging Deleted Items," on page 384.

Outlook generously gives you a number of ways to delete a folder. Perhaps the simplest method is to open the folder you want to remove, choose the File Folder command, and then choose Delete from the submenu. (The Delete command shows the folder name.)

To use any of the following additional methods of deleting a folder, you must first display the Folder List:

- Select the folder in the Folder List, and then click the Delete button on the Standard toolbar.

- Right-click the folder, and then choose Delete from the shortcut menu.

- Select the folder in the Folder List, choose the File Folder command, and then choose Delete from the submenu.

- Select the folder in the Folder List, and then press the Delete key.

- Drag the folder to the Deleted Items folder.

Lounging in Public Folders

In most ways, a public folder is like any other Outlook folder or disk folder. A public folder can contain any type of folder item—a message, an appointment, a contact, a task, a journal entry, a note, a posting, a file, or a form—that an Outlook folder or a disk folder can contain. The purpose of public folders is to allow wide access to folder items that are interesting to everyone in an organization or to a particular group within an organization—for example, a project team or a specific department. Public folders can also be used to organize information by subject matter, which gives people interested in the subject a handy place to browse.

In most public folders, you can read items and add your own items, but you cannot delete items other than those you added. Some public folders are even more restricted—for instance, you might be able to see and read the items but be unable to add any items to the folder. In very restricted cases, the public folder is not available to you at all. The difference has to do with permissions. (See the sidebar "Do You Have Permission?" on the following page.) To open a public folder and read its folder items, you must have permission to do so. To add items to a public folder, you must have permission to create items. In most cases, public folders grant such permission to anyone who has access to them. It is less likely that you'll have permission to create forms for a public folder.

Do You Have Permission?

All public folders can have a level of protection against vandalism and voyeurism. Some public folders are open and available to all Outlook users on your system. Other public folders are limited to people who have a special affiliation with the folder, such as a project team. Still other folders might be available by subscription—that is, you sign up with the group whose conversations are kept in the public folder. And you might even be barred from seeing certain other public folders.

In general, you can read the contents of a folder if you can open the folder. Any time you are restricted from a folder or from performing certain functions in a folder, Outlook lets you know that you're trying to trespass into forbidden territory. If you don't have permission to use a folder, you can't open it. If you don't have permission to post an item to a folder, you'll see an error message when you try to post the item, or the commands you need will be unavailable. If you don't have permission to move or delete a folder or its contents, you'll see a message when you try.

You can check the precise nature of your permissions in the public folder's Properties dialog box. To display this dialog box, right-click the folder in the Folder list and choose Properties from the shortcut menu, or click the folder and choose the File Folder command and then choose Properties from the submenu. In the Properties dialog box, click the Summary tab and review your permissions, which are specified on this tab.

After you review the level of your permissions, you can discuss any changes you want to make with the folder contact listed on the Summary tab in the Properties dialog box. For more information about folder permissions, see "Permissions Tab," on page 446.

Opening Public Folders

Public folders live inside the folder labeled Public Folders on your e-mail server. To view the list of public folders, you must be connected directly to your e-mail server. You can't view public folders while you're offline unless you set up public folder favorites and set the shortcuts for work online and offline. (See "Public Folder Favoritism," on the facing page.)

To open a public folder, take these steps:

1 Click the Other label on the Outlook Bar.

2 In the Other group, click the Public Folders icon.

3   Click the Folder List button on the Standard toolbar if the Folder List is not already displayed.

4   In the Folder List, expand the list of subfolders by clicking the plus sign beside Public Folders. The first level of public folders contains only two folders: Favorites and All Public Folders.

5   To see the list of public folders, click the plus sign next to All Public Folders.

Each folder can contain folder items and subfolders. You'll know that a folder has subfolders if you see a plus sign next to its name in the Folder List. To see the subfolders, click the plus sign. Click any additional plus signs to expand the subfolders. Each folder and subfolder at any level can contain both folder items and additional subfolders.

To read an item in a public folder, simply open the folder and double-click the item. To move to the next folder item from an open item, click the Next Item button on the folder item's toolbar (just as if you were reading e-mail messages). To see the previous item, click the Previous Item button.

From this point on, you can treat items in public folders the same way you treat mail messages, except that you probably won't be able to delete or move the folder items—unless you have administrative privileges, unless you are the owner of the folder, or unless you put the item in the public folder yourself. You can, however, copy any folder item to your Outlook folders and disk folders, and you can save any folder item as a file on one of your disks.

Public Folder Favoritism

Server administrators invariably set up many public folders. Public folders can contain a wide variety of information about topics that fit within a general category. To help you make some sense of it all, your server administrator is likely to also set up several levels of subfolders.

For example, if the public folders on your e-mail system include a folder for Internet newsgroups, the Newsgroups folder probably contains a subfolder for each newsgroup area. Many newsgroups have a large number of subareas, and these subareas can have specialty

V

Bending Folders to Your Will

forums. When you want to check the latest postings to a specific folder, you might have to click (and scroll) many times to get there. Instead, you can set up shortcuts to your favorite public folders.

Outlook provides two tools to help you with the expanse of public folders—the Other group on the Outlook Bar and public folder favorites. Each tool has its own purpose:

■ Setting up a shortcut on the Outlook Bar gives you quick access to a favorite public folder. For details, see "The Outlook Bar," on page 22.

■ Setting up a shortcut to a public folder favorite lets you open that folder without working through the layers of public folders and also lets you see the folder contents while you're working offline. For details about setting up a favorite folder for offline work, see "Setting Up an Offline Folder File," on page 170. Of course, when working offline, the information in a favorite public folder will be only as current as your last synchronization with the public folder to which it's linked. You can also use a shortcut in the Public Folders Favorites folder to quickly open the related public folder: open the Folder List, open the Public Folders Favorites folder, and then open the shortcut.

> **NOTE**
>
> Do not confuse the Public Folders Favorites folder with the Favorites folder on your hard disk. Public Folders Favorites contain shortcuts only to public folders. The Favorites folder on your hard disk contains shortcuts to folders, files, and disks connected to your computer, not to your e-mail system.

Following a Public Folder Conversation

Some number of public folders in your organization will probably be set aside for "conversation"—one person posts a question or an idea, and others respond. Over time, a large number of different but related conversations can exist in a public folder. Setting up subfolders for various conversation topics helps to bring some order to the mass of material, but even subfolders can contain diverse conversations. Following a particular conversation can be difficult because pieces of different conversations arrive in the folder at different times, with pieces of other conversations interspersed.

To solve this problem, Outlook provides By Conversation Topic view, in which you group folder items according to their topics. When you use this view of a public folder, you can readily follow the threads of any conversation from beginning to end.

To follow a thread, do this:

1 Group the folder contents into threads in one of the following ways:

- From the drop-down list of views on the Standard toolbar, choose By Conversation Topic.

- Choose the View Current View command, and then choose By Conversation Topic from the submenu.

2 Locate the thread (group) that you want to follow, and then click the plus sign to expand the thread.

3 Double-click the first item in the thread, and read it.

4 Click the Next Item button on the toolbar in the item window to see the next item in the thread.

5 When you've read the entire thread, click the Next Item button. If the next thread is expanded, Outlook opens the first item in that thread. If that thread is not expanded, Outlook closes the item window. If you have read as much as you need before you reach the end of the thread, click the Close box in the upper right corner of the item window.

Sending Messages to a Public Folder

A public folder can receive e-mail messages as if it were a person on the e-mail system. To be able to send e-mail to a public folder, you need to do the following:

1 In the Folder List, right-click the public folder, and choose Properties from the shortcut menu. You can also open the public folder, choose the File Folder command, and then choose Properties from the submenu.

2 In the Properties dialog box, click the Summary tab.

V

Bending Folders to Your Will

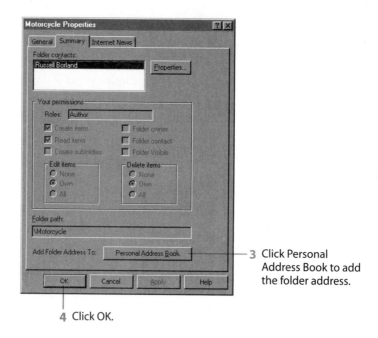

3 Click Personal Address Book to add the folder address.

4 Click OK.

From now on, when you consult the address book, you can find the public folder name in your Personal Address Book, and you can easily send e-mail messages to the folder.

Dealing with Folder Properties

For each folder in Outlook and for public folders for which you have appropriate permission, you can set at least some properties. Each folder has its own unique properties as well as certain properties that are common to all folders.

To set all the properties of a folder, you must have administrative permissions for the folder. Even so, in some cases, you can't set certain properties because they don't apply to the folder. In almost all cases, it is best to set folder properties while you're working online. You can, however, set folder properties for personal folders while you are working offline.

All Outlook folders (except the Contacts folder) have the same four tabs in the Properties dialog box: General, AutoArchive, Administration, and Forms. Server folders have two additional tabs: Permissions and Synchronization. The Properties dialog box of the Contacts folder has a unique tab, Outlook Address Book, instead of the AutoArchive tab. When you create an Outlook folder or copy an Outlook folder, it has the same properties—and therefore the same tabs—as the folder on which it is based. Disk folders have a different set of tabs: see "Disk Folders," on page 449.

The general steps for changing the properties of a folder are as follows:

1 Open the folder.

2 Choose the File Folder command, and then choose Properties For from the submenu. (The Properties For command shows the folder name.)

3 Change the property settings on any or all of the tabs.

4 Click OK.

The following sections illustrate and describe the General, Administration, Permissions, and Outlook Address Book tabs of the Properties dialog box. The remaining tabs are discussed in other sections of this book, as indicated here:

- For details about the AutoArchive tab, see "Setting a Folder's AutoArchive Properties," on page 418.

- For information about the options on the Forms tab, see "Making Forms Available in a Folder," on page 526.

- For details about synchronizing folders and the Synchronization tab, see "Designating Folders for Offline Work," on page 175.

General Tab

The General Tab of the Properties dialog box, shown in Figure 16-1 on the following page, contains information such as the folder name and its description. You cannot change the names of Outlook's standard folders, nor can you change the name or description of a public folder without having the proper permissions. For a custom folder (one that you created), however, you can select the folder's name in the box at the top of the tab and type a new one in its place. In the Description text box, you can type or edit the description of any folder, custom or standard.

FIGURE 16-1.

The General tab of the Properties dialog box.

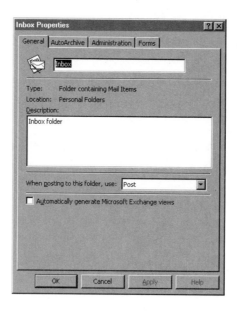

Following is a description of the important features of this tab.

When Posting To This Folder, Use. This list offers two options: Post and Forms. Select Post to use the standard (default) Outlook form for posting in this folder—that is, to use a message form for the Inbox folder, an appointment form for the Calendar folder, and so on. When you select Forms, Outlook opens the New Form dialog box. Select Forms if you want to use a custom form in this folder or a different standard Outlook form. For more information about using this dialog box, see "Opening a Special Form," on page 522.

Automatically Generate Microsoft Exchange Views. If some members of your organization use the Microsoft Exchange client instead of Outlook, turn on this check box so that they can use the views that are set up for this folder. Typically, you'll turn on this check box for a public folder or a folder you share with others who use the Microsoft Exchange client. You'll also want to turn it on if you use the Microsoft Exchange client and Outlook interchangeably.

Administration Tab

The Administration tab is used primarily with public folders. For Outlook folders and for public folders for which you do not have administrative permission, most of the options on this tab are unavailable. If you do have administrative permissions for a folder, you can use this tab to set which view of a folder is used when it is first opened, what happens when you drag and drop an item into the folder, and access permissions as shown in Figure 16-2.

FIGURE 16-2.

The Administration tab of the Properties dialog box.

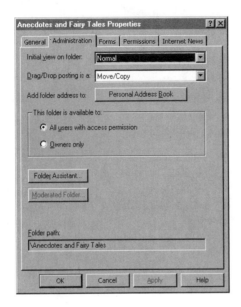

The Initial View On Folder list includes all the built-in views for the folder plus any views you have created for the folder.

The button called Add Folder Address To Personal Address Book (which can also appear on the Summary tab for public folders, depending on your level of permission) lets you add this folder to your Personal Address Book. For information, see "Sending Messages to a Public Folder," on page 441.

Use the Folder Assistant button to set up rules for dealing with the items sent to this folder. The Folder Assistant is similar to the Inbox Assistant. (For information about using the Inbox Assistant to set up rules for folder items, see "Outlook Assistants," on page 38. You can easily apply the information in that section to setting up the rules you want to use with the Folder Assistant.) You can use the Folder Assistant to set up rules to take actions on items sent by or to a particular person, items about a certain subject, or items that contain a particular word or group of words in the body of the message. You can return items to the sender, delete items automatically, reply to items automatically, or forward items.

V

Bending Folders to Your Will

Permissions Tab

(?) SEE ALSO

If you have delegates who work in your Outlook folders on your behalf, you can set up delegate permissions on the Delegates tab of the Options dialog box. For details, see "Delegates Tab," on page 76.

The Properties dialog box for server folders and for public folders for which you have appropriate permissions contains a Permission tab, shown in Figure 16-3. On this tab, you give others permission to open the folders that you want them to see or use.

A server folder is simply a folder in your Mailbox that you access from the server—Outlook automatically sets up the folders in your Mailbox on the server. If you are working from a Personal Folder File (.PST) on your hard disk, you are not accessing the folders from the server, but rather from your own hard disk.

Click Add to add names.

FIGURE 16-3.

The Permissions tab of the Properties dialog box for a server folder.

This box lists names and the role (permission level) assigned to each name.

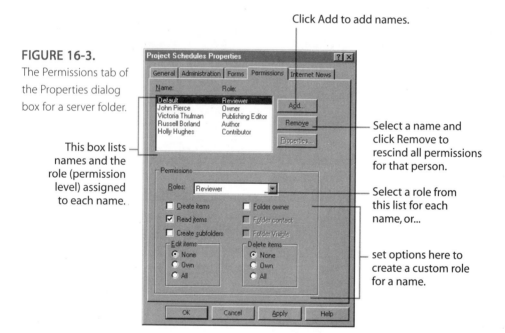

Select a name and click Remove to rescind all permissions for that person.

Select a role from this list for each name, or...

set options here to create a custom role for a name.

On this tab, you can compile a list of names of the people who have permission to use the folder. Each name is assigned a role, and each role has specific privileges attached to it. For instance, someone who has an Author role can create folder items, read folder items, and edit or delete his or her own folder items but cannot create a subfolder and cannot edit or delete the items created by other people. On the facing page, Table 16-1 lists the roles and their respective privileges. (The role None is not listed because this role grants no permissions or privileges.)

TABLE 16-1. Roles and the Privileges They Grant.

Privileges	Author	Contributor	Editor	Owner	Publishing Author	Publishing Editor	Reviewer
Create Items	✔	✔	✔	✔	✔	✔	
Read Items	✔		✔	✔	✔	✔	✔
Create Subfolders				✔	✔	✔	
Folder Owner				✔			
Folder Contact				✔			
Edit Items/None		✔					✔
Edit Items/Own	✔				✔		
Edit Items/All			✔	✔		✔	
Delete Items/None		✔					✔
Delete Items/Own	✔				✔		
Delete Items/All			✔	✔		✔	

Notice that the Folder Visible check box isn't listed in Table 16-1. This is because Folder Visible isn't activated by a role—it's activated only when Read Items is selected in *public* folders. If Read Items is not selected, a message appears stating that a person doesn't have sufficient permission to perform the action. In this case, the person can't create an item and post it to the folder—even when the Create Items check box is selected for that person—because Outlook uses the folder's path to determine where a message should be stored. If the person can't open the folder, Create Items is inaccessible.

When you create a folder in your mailbox, the default role listed is None (no privileges). When you create a public folder, the default role listed is Author. This default applies to everyone who uses your Exchange Server—that is, by default, no one can access your server folder unless you give them permission by adding their name to the list on this tab.

To add a name, click the Add button. Outlook displays the Add Users dialog box, in which you can type or select the name or names you want to add. When you click the Add button in this dialog box and then click OK, Outlook adds the names to the list on the Permissions tab, assigning each the default role (None).

To assign or change the role for a person on the list, select the name, and then select a role from the drop-down list in the Roles box.

Instead of assigning one of the predefined roles to a name, you can assign privileges one by one to that person by setting individual options in the tab's Permissions area. If the resulting combination of privileges is the same as one of the predefined roles, Outlook assigns that role to the person. If the combination of privileges is different from all of the predefined roles, Outlook assigns Custom as the role. (You won't see a Custom role listed in the Roles box; it appears only when you change an assigned role in a way that doesn't match any of the predefined roles.)

 **TIP**

You can change the default role from None to, say, Author or Contributor. But remember that the default role applies to everyone who uses your Exchange Server. If you want to limit access to your folder to only those people you specify on the Permissions tab, leave the default role set to None.

Outlook Address Book Tab

As mentioned earlier, the Properties dialog box for the Contacts folder contains the Outlook Address Book tab instead of the AutoArchive tab. This tab is shown in Figure 16-4.

FIGURE 16-4.

The Outlook Address Book tab of the Contacts Properties dialog box.

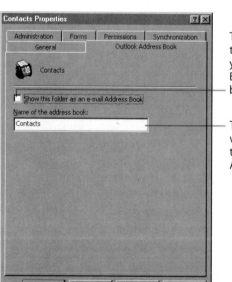

Turn on this check box to add your contacts to your Outlook Address Book; turn off this check box to remove them.

Type the name you want to appear in the Outlook Address Book list.

Turning on the check box labeled Show This Folder As An E-Mail Address Book adds your Contacts folder items to your Outlook Address Book, giving you access to the names, addresses, fax numbers, e-mail addresses, and URLs of the people you list as contacts. You can use contact entries to send messages and faxes, to place telephone calls, to write letters, and to connect to web pages while you're working in another Microsoft Office 97 program.

Oh, No! The Show This Folder As An E-Mail Address Book Check Box Is Not Available!

The check box called Show This Folder As An E-Mail Address Book is not available if you have set up Microsoft Schedule+ 95 as your primary calendar. (See "Use Microsoft Schedule+ 95 As My Primary Calendar," on page 62.) To use your Contacts folder as an e-mail address book, you must choose the Tools Options command and turn off the Use Microsoft Schedule+ 95 As My Primary Calendar check box on the Calendar tab of the Options dialog box. You must then exit and log off Outlook and restart Outlook for this change to take effect. Once you do this, the Show This Folder As An E-Mail Address Book check box will be available, and you can turn it on to use your Contacts folder as an address book.

As an alternative way of setting up your Contacts folder as an address book, open the profile you use for Outlook and add Outlook Address Book as a service. This replaces Schedule+ 95 as your primary calendar and automatically adds your Contacts folder as an e-mail address book. For information about adding a service to a profile, see "Changing a Profile," on page 12.

Although you can't change the name of the Contacts folder itself, you can change the name that appears in your Outlook Address Book. For example, if you want your Contacts list to be called "Buddies" in the Outlook Address Book, type *Buddies* in the Name Of The Address Book box in the Contacts Properties dialog box.

Disk Folders

Disk folders that you set up and view in Outlook have the same properties they have in a My Computer window or a Windows Explorer window. The Properties dialog box for a disk folder contains two tabs: General and Sharing. Figure 16-5 on the following page shows the General tab, which provides a general description of the folder and allows you to set the folder's attributes.

FIGURE 16-5.

The General tab of the Properties dialog box for a disk folder.

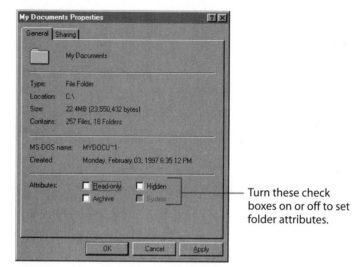

Turn these check boxes on or off to set folder attributes.

On the Sharing tab of a disk folder's Properties dialog box, shown in Figure 16-6, you can specify whether or not the folder will be shared with other people. If you designate it as a shared folder, you can also specify how it will be shared and with whom.

Click here to turn on sharing.

Type a share name.

Add a comment (optional).

FIGURE 16-6.

The Sharing tab of the Properties dialog box for a disk folder.

Click here to turn off sharing.

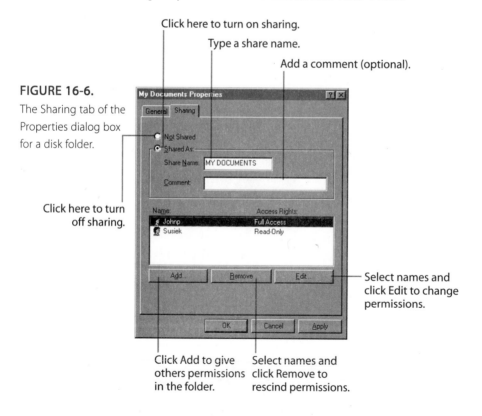

Select names and click Edit to change permissions.

Click Add to give others permissions in the folder.

Select names and click Remove to rescind permissions.

If you want to make a disk folder available to others, click the Shared As option. Then accept or change the share name for the folder. The share name identifies the folder on the network. To help users make sure that they've found the correct folder, you can add a comment that identifies the folder more fully.

> **NOTE**
>
> You can share a folder only if you have administrative control over it. You usually have this control over the folders on a disk that's part of your computer. Also note that you must be connected to your organization's computer network before you can grant permissions.

Even after you share a folder, no one can use it until you grant the appropriate permissions, or access rights. To grant permissions, take these steps:

1 Click the Add button on the Sharing tab.

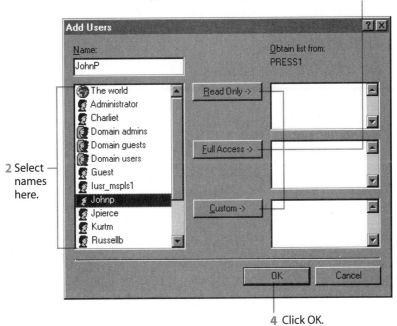

3 Click one of these buttons to assign the appropriate permissions. The names will appear in the appropriate list box on the right.

2 Select names here.

4 Click OK.

After you click OK in the Add Users dialog box, the names of the people to whom you granted access rights appear on the Sharing tab.

V

Bending Folders to Your Will

Columns, Categories, Grouping, Sorting, Filtering, and Custom Fields

Organizing information so that it makes sense is an important part of managing projects and tasks. As you've seen in previous chapters, Microsoft Outlook 97 offers you numerous ways to view your folders and the information they contain. You can choose the view that best meets your needs, one that lets you focus on the most important information in the folder and makes that information clear, readily accessible, and easy to work with. Outlook provides a set of built-in views for each folder, drawn from the five general types of views: table, timeline, card, icon, and day/month/week.

As Chapter 18, "Setting Up Views," will explain, you can modify Outlook's built-in views or even design your own views. To do so, however, you first need to understand the methods and techniques described here, in this chapter, for setting up folders and displaying their contents:

- Choosing which columns of information to display, arranging their order, and formatting them

- Assigning folder items to categories

- Grouping folder items

- Sorting folder items

- Filtering folder items

- Creating your own fields for columns, cards, or individual folder items

All these methods of controlling your views of folder items interact. What you see in a folder depends on the combination of settings you select for columns, categories, grouping, sorting, filtering, and fields. It's almost impossible to describe, at least in fewer than several dozen pages, how all the variations look. In effect, you'll have to experiment with the combinations to come up with the ones that suit your purpose in any given situation.

Setting Up Columns

The table views that are available for Outlook folders arrange folder items in a list with columns that show information about each entry. (Examples include views based on simple lists, such as Phone List, Detailed List, or Notes List, and views that display groups, such as By Contact, By Company, or By Person Responsible.) You can add or remove columns, and you can rearrange the order of the columns to suit your working style, your task needs, or your organization's culture. Also, to view the information more efficiently and effectively, you can adjust the width of the columns to show more information in certain columns or to fit more columns within the width of the folder window.

Adding Columns from the Field Chooser

The Field Chooser command on the View menu displays a window listing the available fields that you can add as columns in a table view. The Field Chooser window gives you a visual means to see and add columns.

 NOTE

> The term "field" simply refers to a location that stores data. Usually a field is used to categorize different types of data so that you can find information quickly.

 SEE ALSO

You can also add a column during the sorting process; see "Sorting with the View Sort Command," on page 469.

You can add columns to a folder view from the Field Chooser as follows:

1 Open the folder, and select a view that has columns (a table view).

2 Choose the View Field Chooser command to display the Field Chooser window:

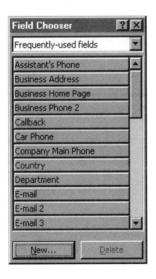

3 From the drop-down list at the top of the Field Chooser window, select a list that contains the column (the field) you want to add. When you select a list, Outlook displays the fields contained in the list in the lower portion of the window. (To find out which lists are available for each folder type, refer to Table 17-1, on page 471. To see examples of the fields contained in each list, refer to Table 17-2, on page 473; the fields listed in this table are similar, though not always identical, to the fields listed in the Field Chooser.)

4 Drag the field name into the folder window, positioning it among the column headings at the location where you want the column to appear. (Outlook displays two red arrows to show you where the column will be inserted.) When you release the mouse button, Outlook adds the column to the folder view, with the field name as the new column heading. Outlook also removes the field name from the Field Chooser.

5 When you've added as many columns as you want, click the Close box in the upper right corner of the Field Chooser window.

★ TIP

If you can't find the column you want to add, you can click the New button in the Field Chooser to create a new field, which you can then add as a column in the folder view. For details, see "Creating a Simple Custom Field," on page 491.

Removing Columns with the Mouse

If you no longer want a column to appear in a folder view, you can easily remove the offending column with the right mouse button and the shortcut menu. Simply right-click the heading of the column you want to remove, and then choose Remove This Column from the shortcut menu.

If the Field Chooser (described in the preceding section) is open when you want to remove a column, you can drag the column heading from the folder window back into the Field Chooser window to remove the column. Outlook deletes the column from the folder view and adds the field name to the list in the Field Chooser.

Rearranging Columns with the Mouse

When you want to quickly move a column to a new position in a folder window, you can point to the column heading and drag it to the new location. As you move the column heading between existing columns, you'll see two red arrows pointing up and down, indicating where the column will be inserted when you release the mouse button. When you do so, the column moves to its new location, and the columns to the right of the new position move to the right to make room.

Managing Columns by Command

The most general way to manage columns in a folder view is by using the View Show Fields command. With this command, you can add columns, remove them, and rearrange them at the same time.

> **NOTE**
>
> You can also use the View Show Fields command to manage fields in card views.

Begin by opening the folder and selecting a view that has columns. Then choose the View Show Fields command to display the Show Fields dialog box, shown in Figure 17-1 on the following page.

V

Bending Folders to Your Will

To add a column,
select the field from
this list and click Add.

To remove a column,
select the field from this
list and click Remove.

FIGURE 17-1.

The Show Fields
dialog box.

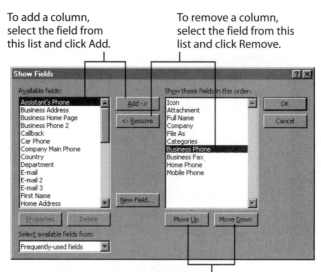

To rearrange columns, select a field name
and then click Move Up to move the column
left in the folder window, or click Move
Down to move the column right in the
folder window. Repeat this step for each
column you want to move.

On the left-hand side of the Show Fields dialog box, you'll see a list
of available fields (columns). On the right-hand side is a list of the
fields that are currently displayed in columns in the folder view. You
can change the list of available fields by selecting a different list in the
Select Available Fields From box. (To find out which lists you can use
for each folder type, refer to Table 17-1, on page 471. To see examples of the fields contained in each list, refer to Table 17-2, on
page 473; the fields listed in this table are similar, though not always
identical, to the fields listed in the Show Fields dialog box.)

 TIP

> If you can't find the column you want to add in the Available Fields list, you
> can click the New Field button in the Show Fields dialog box to create a new
> field, which you can then add as a column in the folder view. For details, see
> "Creating a Simple Custom Field," on page 491.

The Date/Time Fields Dialog Box

If you are using a timeline view of a folder when you choose the View Show Fields command, Outlook displays the Date/Time Fields dialog box rather than the Show Fields dialog box.

In a timeline view—for example, Task Timeline or Message Timeline—Outlook positions folder items on the timeline according to the start and end fields of each item. By default, if a task begins on Monday and is due to be completed on Friday, for instance, Outlook displays a bar indicating this time interval under the appropriate dates on the timeline. For a message, Outlook by default uses the time the message was sent and the time it was received as the time interval. If you want to change the fields used to display folder items on a timeline, you can do so in the Date/Time Fields dialog box:

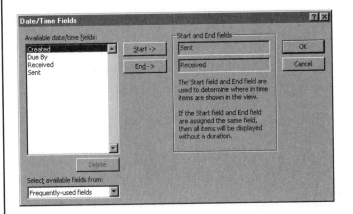

Use the Select Available Fields From box at the bottom of the dialog box to select a list of fields. (To find out which lists are available for each folder type, refer to Table 17-1, on page 471.) Then, from the Available Date/Time Fields list, select the field that you want to use as the item start date, and click the Start button. To change the field that Outlook uses to display each item's end date, select a field from this list and click the End button. For example, if you have significantly modified your tasks—to the point where it's almost like starting over—you might want to use the Modified field to replace the Start field; that is, you might want to tell Outlook to use the date you modified the task to position it on the timeline.

Changing Column Format

With either the mouse or a menu command, you can adjust the width of a column, alter the alignment of information within a column, and generally modify the format of a new column in a folder view.

Changing Column Width

To change column width with the mouse, first position the mouse pointer along the right edge of the column heading for the column that you want to widen or narrow. Then drag the right edge of the column heading to the right to widen the column. Drag the right edge of the heading to the left to narrow the column.

Getting the Best Column Fit

Rather than trying to adjust the width of a column yourself, you can direct Outlook to set the width to best fit the contents of that column. To have Outlook set the best fit for a column width, right-click the column heading and choose Best Fit from the shortcut menu. You can also double-click the right-hand border of a column to set the column width to best fit.

Setting column width with the Best Fit command is usually a temporary arrangement so that you can fully see a particular column's contents. When Outlook sets a column width to best fit, it steals width from the other columns in the folder window. Some columns might even be reduced to a single character's width, which makes them pretty useless. In that case, you might want to remove a column or two or adjust the width of other columns, using the techniques described in the preceding sections.

Changing Column Alignment

By default, the contents of columns in a folder view are left-aligned. You can change the alignment of any column, however, to display the contents right-aligned or centered. To change column alignment, follow these steps:

1 Right-click the column heading.

2 Choose Alignment from the shortcut menu.

3 Choose the alignment you want (Align Left, Align Right, or Center) from the submenu.

Using the Format Columns Command

The Format Columns command on the View menu lets you change the width, the alignment, the heading, and the information format for a single column all in one operation.

To change the format of a column using this command, follow these directions:

1 Open the folder, and select the view in which the column appears.

2 Choose the View Format Columns command. Alternatively, you can right-click the heading of the column you want to format and choose Format Columns from the shortcut menu.

3 Select the column you want to format. **4** Select the format for information. **5** Type a new column heading (label) if needed.

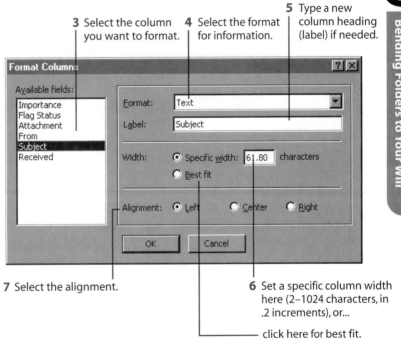

7 Select the alignment.

6 Set a specific column width here (2–1024 characters, in .2 increments), or...

click here for best fit.

8 Repeat steps 2 through 7 for each column you want to format.

9 When you have finished reformatting the desired columns, click OK.

For some columns, you have only one choice in the Format box of the Format Columns dialog box: text. For other columns—namely, date and time columns, number columns, and columns that show importance, attachments, or flags—Outlook provides several format choices. For more information about these formats, see "Creating a Simple Custom Field," on page 491.

Working with Categories

Whether you think of it this way or not, you probably use categories for organizing various activities and written records—shopping lists, reminders, house repairs, friends, pets, and so on. In business, you might have categories of folder items for various projects, personal business, daily tasks, customers, suppliers, orders, billing, and so on. Outlook provides a list of 20 built-in categories for folder items. You can add your own categories too.

To assign a folder item to a category (or to several categories), follow these steps:

1   Open the folder, and select the item. (To assign several folder items to the same category, you can select them at the same time by holding down the Ctrl key as you click each item. To select several consecutive folder items, click the first item and then hold down the Shift key while you click the last item you want to select.)

2   Open the Categories dialog box in one of the following ways:

  • Choose the Edit Categories command.

  • Right-click the folder item, and choose Categories from the shortcut menu.

  • Open the folder item, and click the Categories button on the Options tab in the folder item window.

  • For notes, click the icon in the upper left corner of the note window, and choose Categories from the menu.

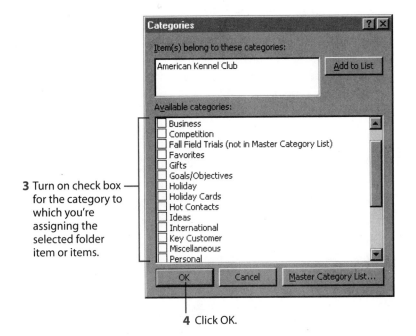

3 Turn on check box for the category to which you're assigning the selected folder item or items.

4 Click OK.

If you want to remove a folder item from a category, the procedure is the same, except that in step 3 you turn off the check box for that category.

Adding Categories to the List

Because you are a unique person, you probably have categories of your own that you'd like to add to Outlook's list. This is easy to do:

1 Open the folder, and select an item that you'd like to assign to the new category.

2 Open the Categories dialog box in any of the ways described in the preceding section.

3 Type the new category name in the Item(s) Belong To These Categories box. If you are adding more than one category, or if any category names already appear in this box, you must separate the names with a comma. If you don't use the comma, Outlook reads the multiple categories as one category.

V

Bending Folders to Your Will

4 Click the Add To List button. (You can skip this step if you won't use this category for any other folder item.) Outlook adds the new category to the list so that you can easily assign other folder items to this new category later. Outlook also adds the new category name to the master category list.

5 Click OK.

Managing the Master Category List

The master category list contains Outlook's built-in list of categories as well as any categories that you've added in the Categories dialog box (as described in the preceding section). In the master category list, you can add categories, remove categories, and reset the category list to the original 20 categories built into Outlook.

To manage the master category list, you must first open the Categories dialog box. In the Categories dialog box, click the Master Category List button to display the Master Category List dialog box:

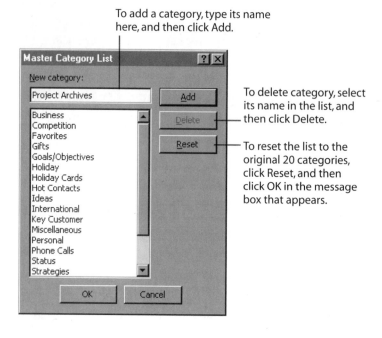

To add a category, type its name here, and then click Add.

To delete category, select its name in the list, and then click Delete.

To reset the list to the original 20 categories, click Reset, and then click OK in the message box that appears.

NOTE

Deleting a category from the Master Category List doesn't affect any items that have already been assigned to that category.

Collecting Related Folder Items

SEE ALSO

An alternative way of collecting related folder items uses a custom field. See the sidebar "Using a Custom Field to Collect Related Folder Items," on page 494.

Messages, calendar items, tasks, contacts, journal entries, and notes can all be assigned to categories. In this way, you can collect all the folder items that relate to a specific project, person, organization, activity, or idea in one place—namely, in a folder for that category.

To set up such a folder, take these steps:

1 Assign each folder item you want to collect to a category that fits the collection. You can use one of Outlook's built-in categories or add your own.

2 Create a new folder for the category. (See "Creating a Folder," on page 431.)

3 Copy the folder items you assigned to the category to this new category folder. (See "Copying a Folder Item," on page 360.)

Now when you want to review or work with these related folder items, you can simply switch to the folder that contains the items in that category.

Grouping

If you've tinkered with views at all, you're already familiar with grouping. Views such as By Category, By Company, or By Location group folder items under headings that correspond to the various entries in the Category, Company, or Location field. For example, By Person Responsible groups task folder items according to the person who is responsible for the task. All "By" views work in a similar way.

Grouping is a way to organize folder items to more easily find and examine similar items. You can group folder items in various ways:

- No groupings. All the folder items appear in a single, undivided list, sorted according to the sorting scheme you select. (See "Sorting," on page 468, for details.)

V

Bending Folders to Your Will

- One level of grouping. Folder items appear within their associated groups under specific headings that can be expanded or collapsed to view or hide the items.

- Two to four levels of grouping. Folder items appear in subgroups under groups or other subgroups. Each level of heading can be expanded or collapsed.

To change the way items are grouped in an open folder, follow these steps:

1 Choose the View Group By command to display the Group By dialog box.

2 In the Select Available Fields From box at the bottom of the dialog box, select the list containing the fields that you want to use for grouping. (To find out which lists are available for each folder type, refer to Table 17-1, on page 471. To see examples of the fields contained in each list, refer to Table 17-2, on page 473; the fields listed in this table are similar, though not always identical, to the fields listed in the Group By dialog box.) Outlook displays the list you select in all four of the drop-down list boxes in the dialog box.

8 For each grouping, choose either Ascending (alphabetical order, earlier time to later time, lower number to higher number) or Descending (the opposite of Ascending).

4 Turn this check box on if you want the grouping to be displayed in a column as well as on the grouping bars.

3 Select a grouping.

5 If you want a second level of grouping, select it here.

6 If you want a third level of grouping, select it here.

7 If you want a forth level of grouping, select it here.

10 Click OK.

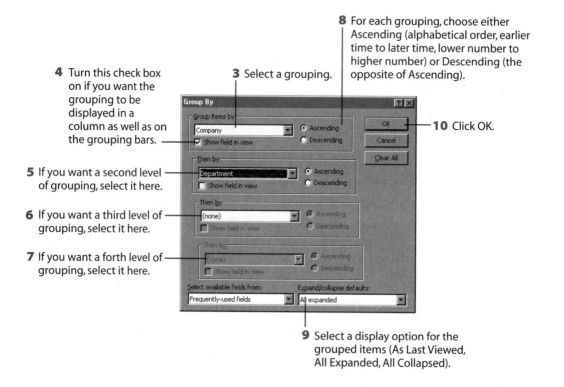

9 Select a display option for the grouped items (As Last Viewed, All Expanded, All Collapsed).

TIP

If you want to group by a visible column, right-click that column heading and then choose Group By This Field from the shortcut menu. To add a subgrouping, repeat this step with a different column.

When you use multiple levels of grouping, Outlook first groups the folder items by the first field you specified as a basis for grouping. Then, within each one of those groups, Outlook creates a subgroup based on the second field, and so on. If a folder item contains no information in the specified field, it is listed first and labeled (None).

TIP

To remove all the groupings from a folder view, open the Group By dialog box and click the Clear All button.

Using the Group By Box

Group By Box

Instead of using the View Group By command or the Group By This Field command on the shortcut menu, you can use the View Group By Box command or the Group By Box button on the Standard toolbar.

When you choose the command or click the button, Outlook adds a Group By box at the top of the folder window, as shown here:

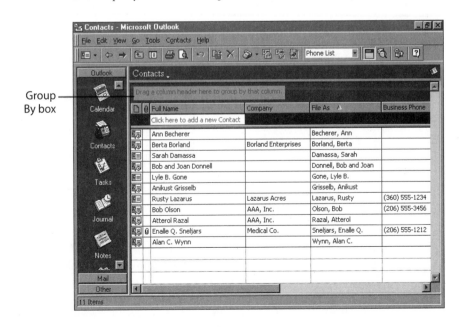

Group By box

To set up a grouping, simply drag a column heading into the Group By box. To set up an additional level of grouping, drag another column heading into the Group By box.

Only visible columns (columns that are set up) are available for this method of setting up groupings. To use fields that aren't set up in columns, you need to use the View Group By command (explained in the preceding section).

Sorting

You can sort folder items in any type of view except timeline and day/week/month views. Outlook gives you two ways to sort folder items: with the mouse and with the View Sort command. You can sort by as many as four sorting fields. For a multiple-field sort, Outlook sorts the folder items by each sorting field in turn. The items are displayed in a single, undivided list in the order you specify. (Unlike grouping, sorting does not add headings or labels to the list.)

Sorting with the Mouse

Sorting with the mouse is quick and convenient, but you can use this method only in a table view (a view with columns for each field of information). You can sort items in either ascending or descending order, as explained in the following list. (Ascending order is alphabetical, earlier time to later time, or lower number to higher number; descending order is the opposite.)

- To sort items in ascending order, click the heading of the column you want to use to sort the items.

- To sort items in descending order, click the column heading a second time.

- To sort items by more than one sorting field, click the column headings in reverse order—that is, begin by clicking the heading of the *last* column you want to sort by, and end by clicking the heading of the *first* column you want to sort by. For example, if you want to sort tasks first by subject, then by priority, and then by the due date, click the Due Date heading first, then the Priority heading, and then the Subject heading.

Sorting with the View Sort Command

The View Sort command gives you more options for sorting than mouse sorting does. Although mouse sorting is quick and easy, you might want to sort folder items by a field that's not visible in the current view of the folder, which you can do only with the View Sort command. You can also use the command to sort in card and icon views as well as in table views.

To sort folder items with this command, follow these steps:

1   Open the folder, and select a table, card, or icon view.

2   Choose the View Sort command to display the Sort dialog box.

3   In the Select Available Fields From box at the bottom of the dialog box, select the list containing the fields that you want to use for sorting. (To find out which lists are available for each folder type, refer to Table 17-1, on page 471; to see the fields contained in each list, refer to Table 17-2, on page 473.) Outlook displays the contents of the list that you select in all four of the drop-down list boxes in the dialog box.

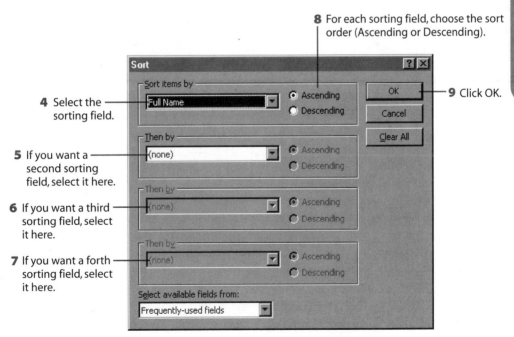

8 For each sorting field, choose the sort order (Ascending or Descending).

4 Select the sorting field.

5 If you want a second sorting field, select it here.

6 If you want a third sorting field, select it here.

7 If you want a forth sorting field, select it here.

9 Click OK.

V

Bending Folders to Your Will

If you select a field for sorting that isn't displayed in the current view of the folder, Outlook asks whether you want to display that field:

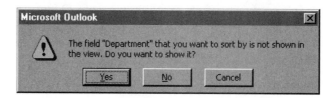

Click Yes to display the field for each item in the view. (If you are using a table view, for instance, this can be a handy way of adding a column to the view.) Click No to keep the current folder view, without displaying the additional field. Whichever choice you make, Outlook can sort items by the fields you choose, whether the fields are visible or not.

> If you select (None) as a sorting key in any box in the Sort dialog box, all the boxes below automatically revert to (None).

Selecting Available Fields

The Select Available Fields From box in the Sort dialog box provides a set of lists containing field names, from which you can select the field you want to sort by. (You'll also find this box and its lists in the Field Chooser, the Show Fields dialog box, and the Group By dialog box, all discussed earlier in this chapter.) Once you've chosen a list in this box, Outlook displays the specific fields contained in that list in the Sort Items By box and the Then By boxes in the Sort dialog box.

The contents of the Select Available Fields From box vary according to the type of folder—that is, the set of available lists varies. Certain general lists such as All Contact Fields, All Mail Fields, All Appointment Fields, and so on are provided for all types of Outlook folders.

All Outlook folders also have lists named Frequently-Used Fields, User-Defined Fields In Folder, and Forms, although the contents of these three lists (the particular fields they contain) vary by folder type. For some folders, you'll also find lists that are specific to those folders: an E-Mail Fields list for the Contacts folder, for instance, or an Info/ Status Fields list for the Tasks folder.

Table 17-1 summarizes the sets of lists you'll find in the Select Available Fields From box for each folder type. (The table refers to "folder type" rather than to specific names of Outlook folders in order to include folders that you create yourself, based on Outlook's built-in folders.) Table 17-1 also lists the default sorting field for each folder.

TABLE 17-1. **Available Lists of Fields and the Default Sorting Field for Each Folder Type.**

Folder Type	List Names	Default Field for Sorting
Inbox: Contains message items (mail)	Frequently-Used Fields, Address Fields, Date/Time Fields, All Mail Fields, User-Defined Fields In Folder, All Document Fields, All Contact Fields, All Appointment Fields, All Task Fields, All Journal Fields, All Note Fields, All Post Fields, Forms	Received
Calendar: Contains calendar items	Frequently-Used Fields, Date/Time Fields, All Appointment Fields, All Document Fields, All Contact Fields, All Mail Fields, All Task Fields, All Journal Fields, All Note Fields, All Post Fields, User-Defined Fields In Folder, Forms	Start (Sorting is not available when viewing a calendar items folder in Day/ Week/Month view.)
Contact: Contains contact items	Frequently-Used Fields, Address Fields, E-Mail Fields, Fax/Other Number Fields, Miscellaneous Fields, Name Fields, Personal Fields, Phone Number Fields, All Contact Fields, User-Defined Fields In Folder, All Document Fields, All Mail Fields, All Appointment Fields, All Task Fields, All Journal Fields, All Note Fields, All Post Fields, Forms	File As

(continued)

TABLE 17-1. *continued*

Folder Type	List Names	Default Field for Sorting
Task: Contains task items	Frequently-Used Fields, Info/Status Fields, Date/Time Fields, All Task Fields, All Document Fields, All Contact Fields, All Appointment Fields, All Mail Fields, All Journal Fields, All Note Fields, All Post Fields, User-Defined Fields In Folder, Forms	(None)
Journal: Contains journal items	Frequently-Used Fields, All Journal Fields, All Document Fields, All Contact Fields, All Appointment Fields, All Task Fields, All Mail Fields, All Note Fields, All Post Fields, User-Defined Fields In Folder, Forms	Start
Note: Contains note items	Frequently-Used Fields, All Note Fields, All Document Fields, All Contact Fields, All Appointment Fields, All Task Fields, All Journal Fields, All Mail Fields, All Post Fields, User-Defined Fields In Folder, Forms	Created
My Computer, My Documents, Favorites: Contains disk files	Frequently-Used Fields, All File Fields, User-Defined Fields In Folder	Name

After you select a list of fields in the Select Available Fields From box, Outlook adds all the fields in that list to the four drop-down list boxes in the Sort dialog box (the Sort Items By box and the Then By boxes). As mentioned earlier, the specific fields in each list sometimes differ, depending on the type of folder you're working in. Table 17-2 shows the list names and all the fields each list offers for sorting in various types of folders.

> **NOTE**
>
> Table 17-2 shows the fields that are available for sorting. The specific fields you'll find on the lists of the same names in the Field Chooser, the Show Fields dialog box, and the Group By dialog box, discussed earlier in this chapter, are quite similar, but they are not identical in all cases.

TABLE 17-2.   The Fields Contained in Each List in the Sort Dialog Box, by Folder Type.

List Name	Fields Available for Sorting, by Folder Type
Frequently-Used Fields	**Message items folder:** Attachment, Cc, Conversation, Conversation Index, Created, Do Not AutoArchive, Due By, Flag Status, From, Icon, Importance, Message Flag, Outlook Internal Version, Received (the default), Sensitivity, Sent, Size, Subject, To **Calendar items folder:** All Day Event, Appt State Flags, Attachment, Created, Duration, End, Icon, Location, Meeting Status, Optional Attendees, Recurrence, Recurrence Pattern, Recurrence Range End, Recurrence Range Start, Recurring, Reminder, Required Attendees, Sensitivity, Show Time As, Start (the default), Subject **Contact items folder:** Assistant's Phone, Attachment, Business Address, Business Fax, Business Home Page, Business Phone, Business Phone 2, Callback, Car Phone, Company, Company Main Phone, Country, Department, E-Mail, E-Mail 2, E-Mail 3, File As (the default), First Name, Full Name, Home Address, Home Fax, Home Phone, Home Phone 2, Icon, ISDN, Job Title, Journal, Last Name, Mailing Address, Mobile Phone, Modified, Office Location, Other Address, Other Fax, Other Phone, Pager, Personal Home Page, Primary Phone, Radio Phone, Sensitivity, State, Telex, TTY/TDD Phone, Web Page **Task items folder:** % Complete, Actual Work, Attachment, Complete, Date Completed, Due Date, Icon, Modified, Owner, Priority, Requested By, Role, Sensitivity, Start Date, Status, Subject, Team Task, Total Work; (None) is the default **Journal items folder:** Attachment, Do Not AutoArchive, Duration, End, Entry Type, Icon, Modified, Sensitivity, Start (the default), Subject **Note items folder:** Color, Created (the default), Icon, Modified, Subject **Disk files folder:** Created, In Folder, Modified, Name (the default), Size, Type
Address Fields	**Message items folder:** Bcc, Cc, From, Have Replies Sent To, Received (the default), To **Contact items folder:** Business Address, Business Address City, Business Address Country, Business Address PO Box, Business Address Postal Code, Business Address State, Business Address Street, City, Country, Department, File As (the default), Home Address, Home Address City, Home Address Country, Home Address PO Box, Home Address Postal Code, Home Address State, Home Address Street, Location, Mailing Address, Office Location, Other Address, Other Address City, Other Address Country, Other Address PO Box, Other Address Postal Code, Other Address State, Other Address Street, PO Box, State, Street Address, ZIP/Postal Code

V

Bending Folders to Your Will

(continued)

TABLE 17-2. *continued*

List Name	Fields Available for Sorting, by Folder Type
Date/Time Fields	**Message items folder:** Defer Until, Due By, Expires, Modified, Received (the default), Sent **Calendar items folder:** Created, Duration, End, Modified, Recurrence Range End, Recurrence Range Start, Remind Beforehand, Start (the default) **Task items folder:** Created, Date Completed, Due Date, Modified, Reminder Time, Start Date; (None) is the default
E-Mail Fields	**Contact items folder:** E-Mail, E-Mail 2, E-Mail 3, File As (the default)
Fax/Other Number Fields	**Contact items folder:** Business Fax, Computer Network Name, File As (the default), FTP Site, Home Fax, ISDN, Other Fax, Telex
Info/Status Fields	**Task items folder:** Actual Work, Owner, Priority, Requested By, Request Status, Status, Subject, Total Work; (None) is the default
Miscellaneous Fields	**Contact items folder:** Account, Assistant's Name, Assistant's Phone, Computer Network Name, Customer ID, Department, File As (the default), FTP Site, Government ID Number, Organizational ID Number, User Field 1, User Field 2, User Field 3, User Field 4
Name Fields	**Contact items folder:** Assistant's Name, File As (the default), First Name, Full Name, Initials, Job Title, Last Name, Manager's Name, Middle Name, Nickname, Referred By, Spouse, Suffix, Title
Personal Fields	**Contact items folder:** Anniversary, Birthday, File As (the default), Gender, Hobbies, Language, Profession, Referred By, Spouse, Web Page
Phone Number Fields	**Contact items folder:** Assistant's Phone, Business Phone, Business Phone 2, Callback, Car Phone, Company Main Phone, File As (the default), Home Phone, Home Phone 2, Mobile Phone, Other Phone, Pager, Primary Phone, Radio Phone, TTY/TDD Phone
All Appointment Fields	**All folders:** All Day Event, Appt State Flags, Attachment, Billing Information, Conversation, Created, Do Not AutoArchive, Duration, End, Icon, Importance, In Folder, Location, Meeting Status, Message Class, Mileage, Modified, Optional Attendees, Organizer, Outlook Internal Version, Outlook Version, Recurrence, Recurrence Pattern, Recurrence Range End, Recurrence Range Start, Recurring, Remind Beforehand, Reminder, Reminder Override Default, Reminder Sound, Reminder Sound File, Required Attendees, Response Requested, Sensitivity, Show Time As, Size, Start, Subject **Message items folder:** adds Received (the default) **Calendar items folder:** Start is the default **Contact items folder:** adds File As (the default) **Task items folder:** (None) is the default **Journal items folder:** Start is the default **Note items folder:** Created is the default

List Name	Fields Available for Sorting, by Folder Type
All Contact Fields	**All folders:** Account, Anniversary, Assistant's Name, Assistant's Phone, Attachment, Billing Information, Birthday, Business Address, Business Address City, Business Address Country, Business Address PO Box, Business Address Postal Code, Business Address State, Business Address Street, Business Fax, Business Home Page, Business Phone, Business Phone 2, Callback, Car Phone, City, Company, Company Main Phone, Computer Network Name, Country, Created, Customer ID, Department, E-Mail, E-Mail 2, E-Mail 3, File As, First Name, FTP Site, Full Name, Gender, Government ID Number, Hobbies, Home Address, Home Address City, Home Address Country, Home Address PO Box, Home Address Postal Code, Home Address State, Home Address Street, Home Fax, Home Phone, Home Phone 2, Icon, In Folder, Initials, ISDN, Job Title, Journal, Language, Last Name, Location, Mailing Address, Manager's Name, Message Class, Middle Name, Mileage, Mobile Phone, Modified, Nickname, Office Location, Organizational ID Number, Other Address, Other Address City, Other Address Country, Other Address PO Box, Other Address Postal Code, Other Address State, Other Address Street, Other Fax, Other Phone, Outlook Internal Version, Outlook Version, Pager, Personal Home Page, PO Box, Primary Phone, Profession, Radio Phone, Referred By, Sensitivity, Size, Spouse, State, Street Address, Suffix, Telex, Title, TTY/TDD Phone, User Field 1, User Field 2, User Field 3, User Field 4, Web Page, ZIP/Postal Code **Message items folder:** adds Received (the default) **Calendar items folder:** adds Start (the default) **Contact items folder:** File As is the default **Task items folder:** (None) is default **Journal items folder:** adds Start (the default) **Note items folder:** Created is the default
All Document Fields	**All folders:** Author, Bytes, Category, Characters, Comments, Company, Creation Time, Document Subject, Edit Time, Hidden Slides, Last Author, Last Saved Time, Lines, Manager, Multimedia Clips, Notes, Pages, Paragraphs, Presentation Format, Printed, Revision Number, Slides, Template, Title, Words **Message items folder:** adds Received (the default) **Calendar items folder:** adds Start (the default) **Contact items folder:** adds File As (the default) **Task items folder:** (None) is the default **Journal items folder:** adds Start (the default) **Note items folder:** adds Created (the default)
All File Fields	**Disk files folder:** Application, Author, Category, Characters, Characters With Spaces, Company, Created, Edited, Format, Hidden Slides, Hyperlink Base, In Folder, Keywords, Lines, Manager, Modified, Multimedia Clips, Name (the default), Notes, Pages, Paragraphs, Printed, Revision, Saved By, Security, Size, Slides, Subject, Template, Title, Type, Words

V

Bending Folders to Your Will

(continued)

TABLE 17-2. *continued*

List Name	Fields Available for Sorting, by Folder Type
All Journal Fields	**All folders:** Attachment, Billing Information, Created, Do Not Auto-Archive, Duration, End, Entry Type, Icon, In Folder, Message Class, Mileage, Modified, Outlook Internal Version, Outlook Version, Sensitivity, Size, Start, Subject **Message items folder:** adds Received (the default) **Calendar items folder:** Start is the default **Contact items folder:** adds File As (the default) **Task items folder:** (None) is the default **Journal items folder:** Start is the default **Note items folder:** Created is the default
All Mail Fields	**All folders:** Attachment, Bcc, Billing Information, Cc, Conversation, Conversation Index, Created, Defer Until, Do Not AutoArchive, Due By, Expires, Flag Status, From, Have Replies Sent To, Icon, Importance, In Folder, Message Class, Message Flag, Mileage, Modified, Outlook Internal Version, Outlook Version, Received, Remote Status, Retrieval Time, Sensitivity, Sent, Size, Subject, To, Tracking Status **Message items folder:** Received is the default **Calendar items folder:** adds Start (the default) **Contact items folder:** adds File As (the default) **Task items folder:** (None) is the default **Journal items folder:** adds Start (the default) **Note items folder:** Created is the default
All Note Fields	**All folders:** Color, Created, Do Not AutoArchive, Icon, In Folder, Message Class, Modified, Outlook Internal Version, Outlook Version, Size, Subject **Message items folder:** adds Received (the default) **Calendar items folder:** adds Start (the default) **Contact items folder:** adds File As (the default) **Task items folder:** (None) is default **Journal items folder:** adds Start (the default) **Note items folder:** Created is the default
All Post Fields	**All folders:** Attachment, Billing Information, Conversation, Conversation Index, Created, Defer Until, Do Not AutoArchive, Expires, From, Icon, Importance, In Folder, Message Class, Mileage, Modified, Outlook Internal Version, Outlook Version, Received, Remote Status, Retrieval Time, Sensitivity, Sent, Size, Subject **Message items folder:** Received is the default **Calendar items folder:** adds Start (the default) **Contact items folder:** adds File As (the default) **Task items folder:** (None) is the default **Journal items folder:** adds Start (the default) **Note items folder:** Created is the default

List Name	Fields Available for Sorting, by Folder Type
All Task Fields	**All folders:** % Complete, Actual Work, Assigned, Attachment, Billing Information, Complete, Conversation, Created, Date Completed, Do Not AutoArchive, Due Date, Icon, In Folder, Message Class, Mileage, Modified, Outlook Internal Version, Outlook Version, Owner, Priority, Recurring, Reminder, Reminder Override Default, Reminder Sound, Reminder Sound File, Reminder Time, Requested By, Request Status, Role, Schedule+ Priority, Sensitivity, Size, Start Date, Status, Subject, Team Task, To, Total Work **Message items folder:** adds Received (the default) **Calendar items folder:** adds Start (the default) **Contact items folder:** adds File As (the default) **Task items folder:** (None) is the default **Journal items folder:** adds Start (the default) **Note items folder:** Created is the default
User-Defined Fields In Folder	**All folders:** The content of this list depends on the fields you've added to the folder that is open when you choose the View Sort command. The list of fields in the Sort Items By box contains at least (None) and the default field for the type of folder. **Disk files folder:** Client, Client Company, Client Name, Company, Company Address, Company City, Company Fax, Company Name, Company Phone, Company State, Company ZIP, Customer Name, Date, Date Completed, Department, Disposition, Division/Department, DocumentEncoding, Due Date, E-Mail, Employee Name, Employee Number, Family Address, Family City, Family Fax, Family Name, Family Phone, Family State, Family ZIP, From, HTML, Interest Rate, Invoice Number, Lender Name, Matter, Name (the default), Number Of Payments, Nwversion, Owner, PO, Principle, Project, Purchase Order Date, Purchase Order Number, Quantity, Reference, Report Title, Sale, Sales, Shared, Size, Statement Number, Title, To, Total Invoice, Total Purchase, Total Reimbursement/Payment, Vendor Name, Version
Forms	**All folders:** Choosing this list opens the Forms dialog box, where you can select forms to add to the open folder. When you select a form, Outlook adds it to the list in the Select Available Fields From box. The fields listed in the Sort Items By box depends on the fields in the form.

Filtering

A filter sets up a screening process that displays some folder items and hides others. The value of a filter is that it gives you an unobstructed and uncluttered view of the folder items you want to see—and *only* those folder items. This limited view makes it easier to analyze the folder items without interference from irrelevant items and the information they contain.

When you set up a filter, you are telling Outlook to display in the folder window only those folder items that meet the criteria you specify. (Folder items that do not meet your criteria are not deleted from the folder; they're simply hidden. When you remove the filter, you can see them again.)

To set up and apply a filter for the current View, you use the View Filter command and the Filter dialog box, shown in Figure 17-2. You can use all three of the tabs in this dialog box to set up criteria for a filter. (As you might notice, the Filter dialog box resembles the Find dialog box, discussed in Chapter 13; see "Searching Folder Contents," on page 372. The processes of setting up a search and setting up a filter are similar in many ways.)

FIGURE 17-2.

The Filter dialog box for the Inbox folder showing the Messages tab.

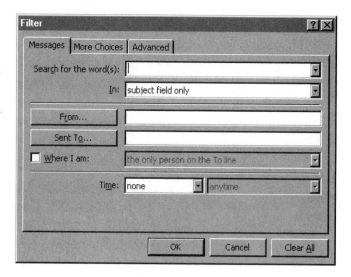

For example, you could use the Filter dialog box shown above in Figure 17-2 to set up a filter for your Inbox folder. Let's say that you want to filter for all messages sent by Jane Doe pertaining to a networking project in which your organization is involved:

1 Open your Inbox folder, and choose the View Filter command.

2 On the Messages tab of the Filter dialog box, type the word *networking* in the Search For The Word(s) box.

3 From the drop-down list in the In box, select Subject Field And Message Body.

4 In the From box, type *Jane Doe.*

5 Click OK to apply the filter.

Now your Inbox folder displays only messages sent by Jane Doe that contain the word *networking* in either the Subject line or the body of the message. Notice that Outlook adds the words *Filter Applied* to the status bar (in the lower left corner of the folder window) and to the right of the folder window's title.

If you want to narrow your filter even further, you can set additional filter criteria on the Messages tab—specifying messages sent during a certain time range, for example—or on either of the two other tabs in the Filter dialog box. (See "Setting Up the More Choices Tab," on page 485, and "Setting Up Advanced Criteria," on page 487, for information about the second and third tabs.) When you set up multiple criteria for a filter, a folder item must meet all of the criteria specified on all of the tabs in order to appear in the filtered view of the folder.

The first of the three tabs in the Filter dialog box varies according to the type of folder that is currently open. For instance, you'll see the Messages tab shown in Figure 17-2 if you are setting up a filter for a folder that contains message items. If you open a different type of folder to set up a filter, Outlook changes not only the name of the first tab in the Filter dialog box but also the options it contains. Table 17-3 on the following page describes the options available on this tab for each type of folder.

V

Bending Folders to Your Will

⭐ **TIP**

You don't have to fill out all the tabs of the Filter dialog box. You can set conditions on any tab of the Filter dialog box either in addition to or instead of conditions you set on other tabs.

TABLE 17-3. Settings on the First Tab of the Filter Dialog Box for Each Folder Type.

Folder Type (and Tab)	Filter Option	Filters For
Inbox: Contains message items (Messages tab)	Search For The Word(s)	Message items that contain the specified words for the field category you select in the In box. (To specify words you used in previous filters, select them from the drop-down list, where Outlook stores them.)
	In	Items containing the specified words in a certain part of the message: Subject Field Only, Subject Field And Message Body, Frequently-Used Text Fields.
	From	Items from particular senders. Type the names, separated by a semicolon or by a comma, or click the From button to select names.
	Sent To	Items you sent to particular recipients. Type the names, separated by a semicolon or by a comma, or click the Sent To button to select names.
	Where I Am	Items sent to you in which you are one of the following: The Only Person On The To Line, On The To Line With Other People, On The Cc Line With Other People. (The Sent To or the From box must contain at least one name before this option becomes available.)
	Time	Items that match the time condition selected in the first Time box and the corresponding time value selected in the second Time box.
	The following time conditions can be selected in the first Time box:	
	None	No time filter applied.
	Received, Sent, Created, Modified	Items that were received, sent, created, or modified during one of these time values: Anytime, Yesterday, Today, In The Last 7 Days, Last Week, This Week, Last Month, This Month.
	Due, Expires	Items that are due or that expire during one of these time values: Anytime, Yesterday, Today, Tomorrow, In The Last 7 Days, Last Week, This Week, Next Week, Last Month, This Month, Next Month.

Folder Type (and Tab)	Filter Option	Filters For
Calendar: Contains calendar items (Appointments And Meetings tab)	Search For The Word(s)	Calendar items that contain the specified words for the field category you select in the In box. (To specify words you used in previous filters, select them from the drop-down list, where Outlook stores them.)
	In	Items containing the specified words in a certain part of the item: Subject Field Only, Subject And Notes Fields, Frequently-Used Text Fields.
	Organized By	Items from particular meeting organizers. Type the names, separated by a semicolon or by a comma, or click the Organized By button to select names.
	Attendees	Items with particular attendees. Type the names, separated by a semicolon or by a comma, or click the Attendees button to select names.
	Time	Items that match the time condition selected in the first Time box and the corresponding time value selected in the second Time box.
	The following time conditions can be selected in the first Time box:	
	None	No time filter applied.
	Starts, Ends	Items whose start or end date corresponds to one of these time values: Anytime, Yesterday, Today, Tomorrow, In The Last 7 Days, In The Next 7 Days, Last Week, This Week, Next Week, Last Month, This Month, Next Month.
	Created, Modified	Items that were created or modified during one of these time values: Anytime, Yesterday, Today, In The Last 7 Days, Last Week, This Week, Last Month, This Month.
Contacts: Contains contact items (Contacts tab)	Search For The Word(s)	Contact items that contain the specified words for the field category of the contact entry you select in the In box. (To specify words you used in previous filters, select them from the drop-down list, where Outlook stores them.)
	In	Items containing the specified words in a certain part of the contact entry: File As Field Only, Name Fields Only, Company Field Only, Address Fields Only, E-Mail Fields Only, Phone Number Fields Only, Frequently-Used Text Fields.

V

Bending Folders to Your Will

(continued)

TABLE 17-3. *continued*

Folder Type (and Tab)	Filter Option	Filters For
	E-Mail	Items for the contacts whose e-mail you specify. Type the e-mail names, separated by a semicolon or by a comma, or click the E-Mail button to select names.
	Time	Items that match the time condition selected in the first Time box and the corresponding time value selected in the second Time box.
	The following time conditions can be selected in the first Time box:	
	None	No time filter applied.
	Created, Modified	Items that were created or modified during one of these time values: Anytime, Yesterday, Today, In The Last 7 Days, Last Week, This Week, Last Month, This Month.
Tasks: Contains task items (Tasks tab)	Search For The Word(s)	Task items that contain the specified words for the field category you select in the In box. (To specify words you used in previous filters, select them from the drop-down list, where Outlook stores them.)
	In	Items containing the specified words in a certain part of the item: Subject Field Only, Subject And Notes Fields, Frequently-Used Text Fields.
	Status	Items that have one of the following status designations: Doesn't Matter, Not Started, In Progress, Completed, Waiting On Someone Else, Deferred.
	From	Task requests received from particular senders. Type the names, separated by a semicolon or by a comma, or click the From button to select names.
	Sent To	Task requests you sent to particular recipients. Type the names, separated by a semicolon or by a comma, or click the Sent To button to select names.
	Time	Items that match the time condition selected in the first Time box and the corresponding time value selected in the second Time box.

Folder Type (and Tab)	Filter Option	Filters For
	The following time conditions can be selected in the first Time box:	
	None	No time filter applied.
	Completed, Created, Modified	Items that were completed, created, or modified during one of these time values: Anytime, Yesterday, Today, In The Last 7 Days, Last Week, This Week, Last Month, This Month.
	Due, Starts	Items that are due or that start during one of these time values: Anytime, Yesterday, Today, Tomorrow, In The Last 7 Days, In The Next 7 Days, Last Week, This Week, Next Week, Last Month, This Month, Next Month.
Journal: Contains journal items (Journal Entries tab)	Search For The Word(s)	Journal items that contain the specified words for the field category you select in the In box. (To specify words you used in previous filters, select them from the drop-down list, where Outlook stores them.)
	In	Items containing the specified words in a certain part of the journal entry: Subject Field Only, Contact Field Only, Subject And Notes Fields, Frequently-Used Text Fields.
	Journal Entry Type	Items of the type you select: All Types, Conversation, Document, E-Mail Message, Fax, Letter, Meeting, Meeting Cancellation, Meeting Request, Meeting Response, Microsoft Access, Microsoft Excel, Microsoft Office Binder, Microsoft PowerPoint, Microsoft Word, Note, Phone Call, Remote Session, Task, Task Request, Task Response
	Contact	Items for particular contacts only. Type the names, separated by a comma, or click the Contact button to select names.
	Time	Items that match the time condition selected in the first Time box and the corresponding time value selected in the second Time box.
	The following time conditions can be selected in the first Time box:	
	None	No time filter applied.

(continued)

V

Bending Folders to Your Will

TABLE 17-3. *continued*

Folder Type (and Tab)	Filter Option	Filters For
	Starts, Ends	Items whose start or end date corresponds to one of these time values: Anytime, Yesterday, Today, Tomorrow, In The Last 7 Days, In The Next 7 Days, Last Week, This Week, Next Week, Last Month, This Month, Next Month.
	Created, Modified	Items that were created or modified during one of these time values: Anytime, Yesterday, Today, In The Last 7 Days, Last Week, This Week, Last Month, This Month.
Notes: Contains note items (Notes tab)	Search For The Word(s)	Note items that contain the specified words for the field category you select in the In box. (To specify words you used in previous filters, select them from the drop-down list, where Outlook stores them.)
	In	Items containing the specified words in a certain part of the note: Contents Only, Subject Field Only
	Time	Items that match the time condition selected in the first Time box and the corresponding time value selected in the second Time box.
	The following time conditions can be selected in the first Time box:	
	None	No time filter applied.
	Created, Modified	Items that were created or modified during one of these time values: Anytime, Yesterday, Today, In The Last 7 Days, Last Week, This Week, Last Month, This Month.
Disk Files: Contains disk file items from folders such as My Computer, My Documents, and Favorites (Files tab)	Named	Disk filenames that contain the specified file type that you selected in the Type Of box. (To specify files that you used in previous filters, select them from the drop-down list, where Outlook stores them.)
	Type Of	Items containing the specified file types: All Files, Office Files, Documents, Workbooks, Presentations, Binders, Databases, and Templates.
	Search For The Word(s)	Disk files that contain the specified words for the field category you select in the In box. (To specify words you used in previous filters, select them from the drop-down list, where Outlook stores them.)

Folder Type (and Tab)	Filter Option	Filters For
	In	Items containing the specified words in a certain part of the message: Any Text Or Property (Including Contents), Contents Only.
	Time	Items that match the time condition selected in the first Time box and the corresponding time value selected in the second Time box.
	The following time conditions can be selected in the first Time box:	
	None	No time filter applied.
	Modified	Items that were modified during one of these time values: Anytime, Yesterday, Today, In The Last 7 Days, Last Week, This Week, Last Month, This Month.

Setting Up the More Choices Tab

The More Choices tab of the Filter dialog box, shown in Figure 17-3, is the same for most types of folders. For a few types, however, as noted in the following summary, some options are grayed out (and therefore unavailable).

FIGURE 17-3.

The More Choices tab of the Filter dialog box.

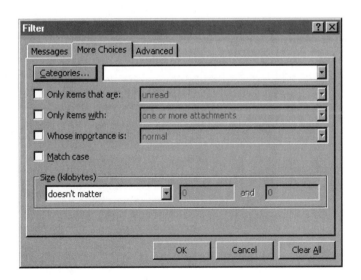

Here's a brief summary of the options on the More Choices tab and how to set them up as filter criteria:

Categories. When you use categories as filter criteria, Outlook displays folder items that have been assigned to the categories you list. Type the category names, separated by a comma, or click the Categories button to select category names in the Categories dialog box. (If you want to specify categories you used in a previous filter, you can select them from the drop-down list, where Outlook stores them.)

Only Items That Are. Turn on the check box, and then select either Read (for folder items that you have already read) or Unread (for folder items that you haven't yet read).

Only Items With. After you turn on this check box, you can select One Or More Attachments (to filter for folder items that contain attachments) or No Attachments (to filter for items that have no attachments). This option is unavailable for folders that contain note items.

Whose Importance Is. This option filters for folder items that have a specific level of importance: High, Normal, or Low. Turn on the check box, and then select a level from the drop-down list. This option is not available for folders that contain contact items, note items, or journal entries.

Match Case. Turn on this check box to display only those folder items whose uppercase and lowercase characters exactly match the uppercase and lowercase characters you typed in the Search For The Word(s) box on the first tab.

Size. You can use this option to restrict the filter to only those folder items whose size, in kilobytes, matches a specified size range. In the drop-down list, select Doesn't Matter if you don't want to filter for a particular size. If you select Equals (Approximately), Less Than, or Greater Than (size conditions), Outlook activates the first box to the right, and you must enter a specific size value. If you select Between, Outlook activates both boxes to the right, and you must enter two size values (the upper and lower end of a size range).

When you set up a filter for a folder that contains disk files, the More Choices tab is a little different. It offers only three options: Match Case, Match All Word Forms, and Size. You can set up the Match Case and Size options exactly as you do for other types of folders. If you choose the Match All Word Forms option, you are in effect widening the scope of your filter criteria to include all files that contain variations of the words you typed in the Search For The Word(s) box on the first tab. For instance, if you've set up the word *create* as a filter criterion in the Search For The Word(s) box, choosing Match All Word Forms means that files containing the text *create, creates, created,* and so on will be displayed in the filtered view.

Setting Up Advanced Criteria

If you need to refine the filter for your folder view beyond the settings available on the first two tabs of the Filter dialog box, you can click the Advanced tab, shown in Figure 17-4, to set up advanced criteria. On this tab, you can select a field, specify a condition and a value for the field, and then have Outlook filter folder items according to this criterion. This tab is the same for all types of folders, including folders that contain disk files. (The More Advanced button is not available for the Disk Files folder type.)

FIGURE 17-4.

The Advanced tab of the Filter dialog box.

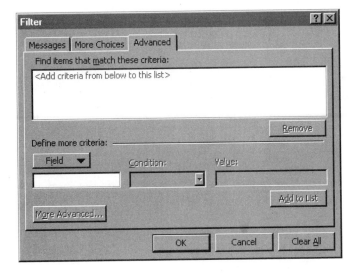

The following steps show you how to set up advanced criteria, using a simple example:

1 In the Filter dialog box, click the Advanced tab.

2 Click the Field button to display a drop-down menu of the available lists of fields.

3 Point to a list name to display a submenu containing all the specific fields on that list that are available for the open folder. As an example, let's say that you want to set up a filter for your Contacts folder that will display all contacts whose business address is in Seattle. In that case, you'd point to the Address Fields list.

4 Click the field you want to use—for this example, click Business Address City. Outlook adds the field name to the box under the Field button and activates the Condition box and the Value box.

5 Choose a condition from the drop-down list in the Condition box. (The set of conditions available in this box depends on the specific field you selected.) For this example, choose Contains.

6 In the Value box, type a value—in this case, type *Seattle*. Outlook activates the Add To List button.

7 Click the Add To List button. Outlook adds the criterion to the Find Items That Match These Criteria box.

8 If you want to add additional criteria, repeat steps 2 through 7. (Remember that when you set up multiple criteria, a folder item must meet *all* the criteria in order to appear in the filtered view.) If you change your mind about including a criterion, select it in the Find Items That Match These box and click the Remove button.

9 Click OK to apply the filter. For the example described here, your Contacts folder will display a filtered view of all contact entries whose Business Address City field contains the word *Seattle*.

Not all fields and conditions require a value (step 6). For instance, let's say that you select Is Empty as the condition in the preceding example. (The filtered view would then display contact entries whose Business Address City field contains no information. In this case, the Value box would be grayed out (unavailable) because no value is required to make sense of that condition. If a condition requires a value, Outlook activates the Value box and does not activate the Add To List button until you've entered the value.

You can enter multiple values in the Value box. For text fields, use the word *and* or a blank space to filter items whose field contents match both values. For instance, to display messages that you've assigned to *both* the categories Key Customer and International, type *Key Customer and International* in the Value box. To display messages that you've assigned to *either* category, use the word *or*, a comma, or a semicolon instead of the word *and*. For date fields—used most often with the conditions On, On Or After, and On Or Before—you can use AutoDate to describe the value. For example, you can assign Birthday for the Field contents, On Or Before as the Condition, and for the value you can type *two days*. The Filter will show only those Contacts whose birthday is on or before today's date.

Turning Off a Filter

To turn off a filter, take these steps:

1 Click the Filter button.

2 In the Filter dialog box, click the Clear All button.

3 Click OK.

Working in Your Own Fields

Outlook gives you the tools you need to create new fields for your folders. You can be creative when you design custom fields, tailoring them to organize your folder information in the way that best meets your unique needs.

When you create a custom field, you must do so for a specific folder. You'll need to create the custom field again in each folder where you want to use it. The custom field name appears in the User-Defined Fields In Folder for the Sort, Filter (Advanced Fields), and Group By options on the View menu.

You can create three kinds of custom fields: simple, combination, and formula.

- Creating a simple field can allow you to add custom information to folder items. You can set up the field as a column in a table view or as a row on a card. For example, you might add a date/time field called Summary Report Submitted in your Tasks folder, in which you can record the date you wrote and submitted a summary of a completed project. You could then add this field as a column in Detailed List view or Completed Tasks view.

- In a combination field, you can combine existing fields so that several pieces of information appear in a single column or a single row in a folder. For example, you might create an Attendees field for your Calendar folder that combines the Optional Attendees and Required Attendees fields, if the distinction between optional and required attendance isn't important or practical in your organization. You could then display the Attendees column in, for instance, Active Appointments view or Recurring Appointments view.

- With a formula field, you can present information with a new or different slant by setting up calculations that involve the information contained in other fields. You might create a formula field for messages, for instance, that shows the number of days since each message was received and its importance icon with any due dates that might occur for the task associated with the message.

Each new custom field must be based on a specific data type—that is, the field must be able to contain the appropriate kind of data: text, numbers, dates, or other data. The basic steps for creating all three types of custom fields are the same, as explained in the following section. Combination and formula fields involve a few additional complications; see "Creating a Combination Field," on page 494, and "Creating a Formula Field," on page 496.

> **NOTE**
>
> You can create custom fields only for table views and card views—not for timeline, day/week/month, note, or icon views.

Creating a Simple Custom Field

To create a simple custom field for a folder, follow these steps:

1 Open the folder for which you want to create a custom field.

2 Select a table view or a card view.

3 Choose the View Show Fields command.

4 In the Show Fields dialog box, click the New Field button.

6 Select the data type. (For a simple field, do not select Combination or Formula.)

5 Type a name for the new field.

7 Select the format.

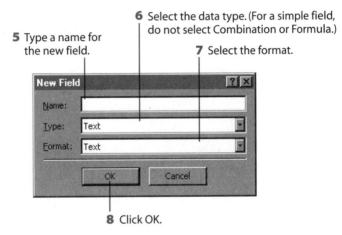

8 Click OK.

9 In the Show Fields dialog box, you can click the Move Up button to move your new field up the Show These Fields In This Order list if you want to adjust the position in which the field will be displayed in the folder window.

10 Click OK in the Show Fields dialog box.

⭐ **TIP**

> The Contacts folder handles custom fields differently. To create a simple custom field for a Contact folder item, double-click the item, click the All Fields tab in the item's window, and then click the New button.

In the following section, you'll find details about how to select a data type and a data type format in the New Field dialog box.

V

Bending Folders to Your Will

Data Types and Standard Formats

When you create a custom field, you select a data type in the Type box of the New Field dialog box. You must base each custom field on a specific data type that is able to contain the kind of information you'll be storing in the field. Table 17-4 lists the data types you can choose.

TABLE 17-4. Data Types for Custom Fields.

Data Type	Use For
Currency	Numbers shown as currency; calculations of money amounts.
Date/Time	Dates and times.
Duration	Numbers. You can enter a duration time as minutes, hours, or days. You can use a standard format to indicate whether duration time is based on a 24-hour day or on the Task Working Hours settings you choose on the Tasks/Notes tab of the Options dialog box (accessed by choosing the Tools Options command). For example, if you have set 10 hours as a work day on the Tasks/Notes tab, entering 15 hours shows as 1.5 days. Values are saved as minutes.
Integer	Nondecimal numbers.
Number	Numbers; mathematical calculations except those involving money amounts. (Use the Currency data type for money.)
Percent	Numbers as a percentage.
Text	Text or combinations of text and numbers (as many as 255 characters), such as addresses and phone numbers.
Yes/No	Data that can be only one of two values, such as Yes/No, True/False, or On/Off. (For example, the Do Not AutoArchive field uses a Yes/No data type.) A Yes/No field can also be displayed as an empty box or a box with a check mark.
Keywords	User-defined fields that you can use to group and find related items, in much the same way you use the Categories field. (See the sidebar "Using a Custom Field to Collect Related Folder Items" on page 494.) If the text contains multiple values, you must separate them with commas. Each value can be grouped individually in a view.

Data Type	Use For
Combination	Combinations of fields and text in a column (table view) or row (card view). You can show each field of the combination or show the first field containing data.
Formula	Calculations using data contained in any field. Use appropriate functions and operators to set up a formula.

For each data type except combination and formula, Outlook provides standard formats that you can choose to format your custom field. Table 17-5 lists these standard formats.

TABLE 17-5.   Some Standard Formats for Data Types.

Data Type	Standard Formats
Currency	$12,345.60 or ($12,345.60) $12,346 or ($12,346)
Date/Time*	Monday, August 4, 1997 8:00 AM
Duration	12h or 12 hours (assumes a 24-hour day) 12h (Work Time) or 12 hours (Work Time) (based on work time set on the Tasks/Notes tab of the Tools Options dialog box)
Integer	1,234 or Computer −2,300K; 2.3M; 2.3 MB
Keywords	Text
Number	All Digits: 1,234.567 or −1,234.567 Truncated: 1,235 or −1,235 1 Decimal: 1,234.6 or −1,234.6 2 Decimal: 1,234.57 or −1,234.57 Scientific: 1235E+03 or −1235E+03 Computer 64K or 128K or 65,536K Computer: 64K or 128 M or 1 GB Computer 64KB or 256MB or 2GB Raw: 12345.67 or −12345.67
Percent	All Digits: 65.4321% Rounded: 65% or −65% 1 Decimal: 64.4% or −64.4% 2 Decimal: 65.43% or −65.43%
Text	Text
Yes/No	Yes or No On or Off True or False Icon—Empty box or Box with a check mark

V

Bending Folders to Your Will

*   There are 16 formats for Date/Time. The format included in this table is provided as an example.

TIP

For a list of standard formats available for a field in a specific view, choose the View Format Columns command. In the Available Fields box, select the field, and then select a format in the Format box. (If you don't find the format you want, you can create a custom format with a formula data type and the Format function; see "Creating a Formula Field," on page 496.)

Using a Custom Field to Collect Related Folder Items

You can create a custom keywords field and use it to group and find related folder items, in much the same way you can use categories to collect related items. (See "Collecting Related Folder Items," on page 465.)

1 Open a folder containing items you want to collect, and select a table view or a card view.

2 Choose the View Show Fields command.

3 In the Show Fields dialog box, click the New Field button.

4 In the Name box of the New Field dialog box, type a name for the new field—for this example, we'll name the field Gather.

5 In the Type box, select Keywords.

6 Click OK to have Outlook add the new field to the folder view.

7 Fill in the new column by typing one or more keywords for each folder item as appropriate. You must separate multiple keywords with a comma.

You can now group folder items by the keywords you've assigned to them. Choose the View Group By Box command, and drag the new column heading up into the Group By area above the columns. Outlook groups the folder items and labels each group with the column heading, a colon, and a keyword. For instance, if you type the keywords *Food, Shelter,* and *Clothing* in the new Gather column, you'll see groups labeled Gather: Food, Gather: Shelter, and Gather: Clothing. (For details about grouping, see "Grouping," on page 465.)

Creating a Combination Field

You can combine simple fields (both built-in fields and custom fields) in a single column or row—the result is called a combination field. For example, you can create a column that combines the City and

State fields in an address list to save space. (For more examples, see Table 17-6, on page 498.)

To create a combination field, follow these steps:

1 Open the New Field dialog box, as explained in "Creating a Simple Custom Field," on page 491 (steps 1 through 4).

3 Select Combination.

2 Type a name for the combination field.

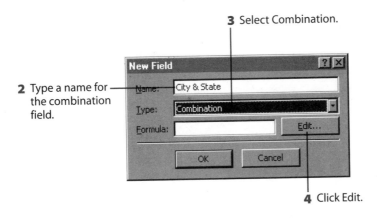

4 Click Edit.

5 Click here to join fields together, or...

click here to show only the first field that has data and to ignore subsequent ones.

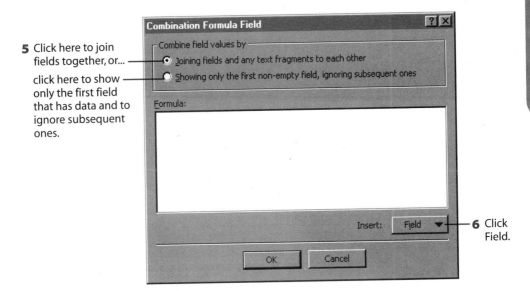

6 Click Field.

7 Point to the field list containing the first field you want to combine. When Outlook displays the list, click the field.

8 Repeat steps 6 and 7 for each field you want to add to the combination.

9 Click OK in the Combination Formula Field dialog box.

10 In the Show Fields dialog box, you can click Move Up to move your new field up the list if you want to adjust the position in which the field will be displayed in the folder window.

11 Click OK in the Show Fields dialog box.

To add or change the information in a combination field, you must add or change the information in the simple fields that make up the combination. For example, if you create a combination field consisting of city and state names, you need to add or change the city name in the simple City field and the state name in the simple State field. You can't directly edit the information in a combination field.

Combination fields use the default format of the data type on which they are based. To display a data type with a custom format, you must create a formula field and use the Format function. (See the following section.)

 NOTE

You cannot sort, group, or filter the contents of a combination field.

Creating a Formula Field

Formula fields combine functions, operators, and fields. To see some examples of formula fields, see Table 17-6, on page 498.

To create a formula field, take these steps:

1 Open the New Field dialog box, as explained in "Creating a Simple Custom Field," on page 491 (steps 1 through 4).

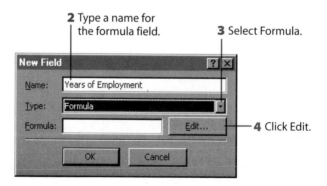

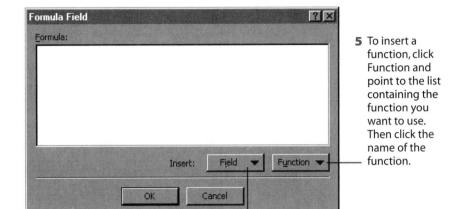

5 To insert a function, click Function and point to the list containing the function you want to use. Then click the name of the function.

6 To insert a field, select the argument in the function that you want to replace. Then click Field, point to the field list containing the field you want to use, and click the field name.

7 Repeat step 5 or step 6 until you have completely built the formula.

8 Click OK in the Formula Field dialog box, and then click OK in the New Field dialog box.

9 In the Show Fields dialog box, click the Move Up button if you want to adjust the position of the field in the list.

10 Click OK in the Show Fields dialog box.

You can use a large number of varied functions in formula fields. Describing all the functions and operators that you can incorporate in formula fields is well beyond the scope of this book, but you can find information about functions, operators, and operator precedence in the Outlook Help file. Click the Office Assistant or open Help and choose Microsoft Outlook Help, and type *functions* or *operators* in the Search box to see an extensive list of topics and comprehensive lists of functions or operators.

If you need to add or change the information contained in a formula field, you must add or change the information in the simple fields that make up the formula. You can't directly edit the information in a formula field.

V

Bending Folders to Your Will

Formula fields are updated any time you change a view. For example, if you change the width of a column, the formula fields are updated.

 **NOTE**

> You cannot sort, group, or filter the contents of a formula field.

Examples of Formula and Combination Fields

Formula and combination fields can be a little tricky, but they can also be extremely useful. Table 17-6 offers a few examples of such custom fields, showing you what the formulas and combinations look like and providing some sample results for each field.

TABLE 17-6. Examples of Formula and Combination Fields, with Sample Results.

What the Custom Field Shows	Custom Field	Sample Result in Custom Field
Number of days since an item was received (formula field)	DateValue (Now())-DateValue ([Received]) & " Day(s)"	6 Day(s)—(if 6 days have elapsed since the date the message was received)
Description of a meeting in your calendar (formula field)	"This meeting occurs" & [Recurrence Pattern] & " in " & [Location]	This meeting occurs every day from 12:00 AM to 1:30 AM in room 10b-3400
Amount charged for a phone call recorded in the Journal at $.75 a minute (formula field)	IIF ([Entry Type] = "Phone call", Format ([Duration] *.75, "Currency"), "None")	$1.50—(if the duration of the call was 2 minutes)
Description of a message flag (formula field)	IIF ([Flag Status] = "2" [Message Flag] & " " & [Due By], "")	Follow up 10/5/97 10:00:00 AM
The first phone number recorded for a contact, in order of appearance in the formula (combination field)	[Business Phone] [Business Phone 2] [Home Phone] [Car Phone]	(555) 555-1234 (555) 555-1234 x564 (555) 555-5000 (555) 555-0000
A description of a field combined with the field itself (combination field)	Task Due: [Due Date]	Task Due: 10/5/97 10:00:00 AM

Changing a Custom Field

You can change a custom field only by changing the format or the formula. You can't change the field name or the data type. If you don't like a field's name or data type, you have to delete the custom field (see "Deleting a Custom Field," on page 500) and then create a new one that suits you.

Here's how to change the format or formula for a custom field:

1 Choose the Show Fields command.

2 If you're using the custom field, remove it from the Show These Fields In This Order list to the Available Fields list. (Either double-click the field name, or select it and then click the Remove button.)

3 Select the field name in the Available Fields list, and then click the Properties button to display the Edit Field dialog box.

4 For a formula field, type a new formula in the Formula box or click the Edit button.

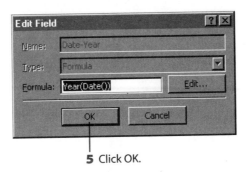

5 Click OK.

6 If you want to use this newly edited custom field in the folder, add it back to the Show These Fields In This Order list. (Either double-click the field name or select it and then click the Add button.)

7 Click OK in the Show Fields dialog box.

> **NOTE**
>
> You can't edit Outlook's built-in fields.

Deleting a Custom Field

If you no longer have a use for a field you created, you might as well get rid of it. To delete a field you created, take these steps:

1 Choose the Show Fields command.

2 If you're using the custom field, remove it from the Show These Fields In This Order list to the Available Fields list. (Either double-click the field name, or select it and then click the Remove button.)

3 Select the field name in the Available Fields list, and then click the Delete button.

4 When Outlook asks you to confirm the deletion, click OK.

5 Click OK in the Show Fields dialog box.

> **NOTE**
>
> You can't delete any of Outlook's built-in fields.

CHAPTER 18

Setting Up Views

Now that you've learned in the preceding chapter about the techniques and features you can use to work with views, you're ready to put it all together. When you set up a view for a Microsoft Outlook 97 folder, you can choose the fields to be included, group and sort the information, and filter the view all in one operation. Later, you can modify the view, rename it, or change its format. You can even decide who can use the view and in which folders they can use it.

Obviously, you'll need familiarity with the topics covered in Chapter 17, "Columns, Categories, Grouping, Sorting, Filtering, and Custom Fields," so you might want to review that chapter briefly before beginning this one. This chapter also includes cross-references to various sections of Chapter 17 to help you make the connections.

Defining a View

When you define a view for a folder, you give the view a name, and you also set up the fields, the sorting, the grouping, and the filtering you want to use in the view. Defining a view involves a series of dialog boxes, as outlined here:

1 Open the folder in which you want to define a new view.

2 Choose the View Define Views command to open the Define Views For dialog box. (Outlook displays the name of the open folder in the title bar of the dialog box.)

3 Click New.

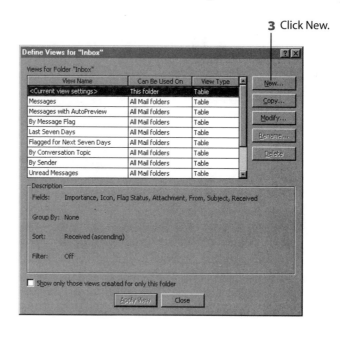

4 Type a name for the new view.

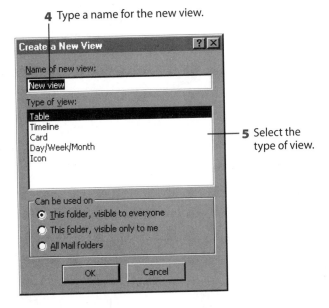

5 Select the type of view.

6 In the Can Be Used On section, select one of the three options to specify where the view can be used and who can use it:

- This Folder, Visible To Everyone makes the view available only in the folder in which you created it. With this option, anyone who has permission to open the folder can choose the view in the drop-down list on the Standard toolbar or on the submenu of the View Current View command.

- This Folder, Visible Only To Me makes the view available only in the folder in which you created it and does not allow other people to use the view. You will be the only person allowed to choose the view; if anyone else has permission to open the folder, they will not find this view listed in the drop-down list on the Standard toolbar or on the submenu of the View Current View command.

- All [Folder Type] Folders makes the view available to all folders that are the same type as the folder in which you created the view. Anyone who has permission to open a folder of this type can use this view to organize items in a similar folder. For example, if you are creating a view for your Inbox, this option will read All Mail Folders, and anyone with permission to open mail folders will be able to use this view.

7 Click OK in the Create A New View dialog box. Outlook displays the View Summary dialog box, which provides a complete description of the view as it currently exists:

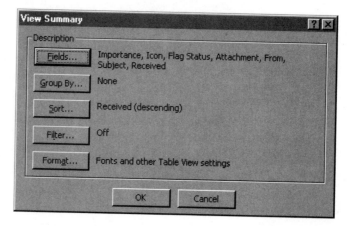

8 To set up the elements of the new view, click any one of the Fields, Group By, Sort, Filter, or Format buttons. Clicking one of the first four of these buttons takes you to a dialog box that should be familiar from Chapter 17; for details about how to use these dialog boxes, see "Managing Columns by Command," on page 457, "Working in Your Own Fields," on page 489, "Grouping," on page 465, "Sorting," on page 468, or "Filtering," on page 477. Clicking the Format button opens the Format View dialog box, discussed in "Formatting Views," on page 509, later in this chapter.

9 When you've finished setting up the elements of the view and closed the relevant dialog boxes, click OK in the View Summary dialog box to close it and return to the Define Views For dialog box.

10 If you want to apply the new view to the currently open folder, click the Apply View button in the Define Views For dialog box.

11 Click the Close button in the Define Views For dialog box.

Outlook also provides a shorter method for creating a new view. Instead of starting from scratch and defining every part of a new view, you can base a new view on the current arrangement of fields, sorting, grouping, and filtering. Let's suppose that you are using a specific folder view (say, Active Appointments view in your Calendar folder) in which you make some changes—maybe you add a new column to the view, rearrange the order of the columns, or set up a filter. When you switch views or close the folder after making a change to the current view, Outlook displays the Save View Settings dialog box:

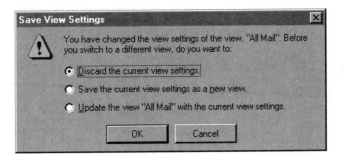

If the changes you made were only temporary and you don't want to use them again, choose Discard The Current View Settings and click OK. But if you'd like to keep the changes, Outlook lets you save them in one of two ways: either by altering the existing view and saving the changes as part of that view or by saving the modifications you've made as a new view (and leaving the existing view unaltered).

If you decide to save the current view settings as a brand new view, choose that option and click OK. Outlook then opens the Copy View dialog box:

In this dialog box, type a name for the new view. Then choose an option from the Can Be Used On section (as explained in step 6 on page 503), and click OK. Outlook adds the new view to the drop-down list on the Standard toolbar and to the submenu of the View Current View command.

Outlook also provides a quick method of updating or discarding the current view. If you've modified the current view and would either like to keep the changes you've made or discard them, choose the same view that you've been modifying from the View Current View submenu. Outlook displays the following dialog box:

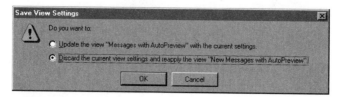

Select the desired option. For example, if you're currently using Messages With AutoPreview view and you want to keep the modifications you've made, choose View Current View, and then choose Messages With AutoPreview from the submenu. In the Save View Settings dialog box, choose the Update The View 'Messages With AutoPreview' With The Current Settings option, and then click OK.

> **NOTE**
>
> Notice that the Save View Settings dialog box that you saw previously has been modified—you can't create a new view from this version of the dialog box. To create a new view, use the View Define Views command and copy the current view to a new view.

Modifying a View

If a view isn't quite right, you can modify it so that it better suits your needs. To modify either a view you created or one of Outlook's built-in views, follow these steps:

1 Open the folder that contains the view you want to change.

2 Choose the View Define Views command to open the Define Views For dialog box.

3 Select the name of the view you want to change.

4 Click the Modify button to open the View Summary dialog box.

5 In the View Summary dialog box, click any one of the Fields, Group By, Sort, Filter, or Format buttons to open the appropriate dialog box(es) and modify the view as needed. (For information about how to use these dialog boxes, see "Managing Columns by Command," on page 457, "Working in Your Own Fields," on page 489, "Grouping," on page 465, "Sorting," on page 468, "Filtering," on page 477, or "Formatting Views," on page 509.)

6 When you've finished modifying the view and have closed the relevant dialog boxes, click OK in the View Summary dialog box to close it and return to the Define Views For dialog box.

7 If you want to apply the modified view to the currently open folder, click the Apply View button in the Define Views For dialog box.

8 Click the Close button in the Define Views dialog box.

V

Bending Folders to Your Will

TIP

To open the View Summary dialog box quickly, right-click a column heading in a table view or right-click anywhere in a timeline view, and then choose the View Summary command from the shortcut menu that appears.

Resetting a Standard View

As just described, you can modify custom views as well as Outlook's built-in views. If you modify a built-in view but later decide that you'd prefer to use Outlook's original version, you can restore the standard settings for that view. Here's how to do it:

1 Open the folder containing the built-in view you want to reset.

2 Choose the View Define Views command.

3 In the Define Views For dialog box, select the name of the view. (The name of the built-in view remains the same, no matter how you modify its various elements.)

4 Click the Reset button. This button is available only when you select a built-in view; you can't reset a custom view.

5 If you want to apply the restored original view to the currently open folder, click the Apply View button in the Define Views For dialog box.

6 Click the Close button in the Define Views For dialog box.

Renaming a User-Defined View

You can easily change the name of a view you created. (Although you can modify Outlook's built-in views, as you saw in the preceding section, you cannot rename them.)

To change the name of a view you created, take these steps:

1 Open the folder that contains the view you want to rename.

2 Choose the View Define Views command.

3 In the Define Views For dialog box, select the view you want to rename, and then click the Rename button.

4 Type the new name for the view.

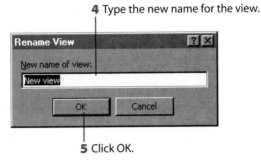

5 Click OK.

6 If you want to apply the renamed view to the currently open folder, click the Apply View button in the Define Views For dialog box.

7 Click the Close button in the Define Views For dialog box.

Formatting Views

As you know, each of Outlook's folders has its own set of built-in views. (And when you create a custom folder based on one of Outlook's folders, that new folder has the same set of built-in views.) Each view is one of these five types:

- Table

- Timeline

- Day/Week/Month (built into the Calendar folder only)

- Card (built into the Contacts folder only)

- Icon (built into the Notes folder only)

As this list implies, some views are designed specifically for certain folders (and for custom folders of the same type). Actually, you can set up any view for any folder—for instance, you could set up a Day/Week/Month view for your Notes folder—but you'll need to judge for yourself how much sense this makes in any given situation.

V

Bending Folders to Your Will

As you've seen in earlier chapters, you can customize views in Outlook in many ways. In addition to defining what folder items a view displays and in what order or groupings it displays them, you can also change the font, add previews, and set other formatting options for the various views.

When you use the View Format View command to change the formatting of a view, as explained in the following sections, the modifications you make in the Format View dialog box apply only to the specific view that is currently on your screen, not to all views of that type. For example, if you change the formatting of the Tasks folder's Simple List view in the Format Table View dialog box, the changes apply only to that view and not to any other table views.

Table Views

A table view, as you've seen throughout this book, displays folder items in rows and columns. Each row contains the information for one folder item; each column contains one piece of information about the item (one field). (For details about working with columns, see "Setting Up Columns," on page 454.)

To format a table view, display the view on your screen and choose the View Format View command. Outlook opens the Format Table View dialog box, shown in Figure 18-1.

FIGURE 18-1.

The Format Table View dialog box.

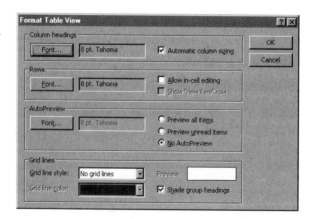

As you can see in the dialog box, Outlook offers numerous options for formatting:

Font buttons. When you click any one of the Font buttons, Outlook opens the Font dialog box, where you can change the font itself, the font style (bold, italic, bold italic, or regular type), the font size, and the script for the font you've chosen (if your computer is set up to work in various foreign-language alphabets). You can make these font changes for column headings, for rows (the contents of each folder item), or for previews (if you choose to display them).

Automatic Column Sizing. Turn on this option to have Outlook size the columns in the view so that all of them fit on the screen. (Some might be abbreviated in order to fit.) If you turn this option off, you might have to scroll to see all the columns in a view or you can size the columns yourself to see the ones you want.

Allow In-Cell Editing. When this option is turned on, you can type or edit directly in the table cells to make changes to folder items. When it's turned off, you cannot edit in the cells and must instead open each folder item to make any changes.

Show "New Item" Row. This option is available only when Allow In-Cell Editing is turned on. When you select it, Outlook adds a row at the top of the table view that allows you to create a new folder item without opening a new folder item window. (The Tasks folder, for example, displays such a "new item" row by default.)

AutoPreview. This Outlook feature allows you to display partial contents of a folder item in the table view so that you can quickly determine what each item contains. For messages, Outlook displays the first three lines of the message body; for other folder items, you see the first three lines of the Notes section of the folder item. You can choose whether to show previews for all items or for unread items only, or you can choose No AutoPreview to eliminate previews and see headings only. (As noted earlier, you can also specify a font for the previews. In addition to setting font, style, size, and script for previews, you can also specify a color and add underlining or strikeouts.)

Grid Lines. You can choose to display grid lines to set off the rows and columns of a table view. If you include the grid lines in the view, you can set both a line style (Small Dots, Large Dots, Dashes, or Solid) and a line color. After you set both these options, Outlook provides a sample grid line in the Preview box.

Shade Group Headings. You'll probably want to leave this option turned on in most cases; it's usually easier to distinguish the headings of grouped items when they're shaded. But you can turn this option off to eliminate the shading if you like.

The default settings in the Format Table View dialog box are not the same for all table views and all folders. For instance, Simple List view in the Tasks folder displays grid lines, allows in-cell editing, and includes a "new item" row by default, whereas Messages view in the Inbox folder (another table view) by default omits grid lines and in-cell editing, and does not contain a "new item" row.

Timeline Views

A timeline view shows the dates in a band across the top of the folder window with the folder items for each date listed below, as shown here in a timeline view for a single day:

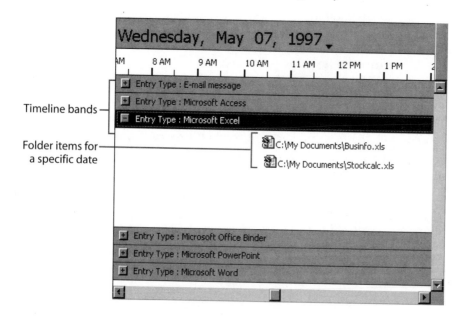

By clicking the Day, Week, or Month button on the Standard toolbar, you can have the timeline band show the folder items in the following ways:

- For a single day, listed by the time

- For a single week, listed by the day

- For a month, listed by the date or by the week of the year—for example, week 14

To format a timeline view, display the view on your screen and choose the View Format View command. Outlook opens the Format Timeline View dialog box, shown in Figure 18-2.

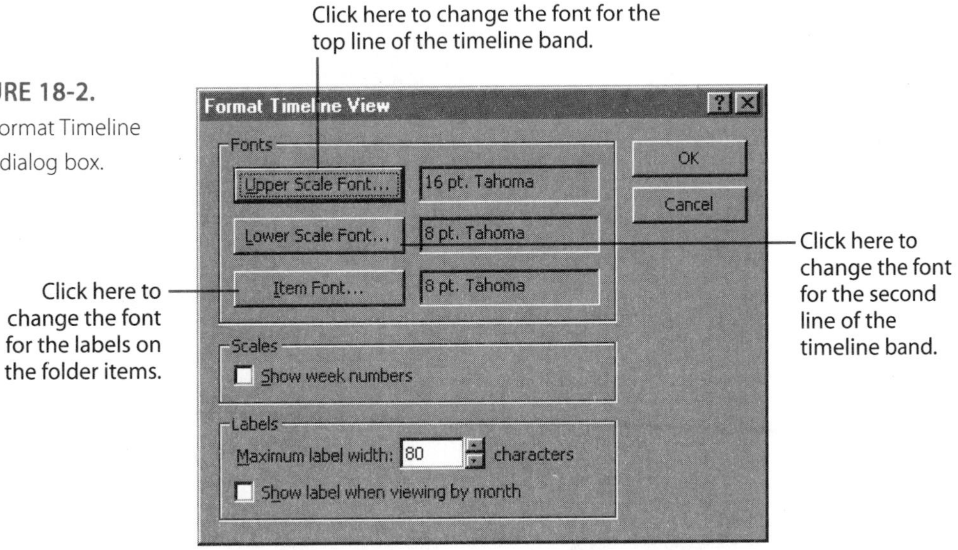

Click here to change the font for the
top line of the timeline band.

FIGURE 18-2.
The Format Timeline
View dialog box.

Click here to
change the font
for the labels on
the folder items.

Click here to
change the font
for the second
line of the
timeline band.

Fonts. As indicated in Figure 18-2, you can click the buttons in this section to set the font, font style (bold, italic, bold italic, or regular type), font size, and script for the font you've chosen (if your computer is set up to work in various foreign-language alphabets). You can make these font changes for the upper or lower scale of the timeline or for the folder items displayed in the view. You cannot change the color of any of these elements in the timeline view.

Scales. Turn on the Show Week Numbers check box if you want to include week numbers in the view. When you turn on this option, Outlook displays the week numbers in the top band of the timeline when you're looking at a single day or week and in the lower band of the timeline when you're looking at a month.

Labels. The options in this section affect the labels (names) of the various folder items that appear under the dates in the timeline. You can set a maximum width for these labels (from 0 through 132 characters). When the timeline displays a month rather than a day or a week, you can choose whether to include or omit the item labels by setting the Show Label When Viewing By Month option.

Day/Week/Month View

? **SEE ALSO**

For information about Day, Week, and Month views which are built into Outlook's Calendar folder, and about elements such as the Date Navigator, see Chapter 7, and also see "Calendar Tab," on page 61.

A day/week/month view displays folder items in a standard calendar arrangement. By clicking the Day, Week, or Month button on the Standard toolbar, you can have the calendar show the items in the following ways:

- For a single date, listed by the time

- For a single week, listed by the day

- For a month, listed by the day

To format a Day, Week, or Month view, display the view on your screen. For example, open the Calendar folder and choose the View Format View command. Outlook opens the Format Day/Week/Month View dialog box, shown in Figure 18-3.

FIGURE 18-3.

The Format Day/ Week/Month View dialog box.

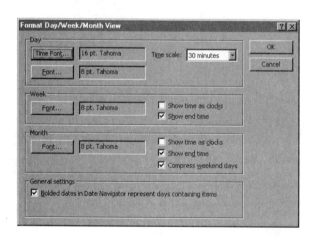

Day. Two options in this section, Time Font and Time Scale, let you reformat the time slots that appear to the left of the appointment (or other folder item) slots on a one-day calendar. If you want to change the look of the hour numbers in the time slots, click the Time Font button to open the Font dialog box, where you can set the font, font style (bold, italic, bold italic, or regular type), font size, and script for the font you've chosen (if your computer is set up to work in various foreign-language alphabets). To alter the span of time represented by each time slot, select a new time interval from the Time Scale drop-down list (5, 6, 10, 15, 30, or 60 minutes). Click the Font button if you want to change the font of the folder items that appear in the appointment (or other folder item) slots.

Week.   When you've set Week view to display a one-week time span, clicking the Font button in the Week section lets you change the font of both the dates and the folder items. If you'd like to see start times for items shown on small clock faces rather than in digits, turn on the Show Time As Clocks check box. To have Outlook display both start and end times for folder items, turn on the Show End Time check box; turn it off to omit the end times.

Month.   When you've set Month view to display a one-month time span, clicking the Font button in the Month section lets you change the font of both the dates and the folder items. The Show Time As Clocks and Show End Time check boxes are available, as they are in the Week section. You can also choose to compress weekend days on the monthly calendar (combining Saturday and Sunday in a smaller space) or to allot equal space to all days of the week.

> **NOTE**
>
> To display the start and end times of appointments in Month view, you must have Show Time As Clocks selected for Month view in the Format View dialog box. Depending on the resolution of your monitor, you might have to hide the Outlook Bar (by selecting View Outlook Bar) and the Folder List (by selecting View Folder List) to display both the start and end times of an appointment.

General Settings.   Turn on the check box in this section if you want dates with folder items to appear in boldface in the Date Navigator; turn off the check box to remove the boldface.

V

Bending Folders to Your Will

Card Views

? **SEE ALSO**

For information about
the specific card views
built into the Contacts
folder, see "Card Views
of the Contacts Folder,"
on page 317.

A card view displays folder items as small cards containing various
fields of information. The two card views that are built into Outlook's
Contacts folder, for instance, show contact information such as addresses and phone numbers on cards that look like rotary file cards
laid out on a desk. You can view a number of cards on the screen at
the same time, with the level of detail that you set up.

To format a card view, display the view on your screen, and choose
the View Format View command. Outlook opens the Format Card
View dialog box, shown in Figure 18-4.

FIGURE 18-4.

The Format Card View
dialog box.

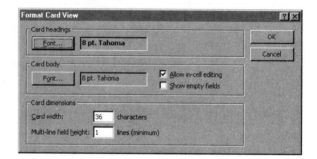

Font buttons. If you want to reformat the card headings (titles) or
the body of the card (the contents of the folder item), click the Font
button in the appropriate section to open the Font dialog box, where
you can change the font, font style (bold, italic, bold italic, or regular
type), font size, or script for the font you've chosen (if your computer
is set up to work in various foreign-language alphabets).

Allow In-Cell Editing. Turn on the check box for this option if you
want to be able to type or edit directly on the card that appears on
your screen in the card view. When this option is turned off, you
cannot edit the fields of information on the card but must instead
open the folder item to make changes.

Show Empty Fields. Turn on this check box if you want each card
to display all the fields for the folder item, whether or not the fields
contain text. Turn off this option to have Outlook show only those
fields that contain information (a more efficient use of screen space
in most cases).

Card Dimensions. You can type a width for the cards, from 3 through 1000 characters. If you type a width that is too large to fit in the window, Outlook resets the card width to the maximum possible for the window. (Note that when you display the Outlook Bar and the Folder List, the maximum width for a card decreases.) In the Multi-Line Field Height box, you can specify the minimum number of lines (1 through 20) that should be allocated to a multiple-line field such as an address field.

You can also use the mouse to change card width in the folder window. When you place the mouse pointer on the vertical dividing line between two columns of cards, the pointer becomes a double vertical line with a two-headed arrow. Drag the dividing line to the left to decrease the card width or to the right to increase the card width. If you widen the cards so that some columns move off screen, Outlook activates a horizontal scroll bar so that you can scroll to see all the cards.

Icon Views

An icon view displays folder items as small images (icons) with text labels. You'll see different icons for different types of folders—the specific icon Outlook shows matches the type of item contained in the folder.

To format an icon view, display the view on your screen and choose the View Format View command. Outlook opens the Format Icon View dialog box, shown in Figure 18-5.

FIGURE 18-5.

The Format Icon View dialog box.

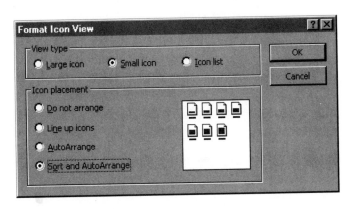

View Type. You can choose to display the icons in the view as large icons, as small icons, or as an icon list. If you select the Icon List option, the options in the Icon Placement section below become unavailable; you can arrange the icons in the window only if you choose the Large Icons option or the Small Icons option.

Icon Placement. You can select any one of the four options in this section. Select Do Not Arrange if you want to arrange the icons yourself, dragging them to any spot in the folder window. The Line Up Icons option lines up the icons according to a preset grid in the folder window, without closing up gaps of space around them. The AutoArrange option arranges the icons in rows and columns, closing any gaps. To have Outlook sort the icons, choose Sort And AutoArrange, which arranges the icons in rows according to the sorting keys you specify in the Sort dialog box. In the box to the right of these options, you can see a small preview of how the icons will be arranged, depending on your choice.

Deleting a View

If you no longer have a use for a custom view, you can delete it from the folder that contains it. (You can delete only those views that you created yourself; you cannot remove Outlook's built-in views.)

1 Open the folder that contains the view you want to delete.

2 Choose the View Define Views command.

3 Select the name of the view in the Define Views For dialog box.

4 Click the Delete button. (This button is available only when you select the name of a custom view.) When Outlook asks whether you're sure you want to delete the view, click the Yes button.

5 Click the Close button in the Define Views For dialog box.

 **NOTE**

If you delete a custom view but then change your mind, you're out of luck—you'll have to re-create the view. Outlook provides no way to retrieve a deleted view.

PART VI

According to Form

Using Forms

Microsoft Outlook 97 uses forms for just about everything. If you have composed and read messages, recorded appointment or meeting times, specified task details, sent task requests and responses, recorded journal entries and notes, or composed postings, you've used forms. For much of what you do in Outlook, you'll rely on standard forms.

In your organization, someone might act as an electronic forms designer. This designer can create standard forms that all members of your organization can use to report information and to order goods and services. These forms are usually referred to as organization forms.

With Outlook's form design tools, you can also create forms of your own for messages, notes, or any other type of Outlook folder item. The form design tools give you the ability to tailor the collection and presentation of information in a way that suits your circumstances and needs. (The next chapter provides the details about creating your own forms; see Chapter 20, "Designing Personal Forms.")

Whenever you create or read a folder item that uses a nonstandard form, Outlook installs the form on your computer and then opens it (while displaying a message telling you what's going on). This installation makes it possible for you and others to read folder items that use any Outlook form, even if it's a private form rather than an organization form.

Opening a Special Form

SEE ALSO
You can save a custom form in a folder, in a forms library, or as a file or a template. See "Saving and Distributing a Form," on page 576, for details.

To use a special form, you simply open it, fill it out, and send it to the appropriate person. Sometimes the trickiest part of this process is opening the form. How you open a custom form depends on where and how you saved it. The following summary explains how to open both custom forms and the sample forms that are supplied with Outlook:

- **If you saved the custom form in the Folder Forms library.**
  Open the folder in which you saved the form, and select the form's name from the item menu. (For most folders, the term "item menu" refers to the menu that is named for the folder—the Tasks menu in the Tasks folder, for instance. In e-mail folders, however, the "item menu" is the Compose menu.)

- **If you saved the form in the Organization Forms library.**
  Open the folder in which you saved the form, and select the Choose Form command from the item menu. Outlook displays the New Form dialog box, which is shown on the facing page.

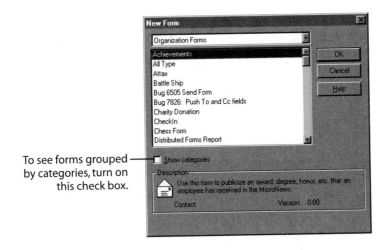

To see forms grouped by categories, turn on this check box.

If necessary, select Organization Forms from the drop-down list at the top of the dialog box. Then select the name of the form you want to open, and click OK.

■ **If you saved the form in the Application Forms library.**
Open the folder in which you saved the form, and select the Choose Form command from the item menu. Outlook displays the New Form dialog box:

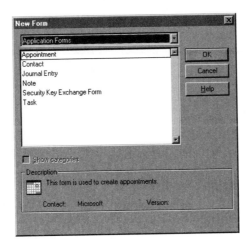

If necessary, select Application Forms from the drop-down list at the top of the dialog box. Then select the name of the form you want to open, and click OK.

■ **If you saved the form in the Personal Forms library.** Open the folder in which you saved the form, and select the Choose Form command from the item menu. Outlook displays the New Form dialog box:

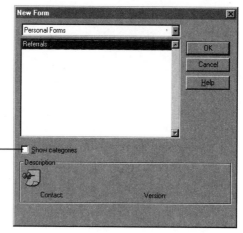

To see forms grouped by categories, turn on this check box.

If necessary, select Personal Forms from the drop-down list at the top of the dialog box. Then select the name of the form you want to open, and click OK.

■ **If you saved the form as a file.** Choose the Find Items command from the Tools menu. Outlook displays the Find dialog box, shown in Figure 19-1 on the facing page.

SEE ALSO
See "Searching Folder Contents," on page 372, for more information about working with the Find dialog box.

In the Look For box, select Files. Then type the name of the file in the Named box, select All Files from the drop-down list in the Of Type box, and click the Find Now button. When the name of the file appears in the lower portion of the dialog box, double-click it to open the form.

FIGURE 19-1.

The Find dialog box.

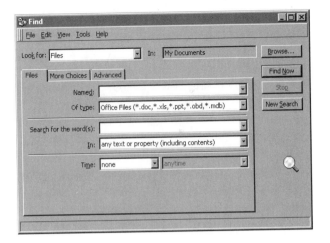

■ **If you saved the form as an Outlook template or if the form is one of the sample forms supplied with Outlook.** Select the Choose Template command from the open folder's item menu. Outlook displays the Choose Template dialog box:

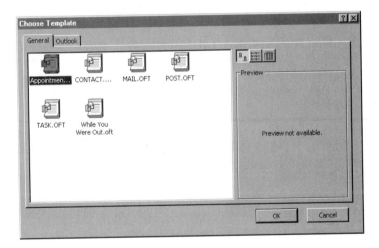

The General tab of the Choose Template dialog box, shown above, contains the templates that are more commonly used by many types of e-mail software, whereas the Outlook tab of the Choose Template dialog box, shown on the following page, contains the templates that are unique to Outlook. Some of these templates integrate the use of Microsoft Word capabilities with the capabilities of Outlook to produce sophisticated forms:

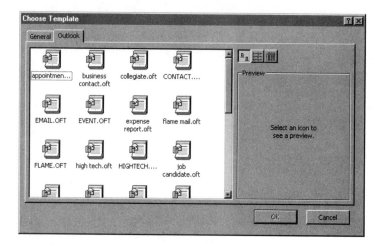

Select the template for the form you want to open, and click OK.

When you open a template form, Outlook starts the program associated with the template, and that program acts temporarily as the editor for the form.

Making Forms Available in a Folder

If you're working in a folder and realize that you need a form that isn't available in the folder, you can add the form to the folder.

You must have editor, publishing editor, or owner permission to add forms to a private shared folder or a public folder. If you have owner permission for a public folder, you can limit the forms that are available to other people who use the folder.

? SEE ALSO

For information about
levels of permissions,
see the sidebar "Do
You Have Permission?",
on page 438, and see
"Permissions Tab," on
page 446.

To make an existing form available in a folder, follow these steps:

1 Open the folder to which you want to add the form, choose the
File Folder command, and select Properties For from the submenu.
(The Properties For command includes the name of the folder.)
Alternatively, you can right-click the folder in the Folder List and
then choose Properties from the shortcut menu. (Click the Folder
List button on the Standard toolbar if the Folder List is not visible.)

2 In the Properties dialog box, click the Forms tab. This tab lists
the forms that you have already installed or copied for this folder,
along with a description of the selected form.

The name of the folder appears here.

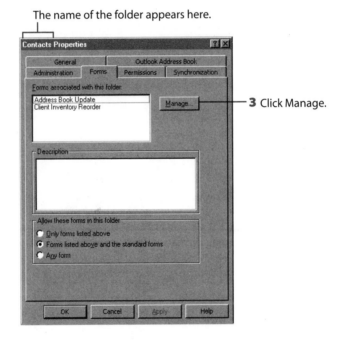

3 Click Manage.

4 When Outlook displays the Forms Manager dialog box, check the
name of the forms library in the drop-down list at the top left of
the dialog box. If you need to switch to a different forms library,
click the Set button to open the Set Library To dialog box.

VI

According to Form

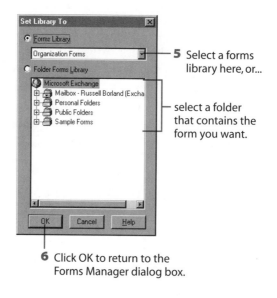

5 Select a forms library here, or...

select a folder that contains the form you want.

6 Click OK to return to the Forms Manager dialog box.

7 Select the form you want to use in the folder.

8 Click Copy to have Outlook list the form in the right-hand box.

To update an installed form to the latest version, select the form in the right-hand list and click Update.

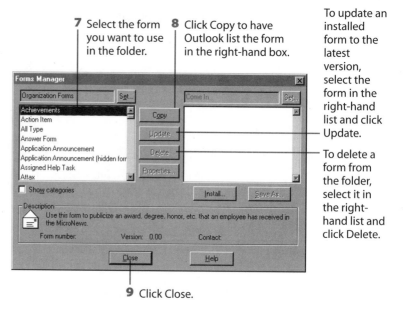

To delete a form from the folder, select it in the right-hand list and click Delete.

9 Click Close.

The form then becomes available in this folder. (Available forms are listed at the bottom of the item menu when you work in the folder.)

TIP

> In public folders, you can also specify the availability of certain forms by selecting an option in the Allow These Forms In This Folder section on the Forms tab of the folder's Properties dialog box.

Changing the Standard Form for a Public Folder

If you control a public folder—that is, if you have owner permission for the folder—you might want to set up a special form as the standard form for items in the public folder. (For information about how to check public folder permissions, see the following section, "Checking Your Public Folder Permission Status.") Here's how to change the standard form for a public folder:

1   Open the folder to which you want to add the form, choose the File Folder command, and select Properties For from the submenu. (The Properties For command includes the name of the folder.) Alternatively, you can right-click the folder in the Folder List and then choose Properties from the shortcut menu. (Click the Folder List button on the Standard toolbar if the Folder List is not visible.)

2   On the General tab of the Properties dialog box, select the form that you want others to use from the drop-down list labeled When Posting To This Folder, Use.

3   Click OK.

Checking Your Public Folder Permission Status

? SEE ALSO

For information about permission levels, see "Permissions Tab," on page 446. Also see the sidebar "Do You Have Permission?", on page 438.

Before you try to add, edit, update, or delete forms in a public folder, you can save yourself some aggravation by checking your permission status for the folder. To check your permissions for a public folder, open the Properties dialog box (as explained in step 1 in the preceding section). Click the Summary tab, and review your permissions, which are specified on this tab. If the Permissions tab appears instead of the Summary tab, you have owner permission. If neither tab appears, you do not have permission to change the public folder properties.

VI

According to Form

Designing Personal Forms

M icrosoft Outlook 97 contains built-in forms for all the types of folder items you find in Outlook folders. In fact, every Outlook folder item is based on a form. Forms provide an easy-to-use and convenient format for distributing and collecting information electronically.

To increase the usefulness of Outlook folders to you and to your organization, you can create your own forms, using the form design tools built into Outlook. When you design a custom form, you can base it either on a built-in form (by beginning with a copy of the form) or on a Microsoft Office 97 file:

- Base a custom form on an existing built-in form to include the features of the built-in form—for example, you can include the components of the Classified Ads form and then modify the fields to match your needs.

- Base a custom form on an Office 97 file to use the tools from another Office program such as Microsoft Excel or Microsoft Word.

To customize a form, you can add or delete fields, options, tabs, and controls. To help you design and set up your form, Outlook provides a number of menu commands as well as a batch of visual tools. The form design tools appear in three locations: the Field Chooser, the Control Toolbox, and the Form Design toolbar in Outlook's form design mode, all of which are discussed in this chapter. After you've finished your custom form, you can save it in an Outlook folder to be used in that folder, in a forms library so that others can access the form, or as a file to be used as a template or as a form in another application.

If the Control Toolbox doesn't automatically display when you open the Form Design tool, choose Control Toolbox from the Form menu.

You can't use Outlook forms in Microsoft Visual Basic or in Microsoft Exchange. In Outlook, however, you can use forms created with the Microsoft Exchange Forms Designer.

Installing Sample Forms

Outlook provides several useful sample forms:

- Classified Ads, used for placing a classified advertisement electronically
- Sales Tracking, on which you can set up information for a sales account
- Training Management, used for describing a course catalog entry
- Vacation Request, which actually consists of several forms for requesting, approving, denying, or reporting vacation
- While You Were Out, used to take a message for an absent co-worker

The While You Were Out form is installed when you set up Outlook; you must install the other forms from the Microsoft Office 97 CD-ROM ValuPack or from the network location from which you installed Office 97. (If you use Microsoft Internet Explorer or another Web browser to access the World Wide Web, you can choose the Help Microsoft On The Web command and then choose Free Stuff from the submenu.)

Here's how to install the sample forms from the Office 97 CD-ROM:

1 Open the ValuPack folder from the CD-ROM, and then open the Template folder.

2 Open the Outlook folder, and then double-click the Outlfrms icon.

3 The installation program tells you where the forms will be installed and how to view them; click OK in the dialog boxes and in the message box displayed by the program.

4 Start Outlook.

5 Choose the File Open Special Folder command, and then choose Personal Folder from the submenu.

6 In the Connect To Personal Folders dialog box, switch to the folder in which Outlook stored the sample forms file FORMS.PST (probably the Program Files\Microsoft Office\Office folder). Select the FORMS.PST file, and click OK. Outlook opens a window that contains the Sample Forms store; you can close this window or work within it if you want.

The Sample Forms store is also available in the original Outlook folder window:

1 Display the Folder List, scroll down the Folder List until you see the Sample Forms folder, and expand the Sample Forms store.

2 Open each subfolder to see the corresponding sample form. When you select the name of a sample form in the Folder List, Outlook adds the name to the bottom of the folder window's item menu (the Compose menu in e-mail folders; in other folders, the menu named for the folder). Choose the name of the sample form from the item menu to open the form.

If you want to customize a sample form for your own use, you can install it in the Personal Forms library; see the instructions in the Read Me file for each sample form.

Creating a Custom Form from a Built-In Form

To create a new form based on a built-in Outlook form, begin by opening an existing folder item (or creating a new item) that uses the built-in form. (Alternatively, you can open a form from another folder or from a forms library; see "Opening a Special Form," on page 522.) Then choose the Tools Design Outlook Form command. Outlook switches to form design mode, displaying the form you've selected, ready for customization, along with the available tools, as shown in Figure 20-1.

FIGURE 20-1.

A blank form in design mode, ready for customization.

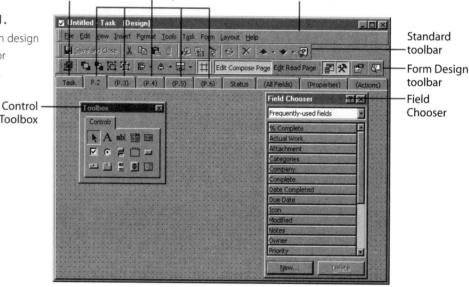

NOTE

You can't create a new form based on a Note.

Once Outlook is in form design mode, you can take the general steps outlined here to create the custom form:

1 Customize the tabs (pages) on the form.

2 Hide or show the form's tabs.

3 Set the form's properties on the Properties tab.

4 Create custom actions for the form.

5 Test the form.

6 Save and distribute the form.

The remainder of this chapter provides specific directions for carrying out these steps.

Creating a Custom Form from an Office 97 File

When you create a new form from an Office 97 file, you must begin by opening an Outlook folder or a public folder—*not* a disk files folder. In fact, you cannot have a disk files folder open for this procedure. Notice that unlike forms designed from a built-in form, Office 97 forms don't enable the Field Chooser or the Control Box, or allow you to customize or hide tabs.

The general steps for creating a custom form from an Office 97 file are as follows:

1 In an Outlook folder or in a public folder, choose the File New command, and then choose Office Document from the submenu. Alternatively, you can simply press Ctrl+Shift+H.

2 Double-click the icon for the type of file on which the new form should be based.

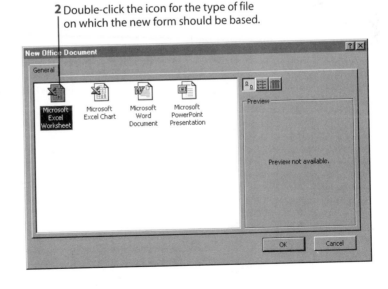

VI

According to Form

3 Outlook displays the message box shown in the following illustration. Choose Post The Document In This Folder if you want to create a form that contains only a Documents tab and that you can post only in this folder. If you choose Send The Document To Someone, the form you create will contain Document, Message, and Options tabs, and you will be able to send the form to someone else.

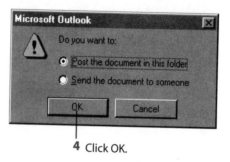

4 Click OK.

5 Choose the Tools Design Outlook Form command. (You might have to expand the menu to view the Design Outlook Form command by moving the mouse pointer over the down-arrow at the bottom of the tools menu.) Outlook displays the document template form, ready for customization. The following example is based on a Microsoft Word file:

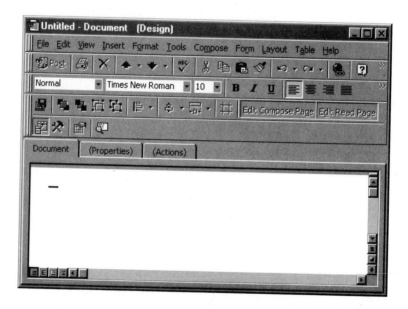

6   Set the form's properties on the Properties tab.

7   Create custom actions for the form.

8   Test the form.

9   Save and distribute the form.

The remainder of this chapter provides specific directions for carrying out these general steps.

Choosing the Compose or Read Page

You can create different forms for sending messages and for reading messages. These two forms are the Compose and Read pages, respectively. When you open a form in design mode, the Compose page and the Read page are synchronized by default, so that when you add a control to a form, it is added to both the Compose and Read pages. To create separate Compose and Read pages, choose Separate Read Layout from the Form menu, then choose which page you wish to edit first. The Compose page opens by default. To edit the contents of the Read page, choose Edit Read Page from the Form menu or click the Edit Read Page button on the Form Design toolbar. You can choose Separate Read Layout from the Form menu again to use synchronized Compose and Read pages but you will see a message warning you that you will lose any changes you made to the Read page.

Customizing Form Tabs

Form pages (their formal name) appear as tabs in a form window. As shown in Figure 20-2, on the following page, most forms have as many as five tabs that you can customize. To display any one of the form's tabs, simply click the tab's name.

VI

According to Form

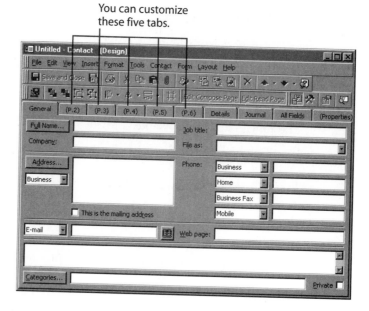

FIGURE 20-2.
A contact form
contains five tabs
that you can
customize.

On mail message and post forms, you can also customize the Message
tab. You can see this tab in Figure 20-3.

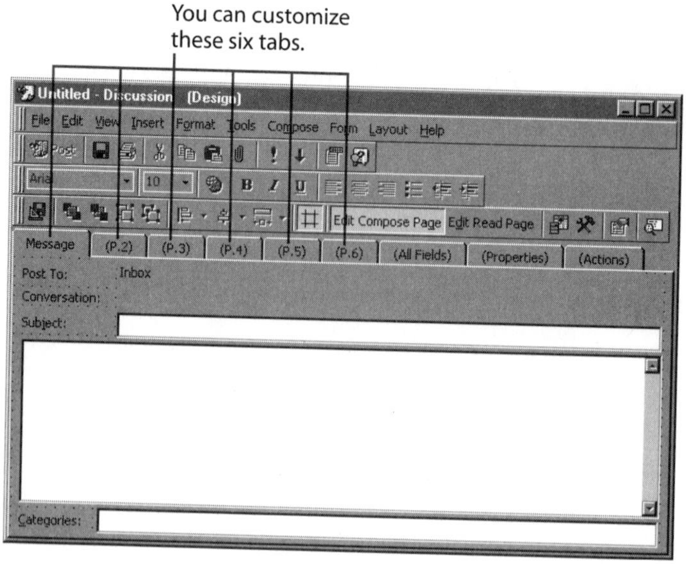

FIGURE 20-3.
You can customize six
tabs on a post form or
a mail message form.

You can customize
these six tabs.

Naming a Form Tab

As you can see in Figure 20-2 and Figure 20-3 (on the facing page), the tabs that you can customize are numbered with "page numbers" in parentheses—(P.2), (P.3), and so on. When you set up a tab, you need to give it a name that describes the kind of information the controls on the tab collect and display. That name then replaces the "P" designation.

You can name a tab as follows:

1   Click the tab you want to name.

2   Choose the Form Rename Page command.

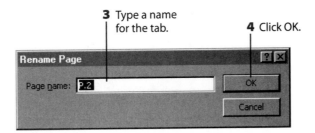

3 Type a name
for the tab.

4 Click OK.

After you name the tab, you'll notice that the tab name is still in parentheses—this is because the tab is still hidden. To display the tab, choose Display This Page from the Form menu.

Adding Fields to a Form Tab

For adding fields to a form tab, Outlook provides a useful design tool called the Field Chooser. The controls in the Field Chooser are text controls. If you don't see the Field Chooser in form design mode, choose the Form Field Chooser command, or click the Field Chooser button on the Form Design toolbar.

When you finish using the Field Chooser, you can hide it by clicking this same button or by choosing the command again.

The Field Chooser window, shown in Figure 20-4 (on the next page), contains a list of available fields that you can add to a tab simply by dragging them onto the tab. If the field you need doesn't appear in the Field Chooser, select a different list of fields from the box at the top of the Field Chooser window or click the New button to create a new field.

FIGURE 20-4.

You can add fields to a form tab from the Field Chooser.

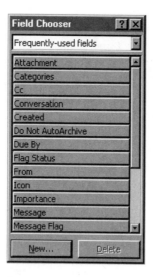

When you drag a field from the Field Chooser onto a tab, Outlook sets up the appropriate type of control (a text control or a check box, for instance), with a text label that shows the name of the field.

The AutoLayout feature automatically places and sizes the field for you, no matter where you drag the field initially. After AutoLayout sets the initial position, you can then change the field's size and drag the field to any location on the tab's grid; see "Placing and Sizing Controls: Form Layout," on page 552. (If you'd prefer to position the field yourself with the initial drag, turn off the Layout AutoLayout command.)

If you need to create a new field for your custom form, click the New button at the bottom of the Field Chooser window. In the New Field dialog box, type the new field's name, and then select a data type and a format for the field. For all the details about creating new fields and choosing data types and formats, see "Working in Your Own Fields," on page 489.

 TIP

If you change your mind after you've added a field to a form tab, you can remove the field by right-clicking it and choosing Delete from the shortcut menu. However, you can't delete the standard fields that come with Outlook.

Viewing All Standard Fields for a Form

You might find it useful to view all the standard fields a built-in form can have (and, by extension, the standard fields that a custom form based on the built-in form can have). To view these fields, follow these steps:

1 Open a folder item that uses the form you're interested in.

2 Choose the Tools Design Outlook Form command to switch to form design mode.

4 Select the All Fields list for the item type.   **3** Click the All Fields tab.

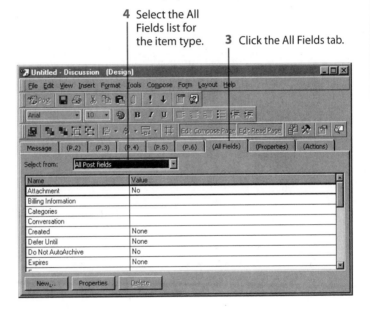

You can also create new fields on the All Fields tab: click the New button at the bottom of the tab to open the New Field dialog box. For help with creating a new field, see "Working in Your Own Fields," on page 489.

For a contact form, you can see all of the standard fields without switching to form design mode. Simply open an item from the Contacts folder and click the All Fields tab in the folder item window. Then select All Contact Fields from the drop-down list.

VI

According to Form

Adding and Removing Other Controls on a Form Tab

In addition to the Field Chooser, the Control Toolbox also provides controls that you can add to a form tab. The Control Toolbox contains the controls that allow you to design your own fields. It operates a little differently—you can click a control to select it and drop it into position on the form, or you can drag the control to the form if you prefer. In general, whether a control comes from the Field Chooser or the Control Toolbox, you work with the control as follows:

1 Click or drag the control onto the form tab.

2 Set the placement and size of the control (explained in "Placing and Sizing Controls: Form Layout," on page 552).

3 Set the control's properties (explained in "Setting Properties for a Control," on page 561).

The next section takes a detailed look at the Control Toolbox. After that, we'll explore the topics of form layout and control properties.

Control Toolbox

As mentioned earlier, the Control Toolbox contains all the basic controls that you can use to design your own fields. For example, the CheckBox control adds a check box to the form with a label area attached for customization (unlike the Field Chooser, which only has controls that contain fields—there aren't any special design features such as check boxes, option buttons, or tabs available). To display the Control Toolbox in form design mode, choose the Form Control Toolbox command, or click the Control Toolbox button on the Form Design toolbar.

When you finish using the Control Toolbox, you can hide it by clicking the Control Toolbox button or by choosing the command again. Figure 20-5, on the facing page, shows the Control Toolbox and the control buttons it contains.

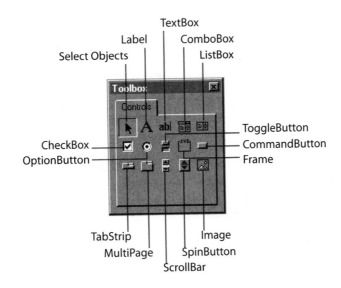

FIGURE 20-5.
The Control Toolbox and its control buttons.

To add a control to a form tab, you can simply drag the appropriate control button from the Control Toolbox onto the tab. Alternatively, as mentioned earlier, you can click the control button in the Control Toolbox, move the mouse pointer onto the tab (where it becomes a crosshair with an icon of the control you selected adjacent to the crosshair), click somewhere on the tab to anchor a corner of the control, and then drag horizontally and vertically away from that point to set the size of the control. You can drag in any direction from the anchored corner. Selecting a control by clicking it in the Control Toolbox also lets you view an icon of the control as you place it, visually aiding you as you design the form. Dragging the actual control only lets you view a box outline of the control.

 **TIP**

> If you change your mind after you've added a control from the Control Toolbox to a form tab, you can remove the control from the tab by right-clicking it and choosing Delete from the shortcut menu.

The following sections discuss each control button in the Control Toolbox.

VI

According to Form

Select Objects. The Select Objects button is usually turned on to allow you to select controls. The only time it is not turned on is immediately after you click another control button in the Control Toolbox. As soon as you place that control on the form tab, the Select Objects button is turned on again. If you click a control button in the Control Toolbox and then decide not to place the control on a form tab, click the Select Objects button to cancel your selection.

Label. Use this control button to place a label control on a form tab. A label control is a caption for another control, identifying the purpose or use of that control.

TextBox. Dragging this control button places a text box on a form tab, in which the person who uses the form can type information.

ComboBox. The ComboBox button lets you add a control that is a combination of a list and a text box. The list contains possible responses from which the user can choose, but the text box portion permits the user to type any response that passes the validation test (if such a test has been set up—see "Setting Properties for a Control," on page 561).

ListBox. Use this control button to add a box that lists the only possible responses; users of the form cannot type different responses. However, users can speed response selection by pressing a letter key on the keyboard (called a keypress). Outlook responds to the keypress by scrolling the list and selecting the first response that starts with that letter. If Outlook doesn't find a response to match the letter, the keypress is ignored.

CheckBox. Dragging this control button places a check box on a form tab. A user can turn on a check box (displaying a check mark) or turn it off (clearing the check mark). Use check boxes on a form tab when several choices can be turned on or off in various combinations.

OptionButton. This control button lets you add an option button to a form tab. A user can click the option button to select an option. Add option buttons to a form tab when only one option out of several can be chosen at any one time.

ToggleButton. Use this control button to add a toggle button, which is designed to turn a feature on or off when the user clicks it.

For example, the Control Toolbox button on the Standard toolbar in form design mode is a toggle button.

Frame. This control button lets you place a rectangle that has a border and a caption on a form tab. You use the frame control to group other controls together as related settings. Many dialog boxes show a group or a section of controls surrounded by a frame.

CommandButton. This control button lets you add a command button to a form tab. A command button is designed to start an action, such as opening or closing a window or a form. An OK button, for example, is a command button that can close one dialog box and that often opens another.

SEE ALSO

For details ab out working with the tab strip and multipage controls, see "Changing Control Toolbox Tabs," on page 546.

TabStrip. Use this control button to place a set of tabs on a form tab. You can name each tab, but you can't add any other features to the tabs. These tabs are intended to work like old-style radio buttons—clicking one makes it the current choice. You could use a tab strip in place of option buttons.

MultiPage. This control button also lets you place a set of tabs (pages) on a form tab. These tabs are similar to the tabs on a form: you can place any other controls on these tabs, and you also see a grid on the selected tab (unlike a tab strip). Use this control to create a form within a form.

ScrollBar. With the ScrollBar button, you can add a scroll bar to a form tab. If you size the scroll bar control to be taller than it is wide, it becomes a vertical scroll bar; if you size it to be wider than it is tall, it becomes a horizontal scroll bar.

SpinButton. Use this control to add a spin button control, which provides arrows for scrolling a list of choices (usually numbers) up or down while the control window remains only one line tall.

Image. If you want to display a picture on a form tab, use the Image control button to place a rectangle on the tab, in which you can show the picture. Then take these steps:

1 Right-click the image control, and choose Advanced Properties from the shortcut menu.

2 In the Properties window, locate and click the entry named Picture.

3 Click the button labeled with three dots at the right end of the box at the top of the window.

4 In the Load Picture dialog box, switch to a folder that contains the picture you want to use, select the picture, and then click the Open button.

In the Properties window, you might also want to check out the PictureAlignment and PictureSizeMode properties. Select each property in turn, and then click the drop-down arrow that appears at the right end of the box at the top of the window. From the list that appears, select the choice that suits the way you want the picture to appear in the image control. You can see the effect of each choice on the picture as you make it.

Changing Control Toolbox Tabs

You can add tabs to a tab strip control, to a multipage control, or to the Control Toolbox window. You can also rename tabs, delete them, or change their order. To change one of these tabs, click the tab name to select it. Then right-click the selected tab name, and choose a command from the shortcut menu. The following sections explain how to use these commands.

Adding tabs. When you right-click a tab strip control or a multipage control and choose the Insert command from the shortcut menu, Outlook adds a new tab to the control. This new tab is named Tab3 (or the next higher number) on a tab strip control; the new tab is named Page3 (or the next higher number) on a multipage control.

Likewise, when you right-click the Control Toolbox and choose the New Page command from the shortcut menu, Outlook adds a new tab to the Control Toolbox and names it New Page.

If the number of tabs you add requires a width greater than the width of the control or the Control Toolbox window, Outlook adds horizontal scroll arrows, as shown on the facing page.

Click the scroll
arrows to view
the tabs that are
not visible.

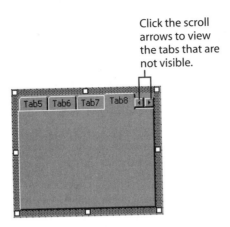

If you widen the control or the Control Toolbox window to fit all the tabs, Outlook removes the scroll arrows.

Deleting tabs. To remove a selected tab from a tab strip control or a multipage control, choose the Delete command from the shortcut menu. Choose the Delete Page command from the shortcut menu of the Control Toolbox to remove a selected tab from that window.

Renaming tabs. When you choose the Rename command for a selected tab, Outlook displays a Rename dialog box. Figure 20-6 shows the Rename dialog box for tab strips and multipage tabs; Figure 20-7, on the next page, shows the Rename dialog box for Control Toolbox tabs. (Each figure shows the steps for renaming these tabs.)

1 Type a name
for the tab.

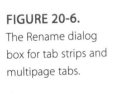

FIGURE 20-6.
The Rename dialog
box for tab strips and
multipage tabs.

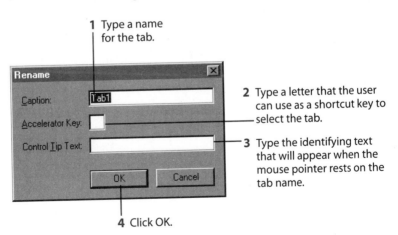

2 Type a letter that the user
can use as a shortcut key to
select the tab.

3 Type the identifying text
that will appear when the
mouse pointer rests on the
tab name.

4 Click OK.

VI

According to Form

NOTE

In the Rename dialog box for tab strips and multipage controls, the accelerator key can be any character. You should, however, select a letter that appears in the tab name. Consider making the initial letter the accelerator key, unless it conflicts with the name of another tab. Outlook underlines the letter in the tab name. To use the accelerator key, the user of the form must hold down the Alt key while pressing the accelerator key.

FIGURE 20-7

The Rename dialog box for Control Toolbox tabs.

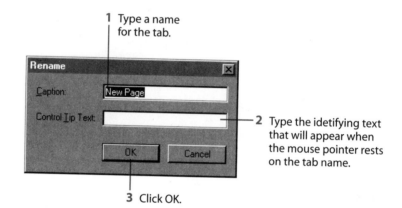

1 Type a name for the tab.

2 Type the idetifying text that will appear when the mouse pointer rests on the tab name.

3 Click OK.

Rearranging tabs. For a multipage control or the Control Toolbox, right-clicking the tab label and then choosing the Move command from a tab's shortcut menu opens the Page Order dialog box, shown here:

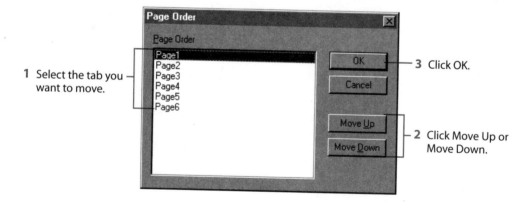

1 Select the tab you want to move.

3 Click OK.

2 Click Move Up or Move Down.

You can select a tab and click Move Up or Move Down to rearrange the order of the tabs as many times as you need before you click OK. Your changes in the Page Order dialog box affect the tabs only after you click OK.

Importing a page.   Choose the Import Page command to import a page of controls for the Control Toolbox. (This command is not available for tab strips or multiple controls.) The Import Page dialog box is a standard Open dialog box in which you locate and select the file that contains the controls you want to add and then click the Open button. Outlook adds a tab named New Page to the Control Toolbox. This new page, or tab, displays the controls that were stored in the file.

Exporting a page.   Choose the Export Page command to save a tab of controls to a file. (This command is available only for the Control Toolbox, not for any of the controls on the Controls tab.) The Export Page dialog box is a standard Save dialog box, in which you open the folder where you want to store the file, type a filename, and then click the Save button.

Changing Control Toolbox Buttons

On any tab of the Control Toolbox, you can add or remove controls and you can change the appearance of the control buttons on the tab. When you right-click a control button, Outlook displays a shortcut menu containing three commands: Custom Controls, Delete (control name), and Customize (control name).

> **NOTE**
>
> The Delete and Customize commands include the name of the control button (Delete TextBox, or Customize ToggleButton, for instance). If you right-click the tab on the background of the Control Toolbox away from a control button (or if you right-click the Select Objects button), only the Custom Controls command will be available on the shortcut menu.

Custom Controls command.   Choose this command to add controls to a Control Toolbox tab or to remove controls. When you choose this command, Outlook opens the Additional Controls dialog box, shown on the following page.

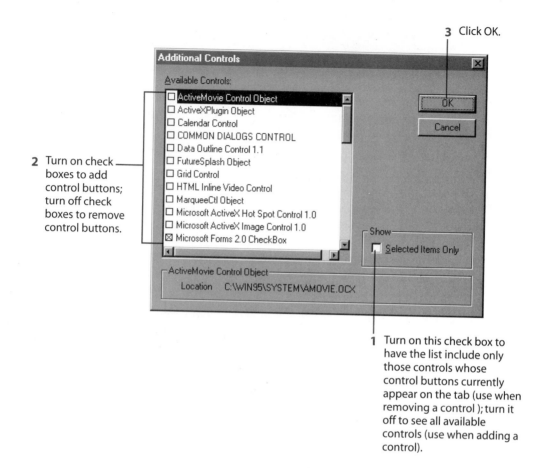

3 Click OK.

2 Turn on check boxes to add control buttons; turn off check boxes to remove control buttons.

1 Turn on this check box to have the list include only those controls whose control buttons currently appear on the tab (use when removing a control); turn it off to see all available controls (use when adding a control).

Delete command.   Choose this command to remove a control from a Control Toolbox tab. (This command does not delete a control from the form tab.)

Customize command.   Choose this command to change the tool tip text (the identifying text that appears when the mouse pointer rests on the button) or the face of the control button. When you click this command on the shortcut menu, you see the Customize Control dialog box, shown on the facing page.

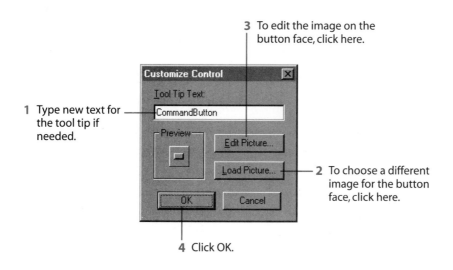

3 To edit the image on the button face, click here.

1 Type new text for the tool tip if needed.

2 To choose a different image for the button face, click here.

4 Click OK.

To replace the image that appears on the face of the control button in the Control Toolbox, click the Load Picture button to load a new picture. Outlook displays the Load Picture dialog box, which is a standard Open dialog box. Locate and select the picture file you want to use, and then click the Open button. You can now edit this new picture if necessary.

To edit the image that appears on the control button, click the Edit Picture button to open the Edit Image dialog box, shown here:

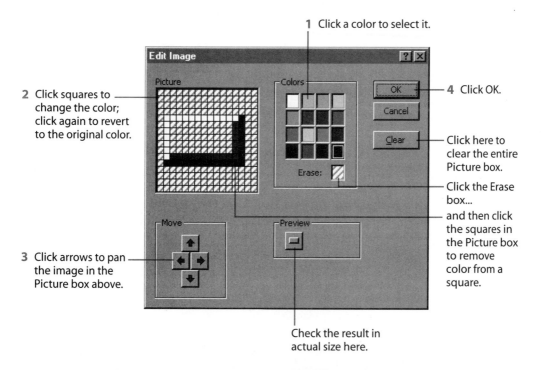

1 Click a color to select it.

2 Click squares to change the color; click again to revert to the original color.

3 Click arrows to pan the image in the Picture box above.

4 Click OK.

Click here to clear the entire Picture box.

Click the Erase box...

and then click the squares in the Picture box to remove color from a square.

Check the result in actual size here.

VI

According to Form

NOTE

When you customize the appearance of a control button, you are not changing the appearance of the control that can be added to a form tab. To change the control on the form tab, you must use the Properties command and the Properties dialog box; see "Setting Properties for a Control," on page 561.

Placing and Sizing Controls: Form Layout

You can position and size controls on a form tab by dragging them with the mouse. To position a control with the mouse, first select the control by clicking it. Then position the mouse pointer anywhere on the control's border except on one of the sizing handles (the small white squares), and drag the control to its new location.

 NOTE

If the Layout Snap To Grid command is turned on, Outlook sets the final position of the control you drag to the nearest grid point. You can turn off Snap To Grid, or you can change the grid size—see "Using the Grid," on page 558.

To size a control with the mouse, first click the control to select it. Then position the mouse pointer on the sizing handle for the direction in which you want to move. (Sizing handles work like the borders of a window.) Drag the sizing handle away from the center of the control to enlarge the control; drag the sizing handle toward the center of the control to shrink it.

You can get help with positioning and sizing a control by right-clicking it (for all controls except MultiPage and Frame) and choosing the applicable command from the shortcut menu, by using the commands on the Layout menu, or by using the buttons on the Form Design toolbar. The Form Design toolbar looks like this:

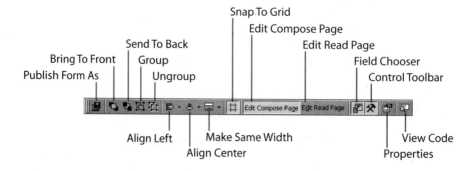

As you can see, many of the toolbar buttons are related to form layout. (Others, such as the Field Chooser button and the Control Toolbox button, should be familiar to you from earlier sections of this chapter; still other buttons are discussed in later sections.)

In the discussion that follows, you'll find that the Layout menu is the most comprehensive source of useful commands for positioning and sizing controls. But in case you prefer to use the control's shortcut menu or the toolbar buttons when possible, I'll let you know when you can do so. Also, as you try out these commands, note that both commands and toolbar buttons are available only when they fit the selection you've made on the form tab. (For instance, the Group command and toolbar button are unavailable when you've selected only one control.)

Selecting Controls on a Form Tab

On the face of it, selecting a control on a form tab is easy: simply click the control.

You can also select several controls at one time, in any of these three ways:

- To select several controls at various positions on the tab, hold down the Ctrl key while you click each control.

- To select a sequence of controls in a row or a column, click the first control in the sequence, and then hold down the Shift key while you click the last control in the sequence.

- To select all the controls at once, either choose the Edit Select All command or press Ctrl+A.

If you have multiple controls selected, how do you release those controls and select only a single control? In most Microsoft Windows 95 applications, you simply click any single control to release the multiple control feature. Form Design mode, however, doesn't work that way. Instead, you click the background of the tab (and not any particular control), and then click the single desired control.

Aligning Controls

The Align feature appears on the Layout menu and on the control's shortcut menu; specific commands are on submenus. On the Form Design toolbar, click the down arrow beside the Align Left button to see the other commands. In general, all the Align commands set the relative alignment of two or more selected controls. Different types of controls enable different alignment selections. For example, a Calendar control only enables Vertical and Horizontal center alignment on the Form Design toolbar, or Align To Grid on the control's shortcut menu.

? SEE ALSO

For details about centering controls on a form tab (and the Align Center toolbar button), see "Centering on the Form," on page 556.

Use the Align Left, Align Right, and Align Center commands only for a vertical selection of controls. Choose Align Left or Align Right to align all selected controls along their left or right edges. Choose Align Center to center selected controls around a midline of the widest control you've selected.

The Align Top, Align Bottom, and Align Middle commands are designed for a horizontal selection of controls. Choose Align Top or Align Bottom to align the selected controls along their top or bottom edges. Align Center centers the selected controls around a midline of the tallest control you've selected.

The Align To Grid command on the control's shortcut menu aligns selected controls with the grid on the form tab. If you've turned off the Snap To Grid command and then dragged a control to a new position, you can choose Align To Grid to ensure that the control aligns with the grid.

Making Controls the Same Size

The Make Same Size feature appears on the Layout menu and on the control's shortcut menu; specific commands are on submenus. On the Form Design toolbar, click the down arrow beside the Make Same Width button to see the other commands. In general, these commands resize a selection of controls relative to one another.

The Width command makes all the selected controls the width of the narrowest control in the selection; the Height command makes all the selected controls the height of the shortest control. To make the selected controls the width of the narrowest control *and* the height of the shortest, choose Both.

Sizing To Fit

Turn on the Size To Fit command on the Layout menu to make the border surrounding the control fit the size of the control. For example, if you have added a label control to your form and you have added text to the label control that doesn't fill up the label box, choose Size To Fit and the label box will resize itself to the size of the text.

Sizing to the Grid

If you change the size of a control when the Snap To Grid command is turned off, the edges of the control could fall between gridlines. Choose the Size To Grid command on the Layout menu to shrink the edges of the control to the nearest gridlines.

Horizontal Spacing

You can find options for horizontal spacing on the Layout menu. The commands on the Horizontal Spacing submenu change the horizontal spacing between two or more selected controls on a form tab. You must select at least two controls before these Horizontal Spacing submenu commands become active.

When you select at least three controls, you can choose the Make Equal command to make the horizontal space between the controls the same width. Outlook divides the total amount of the current horizontal space between the selected controls by the number of gaps between controls and equalizes the space. The leftmost and rightmost controls do not move.

Choose the Increase command or the Decrease command to increase or decrease the horizontal space between two or more controls by the width of one column on the grid. The larger the grid, the more distance Outlook adds or subtracts between the selected controls. You might need to choose the command several times to change the spacing sufficiently.

If you want to remove all horizontal space between selected controls, choose the Remove command from the Horizontal Spacing submenu.

Vertical Spacing

Options for vertical spacing of controls on a form tab appear on the Layout menu. The commands on the Vertical Spacing submenu change the spacing between two or more selected controls. You must select at least two controls before these commands become active.

Choose the Make Equal command to make the vertical space between three or more selected controls the same height. Outlook divides the total amount of the current vertical space between the selected controls by the number of gaps between controls and equalizes the space. Outlook doesn't move the top and bottom controls.

With the Increase command or the Decrease command, you can increase or decrease the vertical space between two or more controls by the height of one row on the grid. The larger the grid, the more distance Outlook adds or subtracts between the selected controls. You might need to choose the command several times to change the spacing sufficiently.

Choose the Remove command from the Vertical Spacing submenu to remove all vertical space between selected controls.

Centering on the Form

If you want to center controls on a form tab, you can use the Center In Form command on the Layout menu or the Align Center button on the Form Design toolbar. Click the down arrow beside the toolbar button to see the two commands Horizontally and Vertically, which also appear on the Center In Form submenu. Choose Horizontally to move selected controls to the horizontal center between the two sides of the tab; choose Vertically to move the controls to the vertical center between the top and the bottom of the form tab.

Arranging Command Buttons

It's a common practice to place command buttons (buttons that initiate actions) either along the right side or along the bottom of a form. To quickly place command buttons at either of these positions on a form tab, choose Layout Arrange and then use the commands on the Arrange submenu. The Arrange submenu commands are active only when you have selected at least one command button. Also note that these commands move only command buttons; if you've selected any other type of control when you choose one of these commands, that control does not move. To place other types of controls at the bottom or right edge of the form tab, you'll need to drag them.

Choose the Right command from the submenu to position all the selected command buttons along the right edge of the form tab. Outlook arranges the buttons in a stack. The order of the buttons relates to their previous vertical positions on the tab: the command button closest to the top of the tab becomes the top button in the stack; the command button closest to the bottom of the tab becomes the bottom button in the stack.

Choosing the Bottom command places all the selected command buttons along the bottom edge of the form tab, arranging them in a row. The order of the buttons relates to their previous horizontal positions on the tab: the command button closest to the left edge of the tab becomes the leftmost button in the row; the command button closest to the right edge of the tab becomes the rightmost button in the row.

 TIP

If you don't like the order in which the command arranges the buttons, you can rearrange the order by dragging the buttons individually. Then choose the command again.

Grouping and Ungrouping

When you collect several controls into a group, you can move or change the group as if it were a single object—for instance, a label and its associated control are often grouped together. Within the group, the controls maintain their positions relative to each other when you move them.

After you've selected the controls you want to group, you can click the Group button on the Form Design toolbar, choose the Layout Group command, or right-click one of the selected controls and choose Group from the shortcut menu.

If you need to make changes to any one of the grouped controls without changing the others, you'll first need to ungroup the controls, making them individual objects again. To do this, select the group and click the Ungroup button on the Form Design toolbar, choose the Layout Ungroup command, or right-click the group and choose Ungroup from the shortcut menu.

Reordering Overlapping Controls

Each control sits in its own "layer" on a form tab. This means that you can position controls to overlap one another. If you do this, however, you'll want to be sure that no important part of a control is hidden by an overlapping control. For example, if a label control overlaps its associated text control, you don't want the label to obscure part of the text control. Also, if you set an icon or a picture on another control, you can choose whether you want the entire image to appear or

VI

According to Form

whether you want part of it obscured. To arrange a stack of overlapping controls, choose the commands on the Layout Order submenu. Two of these commands, Bring To Front and Send To Back, are also available as buttons on the Form Design toolbar. The other two, Bring Forward and Send Backward, appear on the control's shortcut menu.

Choose Bring To Front to place the selected control on top of all other controls at the same position; choose Send To Back to position the selected control under all other controls at the same position. The Bring Forward command moves the selected control on top of the next higher layer of controls at the same position; the Send Backward command moves the selected control beneath the next lower layer of controls at the same position.

Using the Grid

Each form tab is set up with a grid which helps you align controls and sets the size of controls and the spacing between them. When Outlook increases or decreases the vertical or horizontal spacing between controls, it uses increments of space based on the grid size.

When you initially switch to form design mode, the form tabs that you can customize show the grid, and the Snap To Grid command is turned on. The grid size is set to 8 pixels by 8 pixels. You can change all these grid settings.

Show Grid.   The grid is displayed as dots in rows and columns. Choose the Show Grid command on the Layout menu to toggle the display of the grid on and off, or right-click the form tab away from a control and choose Show Grid from the shortcut menu. You might want to hide the grid to see a preview of what the tab will look like when you've finished the form. Showing or hiding the grid doesn't affect the Snap To Grid command.

Snap To Grid.   Choose this command from the Layout menu or click the Snap To Grid button on the Standard toolbar to toggle this feature on or off. You can also right-click the form tab anywhere but directly on the control and choose Snap To Grid from the shortcut menu. When you turn on Snap To Grid, each new control, each move of a control, and each resizing of a control happen relative to the grid. If you want to resize or move a control to a position that's not on the grid, turn off this feature. If you later want to move the control to align with the grid, choose the Layout Align To Grid command. If you want to size the control to the grid, choose the Layout Size To Grid command.

Set Grid Size.   This command appears on the Form menu rather than on the Layout menu. To change the grid size, take these steps:

1   Choose the Form Set Grid Size command.

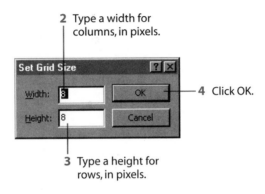

2 Type a width for columns, in pixels.

4 Click OK.

3 Type a height for rows, in pixels.

Using AutoLayout

Outlook's AutoLayout feature automatically places new fields and controls below or to the right of controls that are already on a form tab. (If the control is the first item, it's placed in the top left corner of the tab.) If you prefer to perform the initial placement yourself, turn off the AutoLayout command on the Layout menu. Choose this command again to turn AutoLayout on.

Changing Tab Order

When you're using a finished form, press the Tab key to move from one control to the next. (Press Shift+Tab to move backward through the controls.) The order in which you move among the controls is initially set when you place the controls on the form tab: Outlook establishes the order in which the tab key moves among the controls based on the order in which you added the control. (Tab order has no relationship to the position of the control on the tab.)

But this initial tab order might not be logical or helpful to the user of the form. You might have placed controls and fields on the form tab as the need occurred to you. Or you might have rearranged the controls since their initial placement. For whatever reason, before you finish designing your form you should set the tab order so that the order is logical and useful.

To change the tab order, follow these steps:

1 Choose the Layout Tab Order command.

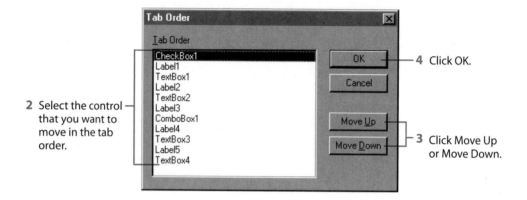

2 Select the control that you want to move in the tab order.

4 Click OK.

3 Click Move Up or Move Down.

The first control listed in the Tab Order dialog box is the first control that is active when a user clicks the tab in the form. The user can press the Tab key to jump to the control that's next down the list. Pressing Shift+Tab jumps to the control that's next up the list.

The tab order list includes all the controls on the tab, whether the controls are enabled or disabled, including labels. Note, however, that when the user of the form presses the Tab key, labels are not activated if you have disabled them. Also, even if you move a label control up the list in the Tab Order dialog box, Outlook moves the disabled label back to the bottom of the list after the user clicks OK.

 **TIP**

If you're planning to change tab order as part of your design process, you'll want to give each control a name that tells you what information it contains or collects. Otherwise, the default names of the controls might not be very helpful. To name controls, use the Display tab of the Properties dialog box, discussed in the following section.

Setting Properties for a Control

Each control has its own set of properties that determine how the control looks and how it functions. You set these properties in the Properties dialog box, which contains three tabs: Display, Value, and Validation. (Note, however, that the Properties dialog box for a multipage control contains only a Display tab; the Value and Validation tabs do not appear.)

You can open the Properties dialog box for a selected control in any of the following ways:

- Right-click the control, and then choose Properties from the shortcut menu.

- Click the Properties button on the Form Design toolbar.

- Choose the Form Properties command.

> If more than one control is selected when you open the Properties dialog box, Outlook displays the dialog box for the "first" control in the selection. The first control is the one that you placed on the form tab first, regardless of its current position on the tab or its position in the tab order.

Setting Up Display Properties

To set up the display properties for a control—that is, to determine how the form's user will view the control—click the Display tab, which is shown in Figure 20-8.

FIGURE 20-8.
The Display tab of the Properties dialog box.

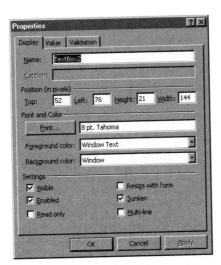

If the Name and Caption boxes are active on this tab, you can type a different name or a different caption for the control. Outlook assigns a default name to every control (TextBox2, for instance), which identifies it to other controls or in code. You might want to assign a more useful name, especially if you plan to alter the tab order. (See "Changing Tab Order," on page 559.) The user does not see this name, however; the "name" displayed to the user is referred to as the caption. The caption is the text displayed in a label. (Outlook also provides a direct method for changing a control's caption text; see "Editing a Control Directly," on page 567.)

The Position settings on the Display tab record the current position and size of the control on the form tab, measured in pixels. After you've dragged a control to its approximate location and sized it with the mouse, you can tweak the position and size by changing the Position settings. The Top box sets the position of the top edge of the control, and the Left box sets the position of the left edge. If you change the Height setting, Outlook moves the bottom edge of the control; if you change the Width setting, Outlook moves the right edge.

⭐ TIP

> To align multiple controls horizontally, give them all the same Top setting. To align them vertically, give them all the same Left setting.
>
> In the Font And Color section of the tab, you can change the font of any text that is part of the control. (Click the Font button to open the Font dialog box.) You can also select foreground and background effects by choosing the Foreground Color or Background Color drop-down arrows. Note that the changes you make here may nullify Font color changes. The Foreground and background effects are available so that you can quickly change the way a button looks based on standard button settings.

At the bottom of the tab, you'll find these general settings for the control:

- Turning on the Visible check box enables the user to see the control on the form; turning off the check box hides the control. For example, if you want to add a timer control to animate a graphic—you would want the timer control to be invisible to the user.

- Turning off the Enabled check box prevents the user from being able to select the control or even to copy its value.

- Turning on the Read Only check box makes the control read-only—that is, the user cannot change the control's value (but can select the control or copy its value).

- Turning on the Resize With Form check box displays the control proportional to the size of the form—for example, if the user makes the form window smaller, the control also becomes smaller.

- Turning on the Sunken check box gives the control a three-dimensional appearance; turning off this check box gives the control a two-dimensional look.

- Turning on the Multi-Line check box allows the user to enter multiple lines in a text box by pressing the Enter key to start each new paragraph—text automatically wraps to the next line.

Setting Up Values

To link the control to a field or to set initial and calculated values, click the Value tab of the Properties dialog box, which is shown in Figure 20-9. For example, you might want to set an option button when Outlook detects a specific value in a list box.

FIGURE 20-9.

The Value tab of the Properties dialog box.

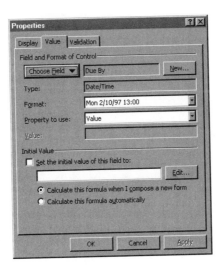

SEE ALSO

You can click the New button on the Value tab to create a new field; for instructions, see "Working in Your Own Fields," on page 489.

In the Field And Format Of Control section of the Value tab, you can click the Choose Field button to see lists of the fields that are available to use with the control. Choose a list, and then choose a specific field from the list. Outlook fills in the name of the field and, in the Type box, shows you the data type on which the field is based. In the Format box, you can choose a format that is appropriate for the type of field you've chosen. (For details about data types and formats, see "Data Types and Standard Formats," on page 492.)

The Property To Use and Value boxes list the properties and values from any published custom or built-in Outlook form. (The properties and values in these two boxes are associated with the field that you choose by clicking the Choose Field button.) It's best not to change these properties and values unless you have much more advanced knowledge of forms than that provided in this chapter.

If you want to set up an initial value for the control, turn on the check box labeled Set The Initial Value Of This Field To, and either type a value in the box below or click the Edit button to create a formula for calculating the value. (See "Setting Up a Formula," on page 566.) Then choose one of the two option buttons to have Outlook calculate the formula when you open a new instance of the form or to have Outlook calculate the formula automatically as values change. (Outlook also provides a direct method for changing the initial value of a control; see "Editing a Control Directly," on page 567.)

NOTE

The types of options you can change in the Value tab depend on the properties of the field you choose to have Outlook evaluate.

Setting Up Validation

To have Outlook validate user entries on the form, click the Validation tab of the Properties dialog box, which is shown in Figure 20-10.

FIGURE 20-10.

The Validation tab of the Properties dialog box.

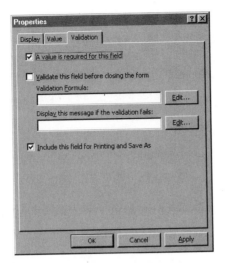

Validation simply ensures that the user has entered the necessary information on the form and that the information is in the correct format. At the top of the tab, you'll see a check box labeled A Value Is Required For This Field. When this option is available, you can turn it on to require a response from the user. Then, if the user leaves the field empty, Outlook will display a message telling the user to enter the information when the user tries to save or close the form.

You can also have Outlook validate the field before closing the form—that is, Outlook checks to be sure that the user input matches the validation test you set up in the Validation Formula box (or the validation formula you specify after clicking the Edit button; see "Setting Up a Formula," on the following page). For instance, if you specify that the user must type a date, and the user types a single digit, the input is not valid, and Outlook displays an error message to the user. You can compose the error message in the text box labeled Display This Message If The Validation Test Fails.

The final option on this tab is Include This Field For Printing And Save As. Turn on this check box if the contents of this field should be printed and saved with the rest of the form. Turn off the check box to omit the field during printing and saving.

Setting Up a Formula

⊘ SEE ALSO

For examples of formulas, see Table 17-6, on page 498. For details about creating your own fields, see "Working in Your Own Fields," on page 489.

You can set up a formula to set an initial value for a control, to construct a validation test for user responses, or to display a message when a response fails the validation test. In all three cases, you click the Edit button (on either the Value tab or the Validation tab of the Properties dialog box) to open a dialog box in which you set up the formula. In all three cases the dialog boxes look the same except for their titles. All three dialog boxes function alike. In any of these dialog boxes, type the formula (text, fields, and functions); enclose the field and function names in square brackets. Click the Field button to select fields; click the Function button to select functions. Then click OK.

Getting Help With Functions and Fields in the Context of Formulas

For help with functions, follow these steps:

1 Press F1 while the Formula dialog box is open.

2 Type *Functions* in the Office Assistant balloon, and click Search.

3 Click the All Functions button.

For help with fields, follow these steps:

1 Press F1 while the Formula dialog box is open.

2 Type *Fields* in the Office Assistant balloon, and click the Search button.

3 If you want information about built-in fields, click the button called About Standard Fields In Microsoft Outlook. If you want information about creating your own fields, click the Create A Custom Field button.

 TIP

Describing all the functions and fields that you can incorporate into a formula is beyond the scope of this book, but you can find detailed information in the Outlook Help file. Open Help, and type *functions* or *fields* in the first box on the Find tab to locate an extensive list of topics and comprehensive lists of all functions or all standard fields.

Editing a Control Directly

Although you can set the caption and the initial value of a control on the Display and Value tabs in the Properties dialog box, you might sometimes prefer a more direct method for editing these settings. You can do this directly on the form tab.

To activate a control for editing, use one of these methods:

- Right-click the control, and select Edit from the shortcut menu.

- Click the control, and then click inside it.

You can type the caption text or the new initial value directly on the control.

> If you have set up a formula to determine an initial value, directly editing the initial value on the control wipes out the formula. In that case, it's preferable to edit the formula; see "Setting Up a Formula," on the facing page.

Setting Advanced Properties for a Control

If you know a little about Visual Basic programming, you might want to try setting advanced properties for a control. When you right-click a selected control and choose Advanced Properties from the shortcut menu, Outlook opens the Properties window, shown in Figure 20-11. This Properties window is very similar to the one used in Visual Basic.

FIGURE 20-11.

You can set advanced properties for a control in the Properties window.

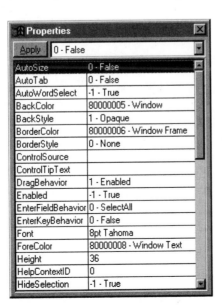

WARNING

> Unless you have some knowledge of Visual Basic programming, it's risky to try to set advanced properties. Without an understanding of what these properties do and what their settings mean, you're likely to wreck your form rather than improve it.

To set a new value for an advanced property in the Properties window, select the property, and then use the box beside the Apply button. For certain properties, you'll be able to type text or numbers in the box. If a down arrow appears at the right end of the box, click it to see a drop-down list of possible choices. If an icon button appears beside the box, click the button to open a dialog box in which you can select an appropriate file (usually an icon or a picture).

Many advanced properties get their settings from your choices in the Properties dialog box. (Some overlap exists between a control's standard properties and its advanced properties.) For example, if you type a caption on the Display tab of the Properties dialog box, that caption appears as the setting for the Caption property in the Properties window. In fact, when you set a value in either location (the dialog box or the window), Outlook sets the same value in the other location after you click the Apply button. (You might have to close the Properties dialog box and then reopen it to see the change.)

TIP

> You can have both the Properties dialog box and the Properties window open at the same time. To do this, open the Properties window first, and then open the Properties dialog box.

Table 20-1, on the facing page, describes some of the advanced properties that you might want to experiment with. Not all these properties apply to all types of controls; depending on the type of control you've selected, some of the properties might not appear in the Properties window. Check marks in the Easy column of the table indicate the properties that you can change in the Properties dialog box as well as in the Properties window.

TABLE 20-1.   Some examples of advanced properties.

Easy	Property Name	Values
✓	Alignment	1 - Right 0 - Left
✓	AutoSize	−1 - True (The control changes size to show the entire contents of the control.) 0 - False (The control remains the same size all the time.)
	AutoWordSelect	−1 - True (Outlook selects entire words when the user selects with the mouse.) 0 - False (The user can select partial words.)
	BorderColor	A name of a window or desktop element chosen from a drop-down list. (Your choice from the list sets the color you've set for the corresponding window or desktop element in the Display dialog box of the Windows 95 Control Panel.)
	BorderStyle	0 - None 1 - Single
✓	Caption	Text that appears in a label
✓	ControlTipText	Text that appears when the mouse pointer rests on a control
✓	Height	Number of pixels that the left edge of the control sits from the left edge of the tab
✓	SpecialEffect	0 - Flat 1 - Raised (This setting is not available in the Properties dialog box.) 2 - Sunken 3 - Etched (This setting is not available in the Properties dialog box.) 6 - Bump (This setting is not available in the Properties dialog box.)
✓	Top	Number of pixels that the top edge of the control sits from the top edge of the tab
✓	Value	Text or formula that sets the initial value
✓	Width	Number of pixels for the width of the control
✓	WordWrap	−1 - True (Outlook wraps text to a new line.) 0 - False (Outlook does not wrap text to a new line.)

VI

According to Form

Hiding or Showing Form Tabs

As noted earlier in this chapter, a form can have as many as five or six tabs. Only standard form tabs whose names do not appear in parentheses (such as the Message tab for an e-mail form) and tabs to which you've added fields or controls are automatically displayed in the finished form. But you can choose whether to hide or display specific tabs, showing the user only those tabs that are useful and hiding the rest.

To hide or show a form tab, click the tab to select it, and then choose the Form Display This Page command to toggle between hiding and showing the tab. If you choose to hide a tab but then later drag a field or control onto it, the tab will no longer be hidden.

Among the form tabs whose names are enclosed in parentheses, the All Fields and Options tabs are usually hidden by default, although you can change the status of these tabs to display them. You cannot show the Properties tab or the Actions tab, however; the Form Display This Page command is unavailable for these two tabs.

Setting Properties for a Form

So far, you've learned how to set properties for individual controls. But you also need to learn how to set the properties of the form itself. To do this, click the Properties tab of the form in form design mode. Figure 20-12 shows the Properties tab for a message form.

FIGURE 20-12.

The Properties tab for a message form in form design mode.

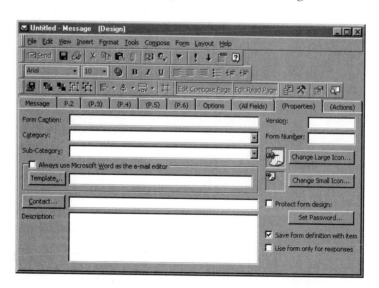

Form Caption. Type a name for the form in this box. This name appears in the title bar of the folder item window when the user opens the form.

Category and Sub-Category. The value of assigning your form to a category and/or a subcategory becomes evident when you select the Choose Form command from the item menu in an Outlook folder. If you have a long list of forms to scroll through in the New Form dialog box, you can turn on the Show Categories check box to group the forms into categories and subcategories, making it easier to find a particular type of item.

Always Use Microsoft Word As The E-Mail Editor. This check box is available only for message forms. If you turn it on, Outlook starts Word as the e-mail editor whenever a user who uses Word as the e-mail editor receives a message based on your form. You can click the Template button to select a specific Word template to use for this form.

> **NOTE**
>
> Setting up a custom form to use Word as the e-mail editor does not affect standard message forms. You can set that option for standard message forms on the E-Mail tab of the Options dialog box; see "E-Mail Tab," on page 51.

Contact. In this box, you can type the name of a person whom users can contact for help with the form or for information about the topic of the form. Alternatively, you can click the Contact button and choose a name from the Select Contact dialog box.

Description. In this text box, you can type a brief description of the form and its purpose. You can also add any short comments about how the form should be used.

Version and Form Number. For your own record keeping, you can assign a number to each form you create by typing the number in the Form Number box. If you revise a form for one reason or another, you might also want to assign a version number in the Version box.

> **> NOTE**
>
> The Contact, Description, Version, and Form Number all appear on the Forms Manager dialog box when you choose the Manage Forms tab from the Tools Options menu. This information also appears in the New Form dialog box, which opens when you select the Choose Form command from a folder's item menu.

Change Large Icon and Change Small Icon.   Each form is represented by a large icon and a small icon. These icons appear in folder windows or on the forms themselves, and they represent the form when you use an icon view to look at the contents of a folder. (See "Icons View," on page 349 and "Icon Views," on page 517.)

Outlook assigns an icon to each form, based on its type, but you can change either of the icons:

1 Click the Change Large Icon button or the Change Small Icon button.

2 In the File Open dialog box, switch to a folder that contains icon files. (The Office and Outlook folders in the Microsoft Office folder, which is inside the Program Files folder, contain icon files.)

3 Select the icon file you want to use, and then click the Open button.

Protect Form Design.   To protect your form with a password, turn on the Protect Form Design check box. When this option is turned on, only users with a password can alter the form. To set up the password, click the Set Password button. Outlook opens the Password dialog box, shown here:

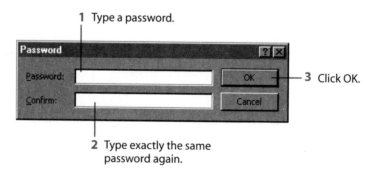

1 Type a password.

3 Click OK.

2 Type exactly the same password again.

Save Form Definition With Item.   If you save this form in a forms library, clear this check box. If you publish your form in a personal folder, select this check box. Forms libraries contain form layout information, so it isn't necessary to save the form layout and definition information with the form.

> When you create a form based on a message form, Outlook automatically turns on the Save Form Definition With Item check box. When you create a form based on any other type of built-in form, Outlook automatically turns off this check box.

Use Form Only For Responses.   If you want the form to be used only for message responses, turn on this check box. You could use a response form for a ballot on which the user can select options or check boxes based on the ballot's choices and send the ballot response form to the originator—this keeps the response information of the same type for all users. On the Actions tab of the form, you can specify the kind of response the form should be used for; see the next section, "Creating Custom Actions for a Form."

Creating Custom Actions for a Form

The Outlook built-in forms perform actions when a user applies an Outlook command to the form. For example, if you choose the Reply command for a message form, Outlook creates a message that looks like a reply. You can add your own custom actions to a form or delete the actions built into an Outlook form.

For more advanced forms, you can set up custom actions. You can use actions to open other forms, even forms of a different type. For example, you can create a message form with an action that opens a contact form. You can also use actions to create new items. For example, you can create a message form with an action that creates a new contact. The new item is created in the open folder, not in the contacts folder.

You can set up an action to appear as a command on the item menu of the form as well as on the Form Design toolbar, or you can set it up to appear as a command on just the item menu.

1 Click the (Actions) page.

FIGURE 20-13.

The Actions tab for a message form in form design mode.

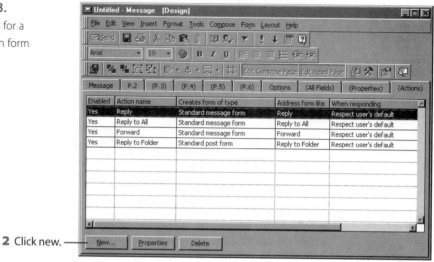

2 Click new.

3 Type a name for this new action.

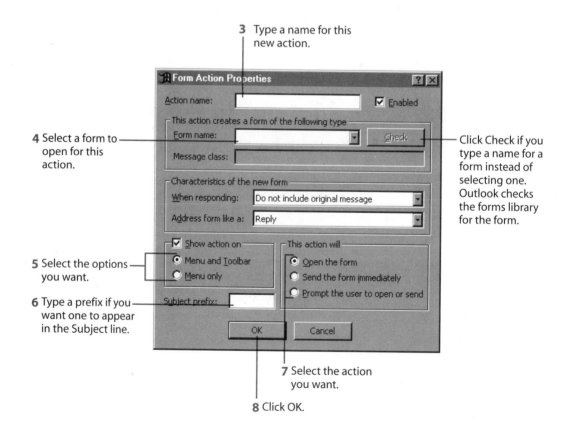

4 Select a form to open for this action.

Click Check if you type a name for a form instead of selecting one. Outlook checks the forms library for the form.

5 Select the options you want.

6 Type a prefix if you want one to appear in the Subject line.

7 Select the action you want.

8 Click OK.

If you later want to change the setup for an action or to change a standard Outlook action, select and double-click the action, and make your changes in the Form Action Properties dialog box. The following table describes some of the options in this dialog box:

When Responding	Select how you want Outlook to handle the original message in the form that's created by this action.
Address Form Like A	Select the style of form you want Outlook to use for the form you selected in the Form Name box. Your choice appears in the form's title bar.
Show Action On	Turn on this check box to display this action as a command, and then select where you want the command to appear.
This Action Will	Select the action you want Outlook to take for the form you selected in the Form Name box. If you click Send The Form Immediately, the user doesn't see the form. In that case, you'd need to select a form that contains all the information that the message must contain.
Subject Prefix	The characters you type here appear at the beginning of the subject line. For example, the subject prefix *RE:* appears on the Reply form.

> **NOTE**
>
> The Properties button and the Properties command on the Form menu are disabled for the standard Outlook actions, as are Reply, Reply To All, and Forward.

Testing a Form

As you design a custom form, you'll want to test it periodically. The simplest way to check the appearance of the form is to switch out of form design mode, back to what is referred to as read view. In read view, you see what the user of the form will see. To switch out of form design mode to read view, choose the Tools Design Outlook Form command. To return to form design mode, choose this command again.

> **NOTE**
>
> In some cases, you might find that you need to save the form or save and publish the form before you can see the changes you've made.

After you've finished designing the form and closed form design mode described in the previous paragraph, you can test the form by opening it, filling it out, and sending it to yourself or posting it to a folder. Then you can open the stored form to check that all its elements work and look the way they're supposed to.

Saving and Distributing a Form

Before you or anyone else can use a form, you have to save it. After you save and publish it, you can then distribute the form to others in your organization. You can save a custom form in the following ways:

- When you want to send the form to other people through e-mail, or if you don't intend to share the form, save it as an item in an open folder.

- When you want to use the form in another program, or if you need to save the form as a template, save it as a .MSG or .RTF file instead of a template file.

- When you want to save the form to a location where it can be readily accessed, save it in a forms library.

> **TIP**
>
> To save a form under a different name, open the form, switch to form design mode, and click the Properties tab. Type the new name in the Form Caption box, and then save the form under a new name.

Saving a Form in the Open Folder

When you save a form in the open folder, it appears there as a folder item. Because a new form doesn't contain identifying information such as the version number or the description, the form appears as a blank entry in the folder. (Usually the form is saved to the Inbox folder.)

To save a form in the open folder, simply choose the File Save command, or click the Save button on the Standard toolbar.

If you use advanced security (encryption and digital signature) for messages, you must be signed on to advanced security before you can save a message. If you don't want the messages sent with a new custom form to be encrypted or digitally signed, switch out of Outlook's form design mode, turn off advanced security, switch back to form design mode, and then save the form. For information about advanced security, see "Security Tab," on page 71, and "Sending a Protected Message," on page 92.

When you save a custom form based on a contact form without entering a name in the File As field (even if this field does not appear on the current version of the form), Outlook notifies you that the File As field is empty. To save a blank form, click Yes. Click No to return to the form. If you add File As text to the form (by typing an entry in a name or a company name field), you don't see this message when you save the form. The form, however, is listed under that entry as its File As name.

Saving a Form as a File

To save a form as a file, take these steps:

1   Choose the File Save As command.

2   In the File Name box, type a name for the form.

3   In the Save As Type box, select a file type. To save the form as an Outlook template, select Outlook Template, and switch to the Templates folder.

4   Click OK.

VI

According to Form

Saving a Form in a Forms Library

You can save a form in any of these three form libraries:

- **Personal Forms library.** You are the only person who can access forms saved in this library. The forms are stored in your mailbox. To use a form from this library, select the Choose Form command from a folder's item menu. In general, these are forms created for your personal use.

- **Folder Forms library.** Everyone in your organization can access forms saved in this library if the forms have been saved in a public folder; only you can access the forms in this library if the forms have been saved in a private folder. If the forms are saved in a library on your hard disk, you can access them only while you work in the folder. These forms are available on the folder's item menu. Use this library to save forms to a specific folder, generally a public folder.

- **Organization Forms library.** Everyone in your organization can access forms saved in this library. The forms are stored on the server. (You must have write permission to save to the server.) These forms are available on a folder's item menu when you select the Choose Form command. Keeping forms in this library makes it easy to distribute and update them.

Here's how to save a form in a forms library:

1 Choose the File Publish Form As command.

2 Type the name of the form.

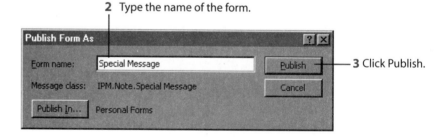

3 Click Publish.

If you want to change the location (library) where the form is stored, click the Publish In button in the Publish Form As dialog box. Outlook opens the Set Library To dialog box, shown here:

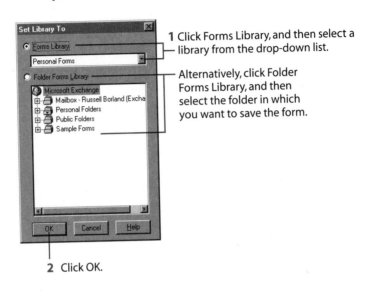

1 Click Forms Library, and then select a library from the drop-down list.

Alternatively, click Folder Forms Library, and then select the folder in which you want to save the form.

2 Click OK.

 TIP

You can use the File Publish Form As command to move a sample form into a forms library.

NOTE

Whenever you make changes to a form that you've shared in a forms library, be sure to republish it. Outlook uses the latest version of the published form in the item menus, so even if you've saved changes to a form that is already listed in a forms library, Outlook doesn't recognize those changes until you publish the updated version. This is an advantage for a forms designer because users can continue to use the current version of the form until you've completed the changes you want to make. Please note when testing changes, that some changes might not be visible until you publish the form.

Sending a Form Through E-Mail

To distribute your form to other people, you might want to send it to them through e-mail:

1 On the Properties tab of the form (in form design mode), turn on the Save Form Definition With Item check box.

2 If you have not already done so, save the form in the open folder. (See "Saving a Form in the Open Folder," on page 576.)

3 Close the form, and then create a mail message.

4 Choose the Insert Item command.

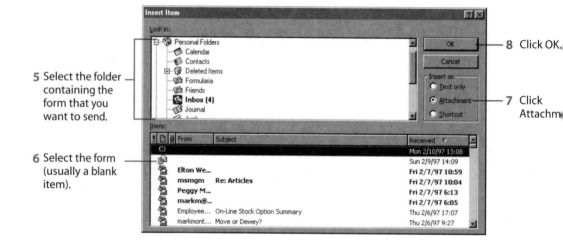

5 Select the folder containing the form that you want to send.

6 Select the form (usually a blank item).

7 Click Attachm▮

8 Click OK.

9 Click the Send button in the message window.

Getting Help for Visual Basic in Outlook

Controls and custom actions are manifestations of Visual Basic programs.

Microsoft Office 97 comes with an additional Help file for Visual Basic in Outlook. To use this Help file, you must first install the Microsoft Outlook Visual Basic Help file:

1 If you have opened Help, quit Help.

2 Insert the Microsoft Office 97 CD or the stand-alone Outlook CD in your CD drive.

3 Open the ValuPack folder, and then double-click the MoreHelp folder.

4 Select the VBAOUTL.HLP and VBAOUTL.CNT files.

5 Copy both files to the \Microsoft Office\Office folder inside the Program Files folder on your hard disk.

6 When Outlook asks whether you want to replace the existing versions of these files, click Yes.

7 To update the table of contents and the index to include the topics in the files you copied, choose the Start Find command, and then choose Files Or Folders from the submenu.

8 In the Named box, type *.gid.

9 In the Look In box, type *C:\Program Files\Microsoft Office\ Office*, and then click the Find Now button.

10 When the filenames appear at the bottom of the dialog box, select them all, and then choose the File Delete command.

If you installed Office or Outlook from a corporate network, ask your network administrator where the ValuPack files are located. If you installed the application from 3.5-inch disks, the ValuPack isn't included. You can find these files on the Microsoft web site, however. If you use Microsoft Internet Explorer or another Web browser to access the World Wide Web, choose the Help Microsoft On The Web command and then choose Online Support from the submenu.

After you've installed this Help file, you can get help for Visual Basic in Outlook as follows:

1 Open any folder item except a note.

2 Choose the Tools Design Outlook Form command.

3 Choose the Form View Code command.

4 Choose the Help Microsoft Outlook Object Library Help command.

VI

According to Form

Microsoft Press Books About Outlook 97 and Office 97

Microsoft Press has the training and support products you need to help you get more from Microsoft Windows 95, Microsoft Office 97, Microsoft Outlook 97, and Microsoft Windows NT Workstation. Whether you're a beginning user, an advanced user, a support professional, or a software developer, Microsoft Press has what you're looking for—from quick-and-easy handbooks and self-paced training guides to desktop references, technical resources, and programming titles.

To locate your nearest source for Microsoft Press products worldwide, visit the Microsoft Press Web site (http://www.microsoft.com/mspress), or contact your local Microsoft office. In the United States, call 1-800-MS-PRESS. In Canada, call 1-800-667-1115. For a quick glance at what's available, review the book summaries that follow.

Books About Outlook

Microsoft Outlook 97 Step by Step
by Catapult, Inc.
ISBN: 1-57231-382-X
A procedural training system with basic information about Outlook.

Microsoft Outlook 97 Field Guide
by Stephen L. Nelson
ISBN: 1-57231-383-8
A concise, graphic, pocket-sized reference with alphabetically listed tasks, terms, and techniques.

Building Applications with Microsoft Outlook 97
by Microsoft Corporation
ISBN: 1-57231-536-9
A results-oriented book that offers both the nonprogrammer and the experienced professional the information, strategies, and sample applications they need to get started building useful groupware and mail-enabled applications almost immediately.

Books About Office 97 That Include Information About Outlook

Microsoft Office 97 Integration Step by Step
by Catapult, Inc.
ISBN: 1-57231-317-X
A procedural training system with basic information about Office 97.

Microsoft Office 97 At a Glance
by Perspection, Inc.
ISBN: 1-57231-365-X
Quick solutions to specific software problems in a graphic, well-organized reference format.

Microsoft Office 97/Visual Basic Step by Step
by David Boctor
ISBN: 1-57231-389-7
A procedural approach to programming.

Microsoft Office 97/Visual Basic Programmer's Guide
by Microsoft Corporation
ISBN: 1-57231-340-4
A programming guide that enables you to build on your knowledge of Visual Basic—the powerful programming language used in most of the Microsoft Office 97 programs—to develop lean and efficient code. This guide helps you become more productive with Visual Basic for Applications. Learn how to create custom commands, menus, dialog boxes, messages, and buttons, as well as display custom online help for all these items.

Running Microsoft Office 97 for Windows, Select Edition
by Michael Halvorson and Michael Young
ISBN: 1-57231-322-6
An in-depth and example-filled guide containing inside tips from software experts.

Microsoft Office 97 Resource Kit
by Microsoft Corporation
ISBN: 1-57231-329-3
A definitive guide about how to install, configure, and support Microsoft Office in your organization. This kit is designed for system administrators, consultants, and power users, and thoroughly covers all aspects of Office 97—whether you run Microsoft Office under Windows 95 or Windows NT Workstation, or on a Macintosh.

Index

M

Macintosh, 157
Mail And Fax dialog box, 10, 12, 13
Mail And Fax icon, 9, 13, 16, 19, 151, 168, 179
Mail group, 22–27, 109
mailto links
    adding, to messages, 105, 107–8
    replying through, 116
Make Equal command, 555
Make New Connection Wizard, 166–68
Make Same Width button, 552
Manage Forms button, 80–81
Manage Forms tab, 79–82, 572
Manually Configure Information Services option, 11
margin settings, for print styles, 407, 409
Mark Complete button, 281
Mark My Comments With option, 60
Mark To Retrieve A Copy button, 199
Mark To Retrieve button, 199, 200
Master Category list, 102
Master Microsoft Exchange Server button, 464
Master Microsoft Exchange Server List dialog box, 464–465
Match Case option, 486
Medium Booklet print style, 394, 399, 405
Meeting Planner tab, 232, 234, 240–42, 244–45, 254–56
meetings
    cancelling, 253
    changing, 238–51
    changing the time of, 240–41
    with contacts, 314
    inviting resources to, 237
    planning, 234–38
    requests, 78–79, 254–56
    setting up, 230–38
    viewing lists of attendees/ resources for, 255–56
Members button, 159
Memo print style, 393, 394, 399, 403, 404

Message Body option, 40
Message Flag button, 102–3, 116
Message Format area, 18
Message Format file format, 118
messages
    adding databases/spreadsheets to, 105
    adding graphics to, 105, 106
    adding mailto links to, 105, 107–8
    adding URLs to, 105, 107
    deleting portions of, 117
    deleting, 59, 109, 201
    downloading, 170, 177, 178, 182–85, 198–201
    filtering, 182–85, 477–89
    flagging, 102–5, 116
    forwarding, 43, 57, 59–60, 70, 117, 275–76
    reading, 57–60, 111–14
    recalling, 109
    replacing, 109
    replying to, 57–59, 70, 99, 114–16
    resending, 109
    saving, 57, 99–100, 117–18
    searching for similar, 381–82
    sending, 53–57, 90–109, 302, 312–14
    sensitivity (priority) levels for, 41–42, 54–55, 97–98
    size limits for, 107
Messages tab, 99, 124, 126, 145, 374, 478–79, 536, 538
Microsoft Equation Editor, 105
Microsoft Exchange Forms Designer, 532
Microsoft Exchange Security Logon dialog box, 75–76, 93, 111
Microsoft Exchange Server, 29, 38, 49, 101
Microsoft Exchange Server, *continued*
    message size limits, 107
    moving folders and, 435
    remote work and, 165, 169–77, 180–86, 192, 194–97
    security and, 71, 75–76, 92–93, 95, 111, 447

Microsoft Exchange Server dialog box, 4, 6, 171–72, 173, 185
Microsoft Fax Properties dialog box, 17, 123–35, 145
Microsoft Fax Status dialog box, 140
Microsoft Fax Status window, 145–46
Microsoft Network (MSN), 6, 12, 150. *See also* online services
Microsoft Office 97, 326, 327, 361–62
Microsoft Web site, 581
Mileage box, 282
MIME (Multipurpose Internet Mail Extensions), 156–57
minus sign (–), 25
modems
    fax, 16–17, 130–34, 145
    installing, 145
    selecting, 50
    using multiple, 168
Modem tab, 17, 130–34
Modify button, 507
Month button, 291, 389, 513, 514–15
Monthly print style, 393, 394, 399, 403, 405
Monthly recurrence pattern, 247, 248–49, 262
Month view, 212, 213, 216, 225, 509, 514–15
More Choices tab, 378, 485–87
MoreHelp folder, 581
mouse. *See also* dragging
    cursors, briefly changing, 52
    rearranging columns with, 457
    removing columns with, 456–57
    sizing controls with, 552
    sorting with, 468
Move Down button, 455
Move Folder dialog box, 434
Move Items dialog box, 358–60
Move To Folder button, 358, 360
Move To Folder command, 359
Move To option, 43
Move Up button, 455, 491

The manuscript for this book was prepared and submitted to Microsoft Press in electronic form. Text files were prepared using Microsoft Word 97. Pages were composed using Adobe PageMaker 6.5 for Windows, with text in Garamond and display type in Myriad. Composed pages were sent to the printer as electronic prepress files.

Cover Artwork

Landor and Assoc.

Interior Graphic Designer

designLab

Electronic Artists

Travis Beaven

Joel Panchot

Compositors

Elisabeth Thébaud Pong

Paul Vautier

Principal Proofreader/ Copy Editor

Cheryl Penner

Indexer

Liz Cunningham

Get the most from the Internet.

The OFFICIAL MICROSOFT® INTERNET EXPLORER BOOK is a self-paced study guide that makes it easy to unlock the full potential of the Internet. Everything you need is in this book-and-disc package—quick and easy, self-paced instruction, plus Microsoft Internet Explorer version 3.0 on CD-ROM.

U.S.A. **$24.95**
U.K. £23.49 [V.A.T. included]
Canada $33.95
ISBN 1-57231-309-9

The OFFICIAL MICROSOFT INTERNET EXPLORER BOOK will help you:

- Install your home page the easy way. Wizards make it simple.

- Make your home page personal with stock quotes, news updates, and dozens of other custom features.

- See and hear Web pages come alive with animation, audio, moving text and graphics, and more—via built-in multimedia support and ActiveX™ controls, including ActiveMovie™.

- Share both discussion and data in real time using built-in NetMeeting™ software.

- Stay on top of all the news—personal and global—with Microsoft Internet Mail and News.

- Keep your conversations and commerce safe. The latest version of Microsoft Internet Explorer lets you safely download programs and controls—and will add support for the Secure Electronic Transactions (SET) specification as soon as it is released.

- Take advantage of unprecedented ease and flexibility for developers, plus unsurpassed legibility for users via HTML enhancements.

Microsoft Press

Learn to create
Outlook™ 97 applications— fast!

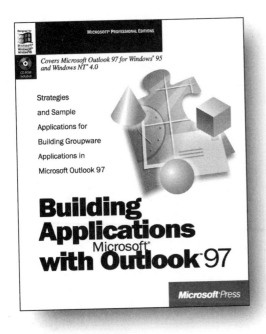

MICROSOFT® PROFESSIONAL EDITIONS

Covers Microsoft Outlook 97 for Windows® 95 and Windows NT™ 4.0

Strategies and Sample Applications for Building Groupware Applications in Microsoft Outlook 97

Building Applications with Microsoft® Outlook 97

Microsoft Press

U.S.A.	**$39.99**
U.K.	£37.49 [V.A.T. included]
Canada	$54.99
ISBN	1-57231-536-9

With its built-in mail client, scheduling, organizing capabilities, and integration with each of the Office 97 applications, Microsoft® Outlook 97 is virtually the heart of Office 97. BUILDING APPLICATIONS WITH MICROSOFT® OUTLOOK 97 covers these topics in detail:

- Applications you can create with Outlook 97
- Outlook 97 design tools
- Extending the use of any module, such as Contacts
- Designing custom applications
- How forms, controls, fields, and folders work
- Using Microsoft Visual Basic® Scripting in Outlook applications
- The Business Card Request Form
- Database access, document tracking, and Help Desk applications
- How to maintain and distribute applications

The companion CD-ROM contains all the source code and files necessary to create and use the sample applications in the book.

BUILDING APPLICATIONS WITH MICROSOFT® OUTLOOK 97 helps you use Outlook Forms to build groupware solutions—fast!

Microsoft®Press

Learn to build high-performance applications for *Windows*® and the *Internet* with *Visual Basic*®!

MICROSOFT® VISUAL BASIC, DELUXE LEARNING EDITION, is a comprehensive training kit that will teach you how to put Microsoft Visual Basic to work building high-performance applications for Windows and the Internet. The kit contains the complete version of Visual Basic 5.0, Learning Edition, and is the easiest way to learn to use it. You choose the training that fits your own learning style—easy-to-follow, interactive, computer-based training with multimedia lessons and exercises, or your choice of two outstanding Visual Basic programming guidebooks.

U.S.A.	**$129.99**
Canada	$174.99
ISBN 1-57231-551-2	

Microsoft®*Press*

Keep things **running** smoothly around the **Office.**

These are *the* answer books for business users of Microsoft Office 97 applications. They are packed with everything from quick, clear instructions for new users to comprehensive answers for power users. The Microsoft Press® *Running* series features authoritative handbooks you'll keep by your computer and use every day.

Running Microsoft® Excel 97
Mark Dodge, Chris Kinata, and Craig Stinson
U.S.A. $39.95   ($53.95 Canada)
ISBN 1-57231-321-8

Running Microsoft® Word 97
Russell Borland
U.S.A. $39.95   ($53.95 Canada)
ISBN 1-57231-320-X

Running Microsoft® PowerPoint® 97
Stephen W. Sagman
U.S.A. $29.95   ($39.95 Canada)
ISBN 1-57231-324-2

Running Microsoft® Access 97
John L. Viescas
U.S.A. $39.95   ($53.95 Canada)
ISBN 1-57231-323-4

Running Microsoft® Office 97
Michael Halvorson and Michael Young
U.S.A. $39.95   ($53.95 Canada)
ISBN 1-57231-322-6

Microsoft®*Press*

IMPORTANT—READ CAREFULLY BEFORE OPENING SOFTWARE PACKET(S). By opening the sealed packet(s) containing the software, you indicate your acceptance of the following Microsoft License Agreement.

MICROSOFT LICENSE AGREEMENT

(Book Companion Disks)

This is a legal agreement between you (either an individual or an entity) and Microsoft Corporation. By opening the sealed software packet(s) you are agreeing to be bound by the terms of this agreement. If you do not agree to the terms of this agreement, promptly return the unopened software packet(s) and any accompanying written materials to the place you obtained them for a full refund.

MICROSOFT SOFTWARE LICENSE

1. GRANT OF LICENSE. Microsoft grants to you the right to use one copy of the Microsoft software program included with this book (the "SOFTWARE") on a single terminal connected to a single computer. The SOFTWARE is in "use" on a computer when it is loaded into the temporary memory (i.e., RAM) or installed into the permanent memory (e.g., hard disk, CD-ROM, or other storage device) of that computer. You may not network the SOFTWARE or otherwise use it on more than one computer or computer terminal at the same time.

For the files and materials referenced in this book which may be obtained from the Internet, Microsoft grants to you the right to use the materials in connection with the book. If you are a member of a corporation or business, you may reproduce the materials and distribute them within your business for internal business purposes in connection with the book. You may not reproduce the materials for further distribution.

2. COPYRIGHT. The SOFTWARE is owned by Microsoft or its suppliers and is protected by United States copyright laws and international treaty provisions. Therefore, you must treat the SOFTWARE like any other copyrighted material (e.g., a book or musical recording) except that you may either (a) make one copy of the SOFTWARE solely for backup or archival purposes, or (b) transfer the SOFTWARE to a single hard disk provided you keep the original solely for backup or archival purposes. You may not copy the written materials accompanying the SOFTWARE.

3. OTHER RESTRICTIONS. You may not rent or lease the SOFTWARE, but you may transfer the SOFTWARE and accompanying written materials on a permanent basis provided you retain no copies and the recipient agrees to the terms of this Agreement. You may not reverse engineer, decompile, or disassemble the SOFTWARE. If the SOFTWARE is an update or has been updated, any transfer must include the most recent update and all prior versions.

4. DUAL MEDIA SOFTWARE. If the SOFTWARE package contains both 3.5" and 5.25" disks, then you may use only the disks appropriate for your single-user computer. You may not use the other disks on another computer or loan, rent, lease, or transfer them to another user except as part of the permanent transfer (as provided above) of all SOFTWARE and written materials.

5. SAMPLE CODE. If the SOFTWARE includes Sample Code, then Microsoft grants you a royalty-free right to reproduce and distribute the sample code of the SOFTWARE provided that you: (a) distribute the sample code only in conjunction with and as a part of your software product; (b) do not use Microsoft's or its authors' names, logos, or trademarks to market your software product; (c) include the copyright notice that appears on the SOFTWARE on your product label and as a part of the sign-on message for your software product; and (d) agree to indemnify, hold harmless, and defend Microsoft and its authors from and against any claims or lawsuits, including attorneys' fees, that arise or result from the use or distribution of your software product.

DISCLAIMER OF WARRANTY

The SOFTWARE (including instructions for its use) is provided "AS IS" WITHOUT WARRANTY OF ANY KIND. MICROSOFT FURTHER DISCLAIMS ALL IMPLIED WARRANTIES INCLUDING WITHOUT LIMITATION ANY IMPLIED WARRANTIES OF MERCHANTABILITY OR OF FITNESS FOR A PARTICULAR PURPOSE. THE ENTIRE RISK ARISING OUT OF THE USE OR PERFORMANCE OF THE SOFTWARE AND DOCUMENTATION REMAINS WITH YOU.

IN NO EVENT SHALL MICROSOFT, ITS AUTHORS, OR ANYONE ELSE INVOLVED IN THE CREATION, PRODUCTION, OR DELIVERY OF THE SOFTWARE BE LIABLE FOR ANY DAMAGES WHATSOEVER (INCLUDING, WITHOUT LIMITATION, DAMAGES FOR LOSS OF BUSINESS PROFITS, BUSINESS INTERRUPTION, LOSS OF BUSINESS INFORMATION, OR OTHER PECUNIARY LOSS) ARISING OUT OF THE USE OF OR INABILITY TO USE THE SOFTWARE OR DOCUMENTATION, EVEN IF MICROSOFT HAS BEEN ADVISED OF THE POSSIBILITY OF SUCH DAMAGES. BECAUSE SOME STATES/COUNTRIES DO NOT ALLOW THE EXCLUSION OR LIMITATION OF LIABILITY FOR CONSEQUENTIAL OR INCIDENTAL DAMAGES, THE ABOVE LIMITATION MAY NOT APPLY TO YOU.

U.S. GOVERNMENT RESTRICTED RIGHTS

The SOFTWARE and documentation are provided with RESTRICTED RIGHTS. Use, duplication, or disclosure by the Government is subject to restrictions as set forth in subparagraph (c)(1)(ii) of The Rights in Technical Data and Computer Software clause at DFARS 252.227-7013 or subparagraphs (c)(1) and (2) of the Commercial Computer Software — Restricted Rights 48 CFR 52.227-19, as applicable. Manufacturer is Microsoft Corporation, One Microsoft Way, Redmond, WA 98052-6399.

If you acquired this product in the United States, this Agreement is governed by the laws of the State of Washington.

Should you have any questions concerning this Agreement, or if you desire to contact Microsoft Press for any reason, please write: Microsoft Press, One Microsoft Way, Redmond, WA 98052-6399.

Register Today!

Return this
Running Microsoft® Outlook 97
registration card for
a Microsoft Press® catalog

U.S. and Canada addresses only. Fill in information below and mail postage-free. Please mail only the bottom half of this page.

1-57231-608-XA   *RUNNING MICROSOFT® OUTLOOK 97*   *Owner Registration Card*

_____

NAME

_____

INSTITUTION OR COMPANY NAME

_____

ADDRESS

_____

CITY   STATE   ZIP

Microsoft *Press*
Quality Computer Books

For a free catalog of
Microsoft Press® products, call
1-800-MSPRESS

BUSINESS REPLY MAIL
FIRST-CLASS MAIL   PERMIT NO. 53   BOTHELL, WA

POSTAGE WILL BE PAID BY ADDRESSEE

MICROSOFT PRESS REGISTRATION
RUNNING MICROSOFT® OUTLOOK 97
PO BOX 3019
BOTHELL WA   98041-9946

Running Microsoft Outlook quick reference card

View Options for Folders

Inbox and Public Folders

View	Format of Messages
Messages	List
Messages With AutoPreview	List showing first three lines of message text displayed
By Message Flag	List grouped by message flag; also shows due date for follow-up action for message flag
Last Seven Days	List of messages that arrived during the last seven days
Flagged For Next Seven Days	List of messages flaged for follow-up actions due within next seven days
By Conversation Topic	List grouped by subject
By Sender	List grouped by sender
Unread Messages	List displaying only messages marked as unread
Sent To	List displaying recipients' names (instead of sender's name)
Message Timeline	Icons arranged on a timeline by date sent

Calendar

View	Format of Calendar Items
Day/Week/Month	Appointments, events, and meetings for one or more days or weeks or for a month; also includes task list on Day and Week views; looks like a paper calendar or a planner
Active Appointments	List of all appointments and meetings (and details about them) beginning today and going into future
Events	List of all events and details about them
Annual Events	List of events that happen once a year and details about them
Recurring Appointments	List of recurring appointments and details about them
By Category	List of all calendar items, grouped by category, and details about them

Contacts

View	Format of Contacts
Address Cards	On individual cards with one mailing address, plus business and home phone numbers
Detailed Address Cards	On individual cards with business and home addresses, phone numbers, and other details
Phone List	List with company name, business and home phone numbers, and business fax number
By Category	Listed by categories and sorted by names that contacts are filed under within each category
By Company	Listed by company with job title, company name, department, business phone number, and business fax number
By Location	Listed by country with company name, state, country, and business and home phone numbers

Tasks

View	Format of Tasks
Simple List	List showing few details to enable quick viewing of completed tasks
Detailed List	List showing many details, including priority and percentage complete
Active Tasks	List of incomplete and overdue tasks
Next Seven Days	List of tasks due in the next seven days
Overdue Tasks	List of overdue tasks
By Category	Listed by category and sorted by due date within each category
Assignment	List of tasks that have been assigned to others, sorted by task owner and due date
By Person Responsible	List, grouped by task owner and sorted by due date for each task owner
Completed Tasks	List showing tasks marked complete
Task Timeline	Icons arrangedon a timeline by start date; tasks without start dates are arranged by due date

Journal

View	Format of Journal Entries
By Type	Icons on timeline grouped by item type
By Contact	Icons on timeline grouped by contact name
By Category	Icons on timeline grouped by category
Entry List	List of all entries
Last Seven Days	List of entries created during the last seven days
Phone Calls	List of phone call entries

Notes

View	Format of Journal Notes
Icons	Icons arranged from left to right by creation date
Notes List	List sorted by creation date
Last Seven Days	List of notes created during the last seven days
By Category	Listed by categories and sorted by creation date within each category
By Color	Listed by color and sorted by creation date for each color

Files

View	Format of Files
Icons	Icons arranged in alphabetical order from left to right by filename
Details	Listed by filename with author, type, size, modification date, and keywords (AutoPreview only)
By Author	Listed by author and sorted by filename with type, size, modification date, keywords, and comments
By File Type	Listed by type and sorted by filename with author, size, modification date, keywords, and comments
Document Timeline	Icons arranged on a timeline by creation date
Programs	List including files that are programs or that are used only by the system— e.g., .EXE or .DLL files

Running Microsoft Outlook quick reference card

Common Actions

Create a folder for items

1 On the File menu, point to New, and then click Folder.
2 In the Name box, enter the folder name.
3 In the Folder Contains box, click the type of items you want the folder to contain.
4 In the Make This Folder A Subfolder Of box, click the location for the folder.

Create a folder shortcut on the Outlook Bar

1 On the Outlook Bar, right-click background of group where you want to add shortcut.
2 Click Add To Outlook Bar on the shortcut menu.
3 In the Folder Name box, click the name of the folder you want to create a shortcut to.

Show or hide the Outlook Bar

On the View menu, click Outlook Bar.

Create a new item from a different type of item

1 Drag the item you want to use to create another type of item onto a shortcut on the Outlook Bar that points to a folder containing the type of item you want to create. For example, drag a message item to the Calendar shortcut.
2 Select the desired options.
3 Click Save And Close.

Create a note from any item

1 Drag the item you want to use to create a note onto Notes.
2 In the note, use the arrow keys to scroll, and then change the text you want.
3 Click the Close button.

Create a contact with new information

1 On the File menu, point to New, and then click Contact.
2 In the Full Name box, type the contact name.
3 Enter the contact information in the remaining fields.
4 Click Save And Close.

Schedule time in your calendar to complete a task

1 Drag the task you want to schedule time for from the Tasks folder to the Calendar folder.
2 On the Appointment tab, select the desired options.
3 Click Save And Close.

Keyboard Shortcuts

Create an item or a file

Action	Key(s)
Appointment	CTRL+SHIFT+A
Contact	CTRL+SHIFT+C
Folder	CTRL+SHIFT+E
Journal entry	CTRL+SHIFT+J
Message	CTRL+SHIFT+M
Meeting request	CTRL+SHIFT+Q
Note	CTRL+SHIFT+N
Post to folder	CTRL+SHIFT+S
Task	CTRL+SHIFT+K
Task request	CTRL+SHIFT+U

Apply formatting

To	Press
Add bold	CTRL+B
Add bullets	CTRL+SHIFT+L
Center	CTRL+E
Add italics	CTRL+I
Increase indent	CTRL+T
Decrease indent	CTRL+SHIFT+T
Left align	CTRL+L
Underline	CRTL+U
Increase font size	CTRL+]
Decrease font size	CTRL+[
Clear formatting	CTRL+SHIFT+Z or CTRL+SPACEBAR

Move around toolbars

Action	Key(s)
Make the menu bar active	F10
Select the next or previous toolbar	CTRL+TAB or CTRL+SHIFT+TAB
Select the next or previous button or menu on the toolbar	TAB or SHIFT+TAB (when toolbar is active)
Open the menu	ENTER (when menu on toolbar is selected)
Perform action assigned to a button	ENTER (when button is selected)
Enter text in text box	ENTER (when text box is selected)
Select option from drop-down list box or drop-down menu on a button	Arrow keys to move through the options in a list or menu; ENTER to select the option you want (when a drop-down list box is selected)

Common operations

Action	Key(s)
Cancel the current operation	ESC
Show ScreenTip for the active item	SHIFT+F1
Expand/collapse a group (with a group selected)	PLUS or MINUS SIGN on numeric keypad
Select	ENTER
Turn on editing in a field (except Icon view)	F2
Move from item to item	UP, DOWN, LEFT, or RIGHT ARROW
Switch to the next tab in an item	CTRL+TAB or CTRL+PAGE DOWN
Switch to the previous tab in an item	CTRL+SHIFT+TAB or CTRL+PAGE UP
Show Address Book	CTRL+SHIFT+B
Dial	CTRL+SHIFT+D
Find	CTRL+SHIFT+F
Next item (with item open)	CTRL+SHIFT+>
Previous item (with item open)	CTRL+SHIFT+<
Mark as read	CTRL+Q
Reply to mail message	CTRL+R
Reply All to mail message	CTRL+SHIFT+R
Switch case (with text selected)	SHIFT+F3
Switch between Folder List and information viewer on right	F6